JURISDICTION AND CROSS-BORDER COLLECTIVE REDRESS

In recent decades, the rise in cross-border law violations has harmed numerous victims around the globe. The damages are often dispersed and low-level. As a result, the private enforcement gap has deepened and collective redress represents an interesting procedural instrument that is able to provide effective access to justice.

This book analyses thoroughly the dominant collective redress models adopted in the EU. Data from 13 Member States has been catalogued and categorised. The research mainly focuses on the consumer law field but frequent references to financial and data protection-related cases are made. The dominant collective redress models are then studied from a private international law perspective. In particular, the book highlights the current mismatch between collective redress on the one hand, and rules on international jurisdiction on the other. Additionally, it notes that barriers to cross-border litigation remain significant for victims and their representatives. The unprecedented empirical study included in this book confirms that statement. Observing that EU measures have not satisfactorily lowered those barriers, the author proposes the creation of a new head of jurisdiction for cases of international collective redress.

This book will be of interest to private international law scholars, researchers, students, legal practitioners, judges and policy-makers. It is a reference point for those with an interest in cross-border collective redress in particular, and private international law in general.

Volume 23 in the series Studies in Private International Law

Studies in Private International Law

Recent titles in the series

Intellectual Property and Private International Law: Comparative Perspectives
Edited by Toshiyuki Kono

Child Abduction within the European Union
Katarina Trimmings

International Surrogacy Arrangements: Legal Regulation at the International Level
Edited by Katarina Trimmings and Paul Beaumont

The Hague Child Abduction Convention: A Critical Analysis
Rhona Schuz

Interregional Recognition and Enforcement of Civil and Commercial Judgments: Lessons for China from the US and EU Law
Jie Huang

The Recovery of Maintenance in the EU and Worldwide
Paul Beaumont, Burkhard Hess, Lara Walker and Stefanie Spancken

Australian Private International Law for the 21st Century: Facing Outwards
Edited by Andrew Dickinson, Thomas John and Mary Keyes

Maintenance and Child Support in Private International Law
Lara Walker

The Choice of Law Contract
Maria Hook

The Nature and Enforcement of Choice of Court Agreements: A Comparative Study
Mukarrum Ahmed

Cross-Border Litigation in Europe
Edited by Paul Beaumont, Mihail Danov, Katarina Trimmings and Burcu Yuksel

Forum (Non) Conveniens in England: Past, Present, and Future
Ardavan Arzandeh

Commercial Issues in Private International Law: A Common Law Perspective
Edited by Vivienne Bath, Andrew Dickinson, Michael Douglas and Mary Keyes

Jurisdiction and Cross-Border Collective Redress

A European Private International Law Perspective

Alexia Pato

•HART•
OXFORD • LONDON • NEW YORK • NEW DELHI • SYDNEY

HART PUBLISHING

Bloomsbury Publishing Plc

Kemp House, Chawley Park, Cumnor Hill, Oxford, OX2 9PH, UK

HART PUBLISHING, the Hart/Stag logo, BLOOMSBURY and the Diana logo are trademarks of Bloomsbury Publishing Plc

First published in Great Britain 2019

A catalogue record for this book is available from the British Library.

Library of Congress Cataloging-in-Publication data

Names: Pato, Alexia, author.

Title: Jurisdiction and cross-border collective redress : a European private international law perspective / Alexia Pato.

Description: Oxford, UK ; Chicago, Illinois : Hart Publishing, 2019. | Series: Studies in private international law ; volume 23 | Based on author's thesis (doctoral – Universidad Autâonoma de Madrid, Facultad de Derecho, 2017) issued under title: Cross-border collective redress in the European union and private international law rules on jurisdiction. | Includes bibliographical references and index.

Identifiers: LCCN 2019007885 (print) | LCCN 2019009385 (ebook) | ISBN 9781509930302 (EPub) | ISBN 9781509930296 (hardback)

Subjects: LCSH: Conflict of laws—Class actions—European Union countries. | Class actions (Civil procedure)—European Union countries.

Classification: LCC KJE983.C62 (ebook) | LCC KJE983.C62 P38 2019 (print) | DDC 347.24/053—dc23

LC record available at https://lccn.loc.gov/2019007885

ISBN: HB: 978-1-50993-029-6
ePDF: 978-1-50993-031-9
ePub: 978-1-50993-030-2

Typeset by Compuscript Ltd, Shannon

'Pour atteindre la vérité, il faut une fois dans la vie se défaire de toutes les opinions qu'on a reçues, et reconstruire de nouveau tout le système de ses connaissances.'

René Descartes

SERIES EDITOR'S PREFACE

I am very pleased to welcome this monograph to the Studies in Private International Law Series. It is the first book in the Series tackling the increasingly important topic of collective redress. Class actions are a notoriously significant part of the US legal process and the writer therefore takes full account of the US system before turning her attention to the various systems in the EU. The book offers a rich and full diet of comparative law on collective redress in the US and the EU. In the latter context the author sets out a clear description of all the key studies, legislative proposals and legislation at the European Union wide level. She argues against harmonisation of the substantive and procedural rules on collective redress in the EU. In doing so she gives appropriate weight to subsidiarity and to the lack of convincing empirical evidence that such harmonisation would give sufficient benefit to the internal market to justify such legislation at the EU wide level.

The author then considers the potential value of private international law solutions to improving collective redress in the EU and explains why she chooses to focus on jurisdiction. The author gives a helpful primer on the relevant jurisdiction rules in Brussels Ia (the domicile of the defendant, the branch jurisdiction, the domicile of any one of multiple defendants when the actions are closely connected, the special jurisdictions on contract and tort, the protective jurisdiction regime for consumers, *lis pendens* and related actions, and, briefly, choice of court agreements). She then considers jurisdictional theory (making good use of the work of the late, great Arthur von Mehren among others) as the context for the really innovative part of the book – her analysis of how the current jurisdiction rules work in relation to the four main types of collective redress in the EU countries. The clear weaknesses the author exposes in the practical application of the current jurisdiction rules in relation to all four of the chosen types of collective redress leads her to make some very clear suggestions for law reform. One of the virtues of the book is the detailed analysis of the existing case law on collective redress by the Court of Justice of the European Union (CJEU) and by many leading courts in Europe including the Amsterdam Court of Appeal.

Her proposals for law reform are based on very extensive reading of primary and secondary sources in a significant range of languages and across many legal systems (in the US and Europe) and the findings from a small empirical study carried out by the author. She advocates creating a new jurisdiction for collective redress by representative bodies in their own domicile but limited to people affected in that national market. The existing alternative of being able to sue in the defendant's domicile for remedies in relation to all the harm done by the defendant to all the members of the group seeking collective redress would be retained. Interestingly the proposed solution has echoes of the CJEU's *Shevill* approach in relation to printed defamation.

The annexes to the book contain very helpful information on the current law on collective redress in the US and in many European systems.

I commend this carefully crafted and thorough book with many insights into the current law and well thought through ideas for law reform.

Paul Beaumont (University of Aberdeen)

ACKNOWLEDGEMENTS

The present book is an updated version of my Ph.D. thesis, which I defended at the *Universidad Autónoma de Madrid* (UAM) in September 2017. I warmly thank my supervisor Elena Rodríguez Pineau for her continuous support, kindness and dedication. As my 'academic mother' – *Doktormutter* as Germans say –, she gave me the necessary tools to grow up and eventually become an accomplished law researcher. My gratitude also goes to my co-director, Miguel Virgós Soriano, who gave me good and instructive advice.

My sincere thanks also go to Elisa Torralba Mendiola and María Jesús Elvira Benayas for their useful feedback on earlier drafts of this thesis. I equally thank Marta Requejo and Laura Ervo for drafting the reports that enabled me to obtain the international law certificate delivered by the UAM. I hope that one day I will become as strong, kind and skilled as those women. I express extensive gratitude to Yolanda Moreno who patiently and efficiently corrected my English.

I am very grateful to Francisco Garcimartín Alferéz, Fernando Gascón Inchausti and Eva Lein, who took the time to read and evaluate my Ph.D. thesis. Their invaluable comments helped me to further hone my analyses. Gratitude is extended to Matthias Weller for his support during the book's publication process.

I thank my family, friends, as well as my business angels who believed in this project. A special thanks to my roommate Izzy McCarthy for making me laugh in difficult times. Thanks to my much-loved friends Lucie Martin, María Cruz de Miguel Portero and Larisa Hancu for their unconditional support and beautiful friendship. Thanks to Richard Beckmann and Luc von Danwitz for making life in Bonn brighter.

Last but by no means least, my gratitude goes to the editorial team of Hart Publishing for making the publication of my thesis possible. I have tried to state the law as it stood on August 2018.

I dedicate this book to my beloved brother Kevin, my source of strength, love and inspiration.

Alexia Pato

Bonn, November 2018

CONTENTS

ABBREVIATIONS

AAA	American Arbitration Association
ACCP	Austrian Civil Code of Procedure
ADR	Alternative Dispute Resolution
ALI	American Law Institute
ATE	After the event insurance
BC	Brussels Convention
BCCP	Bulgarian Code of Civil Procedure
BEUC	Bureau Européen des Unions de Consommateurs
BI	Brussels Regulation (Regulation 44/2001)
BIa	Brussels Regulation (recast) (Regulation 1215/2012)
BTE	Before the event insurance
CADR	Consumer Alternative Dispute Resolution
CAFA	Class Action Fairness Act 2005
CDC	Cartel Damage Claims
CJEU	Court of Justice of the European Union
CMA	Competition and Markets Authority
CPR	Civil Procedure Rules (United Kingdom)
DC	District Court
DCC	Dutch Civil Code
DCCP	Dutch Civil Code of Procedure
EC	European Communities
ECC	European Consumer Centre
EFTA	European Free Trade Association
esp.	especially
EU	The European Union

FCC	French Consumer Code
ff.	following
GCCP	German Code of Civil Procedure
GDP	Gross domestic product
GDPR	General Data Protection Regulation (Regulation 2016/679)
GLO	Group Litigation Order
GPA	Group Proceedings Act 2002
ICC	Italian Consumer Code
ILA	International Law Association
KapMuG	Kapitalanleger-Musterverfahrensgesetz (Capital Market Model Proceedings Act)
KSchG	Konsumentenschutzgesetz (Consumer Protection Act)
LCJI	Ley de cooperación judicial internacional (International Cooperation Act)
MDL	mutli-district litigation
No	number
ODR	online dispute resolution
SMEs	small and medium-sized enterprises
SLCP	Spanish Law of Civil Procedure
SPV	Special purpose vehicle
TEC	Treaty establishing a European Community
TFEU	Treaty on the functioning of the European Union
UKlag	Unterlassungsklagengesetz (Act on Injunctive Relief for Consumer Rights and Other Violations)
US	The United States
v or v.	versus
WCAM	Wet Collectieve Afwikkeling Massaschade (Act on Collective Settlement of Mass Damages)

TABLE OF CASES

US Case Law

Case Law of Member States

Austria

Spain

Germany

The Netherlands

The United Kingdom

EU Case Law

TABLE OF NATIONAL LAWS

Austria, Consumer Protection Act and Civil Code of Procedure
www.jusline.at/Konsumentenschutzgesetz_(KSchG).html.
www.jusline.at/Zivilprozessordnung_(ZPO).html.
Belgium, Economic Code (Book XVII)
www.ejustice.just.fgov.be/cgi_loi/change_lg.pl?language=fr&la=F&table_name=loi&cn=2013022819.
Bulgaria, Code of Civil Procedure
kenarova.com/law/Code%20of%20Civil%20Procedure.pdf.
Finland, Group Action Act 2007
www.finlex.fi/fi/laki/kaannokset/2007/en20070444.pdf.
France, Consumer Code
www.legifrance.gouv.fr/affichCode.do?cidTexte=LEGITEXT000006069565.
Germany, Capital Market Model Proceedings Act 2005, Act on Injunctive Relief for Consumer Rights and Other Violations and Legal Services Act
www.gesetze-im-internet.de/kapmug_2012.
www.gesetze-im-internet.de/uklag.
www.gesetze-im-internet.de/rdg.
Italy, Consumer Code
www.altalex.com/documents/news/2013/12/09/associazioni-dei-consumatori-e-accesso-alla-giustizia#parte5.
The Netherlands, Civil Code and Civil Code of Procedure
www.dutchcivillaw.com/civilcodegeneral.htm.
www.dutchcivillaw.com/civilprocedureleg.htm.
Portugal, Law 83/95 of 31 August 1995
www.pgdlisboa.pt/leis/lei_mostra_articulado.php?nid=722&tabela=leis.
Spain, Rules of Civil Procedure
www.boe.es/buscar/act.php?id=BOE-A-2000-323.
Sweden, Group Proceedings Act 2002
www.government.se/government-policy/judicial-system/group-proceedings-act.
The United Kingdom, Rules of Civil Procedure (Part 19) and Enterprise Act 2002
www.justice.gov.uk/courts/procedure-rules/civil/rules/part19.
www.legislation.gov.uk/ukpga/2002/40/contents.

Introduction

I. The Rise of Mass Damages and the Corresponding Private Enforcement Gap

In the wake of globalisation and the rise of new technologies, international commercial activities around the globe have intensified. It is increasingly common for companies to offer products or services abroad, and for consumers to shop in other states. Within the European Union (EU), this internationalisation process is further enhanced by the market integration policy. In this vein, the EU has undertaken various measures in order to foster consumer confidence and stimulate cross-border activities. This is justified since consumers represent fundamental players of the internal market.

Simultaneously, the desire to engage in cross-border commerce has created new kinds of abusive behaviours. Henceforth, illegal practices may affect numerous consumers around the globe. Additionally, damages are often dispersed and low. Typically, inflated prices stemming from EU-wide cartels may affect a high number of victims domiciled in distinct Member States. Mass accidents such as plane crashes or shipwrecks generate multiple damages for victims from many different countries. Finally, a company selling products or services internationally and whose terms and conditions contain unfair terms can affect clients from all over the world. Despite the increasing frequency of international commercial interactions involving weak parties, such as consumers, the development of effective procedural vehicles that would enable them to enforce their rights is slow. To such extent that these often renounce the protection of their rights – either judicially or extra-judicially. This is typically the case when their harm is only a minor amount, so that going to court is unthinkable.

Therefore, a private enforcement gap persists, which can be characterised by a difference between the theoretical possibilities to obtain redress drafted by the legislator and the reality experienced by consumers in daily life.[1] As a result, the EU institutions have taken various legislative measures in order to solve this problem. For example, the Small Claims Procedure[2] was enacted and the use of Alternative Dispute Resolution (ADR) mechanisms in consumer matters is encouraged.

[1] This difference has been highlighted in the Green Paper on Access of Consumers to Justice and the Settlement of Consumer Disputes in the Single Market COM (93) 576 final, 5.

[2] Council Regulation (EC) 861/2007 of 11 July 2007 establishing a European Small Claims Procedure [2007] OJ L199/1.

It is believed that these measures should boost consumer confidence and facilitate cross-border trade. Collective redress too represents an interesting instrument that may fulfil the above-mentioned enforcement gap. Thanks to this procedural tool, the resources of the judicial power are spared. Furthermore, the collectivisation of proceedings is beneficial to the defendant who does not have to face a multiplicity of trials in different Member States. In other words, the defendant is able to achieve closure. As for victims, they can reach important economies of scale by bundling their claims, as the costs generated by the proceedings are spread among them.

II. Collective Redress to the Rescue

The notion of collective redress covers different situations: on the one hand, this instrument enables victims to bundle their individual claims. On the other hand, collective redress also encompasses actions seeking the protection of general interests, such as the preservation of the environment against air pollution, or the protection of market conditions against the use of unfair terms. Often, representative entities, such as consumer associations or public authorities, are entrusted with the task of defending those interests. For the sake of this book, collective redress covers both types of actions. When those actions are coupled with an ADR mechanism, they are also taken into consideration. However, collective redress actions in the arbitration field fall outside such scope. Finally, although the American class action differs from EU forms of collective redress, the class action model is included within the notion of collective redress for comparative law purposes. By adopting a broad notion of collective redress, this research project undertakes an exhaustive analysis of the different procedural instruments adopted in all Member States of the EU. Naturally, the concept of collective redress, if introduced in a specific legislative act, may be defined in a more restrictive manner.

Today, many countries around the globe have adopted some kind of collective redress mechanism. Notably, the most accomplished system is the class action device of the United States (US). Chapter 1 thoroughly analyses and describes the history, structure and goals of the US class action. It is an efficient mechanism that may serve as a model for other states. The negative consequences linked to the use of class actions are equally interesting to observe. Historical considerations underline that the creation of the class action device is consistent with the American culture and legal environment. It has been and still is a powerful tool, which fosters access to justice. For this reason, the American device is a useful starting point to study collective redress. Furthermore, the solutions adopted by the US legislator in order to tackle some procedural issues triggered by class actions will constitute a source of inspiration, especially for the construction of chapter 4.

In the EU, however, Member States decided to follow their own path and have adopted heterogeneous collective redress instruments. As chapter 2 shows, most Member States took the US class action as a 'counter-model', as they feared the abusive use of this procedural device. This has undeniably created efficiency issues, which may be due, either to their inherent structure, or to external factors, such as lack of funding. Subsequent legislative reforms have tried to reduce those inefficiencies in the last years (chapter 2, I.A.).

Structural differences between collective redress tools in the EU are illustrated in the Table of Annex II, which collects most instruments adopted so far by Member States. Despite the great variety of those instruments, it was possible to sort them out and create four categories of collective redress that predominate in the EU, namely the representative model, the class action model, the test case model and the Dutch model (chapter 2, I.E.). These categories facilitate the analysis in chapter 3.

Even though national legislators have boosted the private enforcement of collective rights, access to justice remains unsatisfactory. This is especially visible in cross-border cases, where language differences and high costs are coupled with the numerous procedural and financial barriers hindering domestic litigation (chapter 2, II.B.i.).

III. Efforts at the EU Level

At the EU level, measures have only fostered access to justice in a limited manner. In 2013, a non-binding Recommendation was issued, which establishes common principles that collective redress mechanisms should follow (chapter 2, II.A. and II.B.ii.a.). Additionally, a Directive on representative actions is in the legislative pipeline (chapter 2, II.A. and II.B.ii.b.). Opponents to collective redress have raised many objections that question the implementation of collective redress in the EU. Chapter 2 examines two of these objections, namely the competence of the EU to undertake a legislative measure and the potentially superior role of ADR. Furthermore, collective redress actions entailing international components, which should increase in light of the ongoing globalisation and digitalisation process, generate additional difficulties: for example, issues of applicable law may appear if claimants of different states are involved in collective redress proceedings; notice to members about the existence of a collective redress action might be costly and difficult to achieve where consumers' identity is unknown; finally, the question of recognition and enforcement of collective redress judgments and settlements is still surrounded by legal uncertainty, especially if proceedings are opt-out based or punitive damages are allocated.

The documents issued by EU institutions show that private international law has been a secondary concern. On the one hand, the Recommendation of 2013 seems to aim at harmonising the structure of collective redress mechanisms. On the other hand, the Directive on representative actions amends certain procedural rules in order to facilitate cross-border litigation. In any case, the reform of procedural aspects seems to be the goal of the EU's measures. Nevertheless, chapter 2 calls into question the effectiveness of such approach (II.C.ii.). Rather, it is argued that a private international law solution would appropriately deal with cross-border obstacles that impede consumers to start collective redress actions abroad and hence, support access to justice.

IV. Delineation of the Material Scope

The present work aims at facilitating the start of cross-border collective redress actions in the EU, through the construction of appropriate private international law rules on jurisdiction. Even though questions regarding applicable law or recognition and enforcement are important, rules on jurisdiction should be clarified first, since they directly affect access to justice. In light of the above, the Regulation 1215/2012 (hereafter, BIa or the Brussels Regulation recast),[3] which is applicable in commercial and civil cases, is the central piece of this work. To be more specific, chapter 3 analyses how EU private international law rules on jurisdiction apply to the four categories of collective redress mechanisms described in chapter 2. Where possible, judgments rendered by national courts in collective redress cases entailing an international component are referred to. Nevertheless, this has been a tricky exercise, since these actions are not widespread and no register catalogues them.

Heretofore, jurisdiction has turned out to be a problematic question: in the absence of a supranational authority to address cross-border collective redress cases, overlapping proceedings, forum shopping and confusion dominate. The traditional two-party-proceedings paradigm, on which the Brussels regime is based, does not match collective redress that involves a plurality of parties. However, the recast of the Brussels Regulation did not take the opportunity to tackle jurisdictional issues regarding cross-border collective redress. Due to the patent unsuitability of the BIa to collective redress actions, centralisation of the dispute in a single forum is often not possible. Even when private international law allows it, many barriers to litigation in courts located abroad still impede the bundling of claims or the defence of general interests in a unique location.

In substance, this work primarily concentrates on consumer matters. According to Article 17 BIa, a consumer is a natural person acting outside the scope of his profession. On the one hand, such delimitation is too restrictive as cross-border harms may also involve investors, data subjects or victims of environmental pollution, to mention just some examples. Collective redress is an interesting procedural tool for tort law cases. On the other hand, however, tort is an overly broad field

[3] Council Regulation (EU) 1215/2012 of 12 December 2012 on jurisdiction and the recognition and enforcement of judgments in civil and commercial matters [2012] OJ L351/1.

of law, which is difficult to manage for legislative purposes as it involves many different types of victims with different procedural positions. Therefore, further delineation is needed.

Additionally, the use of collective redress as an instrument to repair harms to general interests does not perfectly fit the notion of 'consumer', since no individual victim can be identified in those cases. Somehow, general interests transcend the concept of consumer, which seems to require the individualisation of the damage. Therefore, a broad material scope that covers consumers at large is initially adopted in this book. Specific references to investors and data subjects are included, even if these actors fall out of the scope of section 4 BIa. The suggested proposal for a specific forum regarding collective redress actions will eventually draft a more precise delimitation of the material scope.

The use of collective redress in competition law matters would have been an interesting question for this research project to tackle. Nevertheless, the appropriateness of a jurisdictional ground depends, among other things, on the equilibrium between parties' rights and the potential need for protection of the weakest party. In light of this, the situation of both the claimant and the defendant, is an important factor to determine where the best place to initiate proceedings is. However, actors involved in consumer and competition law cases are different: in particular, competition law infringements are not restricted to consumers but rather affect a broader range of victims such as SMEs and even large corporations. In this case, the procedural balance between parties is different from consumer disputes. Furthermore, the determination of a forum also depends on the equilibrium between public and private enforcement. Conversely to the consumer law field, the role of the EU Commission in competition law notably reinforces public enforcement. In light of the above, jurisdictional questions surrounding collective redress actions in the competition law field should be the object of an independent investigation. The result might well be that players in this field of law should be able to litigate in the same forum suggested in the last chapter of this book. Be that as it may, an autonomous assessment is needed.

V. Towards the Construction of an Appropriate Regime on International Jurisdiction in Collective Redress Cases

The last chapter of this book examines whether the available jurisdictional grounds of the BIa are appropriate for collective redress actions (chapter 4, I.A. and B.). Additionally, it investigates whether the different proposals for reform might bring some coherence to the current private international law landscape (chapter 4, I.C.). Specifically, proposals drafted by private organisations and the literature, as well as the solutions adopted by national legislators, are assessed.

Chapter 4 concludes that a specific forum for collective redress actions should be created (II.B.). In order to propose such a forum, the fundamental principles of the private international law discipline are relied on. Furthermore, the policy objectives pursued by the EU are taken into account. The objective is to draft a realistic and easy-to-implement proposal that fosters access to justice. Besides, such a proposal should not alter the rights of the defendant. In order to convince the reader that the specific, suggested forum is valuable, it is compared with competing solutions. Some specific elements that would have to be clarified in case the proposal is adopted are presented.

1

Back to the Origin: The US Class Action

The American class action is considered as the precursor of all modern mechanisms of collective actions. Because of its years of experience, some state that the US class action constitutes a reference system upon which other collective private enforcement systems should rely.[1] This does not mean that national legislators should merely mimic the American device or transplant it, as it stands, into their legal order. However, the study of this instrument is a mandatory step for anyone who wishes to understand the private enforcement of collective rights. In light of this, the present research project naturally starts with an analysis of the US class action. This exercise serves different purposes.

To start with, a look at the abusive exploitation of the US class action explains the EU deep-rooted antipathy against the American device. For example, the EU Commission publicly stated that

> any measures for judicial redress need to be appropriate and effective (…). Therefore, they must not attract abusive litigation (…). Examples of such adverse effects can be seen in particular in 'class actions' as known in the United States. The EU approach to collective redress must thus give proper thought to preventing these negative effects and devising adequate safeguards against them.[2]

So much so, that the Commission recommends Member States to adopt collective redress procedural tools with opposite structural features than its American homologue.[3] In this sense, the Commission's recommendations are 'more reactive

[1] J López Sánchez, *El sistema de las* class actions *en los Estados Unidos de América* (Editorial Comares, 2011) 1–2 ('se presenta como una primera referencia para determinar las pautas sobre las que debe construirse el régimen de la tutela jurisdiccional colectiva. Esto no significa que deban ser entendidas como el norte hacia el que deba encaminarse toda reforma, pero sí que son paso obligado para el estudio de las formas colectivas de tutela'). See also L Carballo Piñeiro, *Las acciones colectivas y su eficacia extraterritorial – Problemas de recepción y transplante de las class actions en Europa* (De conflictu legum. Estudios de Derecho Internacional Privado, 2009) 23.

[2] Commission, Towards a European Horizontal Framework for Collective Redress COM (2013) 401 final 3.

[3] Whereas the US class action is based on an opt-out system, allows punitive damages, gives any claimant standing to sue and permits a no win no pay financing system, the Commission recommends the adoption of collective redress instruments based on an opt-in system (an opt-out-based instrument is possible only in exceptional cases) that ban punitive damages, limit standing to sue and restrict funding possibilities. *Cf* r 23 of the American Federal Rules of Civil Procedure examined below and the

than proactive'.[4] Nevertheless, the fear generated by the US class action is often exaggerated. The distinct and specific features of the US legal system indicate that an abuse of collective redress actions in Europe is rather unlikely.

Additionally, the US class action has served as a basis for the construction of many national collective redress instruments in Europe: sometimes as an example,[5] sometimes as a counterexample.[6] In light of this, certain procedural choices, which have been made at the national level, become understandable if one surveys the American device's functioning. Furthermore, because Member States adopted heterogeneous collective redress instruments, it is difficult to provide a uniform definition of such a concept. Consequently, the term 'collective redress' becomes easier to grasp when compared to a well-known procedural tool that has been and can be investigated. Chapter 2 of this research project takes that reality into account by defining EU collective redress mechanisms in comparison to the US class action.

Besides, the reaction of the US legislator to the procedural complexities generated by class actions represents a valuable information for the creation of future collective redress tools, as other states may apprehend the emergence of similar difficulties.[7] In other words, because foreign legal orders may benefit from the American system's expertise and maturity, they do not start from scratch: they can build up on the US experience by extracting the best of the American class action and avoiding its deficiencies.

Finally, a look at inter-state jurisdictional issues in class action proceedings will support the analysis of EU private international law questions in the next chapters. As explained below, class actions involving defendants and victims from different states generated important jurisdictional concerns that both the legislative and the judicial powers have attempted to resolve as they arose. The solutions given to those problems constitute an important source of inspiration for the development of appropriate private international law rules on collective redress on the other side of the Atlantic.

Chapter 1 first describes the core features of the US class action, as well as the legal environment that surrounds and influences its development (I.). The second part of this chapter focuses on fundamental preliminary questions, namely the suitability of a class action in comparison to alternative instruments and the selection of the appropriate forum (II.). Following this, Rule 23 of the

Commission Recommendation of 11 June 2013 on common principles for injunctive and compensatory collective redress mechanisms in the Member States concerning violations of rights granted under EU Law (ch 2, II.B.ii.b).

[4] SI Strong, 'Regulatory Litigation in the European Union: Does the U.S. Class Action have a New Analogue' (2012) 88(2) *Notre Dame Law Review* 899, 959.

[5] eg in the Netherlands, Portugal, Norway and Sweden.

[6] Most notably in France and Germany.

[7] HL Buxbaum, 'Class Actions, Conflict, and the Global Economy' (2014) 21 (2) *Indiana Journal of Global Legal Studies* 585, 587.

Federal Rules on Civil Procedure, which codifies the federal class action system, is examined (III.). Then, selected procedural consequences that the certification of a class action triggers are highlighted, such as the opt-out system, the effects of a class action judgment or settlement and the allocation of costs and attorney's fees (IV.). This chapter ends with a conclusion (V.).

I. A Primer on Class Actions

A. The Basic Features of the American Legal System

Class actions, as any procedural instrument, do not evolve in a vacuum. In fact, the development of procedural law is tightly linked to the political, economic and social context in which it is implemented. In light of this, it appears appropriate to start this chapter with a survey of the US legal system. As mentioned below, the American legal environment explains the existence and the current form of the class action device. In particular, two specific features of the US legal system influence the development of class actions: the federal structure of the judiciary system and the litigation culture.

To start with, the United States' judiciary organisation is based on the federalist model:[8] accordingly, the 50 states of the United States, as well as the federal government have their own court system.[9] Pursuant to Article III of the US Constitution, it is for Congress to establish the federal court system. Since 1891, the judiciary federal power is a pyramidal organisation composed of three levels: district courts are the tribunals of first instance; circuit courts hear cases on appeal and the US Supreme Court reviews decisions of the federal courts of appeals, as well as certain questions decided by the highest state courts.[10] As regards the state judiciary organisation, it is rather heterogeneous given that each state can establish courts as it deems convenient. However, some similarities can be pointed out: every state has a bunch of first instance courts – often called inferior courts – and appellate courts, as well as a supreme court.[11]

The federalist context that characterises the US judicial organisation influences the class action device: indeed, the dual court system means that class action plaintiffs will often have more than one forum available to bring their lawsuits.

[8] Federalism is the result of Americans' distrust in the concentration of power in the hands of a few. Historically, the rejection of the British domination, coupled with the existing disorder among colonies – partly due to the great diversity of the American population – created an antagonistic social situation: the need for a government and stability on the one hand, and the desire to remain free on the other. Federalism and reliance on litigation are the direct result of this opposition (SN Subrin and MYK Woo, *Litigating in America – Civil Procedure in Context* (Aspen Publishers, 2006) 8–11).

[9] LJ Silberman et al, *Civil Procedure: Theory and Practice*, 4th edn (Wolters Kluwer, 2013) 2.

[10] JB Oakley and VD Amar, *American Civil Procedure: A Guide to Civil Adjudication in US Courts* (Kluwer Law International, 2009) 37–41.

[11] ibid 41–43.

As a result, forum shopping and parallel litigation are general features of the American legal system.[12] For the sake of this investigation, special attention is given to multistate class actions – ie actions that involve the legal order of various states –, as they trigger questions comparable to the ones generated in EU cross-border collective redress cases.

Another consequence of federalism is the regulation of civil procedure, both at the federal and state level. The Federal Rules of Civil Procedure, adopted in 1938, harmonise the procedure in federal courts.[13] Even though states have the power to draft their procedural rules, their design has either been influenced by the Field Code[14] or the Federal Rules of Civil Procedure. However, procedural rules at both levels essentially look like each other. Because the United States is a common law system, specific attention must also be given to case law.

As far as the class action device is concerned, this means that it is regulated at both, federal and state levels. Therefore, different procedural rules apply to the class action suit depending on the forum chosen. At the federal level, the class action procedure is regulated in Rule 23 of the Federal Rules of Civil Procedure.[15] As for states, most of them have decided to closely follow the federal model.[16] For this reason, this work will principally focus on the federal procedure and set aside local specificities. Additionally, this work will make reference to the most important case law that influenced the development of the class action device.

Furthermore, the United States has been relying on litigation as a powerful tool of accountability and enforcement of rights. In this jurisdiction, parties and their counsel[17] are responsible for establishing the facts, framing the dispute and presenting the relevant evidence.[18] Conversely, judges are usually passive. This dispute resolution system based on lawyer-dominated litigation is also called 'adversarial legalism'.[19]

Because the adversarial model essentially rests upon lawyers, an active market has developed around the legal profession. Today, American lawyers are described

[12] This often triggers strategic forum selection (below B.ii.).

[13] The full text is available on the website of the Legal Information Institute of Cornell University Law School, available at www.law.cornell.edu/rules/frcp. All websites mentioned in the following footnotes have been accessed on 5 October 2018.

[14] The American judicial system inherited the division between common law and equity courts from the British. These courts usually applied different rules of procedure. In 1848, the state of New York enacted a Code of Civil Procedure – the Field Code – that merged and simplified the common law and equity systems. Today, the influence of the Field Code is still palpable in many states (see Oakley and Amar, *American Civil Procedure* (n 10) 25–26; Subrin and Woo, *Litigating in America* (n 8) 43–57).

[15] The text of this provision is reproduced in Annex I.

[16] TD Rowe, 'State and Foreign Class-Action Rules and Statutes: Differences From – And Lessons For? – Federal Rule 23' (2007) 35(1) *Western State University Law Review* 101, 101.

[17] The terms 'counsel', 'attorney' and 'lawyer' are used interchangeably.

[18] S Sherry and J Tidmarsh, *Essentials Civil Procedure* (Aspen Publishers, 2007) 34–38.

[19] RA Kagan, *Adversarial Legalism – The American Way of Law* (Harvard University Press, 2003) 9, 15.

as 'entrepreneurs', due to their central role in litigation and the legal system in general.[20] According to Coffee,[21] entrepreneurial litigation is the result of the unique American conception of justice on the one hand, and important legal developments that took place in the nineteenth century on the other – like the development of the American rule on costs and contingency fees. As a result, the lawyer was, and still is, perceived as the guardian of citizens' rights. Eventually, US courts adopted essential doctrines, which became the pillars of entrepreneurial litigation. Among them: (1) the acceptance of contingency fees; (2) the adoption of the 'American rule' on costs; and (3) the development of the 'common fund' doctrine[22] (below IV.C.). The predominant role of attorneys further increased when these obtained the right to litigate in protection of a public interest and thus, to supplement public enforcement. This refers to the 'private attorney general' institution.[23]

Within the class action system, the plaintiff's attorney is also considered as a private attorney general in the sense that he defends the interests of a community.[24] At the same time, the private attorney general faces severe criticism: in the class action system, for instance, the lack of control from the representative plaintiff over the attorney, combined with the lack of alignment of their interests, often encourages lawyers to satisfy greedy ambitions at the expense of the class.[25]

B. Definition and Characteristics

The US class action[26] is a procedural tool whereby a representative plaintiff[27] litigates on behalf of similarly-situated members – forming a class – before a court.

[20] GC Hazard and M Taruffo, *American Civil Procedure – An introduction* (Yale University Press, 1993) 87–88.

[21] JC Coffee, *Entrepreneurial Litigation: its Rise, Fall, and Future* (Harvard University Press, 2015) 9–29.

[22] ibid 11–12.

[23] ibid 14.

[24] For more explanations on the different types of private attorneys general, see WB Rubenstein, 'On What a "Private Attorney General" Is – and Why Does it Matter?' (2004) 57(6) *Vanderbilt Law Review* 2129, 2142–55.

[25] See JC Coffee, 'Rescuing the Private Attorney General: Why the Model of the Lawyer as Bounty Hunter is Not Working' (1983) 42(2) *Maryland Law Review* 215, 230–36, who presents the different factors that cripple adequate private enforcement by the private attorney general.

[26] The definition and description of the American class action is a compilation of different sources: R Mulheron, *The Class Action in Common Law Legal Systems – A Comparative Perspective* (Hart Publishing, 2004) 3; WB Rubenstein, *Newberg on Class Actions*, 5th edn (Eagen, West, December 2016 update) para 1:1, available on WestlawNext; JM McLaughlin, *McLaughlin on Class Actions: Law and Practice*, 13th edn (Thomson West, October 2016 update) para 1:1, available on WestlawNext.

[27] The terms 'representative plaintiff', 'class representative', 'named plaintiff', or simply 'representative' are used interchangeably.

The bundling of analogous claims in a single suit enables courts to resolve tens, hundreds or even millions of cases at once. When potential claimants are numerous and their factual and legal situation is similar enough, then the opportunity to try a myriad of claims all at once becomes attractive for all participants: for plaintiffs because the aggregation of their claims divides the costs of bringing a lawsuit, and thus makes access to court possible. Moreover, opt-out-based class actions represent an interesting way to compensate rational apathy;[28] for defendants thanks to class actions, they avoid the financial burden of litigating multiple individual claims in different locations; and for the judicial power, class actions may spare its resources. Typically, the class action is considered an adequate procedural vehicle in the following illustrative examples: consumers oppressed with unauthorised charges sue telecommunication companies in order to recover their money; employees subjected to systematic race discrimination bring a suit against their employer; investors who purchased overvalued stock due to misleading information start litigation against the company; purchasers of a defective product sue the company liable; and patients injured by the effects of a prescribed drug bring a lawsuit against the manufacturer.

Usually, extensive research by specialised law firms precedes the filing of a class action:[29] these firms scrutinise the news and examine reports in search of the next successful case. In broad outline, law firms will look for cases involving 'large-scale, uniform harm, preferably one in which the harm per person is too small to justify individual lawsuit'.[30] Attorneys play a primary role in class actions not only for their investigative and legal skills but also for their financial support.[31] Ordinarily, attorneys only get their investment reimbursed if the class action succeeds. This makes the business highly risky but the rewards for class counsel take that risk into account. The financial incentives built up by the procedural system push lawyers to undertake class actions. However, they also create potential conflicts of interest between the class and their attorney.

Once the class action is lodged, a specific procedure tailored to multi-party litigation is triggered. As previously mentioned, Rule 23 of the Federal Rules on Civil Procedure governs cases at the federal level. This provision sets up different kinds of class actions according to the remedies sought,[32] establishes the conditions for the group of claimants to proceed as a class and details the procedural specificities applicable to the class action.

[28] As R van den Bergh and LT Visscher explain 'even though it may be beneficial to society, individual consumers will not initiate enforcement actions, since potential plaintiffs are driven only by private gain, which could be lower than the expenses of their claims. From their point of view, not bringing any claim is perfectly rational; this problem is generally known as "rational apathy"'. See R van den Bergh and LT Visscher, 'The Preventive Function of Collective Actions for Damages in Consumer Law' 2008 (1) 2 *Erasmus Law Review* 5, 14.

[29] Like Milberg LLP, The Mills Law Firm or Lieff Cabraser Heimann & Bernstein.

[30] B Anderson and A Trask, *The Class Action Playbook*, 2nd edn (Oxford University Press, 2012) 73.

[31] For an overview of the profession in the United States, see Subrin and Woo (n 8) 25–36, esp 33–36.

[32] Under rr 23(b)(2) and (b)(1)(A), claimants seek injunctive or declaratory relief. As for rr 23(b)(3) and (b)(1)(B), they allow claims for damages. These categories are further detailed below.

From a structural perspective, the class action is led by a representative plaintiff – usually selected by the class counsel – who represents similarly-situated members and litigates on their behalf. The representative must be a plaintiff whose factual and legal situation share similarities with the rest of the class. As for remaining class members, they are automatically bound by the court's final judgment without participating in the class action. This is at odds with the procedural principle whereby a person cannot be bound by the outcome of proceedings in which he/she did not take part.[33] For this reason, the American class action has been highly criticised, mostly by foreign legal professionals. Often, absent members are unaware of the existence of a class action, but their apathy nevertheless triggers a change in their legal position. As the saying goes, silence means consent. This result is quite puzzling: how could someone change his or her legal situation or be bound by a decision without lifting a finger?

With this in mind, some safeguards must necessarily be put in place in order to protect absent class members, who will not have their day in court but will nevertheless be subject to the preclusive effect of the class action judgment or settlement. This goal is achieved if members are offered appropriate notice and in some cases, a right to opt out. The rationale of the notice requirement is to inform these members about the existence of the class action and the legitimacy of the right to opt out is to allow members to start an individual action if they want to. The opportunity to opt out is normally provided when the class is not perfectly cohesive; this means that dissimilarities between claimants still subsist and justify the set-up of an opt-out regime.

Finally, although a class action may theoretically end up with a court's judgment, it has to be emphasised that, most of the time, parties settle.[34]

i. Rationale: Judicial Efficiency and Access to Justice

There are two driving forces behind the class action device: judicial efficiency and access to justice. To begin with, the bundling of similar claims into a single lawsuit spares judicial resources and, thus, contributes to judicial economy. This was the predominant virtue attached to the class action device according to legal professionals of the nineteenth century.[35]

Furthermore, class actions have the power to foster access to courts. Indeed, thanks to class actions the costs of proceedings are divided among all the members

[33] Rubenstein, *Newberg on Class Actions* (n 26) para 1:1. McLaughlin, *McLaughlin on Class Actions* (n 26) para 1:1.

[34] See eg HM Downs, 'Federal Class Actions: Diminished Protection for the Class and the Class and the Case for Reform' (1994) 73 *Nebraska Law Review* 646, 684, who concludes that 'a study of all class actions in the Northern District of California from 1985 to 1993 reveals that over 80% were resolved by settlement'; Kagan, *Adversarial Legalism* (n 19) 109.

[35] Coffee, *Entrepreneurial Litigation* (n 21) 53; A Homburger, 'Private Suits in the Public Interest in the United States of America' in A Homburger and H Kötz (eds), *Klagen Privater im öffentlichen Interesse*, Arbeiten zur Rechtsvergleichung, vol 68 (Metzner, 1975) 24.

of a class. In light of this, it becomes interesting for small value claimants[36] to litigate. Put it differently, class actions improve access to justice for claimants who would otherwise not have access to court if they were required to litigate on an individual basis. Notably, this objective was at the heart of Rule 23 in its 1966 version: in *Mace v. Van Ru Credit Corp.*, the court highlighted that

> the policy at the very core of the class action mechanism is to overcome the problem that small recoveries do not provide the incentive for any individual to bring a solo action prosecuting his or her rights. A class action solves this problem by aggregating the relatively paltry potential recoveries into something worth someone's (usually an attorney's) labor.[37]

In light of this, the class action device has been used as a vehicle to enforce public interests and civil rights in particular. From the 1960s onwards, class actions for injunctive relief were brought in order to impede desegregation practice in public schools,[38] improve prisoners' life conditions, as well as child welfare agencies services,[39] or refrain employment discriminations.[40]

Some consider that the social context of the 1960s in the United States put pressure on the legislative power to provide more efficient and accessible enforcement tools. This led the American legislator to reform the class action device in 1966.[41] In particular, the call from black society for greater equality, the distrust of consumers in the fair and transparent functioning of the market, and the rise of environmental protection movements primarily influenced a proposal for change.[42] However, the most sceptical declare that the reform of 1966 was essentially technical. In this vein, the objective was to improve the wording of the provision and clarify certain issues more than to respond to a social demand. As Miller states, 'the draftsmen conceived the procedure's primary function to be providing a mechanism for securing private remedies, rather than deterring public wrongs or enforcing broad social policies'.[43]

Yet, it has to be emphasised that access to justice and judicial efficiency do not always go hand in hand. An uncontrolled desire to vindicate all possible claims that would otherwise not be litigated if they had to proceed on an individual basis can

[36] Also called negative value claimants. These are plaintiffs whose claims are worth a very small amount of money.

[37] *Mace v. Van Ru Credit Corp.*, 109 F.3d 338, 344 (7th Cir 1997).

[38] See eg *Brown v. Board of Education of Topeka*, 347 US 483 (1954).

[39] See eg *Marisol A. v. Giuliani*, 929 F. Supp 662 (DC New York 1996).

[40] For an overview of areas where civil rights class actions were brought, see J Greenberg, 'Civil Rights Class Actions: Procedural Means of Obtaining Substance' (1997) 39 *Arizona Law Review* 575, 575–86.

[41] Notably, the US legislator got rid of the three categories contained in the previous version of r 23 that were difficult to interpret and distinguish. Instead, the new provision provides a new tripartite structure that is still in force today.

[42] SC Yeazell, *From Medieval Group Litigation to the Modern Class Action* (Yale University Press, 1987) 240–45.

[43] AR Miller, 'Of Frankenstein Monsters and Shining Knights: Myth, Reality, and the "Class Action Problem"' (1979) 92 *Harvard Law Review* 664, 669.

overburden courts and create backlogs.[44] In this case, efficiency would be relatively diminished at the expense of other valuable cases. Citing Professor McGovern, Rabiej presents this problem in an illustrative and interesting way:

> History teaches that when Rule 23 is amended to make it more efficient, more persons will participate in class actions. Professor Francis McGovern (…) characterizes the ironic consequence of enhancing a litigation procedure as the 'freeway effect'. If you build a better highway, more drivers will be drawn to it, creating more congestion. The analogy to automobile congestion is apt. If you build a better Rule 23 to make class actions more efficient, more litigants will be attracted to it, expanding the courts' workloads and the judiciary's administrative burdens.[45]

Additionally, an enhanced access to justice could threaten defendants with unmeritorious claims, ie claims that are weak on the merits. Therefore, some balance between efficiency and access to justice must be achieved.

ii. Functions: Compensation and Deterrence

The class action is a powerful procedural tool that forces potential wrongdoers to internalise the cost of their unlawful conduct. It can be said that the threat of class action proceedings acts as the sword of Damocles over defendants' heads. In the United States, the deterrence effect of class actions replaces, or at least, complements public law enforcement and sanctions that cannot alone discourage harmful social conducts.[46] As the Supreme Court stated: 'The aggregation of individual claims in the context of a class wide suit is an evolutionary response to the existence of injuries unremedied by the regulatory action of government'.[47] In other words, class actions impose market discipline.

However, because class actions are frightening in terms of costs and stakes, some argue that they put unjustified pressure on the defendants who are 'forced' to settle.[48] In this sense, class actions may lead to blackmail settlements. This can be explained by the tremendous financial consequences that such actions trigger. For example, the defendant is required to bear the cost of extensive discovery, he/she is exposed to tremendous damages, and the length of trial usually calls for an important investment of time and money in order to prepare a strong defence. Additionally, the opt-out mechanism greatly increases the scope of the class, as absent members are automatically bound by the court's decision. In other words, while in separate individual proceedings the defendant has the same at stake as

[44] K Dam, 'Class Actions: Efficiency, Compensation, Deterrence and Conflict of Interest' (1975) 4 *The Journal of Legal Studies* 47, 49–54.

[45] JK Rabiej, 'The Making of Class Action Rule 23 – What Were We Thinking?' (2005) 24 *Mississippi College Law Review* 323, 327–28.

[46] Rubenstein (n 26) para 1:8.

[47] *Deposit Guar. Nat'l Bank of Jackson v. Roper*, 445 US 326, 339 (1980).

[48] C Silver, 'We're Scared to Death: Does Class Certification Subject Defendants to Blackmail?' (2003) 78 (4) *New York Law Review* 1357, 1357–430.

each plaintiff, class actions raise the bet and oblige the defendant to risk a lot of money in one shot. However, others argue that the possibility for defendants to settle without paying punitive damages and admitting any liability undermines the deterrent effect of class actions.[49]

In reaction to this, Judge Posner, in the leading case *In re Rhone-Poulenc Rorer Inc.*, used the settlement pressure experienced by the defendant as argument in order to refuse the case to proceed as a class action (decertification).[50] In this case, a group of haemophiliacs were contaminated by HIV, after using the defendant's blood supply previously infected by the virus. Victims brought some 300 lawsuits – in state and federal courts – representing around 400 claimants. The United States District Court of Northern Illinois certified a class containing a portion of the haemophiliacs infected by HIV. The defendant responded by writing a petition of mandamus[51] in the Court of Appeals for the Seventh Circuit. Judge Posner, writing for the majority opinion, granted the writ of mandamus and ordered the decertification of the class. In support of his decision, Judge Posner essentially stated that defendant facing class proceedings was threatened with bankruptcy, while it would not be the case if individual lawsuits were brought. Moreover, separate proceedings are preferable to a class action when the defendant is faced with high value claims. The *Rhone-Poulenc* decision has been highly criticised. The most striking argument against the Court of Appeals' reasoning is that no legal basis or precedent case law supports its theory.[52] Indeed, nothing in Rule 23 allows a court to deny certification – or decertify – a class on the basis that defendant is under pressure to settle.

Compensation is the other objective of the class action. However, depending on the type of action, compensation is not always a priority. Typically, the function of class actions composed of small value claimants is to deter unlawful conducts. In these cases, compensation only plays a secondary role.[53] Ultimately, the compensatory function of class actions has been called into question.[54] Among other things, it is alleged that greedy attorneys often pocket large fees and leave class members with almost nothing. Unfortunately, there is little empirical research on this topic because the information is difficult to obtain and compile.

[49] LS Mullenix, 'Ending Class Actions As We Know Them: Rethinking the American Class Action Rule' (2014) 64 *Emory Law Journal* 399, 420–21.

[50] The class was first certified, ie allowed to proceed as a class, in the United States District Court of Northern Illinois (*Wadleigh v. Rhone-Poulenc Rorer Inc.*, 157 F.R.D. 410 [DC Northern Illinois 1994]) and then decertified, ie not allowed to proceed as a class, by the Court of Appeals of the Seventh Circuit (*In the Matter of Rhone-Poulenc Rorer Inc.*, 51 F.3d 1293 [7th Cir 1995]).

[51] A writ of mandamus is 'a writ issued by a court to compel performance of a particular act by a lower court or a governmental officer or body, usu(ally) to correct a prior action or failure to act' according to BA Garner, *Black's Law Dictionary*, 9th edn (Thomson Reuters, 2009).

[52] A Kanner and T Nagy, 'Exploding the Blackmail Myth: A New Perspective on Class Action Settlements' (2005) 57 *Baylor Law Review* 681, 687.

[53] BT Fitzpatrick, 'Do Class Action Lawyers Make Too Little?' (2010) 158 *University of Pennsylvania Law Review* 2043, 2047.

[54] Mullenix, 'Ending Class Actions As We Know Them' (n 49) 418–20.

However, a recent investigation undertaken in this field by Professors Fitzpatrick and Gilbert draws positive conclusions on the compensation role of class actions.[55] The authors gathered data from over 15 federal consumer class actions (most of which were actions for damages). In particular, they compared the average pay-out consumers received in comparison with the amount of their damages. The results show that many class members received compensation representing up to 65 per cent of their actual damage, which is promising. In light of this, empirical evidence demonstrates that 'a majority of class members received a fair return on even small expected damages'.[56]

II. Pre-Certification Questions

A. Class Action and its Alternatives

Once a potential class action case is identified, plaintiffs' lawyers must first examine if class action is the most adequate procedural vehicle to litigate said case. The appropriateness of other instruments like joinder, multi-district litigation, consolidation, or ADR procedures should also be considered. For example, if the potential class is composed of less than 20 members all domiciled in the state of California, then joinder might appear as being the most suitable tool. Through joinder, each claimant keeps control over the proceedings.[57] When pending trial cases present a common issue of fact or law, the court may exercise its discretion to decide to consolidate suits mostly for efficiency purposes. For example, when the testimony of a witness is useful for various cases, consolidation enables the court to hear him/her only once.[58] Additionally, consolidation is a useful tool to avoid inconsistent judgments.[59] As for multi-district litigation (MDL), it is a procedure whereby dispersed cases from different federal districts are transferred to a single court for pre-trial management efficiency purposes.[60] In principle, MDL is appropriate for complex cases presenting common issues of fact or law. The transferee court is able to rule on questions like pre-trial discovery or jurisdictional issues.[61]

Plaintiffs' lawyers must then consider the potential use of ADR mechanisms and arbitration in particular. Recently, arbitration providers in the United States have reduced arbitration costs in order to make this system attractive for consumer

[55] BT Fitzpatrick and RC Gilbert, 'An Empirical Look at Compensation in Consumer Class Actions', Vanderbilt Public Law Research Paper No 15-3 and Vanderbilt Law and Economics Research Paper No 15-6 (2015), available at papers.ssrn.com.

[56] ibid 21.

[57] RH Klonoff, *Class Actions and Other Multi-Party Litigation in a Nutshell*, 3rd edn (Thomson West, 2007) 370.

[58] ibid 408.

[59] ibid.

[60] ibid 412.

[61] ibid 414.

and employment matters.[62] In this vein, individual arbitration proceedings have gained advantages that now compete directly with the judicial system.[63] Besides, the relatively recent transplant of class actions into the arbitration playfield has been hotly debated,[64] as these institutions possess different and sometimes even contradictory characteristics: while arbitration facilitates informal, streamlined proceedings[65] the mix of class action with arbitration sacrifices arbitration's informality and 'makes the process slower, more costly, and more likely to generate procedural morass'.[66] A more in-depth examination of this topic is provided below (chapter 2, II.C.i.a.).

Ordinarily, attorneys resort to class actions when a large number of victims share common issues of fact or law. Usually, when damages are high, a class action may not be appropriate because individual specificities will often predominate. Moreover, if stakes are high, plaintiffs could be reluctant to transfer their decisional power to a representative. Indeed, they often prefer to keep control over their case.

B. Jurisdiction

If the class action is the best procedural tool to 'drive' the substance of the case, the next step consists in drafting the complaint. At this point, important questions arise.[67] For example, lawyers must clearly delineate the scope of the class and

[62] See eg the fee schedule of the American Arbitration Association (AAA) included in the Consumer Arbitration rules, available at www.adr.org/sites/default/files/Consumer%20Rules.pdf.

[63] Regarding this debate, see, among many others, ME Budnitz, 'The High Cost of Mandatory Consumer Arbitration' (2004) 67 *Law and Contemporary Problems* 133, 150–56; CR Drahozal, 'Arbitration Costs and Forum Accessibility: Empirical Evidence' (2008) 41(4) *University of Michigan Journal of Law Reform* 813, 813–41; T Eisenberg and E Hill, 'Arbitration and Litigation of Employment Claims: An Empirical Comparison' (2004) *Dispute Resolution Journal* 44, 44–45; MB Farmer, 'Mandatory and Fair? A Better System of Mandatory Arbitration' (2012) 121 *Yale Law Journal* 2346, 2352–60; HM Kritzer and JK Anderson, 'The Arbitration Alternative: A Comparative Analysis of Case Processing Time, Disposition Mode, and Cost in the American Arbitration Association and the Courts' (1983) 8(1) *The Justice System Journal* 6, 6–19; TJ St Antoine, 'Mandatory Arbitration: Why It's Better Than It Looks' (2008) 41(4) *University of Michigan Journal of Law Reform* 783, 790–96; DS Schwartz, 'Mandatory Arbitration and Fairness' (2009) 84(3) *Notre Dame Law Review* 1247, 1247–341; JR Sternlight, 'Creeping Mandatory Arbitration: Is It Just?' (2005) 57 *Stanford Law Review* 1631, 1648–58; PB Rutledge, 'Whither Arbitration?' (2008) 6 *The Georgetown Journal of Law & Public Policy* 549, 556–60.

[64] When the Supreme Court issued the *Green Tree v. Bazzle* judgment (539 US 444 [2003]), many perceived that class actions and arbitration were compatible in the eyes of the Supreme Court. However, said Court later clarified its previous case law in *AT&T Mobility LLC v. Concepcion* (563 US 333 [2011]) by explicitly validating the use of class action waiver clauses in consumer contracts. As a result, in an attempt to solve the uncertainty surrounding consumer arbitration – including class arbitration –, the Arbitration Fairness Act has been regularly submitted to the US Congress – the last time being in 2017. This legal text would essentially consist in an amendment of the Federal Arbitration Act forbidding pre-dispute agreements concluded with consumers.

[65] *AT&T Mobility LLC* (n 63) 334.

[66] ibid.

[67] Anderson and Trask, *The Class Action Playbook* (n 30) 76–94.

carefully select the defendant(s). Additionally, they have to choose the plaintiff who will represent the whole class. One of the most important questions at this time of the litigation process and for the sake of this research project is the selection of the forum where the class action suit has to start. In this context, inter-state jurisdictional questions are interesting to analyse since similar problems may occur between the Member States of the EU.

Consequently, the next paragraphs include an excursus on US jurisdictional rules (i.). Then, particular questions regarding jurisdiction in class actions are highlighted (ii.). Some comments on the Class Action Fairness Act (CAFA), which partially reformed the US jurisdictional system, close this sub-section (iii.).

i. A Primer on Jurisdictional Rules in the US

Rules that establish jurisdiction in the United States are quite different from the ones available in the EU. To start with, each state enjoys a two-tier court system and thus, two types of rules on allocation of jurisdiction are available: one at the state level and the other at the federal level.[68] This bunch of rules is not exclusive but concurrent.[69]

Federal and state courts have jurisdiction over a case if they possess personal jurisdiction against the defendant (*in personam*) or his property (*in rem* or *quasi in rem*).[70] Specifically, state courts have general *in personam* jurisdiction over residents, people present in the state's territory, as well as people who consent to the court's jurisdictional power, to mention just a few connecting factors. Alternatively, a state court may have jurisdiction over absent defendants who have minimum contacts (long-arm statutes) with the territory.[71] This jurisdictional power may be specific, meaning that a single act affecting the state can constitute a valid ground for a court to establish jurisdiction, or general, inasmuch as the defendant entertains systematic and continuous contacts with said state.[72] In this case, any cause of action may be raised against the defendant. Furthermore, state courts might have *in rem* or *quasi in rem* jurisdiction over the defendant's property. On the one hand, *in rem* cases aim at determining the ownership over a property *erga omnes*; on the other hand, in *quasi in rem* cases, jurisdiction is linked to a certain property pertaining to the defendant and the effect of a judgment is limited to the parties involved in the proceedings. It is important to underline that only *in personam* jurisdiction creates a personal obligation on the defendant. Conversely, the defendant's liability in *in rem* or *quasi in rem* cases is limited to the property

[68] J Fleming, GC Hazard and J Leubsdorf, *Civil Procedure*, 5th edn (Foundation Press, 2001) 57–60.

[69] Rubenstein (n 26) para 6:3.

[70] The explanations regarding the different types of jurisdictional connecting factors (*in personam*, *in rem* and *quasi in rem*) stem from different sources: RD Freer, *Civil Procedure*, 3rd edn (Wolters Kluwer, 2012) 42–49; FE Scoles et al, *Conflict of Laws*, 3rd edn (West Group, 2000) 281–97; Subrin and Woo (n 8) 71–97.

[71] *International Shoe Co. v. Washington*, 326 US 310 (1945).

[72] Rubenstein (n 26) para 6:26.

thanks to which jurisdiction is established. In all cases, the Due Process Clause (Fourteenth Amendment of the US Constitution) limits the states' power to assert personal jurisdiction.

As for federal courts, their personal jurisdiction is based on state rules on jurisdiction.[73] This means that the federal courts of Massachusetts have to look at state provisions in order to examine if a Massachusetts state court could potentially have jurisdiction over a specific case. If the answer is yes, then federal courts have personal jurisdiction too.

Then, state courts possess original subject matter jurisdiction over all potential cases.[74] Specifically, this means that state courts have jurisdiction over any matter that has not been 'taken over' by Congress. However, it is useful to mention that some specialised courts exist at the state level that have limited subject matter jurisdiction.

As for federal courts,[75] according to Article III, § 2 of the US Constitution, they have subject matter jurisdiction in nine situations of which the most important are mentioned: diversity citizenship – this is when the dispute involves parties from different states and is worth more than USD 75,000 – and the existence of a federal question – that refers to cases which arise under a federal statute, such as securities or antitrust disputes.

As far as class actions are concerned, significant questions on jurisdiction arise in multistate class proceedings. These are class actions involving parties from different states of America. However, not all situations are problematic: for example, when the defendant is headquartered in the state where a nationwide or single-state class action starts, courts will not face any particular issue in asserting jurisdiction since residence establishes a strong link with a state's territory. More challenging is the situation where a non-resident defendant faces a nationwide class action in a given forum. As explained in the above paragraphs, a state court is only able to base its jurisdictional power on a long-arm statute. In other words, jurisdiction may only be asserted if the defendant has minimum contacts with said state. This type of jurisdiction may be specific or general. In case a specific jurisdictional power exists, it might be difficult for courts to acquire jurisdiction over claims that did not take place on the state's territory and affect victims located in a sister-state or even abroad.

For example, such a situation arose in the *Daimler* case,[76] where Argentinean residents brought a class action suit in the District Court for the Northern District of California against DaimlerChrysler AG, located in Stuttgart (Germany). The plaintiffs alleged that an Argentinean subsidiary of the company violated various US laws by kidnapping, torturing, detaining or killing its employees during the 'Dirty War' in Argentina. According to the plaintiffs, the District Court

[73] Scoles et al, *Conflict of Laws* (n 70) 316.
[74] Rubenstein (n 26) para 6:3.
[75] Scoles et al (n 70) 320; Rubenstein (n 26) para 6:2.
[76] *Daimler AG v. Bauman et al*, 571 US ___ (2014).

had general jurisdiction over the defendant based on the Californian long-arm statute.[77] To be more precise, they argued that the Californian subsidiary of Daimler, namely Mercedes-Benz USA, LLC incorporated in Delaware, distributed cars in California and hence, entertained significant contacts with said state.

In this vein, general jurisdiction would allow any plaintiff to present any claim in the District Court of California. Along the same line of reasoning, general jurisdiction would also enable nationwide class actions against a non-resident defendant, supposing that he/she has tight contacts with said state. However, the US Supreme Court, which granted certiorari, rejected this far-fetched interpretation, as it considered that it violated the Due Process Clause. Citing its previous case law, the Supreme Court explained that

> [a] court may assert general jurisdiction over foreign (sister-state or foreign-country) corporations to hear any and all claims against them when their affiliations with the State are so 'continuous and systematic' as to render them essentially at home in the forum State.[78]

In the case at issue, however, the Supreme Court concluded that Daimler's contacts with California were too slim for general jurisdiction to be allocated to the courts of that state.[79]

Another challenging situation occurs when multistate class actions involve plaintiffs from different states of America. At first, it was unclear whether the criteria regarding personal jurisdiction over the defendant – like presence on the territory or minimal contacts – should equally apply to plaintiffs.[80] In *Shutts*,[81] the Supreme Court held that the due process protection provided to defendants should not be the same for plaintiffs, as the burden placed on them is not the same. For instance, contrarily to the plaintiff, the defendant

> must generally hire counsel and travel to the forum to defend itself from the plaintiff's claim, or suffer a default judgment. The defendant may be forced to participate in extended and often costly discovery, and will be forced to respond in damages or to comply with some other form of remedy imposed by the court should it lose the suit. The defendant may also face liability for court costs and attorney's fees.[82]

Because out-of-state absent class members do not face such a burden, they can be attracted in the court of another state under more lenient conditions.[83]

[77] See s 410.10 of the California Code of Civil Procedure.

[78] *Daimler* (n 76) 754.

[79] Due to the result of the *Daimler* case, other theories attempt to reinforce jurisdiction over non-resident defendants for claims, which arise outside a given state territory. These are explained by Rubenstein (n 26) para 6:26.

[80] BA Winters, 'Jurisdiction over Unnamed Plaintiffs in Multistate Class Actions' (1985) 73(1) *California Law Review* 181, 181–211.

[81] *Phillips Petroleum Co. v. Shutts*, 472 US 797 (1985).

[82] ibid 808.

[83] Scoles et al (n 70) 437–38; Klonoff, *Class Actions and Other Multi-Party Litigation in a Nutshell* (n 57) 186–89.

Now, would the situation differ if plaintiffs located in foreign states – like in a Member State of the EU – participated in an American class action? US courts have dealt with this particular question. Overall, the rule is as follows: if it is likely that the courts of the foreign state of which class members are citizens will recognise the US class action judgment or settlement, these members are included in the class.[84] Conversely, if it is unlikely that the foreign courts will recognise the outcome of a US class action, then foreign class members are excluded from class proceedings.[85] Usually, the superiority requirement of Rule 23 is the ground defeating transnational class actions.[86] The rationale behind the above-mentioned principle is the fear of submitting the defendant to re-litigation in case foreign claimants are not satisfied with the outcome of a US class action.[87]

This principle was first established in *Bersch*,[88] where a US citizen litigated against IOS – incorporated in Canada –, alleging that the firm violated US securities laws. The named plaintiff represented a class including mostly EU litigants. The Court of Appeals ruled that 'while an American court need not abstain from entering judgment simply because of a possibility that a foreign court may not recognize or enforce it, the case stands differently when this is a near certainty'.[89] Here, experts' reports demonstrated that a US judgment would not be recognised in England, Germany, Switzerland, Italy and France, even if proper notice and the right to opt out was sent to the foreign class members.

[84] Note that American courts use the words 'recognition' and 'preclusion' interchangeably, which is confusing since those terms refer to different concepts. However, Wasserman clarifies that US courts usually analyse whether a judgment or settlement will be recognised abroad and set aside questions regarding their preclusive effect (R Wasserman, 'Transnational Class Actions and Interjurisdictional Preclusion' (2011) 86(1) *Notre Dame Law Review* 313, 315–16).

[85] L Sandstrom Simard, 'Foreign Citizens in Transnational Class Actions' (2011) 97(1) *Cornell Law Review* 87, 88.

[86] MP Murtagh, 'The Rule 23(b)(3) Superiority Requirement and Transnational Class Actions: Excluding Foreign Class Members in Favor of European Remedies' (2011) 1 *Hastings International and Comparative Law Review* 1, 6; Sandstrom Simard, 'Foreign Citizens in Transnational Class Actions' (n 85) 89.

[87] Murtagh, 'The Rule 23(b)(3) Superiority Requirement and Transnational Class Actions' (n 86) 8–9; R Mulheron, 'The Recognition, and Res Judicata Effect, of a United States Class Actions Judgment in England: A Rebuttal of Vivendi' (2012) 75(2) *Modern Law Review* 180, 185.

[88] *Bersch v. Drexel Firestone, Inc.*, 519 F.2d 974 (2nd Cir 1975).

[89] ibid 996–97. After the *Bersch* judgment, the likelihood of recognition was softened: to be more specific, the 'near certainty' requirement was replaced by a probability test. In *In re Vivendi Universal, S.A. Securities Litigation*, 242 F.R.D. 76 (DC Southern District of New York 2007), the DC stated that '[w]here plaintiffs are unable to show that foreign court recognition is more likely than not, this factor weighs against a finding of superiority and, taken in consideration with other factors, may lead to the exclusion of foreign claimants from the class. The closer the likelihood of non-recognition is to being a "near certainty", the more appropriate it is for the Court to deny certification of foreign claimants' (95). Relying on expert declarations regarding the potential recognition of a class action judgment, the District Court certified a class encompassing claimants from France, England and the Netherlands (105) (Wasserman, 'Transnational Class Actions and Interjurisdictional Preclusion' (n 84) 313–14). This approach was confirmed in *In re Alstom SA Securities Litigation*, 253 F.R.D. 266 (DC Southern District of New York 2008).

Various arguments are often advanced in order to prove that Member States' courts may not recognise an American judgment or settlement:[90] in particular, issues regarding the opt-out nature of the American class action device are often raised as a barrier to recognition pursuant to public policy grounds.[91] Then, some Member States submit the recognition and enforcement of class action judgments or settlements to the control of US courts' jurisdictional power. However, many express that such courts might not extend jurisdiction so as to reach EU absent class members.[92] At least, doubts are allowed. Finally, the allocation of punitive damages under the US legal system might threaten the recognition and enforcement of class actions judgments or settlements abroad.[93]

ii. Strategic Forum Selection and Parallel Litigation

Because of the two-layered US court system, it is common that various courts at different levels simultaneously have jurisdiction over a similar case.[94] Criteria used to establish jurisdiction are often elastic and allow judges a discretionary margin of interpretation. As a result, the opportunity for 'forum shopping' in the United States is high. Moreover, because procedural and substantive laws are diverse, selecting the right forum is a fundamental strategic step.

Depending on the nature of a case, various fora could be available to attorneys and victims willing to bring a class action lawsuit. Because each conflict is unique,

[90] For an interesting analysis of the question in the Netherlands, France, United Kingdom, and Germany, see T Arons, 'Recognition of US Class Actions or Settlements in Europe' (2015) 3 *European Company and Financial Law Review* 462, 462–87.

[91] S Bariatti, 'Recognition and Enforcement in the EU of Judicial Decisions Rendered Upon Class Actions: The Case of U.S. and Dutch Judgments and Settlements' in F Pocar et al (eds), *Recasting Brussels I*, Studi e Pubblicazioni della Rivista di Diritto Internazionale Privato e Processuale 76 (CEDAM, 2012) 321–23; I Buschkin, 'The Viability of Class Action Lawsuits in a Globalized Economy – Permitting Foreign Claimants to Be Members of Class Action Lawsuits in the U.S. Federal Courts' (2005) 90(6) *Cornell Law Review* 1563, 1579–80; GW Johnson, 'Rule 23 and the Exclusion of Foreign Citizens as Class Members in U.S. Class Actions' (2012) 52(4) *Virginia Journal of International Law* 963, 971; Murtagh (n 86) 7–8; A Pinna, 'Recognition and Res Judicata of US Class Action Judgments in European Legal Systems' (2008) 1(2) *Erasmus Law Review* 31, 40–59.

[92] Bariatti, 'Recognition and Enforcement in the EU of Judicial Decisions Rendered Upon Class Actions' (n 91) 324–25; Buschkin, 'The Viability of Class Action Lawsuits in a Globalized Economy' (n 91) 1579; Mulheron, 'The Recognition, and Res Judicata Effect, of a United States Class Actions Judgment in England' (n 87) 197–210; Pinna, 'Recognition and Res Judicata of US Class Action Judgments in European Legal Systems' (n 91) 56–59; M Requejo Isidro and M Otero Crespo, 'Collective Redress in Spain: Recognition and Enforcement of Class Action Judgments and Class Settlements' in D Fairgrieve and E Lein (eds), *Extraterritoriality and Collective Redress* (Oxford University Press, 2012) 320–22, but see the recent enactment of Art 47 of the Law on International Cooperation in Civil Matters (*Ley 29/2015, de 30 de julio, de cooperación jurídica internacional en materia civil*) as well as the interesting comments of F Garcímartin, Reconocimiento en España de las class actions extranjeras: el nuevo artículo 47 LCJI, (04.09.2015) *Almacén de Derecho*, available at almacendederecho.org/reconocimiento-en-espana-de-las-class-actions-extranjeras-el-nuevo-articulo-47-lcji/ and F Gascón Inchausti, 'Reconocimiento y ejecución de resoluciones judiciales extranjeras en la ley de cooperación jurídica internacional en materia civil' (2015) 7(2) *Cuadernos de Derecho Transnacional* 158, 169–70.

[93] Bariatti (n 91) 323–24; Buschkin (n 91) 1578–79.

[94] GP Miller, 'Overlapping Class Actions' (1996) 71 *New York University Law Review* 514, 527.

class counsels have to investigate which court could best match their case. The following paragraphs examine some of the elements guiding attorneys' choice of forum.[95] When two or more state courts have jurisdiction to rule on a case, attorneys will usually look at the political environment, the presence of judges with particular expertise, the substantive state law in force, and other state specificities.[96]

This automatically generates questions regarding the emergence of parallel or duplicative proceedings. First and foremost, it has to be underlined that no statute governs parallel litigation. Instead, US courts have developed rather flexible instruments that foster coordination and coherence. In such a context, class action proceedings may overlap in different scenarios.

In the first place, when different class actions are brought in federal courts, relatively effective tools enable courts to coordinate them. The most obvious one is the centralisation of pre-trial issues in the MDL Panel in order to avoid inconsistencies and waste of resources.[97] In the second place, federal judges might prefer to simply coordinate their proceedings.[98] Finally, federal courts also have the power to enjoin the start of parallel and overlapping proceedings in other federal courts by issuing injunctions.[99]

However, when various class actions are pending in both federal and state courts, the injunction system is limited – federal courts can only preclude the filing of future actions in state courts.[100] Instead, federal judges may decide to stay or

[95] An interesting study shows that leading arguments influencing attorneys' choice of a particular forum are: the predisposition of courts to rule in favour of a party; the source of law (state or federal) supporting class claims; and the connection of members to a certain State (TE Willing and SR Wheatmann, 'Attorney Choice of Forum in Class Action Litigation: What Difference Does it Make?' (2006) 81(2) *Notre Dame Law Review* 591, 611–12).

[96] eg California is well known for its arsenal of provisions protecting consumers' rights. Therefore, starting a class action lawsuit against a telecommunication company in this state could be a favourable forum, if available. Furthermore, class counsel could take advantages or avoid some important state specificities: eg Mississippi has no class action procedural rule; Illinois does not impose any superiority requirement for damages class actions; South Carolina does not allow negative value class actions; and in some states, the burden to pay costs of notice relies on the defendant contrary to federal rules. In case a plurality of federal courts have the competence to hear the case at stake, counsel will pay special attention to judicial predisposition and judges' expertise. Sometimes, attorneys may have the choice to go to state or federal courts according to the nature of the case. Statistically, cases remain in state courts when: local judges show a favourable predisposition towards the attorney's client; claims are essentially based on state substantive law; and a large majority of claimants reside within the territory of a single state. On the other hand, counsel will be inclined to shift to federal courts if they identify a judicial predisposition towards their client, claimants come from various states, and claims trigger federal questions of law (Anderson and Trask (n 30) 76–82; Rowe, 'State and Foreign Class-Action Rules and Statutes' (n 16) 101–26; Willing and Wheatmann, 'Attorney Choice of Forum in Class Action Litigation' (n 95) 612–13).

[97] Manual for Complex Litigation (2004), para 20.13, 219–27, available at https://public.resource.org/scribd/8763868.pdf.

[98] ibid, para 20.14, 227–28.

[99] EF Sherman, 'Class Actions and Duplicative Litigation' (1987) 62(3) *Indiana Law Journal* 507, 518–27.

[100] ibid, para 20.32, 238; Miller, 'Overlapping Class Actions' (n 94) 531–32; Sherman, 'Class Actions and Duplicative Litigation' (n 99) (528–33; CA Wright and AR Miller, *Federal Practice & Procedure* (Thomson Reuters West, April 2017 update), para 4212, available on WestlawNext. The converse situation, whereby a state court would enjoin pending federal proceedings, is unlikely to happen.

dismiss the case.[101] Alternatively, removal in federal courts is another potential instrument that fosters centralisation of actions and, hence, limits the emergence of duplicative actions.[102] As explained below, thanks to the Class Action Fairness Act, removal is facilitated (II.B.iii.). Notably, evidence shows that federal and state judges sometimes use informal communication tools in order to coordinate their cases.[103] Finally, state courts may decide to stay proceedings pending before them when a similar class action has started in a federal court.[104]

Lastly, pending class actions in different state courts is the most interesting situation, as it triggers similar questions to the ones that could potentially appear between various EU Member States. Here, state courts may suspend proceedings when a sister-state court must rule on a similar case.[105] Then, injunctions are also possible although this instrument seems to be relatively unfriendly, since it obliges out-of-state courts to refuse jurisdiction over a case.[106]

In all cases, US courts can always deny certification of a class when it overlaps with a similar action pending in another court. This possibility is examined under the superiority requirement.[107]

iii. The Impact of the Class Action Fairness Act on Jurisdictional Questions

The introduction of CAFA[108] in 2005 altered strategies regarding forum selection to a certain extent. The purpose of this law is to eliminate abusive conduct affecting the rights of both plaintiffs and defendants that have been contaminating the class action. However, it is commonly acknowledged that CAFA is beneficial for defendants inasmuch as they usually prefer to go to federal courts, which are deemed to treat motions for certification more scrupulously.[109] Thanks to CAFA a new diversity standard to bring class action suits in federal courts was adopted (section 1332 of the US Code).

Henceforth, plaintiffs' flexibility for choosing the most favourable forum is limited. Indeed, this legislation gives federal courts original jurisdiction on class actions encompassed in its material scope. Alternatively, defendants may transfer

[101] Manual for Complex Litigation (n 97) para 20.32, 238–39; Miller (n 94) 528–29.
[102] Miller (n 94) 530–31.
[103] Manual for Complex Litigation (n 97) para 20.313, 235–38.
[104] Miller (n 94) 532–33.
[105] ibid 521–22.
[106] ibid 523–25.
[107] Sherman (n 99) 510–17.
[108] The full text of the Class Action Fairness Act is available at www.congress.gov/bill/109th-congress/senate-bill/5/text.
[109] Anderson and Trask (n 30) 104; in their study, Willing and Wheatman ((n 95) 615–18) exposed that defendants' preference for federal courts over state courts is predominantly guided by the following factors: attorneys' and clients' general preference for federal courts and the stringency according to which the court usually examines class certification.

a state class action to federal courts (removal) if they deem convenient. As a result, plaintiff attorneys' strategies shifted with the introduction of the CAFA: prior to that, counsel were usually looking for the most advantageous state court – also called judicial hellholes. This gave rise to abuses since local courts sometimes apply the law inconsistently, tend to favour resident plaintiffs over out-of-state defendants and are subject to political bias.[110] Besides, the general rules on diversity applicable at that time hindered the defendant's removal of the case to federal courts because of their strict conditions:[111] first, complete diversity was required. This means that a case might be removed to a federal court only if all named plaintiffs were from a different state from all the defendants. Second, the amount of the dispute had to be higher than USD 75,000 per claimant. These conditions could be circumvented by class counsel with no particular trouble if, on the one hand, he/she selected a named plaintiff domiciled in the same State as the defendant and, on the other hand, capped the amount sought by claimants.[112] In order to re-establish the procedural equilibrium between the parties, CAFA shifted the original jurisdiction rule and facilitated removal for cases entering into its material scope.

Today, when a case presents diversity elements, it is foreseeable that the defendant will remove the case to federal courts because the conditions for removal are easier to fulfil. Specifically, any suit that fulfils CAFA's requirements, but is nevertheless filed in state courts, can be transferred to federal courts if:[113] (1) the class includes at least 100 members; (2) minimal diversity exists; and (3) the aggregated amount in dispute exceeds USD 5 million. It must be clarified that there is minimal diversity when at least one member of the class comes from a different State from that of the defendant. Then, the amount in dispute corresponds to the amount of all the claims put together. Additionally, section 1146 of Title 28 of the US Code states that any defendant willing to remove a case to federal courts must 'file in the district court of the United States for the district and division within which such action is pending'. This implies that plaintiffs' counsel is 'tied up' to the federal court of the district in which the lawsuit is originally brought. In light of this, when class counsel senses that the case will be removed, he/she should consider filing the suit directly in federal court in order to have a chance to select the most appropriate forum.[114] In this situation, attorneys will take into account the substantive law applicable to the case and the presence of expert judges.[115] Finally, it has to

[110] See the report submitted by Mr Specter from the Committee on the Judiciary on the Class Action Fairness Act 2005 (2005) 4–5, available at www.congress.gov/congressional-report/109th-congress/senate-report/14/1.

[111] McLaughlin (n 26) paras 2:2 and 2:4.

[112] These strategic moves are encompassed under the concept of 'artful pleading'. See A Andreeva, 'Class Action Fairness Act of 2005: The Eight-Year Saga is Finally Over' (2005) 59 *University of Miami Law Review* 385, 394–98; Klonoff (n 57) 216.

[113] Klonoff (n 57) 214–15.

[114] HM Erichson, 'CAFA's Impact on Class Action Lawyers' (2008) 156 *University of Pennsylvania Law Review* 1593, 1611.

[115] ibid 1612.

be highlighted that CAFA sets up some exceptions to the general rule explained above, when the case possesses a strong connection with a given state.[116]

III. Class Certification

Certification is the nucleus of class action litigation.[117] This step will either drop the class action procedure down or give a powerful leverage to the class against the defendant who will feel an important pressure to settle. From a procedural perspective, the class representative bears the burden of proving that all conditions for certification are met. At the federal level, Rule 23 of the Federal Rules of Civil Procedure establishes common requirements that plaintiffs must fulfil if they want to proceed as a class (B.). Depending on the type of class action (A.), additional or different requirements must be fulfilled (C. and D.).

A. The Tripartite Structure of Rule 23

To begin with, Rule 23(a) sets forth four prerequisites that any potential class has to meet for its certification motion to be granted by a court. According to this provision, the class must be so numerous as to make joinder impracticable (numerosity); must present common issues of fact and law (commonality); be adequately represented by a lead plaintiff (adequacy of representation) whose claims are typical of the members of the class (typicality). Then, Rules 23(b)(1), (2) and (3) list three class action categories and their specific requirements. These class action types may be classified according to the remedies that they provide: first of all, injunctive or declaratory relief – Rule 23(b)(2) and (b)(1)(A) – is often sought in cases involving civil rights or institutional reforms. Examples of these particular suits cover discrimination or pollution allegations, and suits aiming at preventing some government action.[118] The specificity of these class actions is that their priority consists in maintaining coherence in the defendant's interest.[119] As a consequence, if the polluting nature of a certain product used by the defendant

[116] Klonoff (n 57) 218–21; McLaughlin (n 26) para 12:6. In particular, s 1332(d)(3) of the US Code states that when more than one-third but less than two-thirds of the class members are citizens of the forum state and the defendant is also domiciled in said state, then the federal court may decline jurisdiction after considering various factors. eg jurisdiction might be rejected where an inter-state interest is at stake or where the law of the state where the class action suit has been filed is the only one to apply to the whole class. s 1332(d)(4) of the US Code obliges the court to decline jurisdiction in certain cases. Notably, when more than two-thirds of the class members, as well as the primary defendants are domiciled in the forum state, jurisdiction has to be rejected.

[117] Klonoff (n 57) 136.

[118] NM Pace, 'Class Actions in the United States of America: An Overview of the Process and the Empirical Literature', National Report 9–10 (2007), available at globalclassactions.stanford.edu/sites/default/files/documents/USA__National_Report.pdf.

[119] ibid 10.

is to be assessed, this question should be resolved uniformly, so that the defendant is not in the position of having to comply with contradictory judgments. In order to guarantee this consistency, class action suits under Rule 23(b)(2) and (b)(1)(A) do not allow members to opt out of the class.[120] Logically, if no opt-out is possible, no notice to absent members is required.[121] For this reason, these specific suits are called 'mandatory' class actions. Second of all, claims seeking monetary compensation – Rule 23(b)(3) and (b)(1)(B) – include two different cases: on the one hand, Rule (b)(1)(B) concerns the particular situation in which defendant has limited funds and, thus, is not able to satisfy all the class members' claims.[122] One can think about a defendant in a situation of insolvency and whose assets are not sufficient to reimburse all creditors. Under normal circumstances, the first litigants would obtain full monetary compensation while late claimants would be left with nothing. As a result, the law states that no opt-out mechanism is available in order to protect the subsequent or late litigants from receiving no compensation at all.[123] Thanks to the mandatory nature of the limited fund suit, a pro rata distribution among the whole class is possible.[124] On the other hand, Rule 23(b)(3) class actions will proceed only if the judge finds that common issues of fact or law predominate and that a class action is the superior means to solve the conflict at stake. These additional requirements elevate the threshold of class certification. Class actions related to mass torts, securities fraud or misrepresentation, financial harm in employment matters, antitrust and consumer fields are usually brought under the (b)(3) category.

It has to be underlined that these class action categories may 'overlap'. For example, plaintiffs may seek injunctive relief – pursuant to Rule 23(b)(2) or (b)(1)(A) – and compensation for their damage – according to Rule 23(b)(3) – at the same time. In this case, the class action is called 'hybrid' as it concerns two of the above described categories. Therefore, what requirements should be imposed on these actions? The answer is not clear.[125] In all cases, it seems that plaintiffs usually prefer to certify the whole class under the (b)(1) or (b)(2) category as their requirements are not as stringent as those of (b)(3) class actions for plaintiffs.[126]

B. Prerequisites under Rule 23(a)

Here are the requirements for certification that any class action must fulfil.

[120] ibid.
[121] ibid.
[122] The specific requirements imposed by r (b)(1)(B) are developed by case law (specifically, see *Ortiz v. Fibreboard Corp.*, 527 US 815 [1999]): in order for this provision to apply there must be: (1) a fund with definite limits; (2) all of which would be devoted to pay outstanding claims; (3) on a pro rata basis.
[123] As Rubenstein states: 'If class members could opt out and pursue their own claim elsewhere, the entire purpose of aggregating the claims into one proceeding would be defeated: the opt-out litigants could deplete the fund to the detriment of the rest of the claimants'. (Rubenstein (n 26) para 4:16).
[124] Rubenstein (n 26) para 4:23.
[125] ibid para 4:38.
[126] Klonoff (n 57) 82–83, 93.

i. Numerosity

Numerosity requires the class to be composed of a plurality of claimants. The assessment of such a condition is not mathematical, but has to be assessed on a case-by-case basis. From a quantitative point of view, no magic number acts as a bottom-line for certification.[127] However, the opportunity for litigants to join their claims is a good indicator: if litigants are able to aggregate their suits through the mechanism of joinder, then a class action may not be indispensable in order to guarantee claimants their day in court. To put it differently, class certification becomes desirable if joinder is unmanageable – but not necessarily impossible – because of the high number of claimants. This will be the case if members are geographically widespread or cannot be individually identified without difficulty.[128] Qualitatively speaking, various factual circumstances influence numerosity. For example, one should take into account the geographical dispersion of the members of the class[129] or the particularly modest amount of each claim.[130] When subclasses are set up, they must also fulfil the numerosity requirement.[131]

ii. Commonality

For the commonality requirement to be satisfied, at least one question of fact or law must be common to the class.[132] Furthermore, at least one of the common issues at stake must be central to the case.[133] This last condition is nothing but a certain type of predominance.[134] When cases present questions of fact and law that are common, then single adjudication of similar claims is preferable to a myriad of individual suits for judicial efficiency purposes.[135]

One cannot approach commonality without examining the *Wal-Mart v. Dukes* decision rendered by the US Supreme Court.[136] This decision concerns a class of one and a half million women who alleged gender discrimination against their employer. In particular, the class sought injunctive and declaratory relief, punitive damages and backpay against Wal-Mart, whose local managers allegedly exercised a discretionary power on pay and promotion policies favouring men over women

[127] Anderson and Trask (n 30) 23–25; Silberman et al, *Civil Procedure: Theory and Practice* (n 9) 1014. However, an examination of case law reveals that certification of a class composed by less than 25 members will rarely be certified (see McLaughlin (n 26) para 4:5, fn 25).

[128] McLaughlin (n 26) para 4:6.

[129] Anderson and Trask (n 30) 24.

[130] Klonoff (n 57) 36–37.

[131] Rubenstein (n 26) para 3:16; Manual for Complex Litigation (n 97) para 21.23, 272.

[132] Rubenstein (n 26) paras 3:20–21; Silberman et al (n 9) 1015.

[133] Rubenstein (n) para 3:22; Silberman et al (n 9) 1015.

[134] AB Spencer, 'Class Actions, Heightened Commonality and Declining Access to Justice' (2013) 93 *Boston University Law Review* 441, 470.

[135] McLaughlin (n 26) para 4:7.

[136] *Wal-Mart Stores, Inc. v. Dukes*, et al, 564 US 338 (2011).

and thus, violating the Civil Rights Act of 1964.[137] In this case, the Court ruled that common questions of fact and law were not present. According to Justice Scalia – writing for the majority opinion –, the plaintiffs failed in their attempt to demonstrate that Wal-Mart's management applied a corporate policy generating gender discrimination.[138] Indeed, claims could 'stick' together only if the plaintiffs proved the existence of a uniform and automatic discrimination policy on behalf of the defendant.[139] The *Wal-Mart* court ruled that too many disparities were present in the case at stake for the class to be certified.[140]

It is commonly acknowledged that the *Wal-Mart* decision enhanced the threshold of the commonality requirement: pre-*Wal-Mart*, this standard was easy to meet. However, in *Wal-Mart*, the Supreme Court imposed a heightened burden of proof on plaintiffs regarding commonality:[141] in particular, the violation of a similar law provision that harmed members of the class is not a sufficient proof for commonality purposes.[142] Additionally, the class must demonstrate that it suffered the same injury. This would be the case if the same manager imposed a discriminatory policy in a similar manner to the class.[143]

iii. Typicality

As Rule 23(a)(3) states, typicality requires the representative plaintiff to have claims and defences that correspond to those of the class, so that proving his/her case simultaneously proves the case of the entire class. However, perfect similarity of claims and defences is not necessary: small factual disparities or differences in the amount of damages claimed does not strike down typicality.[144] The rationale of the typicality requirement is to align the interests of the named plaintiff with those of the class. Indeed,

> if the representative's case were stronger than the typical class member's, it would be unfair to the defendant to generalize the class relief based on that claim; if it were atypically weak, it would be unfair to the class to have its fate tied to such a sample.[145]

For example, the representative plaintiff will be atypical if unique – or individually targeted – defences might be raised against him.[146] This could consequently

[137] ibid 2547–48.
[138] ibid 2554–57.
[139] *General Telephone Co. of Southwest v. Falcon*, 457 US 147 (1982). In this case, the Supreme Court held that the experience of a single plaintiff was not sufficient for the commonality requirement to be met. In light of this, the plaintiffs could either show that the defendant's hiring and evaluating testing procedure was discriminatory, or that the defendant operated under a general discriminatory policy.
[140] *Wal-Mart* (n 136) 348–60.
[141] Spencer, 'Class Actions, Heightened Commonality and Declining Access to Justice' (n 134) 463–64.
[142] *Wal-Mart* (n 136) 349–50.
[143] McLaughlin (n 26) para 4:7.
[144] ibid para 4:17.
[145] Silberman et al (n 9) 1015.
[146] McLaughlin (n 26) para 4:18.

distract the court from common and typical issues and forces the named plaintiff to spend time on litigating its own interests rather than those of the entire class.[147]

iv. Standing to Sue and Adequacy of Representation

A plaintiff is able to represent the interests of a class if: (1) he/she has standing to sue; (2) he/she is a member of the class; and (3) he/she adequately represents absent class members. While the first requirement stems from Article III of the US Constitution and is a mandatory step for every kind of lawsuit, Rule 23(a) incorporates the last two conditions.

In order to have standing to sue, the named plaintiff must first have suffered an injury in fact, this means a violation of a protected interest.[148] Then, he/she has to show the causal link existing between the alleged injury and an unlawful conduct.[149] Finally, a favourable judgment must result in redress of the injury caused to plaintiff.[150] It must be highlighted that absent class members do not have to prove that they have standing to sue.[151] In light of this, contrarily to what happens in the EU, entities such as consumer associations in principle cannot act on behalf of the class if they did not suffer any injury.[152]

From federal Rule 23(a), it can be inferred that the potential named plaintiff has to be a member of the class.[153] This requirement is logical since the representative plaintiff has to protect the interests of the class and the judgment or settlement that will result from his/her case will be applicable to absent members. Therefore, a certain degree of similarity is necessary and expressed by the condition of affiliation to the class. The same can be inferred from the commonality and typicality requirement.

Finally, the named plaintiff must adequately represent the interests of absent class members. Contrarily to the commonality and typicality requirements, adequacy of representation is a subjective test, whereby a court examines if the representative plaintiff is likely to represent the interests of the class, or will rather

[147] ibid.
[148] ibid para 4:28.
[149] ibid.
[150] ibid.
[151] ibid.
[152] Wright and Miller, *Federal Practice & Procedure* (n 100) para 1761 ('The most difficult problems in applying the class-membership prerequisite have arisen in the context of actions brought by or against an association seeking to act as the representative of its members. Several courts have noted that the association is not requesting any relief for itself and therefore is not a member of the class it purports to represent. As a result, these courts have held that a union or cooperative association cannot bring a class action to protect the rights of its members, even though the association well may be the most appropriate representative for doing so'). Conversely, in public interest actions, ie actions brought by a person against the government or one of its branches, the plaintiff does not have to demonstrate adequacy of representation or typicality in order to defend a general interest (Homburger, 'Private Suits in the Public Interest in the United States of America' (n 35)).
[153] McLaughlin (n 26) para 4:28.

be distracted by selfish concerns.[154] In light of this, the court must detect if potential conflicts of interests between the representative and the class exist. There will generally be an inadequate representation when: representative plaintiff suffers from a current injury while some members of the class might suffer from a future injury;[155] part of the class seeks enforcement of an agreement while some members do not want it to be enforced;[156] a shareholder and director brings a class action on behalf of all the shareholders of a company, which allegedly violated federal securities laws.[157]

Adequacy of representation plays a fundamental role within the class action system, as it expands the preclusive effect to absent class members which are not formally parties to the class action. In fact, adequate representation is a *sine qua non* condition for class members to be bound by the outcome of the class action: indeed, because unnamed plaintiffs will not have their day in court, but will nevertheless be bound by the class judgment or settlement, due process requires that absent members are adequately represented and, in certain cases, that they are duly notified their right to opt out.[158]

Besides regulating the relationship between the named plaintiff and class members, adequacy of representation also mandates class counsel to be adequate. The rationale behind class counsel's adequacy is that he/she represents clients who were not able to appoint him. Therefore, courts have to make sure that the attorney in charge of the class action is able to defend absent members' interests (Rule 23(g)(4)). It is important to note that because class counsel represents the class, the named plaintiff cannot discretionarily fire class counsel and the case cannot be settled by the latter's approval.[159] If no counsel fulfils the requirements of Rule 23(g), then the court has discretion to decide whether to dismiss the case or to examine whether other candidates could be fit for the job.[160] According to Rule 23(c)(1)(B), class counsel has to be appointed at the time of the certification.

In principle, the adequacy of class counsel is presumed. Consequently, courts will usually focus on the elements that could negatively put into doubt the attorney's capacity to lead the class action case.[161] Among other things, the counsel's lack of knowledge of procedural or substantive law aspects of the case, as well as a lack of experience, could call into question his/her adequacy. Courts will also look at the attorney's resources to finance the class action, the quality of his/her briefings and the timeliness of motion practice, and the existence of potential ethical violations. Then, courts must examine if conflicts of interest affect the relationship between the class counsel and the class – including the named plaintiff. This will

[154] López Sánchez, *El sistema de las* class actions *en los Estados Unidos de América* (n 1) 22.
[155] See eg *Amchem Products, Inc. v. Windsor*, 521 US 591 (1997).
[156] See eg *Hansberry v. Lee*, 311 US 32 (1940).
[157] *Kornick v. Talley*, 86 F.R.D. 715 (DC Northern District of Georgia 1980).
[158] Freer, *Civil Procedure* (n 70) 773–76.
[159] Rubenstein (n 26) para 3.82; McLaughlin (n 26) para 4:37.
[160] Rubenstein (n 26) para 3.87.
[161] Rubenstein (n 26) paras 3:73–79.

be the case if class counsel claims to represent various sub-classes with different interests or works for the same clients in two different class suits, which enables him/her to gain experience from the first lawsuit to the detriment of the class. Regarding the relationship with the class representative, class counsel should not have any close relationship with him/her, as it could impede him/her from effectively monitoring class counsel.

The increasing focus on class counsel's adequacy highlights the decreasing practical role of the named plaintiff in the class action system. In fact, it is acknowledged that class counsel is the 'true' representative of the class. On the contrary, it appears that the representative is 'at best a volunteer, and at worst a solicited puppet of the class lawyer'.[162]

C. Rule 23(b)(3)

Rule 23(b)(3) regarding class actions for damages imposes two additional requirements for certification purposes.

i. Predominance

The predominance requirement is neither defined by Rule 23 nor by case law.[163] As a result, courts have been applying this criterion in a different fashion. Overall, predominance requires courts to weigh the common issues of a dispute and compare them with individualised ones.[164] Specifically, the assessment of predominance is twofold: first of all, factual predominance exists when the members of the class present similar evidentiary issues.[165] This will not be the case if plaintiffs must individually prove a certain chain of causation, have to demonstrate reliance or have affirmative defences that differ from the rest of the class.[166] Second of all, legal predominance will often be challenged if different state laws apply to members' claims litigated in a federal court. In this situation, if the various legislations cannot be uniformly applied, then the predominance test fails.[167]

ii. Superiority

In a class action suit for damages, the court must examine if the class action device is the most efficient and fair procedural tool to 'drive' the case. Rule 23 establishes

[162] JW Burns, 'Decorative Figureheads: Eliminating Class Representatives in Class Actions' (1990) 42 *The Hastings Law Journal* 165, 190.
[163] Klonoff (n 57) 97.
[164] ibid 96.
[165] Anderson and Trask (n 30) 43.
[166] ibid 44–46.
[167] ibid 46–49.

some elements that courts have to take into account in order to assess the superiority requirement. These factors are not mandatory conditions, but rather guidelines. To start with, courts must inquire into the individual plaintiffs' interest to control litigation. Ordinarily, when the value of a claim is high, each claimant has an interest in litigating his/her case on a separate and independent basis – or through joinder.[168] On the contrary, negative value suits are usually appropriate for aggregation through Rule 23. The second factor establishes that the presence of parallel individual lawsuits challenges the superiority requirement. Indeed, if some plaintiffs decided to bring their own lawsuit, this means that individual proceedings might be the best way to litigate the case at stake.[169] Then, courts must assess the appropriateness of aggregating claims in a single forum. For example, the geographical dispersion of claimants, evidence and witnesses, as well as the applicability of various state laws, plead against superiority.[170] Lastly, the manageability of a potential class action has to be explored. This includes difficulty in giving notice, logistical problems that the application of different state laws may trigger, and the processing of the information for a jury trial in case there is one.[171]

The application of this requirement – along with commonality and predominance – has been challenged with the rise of mass tort cases between the 1970s and the 1990s,[172] which threatened courts by their magnitude. In such a context, the US civil justice system experienced great difficulties in finding the appropriate procedural tool capable of 'driving' these cases to litigation. When courts faced the first class action mass tort suits, their reaction was somewhat sceptical. Specifically, courts denied certification on a regular basis arguing that mass tort litigation did not fit the class action device and that common issues did not predominate. Indeed, they argued that the individualised issues that characterised mass tort cases made it inappropriate to use Rule 23.[173] In light of this, during the first decades following the 1966 reform, mass tort cases were simply consolidated or aggregated for pre-trial purposes under the MDL mechanism. Needless

[168] Klonoff (n 57) 105–06; Anderson and Trask (n 30) 50–51.
[169] Klonoff (n 57) 107–08; Anderson and Trask (n 30) 51.
[170] Klonoff (n 57) 108; Anderson and Trask (n 30) 51–53.
[171] Klonoff (n 57) 108–10; Anderson and Trask (n 30) 53–54.
[172] In an attempt to define or at least display the characteristics of mass tort cases, the Manual for Complex Litigation makes a distinction between single incident mass torts and dispersed mass torts. The first category encompasses situations in which the source of the damage is similar for all victims, such as the collapse of a construction – like the Hyatt Skywalk Collapse –, fire building – like the Beverly Hills Supper Club fire – and shipwreck. The second category concerns cases in which damages to victims are widespread and usually stem from a repetitive unlawful behaviour of the defendant. Examples include use of drugs whose secondary effects are harmful – notably MER-29, Bendectin and DES –, the marketing of defective products – like the Dalkon Shield, an intrauterine contraceptive device, or silicone breast implant – and exposure to toxic substances – eg asbestos or Agent Orange (DR Hensler and MA Peterson, 'Understanding Mass Personal Injury Litigation: A Socio-Legal Analysis' (1993) 59 *Brooklyn Law Review* 961, 970–1013; Manual for Complex Litigation (n 97) 342–48).
[173] Advisory Committee Notes, available at www.law.cornell.edu/rules/frcp/rule_23.

to say, these two instruments were relatively inadequate for mass tort litigation.[174] In the 1980s, however, courts were forced to capitulate due to their inability to tackle the increasing number of mass tort suits.[175] In light of this, important mass tort suits proceeded as class actions during this period. Among others, cases related to exposure to asbestos and Agent Orange[176] were certified, as well as a class composed of women victims of the Dalkon Shield device. Concerned about the excesses generated by mass tort litigation, a complex reform of Rule 23 started at the beginning of the 1990s.[177] Eventually, a provision for interlocutory appeal, namely Rule 23(f), which enables parties to contest an order granting or denying of certification was adopted.

D. Settlement Classes

The American system has a strong policy of favouring the resolution of disputes through settlement, as it means savings in costs, time and judicial resources.[178] The fact that most of class action cases settle confirms the success of such a policy goal. Besides, it is not uncommon that cases settle before plaintiffs even move for certification.[179] In this context, courts have been developing a new practice: they have been certifying cases for settlement purposes only.

The legal system contained in Rule 23 establishes a twofold regime applying to settlements that occur either after, or concurrently with class certification. In those cases, Rule 23(e) requires courts to review the parties' agreement and examine if it is 'fair, reasonable and adequate'. If these conditions are fulfilled, the settlement is then notified to absent members, disregarding the kind of lawsuit brought. Rule 23(b)(3) members are offered an opportunity to opt out. It is useful to mention that when too many members opt out of the settlement, then the defendant often preserves a contractual right to cancel the whole transaction. Indeed, closure allows the defendant to protect him- or herself against repetitive subsequent litigation. If settlement arises at the time of certification, then courts will usually require parties to perform a single certification and proposal of settlement notice. Hearings are combined as well.[180]

[174] Indeed, consolidation still requires parties to present their own proof or argument (Anderson and Trask, n 30, 8), which does not favour judicial economy, and MDL is limited to pre-trial procedure and federal cases.

[175] Klonoff (n 57) 298.

[176] *In re 'Agent Orange' Product Liability Litigation* (100 F.R.D. 718 [DC Eastern District of New York 1983]), the District Court of New York certified a class of victims who were exposed to a toxic herbicide. The Second Circuit upheld the certification (818 F.2d 145 [2d Cir 1987]).

[177] DR Hensler et al, *Class Action Dilemmas – Public Goals for Private Gains* (Rand Institute for Civil Justice, 2000), ch II, 25–37, available at www.rand.org/pubs/monograph_reports/MR969.html.

[178] Rubenstein (n 26) para 13:44.

[179] McLaughlin (n 26) para 6:3.

[180] ibid para 6:3.

In light of this, questions arise regarding settlement classes concluded before certification: on the one hand, one may advocate the application of Rule 23(e) to 'early birds'. On the other hand, it could be convenient to apply the more stringent requirements of Rule 23(a) and (b) to certification of classes for settlement purposes. While judgments dealing with settlement classes firstly opted for the first approach, later case law challenged this solution: in *In re General Motors Corp.*,[181] the Third Circuit held that settlement classes should meet Rule 23(a) conditions in order to be approved by the court. Moreover, in *Amchem Products, Inc. v. Windsor*,[182] the Supreme Court added that Rule 23(b)(3) requirements – apart from manageability – should also be met by the settlement class.

Certainly, the application of stringent requirements to settlement classes hinders the conclusion of agreements between parties. Nevertheless, the solution upheld by the Supreme Court is desirable as it better protects absent class members' rights. The reasoning goes as follows: classes that are certified for settlements purposes only under lenient requirements may never be litigated if they do not fulfil Rule 23(a) or/and (b) conditions. If this is the case, it is doubtful that the negotiations leading to settlement will be held at arm's length.[183] As the defendant knows that there is no viable alternative to settlement, his/her power of negotiation is strengthened. In this vein, defendant could settle the case for peanuts. To sum up, without the threat of an actual class action, the playing field is not levelled and plaintiffs' counsel may not be in a position to get a good deal for the whole class.

In light of this, the settlement phase is a fertile ground for collusion.[184] Specifically, collusion arises when both defendant and class counsel – sometimes the named plaintiff is also involved – conclude a settlement favourable to them but prejudicial to absent class members. In practice, collusive techniques result in cheap settlements and protection from future potential lawsuits for defendants and high fees for class counsel.[185] Some examples of collusion practices involve

[181] *In re General Motors Corp. Pick-Up Truck Fuel Tank Products Liability Litigation*, 55 F.3d 768, 799–800 (3d Cir 1995).

[182] *Amchem Products* (n 155) 619.

[183] S Issacharoff, 'Class Action Conflicts' (1997) 30 *U.C. Davis Law Review* 805. Issacharoff develops this argument in his paper regarding the potential enactment of r 23(b)(4) by Congress. According to this provision, a class should be certified if 'the parties to a settlement request certification under subdivision (b)(3) for purposes of settlement, even though the requirements of subdivision (b)(3) might not be met for trial'. The author states that 'the lawyer who has entered into negotiations on the basis of a settlement class that could never have been tried is in a weak position to hold out'. And then adds: 'since the active agent in consenting the creation of the class is the defendant, there is a significant risk that a defendant will seek to undercut legitimate class actions through collusive behavior with alternative plaintiffs' counsel'.

[184] B Hay and D Rosenberg, 'Sweetheart and Blackmail Settlements in Class Actions: Reality and Remedy' (2000) 75(4) *Notre Dame Law Review* 1377, 1389.

[185] J Bronsteen, 'Class Action Settlements: An Opt-In Proposal' (2005) 4 *University of Illinois Law Review* 903, 904.

reverse auctions,[186] the inclusion of future claimants within the class,[187] coupon settlements[188] and clear sailing agreements.[189]

These types of agreements take place due to the convergence of various factors: first, class settlement information greatly escapes from courts' control.[190] It may be difficult for judges to determine if a settlement is fair, reasonable and adequate because this agreement is concluded under non-adversarial conditions. Furthermore, it is commonly acknowledged that courts have an incentive to clear their already crowded dockets. In this vein, judges may be tempted to accept settlements situated on the borderline of fairness. Then, class counsel is able to control the negotiations as he/she deems fit because of the named plaintiff's lack of incentive to monitor him/her. Most of the time, the cost of supervising class counsel will outweigh the value of representative plaintiff's claim. Lastly, when attorneys' fees are based on a percentage of recovery approach, conflicts of interest between counsel and the class may appear. In this case, attorneys are inclined to settle quickly

[186] Before any class is certified, the defendant who is sued in various class actions will often make potential class counsels compete between them and settle the case with the one offering the most interesting deal (RL Marcus, 'The Big Bad Wolf: American Class Actions' in V Harsági and CH van Rhee (eds), *Multi-Party Redress Mechanisms in Europe: Squeaking Mice?* (Intersentia, 2014) 41). This represents a valuable mechanism for defendants as the first class action being settled has a preclusive effect on other subsequent claims. As for plaintiffs' attorneys, they are pushed to make undervalued bids in order to be elected class counsel and pocket the corresponding fees (Hay and Rosenberg, 'Sweetheart and Blackmail Settlements in Class Actions' (n 184) 1391).

[187] With the rise of mass tort cases, defendants have tried to include future potential claimants within the class definition. These are victims who suffered from exposure to a harmful product – like asbestos – but whose injuries have not appeared yet (Klonoff (n 57) 305–06). Thanks to this strategy, closure is achieved and the defendant protects him- or herself from subsequent litigation. As Latz explains, settlements of classes involving futures offer 'the defendant an opportunity to purchase res judicata and thereby foreclose subsequent claims against it' (TW Latz, 'Who Can Tell the Futures? Protecting Settlement Class Action Members Without Notice' (1999) 85 *Virginia Law Review* 531, 549).

[188] In a coupon settlement, the defendant offers discounts on the future acquisition of his products or services as a compensation for plaintiffs' damages (GP Miller and LS Singer, 'Nonpecuniary Class Action Settlements' (1997) 60(4) *Law & Contemporary Problems* 97, 102). Coupons are supplied instead of cash payment, which represents a great opportunity for the defendant: coupons guarantee future clients at a quite cheap cost (TJ Power, 'Tearing Down a House of Coupons: CAFA's Effect on Class Action Settlements' (2012) 9 *University of Saint Thomas Law Journal* 906, 915). However, coupon settlements have been abusively used as a means to provide class counsel with tremendous high fees. Finally, it has to be underlined that the use of coupons is restricted since the entry into force of CAFA (SB Hantler and RE Norton, 'Coupon Settlements: The Emperor's Clothes of Class Actions' (2005) 18 *Georgetown Journal of Legal Ethics* 1343, 1345). For examples of coupon settlements, see J Brendan Day, 'My Lawyer Went to Court and all I Got Was This Lousy Coupon! The Class Action Fairness Act's Inadequate Provision for Judicial Scrutiny over Proposed Coupon Settlements'(2008) 38 *Seton Hall Law Review* 1085, 1098–105.

[189] Through a clear sailing agreement, the defendant promises not to challenge attorneys' fees if they remain under a certain threshold. When a court is confronted with a clear sailing provision, this should 'ring a bell': it means that negotiations were undertaken between the class counsel and the defendant. These agreements are potentially collusive (WD Henderson, 'Clear Sailing Agreements: A Special Form of Collusion in Class Action Settlements' (2003) 77(4) *Tulane Law Review* 813, 814).

[190] Hay and Rosenberg (n 184) 1390.

in order to optimise hourly return and avoid the risks that an unsuccessful trial would incur.[191]

IV. Post-Certification Steps

A. Notice and Opt-Out Rights

Together with opt-out rights, notice is an essential tool of the class action mechanism. It serves two fundamental purposes:[192] first, people who do not opt out of a class after having been adequately notified are presumed to consent to a court's jurisdiction. Second, notice expands the *res judicata* effect of a judgment to all absent class members even though these did not participate in the trial. In this vein, the legitimacy of class actions rests on representation, adequate notice and the right to opt out. Notably, notice is required when: (1) a class is certified under Rule 23(b)(3); or (2) a settlement has been reached.

In the first place, Rule 23(c)(2) sets up a two-tiered regime for notice to absent class members in accordance with the type of relief sought: for (b)(1) and (b)(2) classes, the court 'may direct appropriate notice to the class'. As for (b)(3) classes, the 'best notice that is practicable under the circumstances, including individual notice to all members who can be identified through reasonable effort' is required. It is readily apparent that notice to class members pursuant to Rule 23(b)(3) imposes more stringent requirements than for injunctive and declaratory relief or limited fund actions. That can be explained by the fact that (b)(1) and (b)(2) class actions do not provide for an opt-out mechanism and, therefore, the justification of notice is sensibly lessened. In this vein, notice to class members represents a mere occasion to monitor proceedings and assure adequacy of representation.[193] The opportunity, the form and the content of notice in mandatory class action suits is left to the discretion of the court. In any event, however, courts rarely notify (b)(1) or (2) class members when costs outweigh its benefits.[194]

[191] Downs, 'Federal Class Actions' (n 34), 665. An example extracted from GP Miller, 'Some Agency Problems in Settlement' (1987) 16 *The Journal of Legal Studies* 189, 200 illustrates this point: 'Suppose that the defendant has proposed a settlement of $100,000, the attorney is working on a 40% contingent fee, the attorney's future costs are $15,000, the probability of success is 50%, and the expected judgment if plaintiff prevails is $250,000. The attorney would find it rational to settle since his or her return from settlement of $40,000 (.4 × $100,000) exceeds his or her return from trial of $35,000 ((.4 × .5 × $250,000) – $15,000). From the client's point of view, however, a settlement at this figure would not be desirable. The client's return from this settlement is $60,000, an amount well below the client's expected gain from trial of $75,000'.

[192] *Phillips Petroleum* (n 81) 812–14; T Eisenberg and GP Miller, 'The Role of Opt-Outs and Objectors in Class Action Litigation: Theoretical and Empirical Issues' (2004) 57(5) *Vanderbilt Law Review* 1529, 1534–35.

[193] Manual for Complex Litigation (n 97) para 21.311, 287.

[194] ibid.

In contrast, damages class actions require that individual notice is given to identifiable members in order to offer them the opportunity to opt out of the class.[195] If identification is impossible through reasonable effort, then the best notice practicable under the circumstances should be delivered. This last requirement encompasses publication of notice in local newspapers within the geographical area of potential class members, on specific Internet websites, and in consumer or financial magazines.[196] The content of notice to classes under Rule 23(b)(3) is detailed in Rule 23(c)(2)(B). Importantly, notice has to be written in an understandable and clear fashion for laypersons. Lastly, it has to be highlighted that the costs incurred by the notice requirement are in principle borne by plaintiffs in the two regimes explained above.[197]

In the second place, Rule 23(e)(1)(B) states that the court must 'direct notice in a reasonable manner' to class members that would be bound by a settlement taking place after certification. This provision is applicable to all categories of class actions – (b)(1), (b)(2) and (b)(3). The Manual for Complex Litigation clarifies that settlement notice must be delivered in a similar way as notice for certification.[198] Furthermore, courts may refuse to approve the settlement if parties did not offer absent members a second opportunity to opt out of the class.[199] This will generally be the case when the information provided has changed since the certification of the class and the right to opt out after certification notice expired. In this case, parties should be able to reassess their desire to be part of the class or not.[200]

B. Effect of Class Action Judgments and Settlements

Among the effects that class action judgments and settlements trigger, issues regarding their binding effects are the most important ones. Since the American system possesses flexible rules on jurisdiction that may generate parallel proceedings, defining the preclusive effect of judgments or settlements is vital. As mentioned above, US jurisdictional rules are concurrent rather than exclusive. Questions arise when a party to a class action subsequently starts individual proceedings

[195] The necessity of individual notice has been interpreted in a strict fashion by courts. According to *Eisen v. Carlisle & Jacquelin*, 417 US 156 (1974), notice must be given to each member no matter how big the class is.

[196] Manual for Complex Litigation (n 97) para 21.311, 288.

[197] *Oppenheimer Fund, Inc. v. Sanders*, 473 US 340 (1978). Nevertheless, in certain circumstances, eg when the defendant is in a better position to undertake notice to class members, courts can shift the costs onto it. Typically, this will be the case if, in a consumer class action, the defendant possesses a register of all its customers and it would be easy for it to send them notice together with bills or other routine documents. However, because this practice could be prejudicial to the defendant and violate its rights under the First Amendment, imposing notice costs on the defendant must be the *ultima ratio* (Manual for Complex Litigation, n 97, para 21.312, 296).

[198] Manual for Complex Litigation (n 97) para 21.312, 294.

[199] The first opportunity to opt out is offered when the class is certified.

[200] Manual for Complex Litigation (n 97) para 21.611, 312–13.

in order to defeat the previous ruling and obtain a different outcome. The court hearing the posterior suit has to examine to which extent the preclusive effect of the first class action judgment or settlement bars the plaintiff or defendant from re-litigating a claim or issue. The preclusive effect of judgments is examined below, as well as some issues specifically related to settlements.

General theory on preclusion establishes that a court's decision has a binding effect on parties.[201] Consequently, these cannot re-litigate their case. The rationale of this solution is simple: if parties could continuously go back to court, judicial resources would be wasted, inconsistent judgments could be rendered and the defendant would be obliged to dedicate his/her time and resources to litigate the case repeatedly.[202] The concept of preclusion has two components: first, claim preclusion – or *res judicata* – forbids parties to a judgment to engage in subsequent litigation over causes of action[203] that already have been litigated or could have been raised in a prior judgment.[204] As for issue preclusion – or collateral estoppel –, it bars re-litigation of a case's specific issue even if the cause of action is different.[205] There are two different forms of collateral estoppel: it is mutual when parties to the second proceedings are identical and non-mutual when one of them did not take part in the initial lawsuit.[206] In the class action context, even if absent members are technically not parties to a court's judgment, they are considered as such for the purpose of preclusion, unless they opt out.[207] There are two ways for class members – who did not opt out – to challenge the preclusive effect of a judgment: first of all, the lack of adequate notice neutralises preclusion;[208] secondly, class members will be bound only if their interests were adequately represented.[209] With this in mind, the most controversial issues presented to US courts regarding the preclusive effect of class action judgments are examined.

To start with, courts have been confronted with cases in which members who opted out of a previous class action then tried to benefit from a favourable initial judgment in subsequent proceedings.[210] In other words, they tried to 'free-ride'

[201] Fleming, Hazard and Leubsdorf, *Civil Procedure* (n 68) 675–76.

[202] DL Bassett, 'Just Go Away: Representation, Due Process, and Preclusion in Class Actions' (2009) 5 *Brigham Young University Law Review* 1079, 1097.

[203] The scope of this term is difficult to frame. It can be approximated to 'claim' or 'demand'. The Restatement Second of Judgments – which is a source for interpretation published by the ALI – offers some guidance by stating that the cause of action or claim 'includes all rights of the plaintiff to remedies against the defendant with respect to all or any part of the transaction' (cited by Fleming, Hazard and Leubsdorf (n 68) 687–88).

[204] Fleming, Hazard and Leubsdorf (n 68) 675–76.

[205] ibid 676.

[206] Klonoff (n 57) 232.

[207] *Hansberry* (n 156) 40.

[208] Klonoff (n 57) 229–30; *Phillips Petroleum* (n 81).

[209] Klonoff (n 57) 229–30. However, this author exposes that some federal courts have been reluctant to review state courts' analysis of the adequacy of representation standard through collateral estoppel. Wright and Miller (n 100) para 4455.

[210] Klonoff (n 57) 232–33; Wright and Miller (n 100) para 1789.

on the class action suit. In this context, the question is whether non-parties can benefit from the binding effect of the class action through non-mutual collateral estoppel. Conversely, defendants have tried to use favourable class judgments against opt-outs on the same basis.[211] Although the judicial trend is to reject the possibility to claim issue preclusion in those cases, some courts have allowed it.[212]

Another question is whether a federal court's denial of class certification constitutes a final judgment barring future class litigation in state courts. If the answer is negative, then the plaintiff's counsel could file various class actions in different state courts having jurisdiction – and there will be numerous potential fora if the case has a nationwide scope – until one judge finally certifies the class. This issue has been parsimoniously resolved by lower courts: while some of them consider that 'class members' are not bound by a denial of certification, as they are not parties to a class, others have rejected subsequent certification on grounds of comity.[213] In 2011, the US Supreme Court ruled that a denial of certification issued by a federal court should not bar the filing of a subsequent class action in a state court, although the class represented and the allegations were the same.[214] The Supreme Court concluded in this manner, since distinct procedural laws applied to the case. Additionally, the representative plaintiffs were not the same in the federal and the state class action.

As far as class action settlements are concerned, two kinds of effects may impede re-litigation: release and claim preclusion.[215] Release is a contractual abandonment of certain claims by the parties.[216] The consequence is that they cannot re-litigate them in subsequent proceedings. Through this mechanism, parties are able to achieve a broader closure than in a class action judgment, since they can even agree on elements that cannot be litigated in court.[217] When a court approves a class action settlement, it issues a judgment that entails a preclusive effect. In this context, the Supreme Court ruled that a settlement concluded at the state level that involves state and federal claims could not be ignored by federal courts.[218] In other words, the conclusion of an agreement in state courts may obstruct the start of a federal class action, given its preclusive effect.

C. Costs and Fees

In the United States, the general principle regarding costs, referred to as the 'American rule', states that each party has to bear her own attorney's fees.[219]

[211] Klonoff (n 57) 232.
[212] Klonoff (n 57) 233; Wright and Miller (n 100) para 1789.
[213] Anderson and Trask (n 29) 271–72; Klonoff (n 57) 237–39.
[214] *Keith Smith, et al v. Bayer Corporation*, 564 US (2011).
[215] McLaughlin (n 26) para 6:29.
[216] ibid.
[217] ibid.
[218] *Matsushita Elec. Indus. Co., Ltd. v. Epstein*, 516 US 367 (1996).
[219] SC Yeazell, *Civil Procedure*, 8th edn (Aspen Casebook Series, 2012) 316–17.

According to this principle, the winning party is only entitled to recover part of his/her costs – these are court filing fees, expert fees and discovery costs among others – under Federal Rule of Civil Procedure 54(d)(1).[220] Contrary to the 'English rule', under which the losing party has to cover the winner's costs, the US policy over cost distribution among parties makes litigation more attractive for plaintiffs: even if plaintiffs lose their case, they do not face the risk of having to cover their adversary's costs. On the negative side of the balance, however, because counsels' fees are particularly high in the United States, the American rule might bar claimants, whose claim is strong but small, from having access to justice.[221] It must be underlined that sometimes, attorneys' fees are paid by the defendant when a fee-shifting statutes exists; this is a rule of law obliging the losing party to reimburse attorney's fees to the counterparty, which is an exception to the American rule.[222]

The class action device generates some specific issues regarding the payment of costs and fees: theoretically, only the representative plaintiff should be held liable to pay the attorney's fees in his or her capacity as party to the proceedings. However, one senses that this result would be unfair because absent class members benefit from the class judgment. In this context, it is reasonable to infer that they should help to finance the attorney's fees. Accordingly, the common fund doctrine, which is predominantly applied in class actions, fixes this unsatisfactory situation. It is another exception to the American rule. Pursuant to this doctrine, lawyers who create a fund that benefits a group of absent litigants are entitled to extract a fee from it. Otherwise, third-beneficiaries would be unjustly enriched if they could escape from paying attorney's fees for the work that has been performed.[223] Another issue is the fact that absent class members cannot directly negotiate an agreement on fees – also called a retainer agreement – as they can in individual litigation. As a result, the legislation on class action imposes on courts a duty to assess the reasonableness of the fees awarded to class counsel in order to protect the class according to Rule 23(h).[224]

As regards the appropriate methodology to calculate fees coming from a common fund or otherwise, Rule 23(h) does not offer any guidance. Traditionally, two methods are used in order to calculate those fees: (1) the lodestar method; and (2) the percentage of the fund method. Under the lodestar method, attorney's reasonable hours spent on the case are multiplied by an hourly rate. Then an upwards or downwards adjustment is done in order to take into account either the complexity of the case, the risks and the quality of the lawyer's services or, on the

[220] Freer (n 70) 9–12, 193.

[221] Kagan (n 19) 123, 239; Yeazell, *Civil Procedure* (n 219) 316–18.

[222] Yeazell (n 219) 335–36.

[223] Silberman et al (n 9) 1053; Rubenstein (n 26) para 15:53; McLaughlin (n 26) para 6:24; Klonoff (n 57).

[224] r 23(h), which refers to r 54(d)(2), sets up the procedural steps regarding the allocation of attorney's fees. Specifically, said provision requires class counsel to ask for fees through a motion that has to enunciate the provision on which the request is based; the amount sought including time records and hourly rates; and disclose the existing agreements regarding attorney's fees.

contrary, the waste of time and the inadequacy of the documents to mention just a few factors.[225] As for the percentage method, it attributes attorneys a percentage of the damages award. In practice, a percentage of 20–30 per cent is usually acceptable depending on the specificities of the case.[226]

Consequently, court intervention in order to control the fairness of class counsel's fees limits parties' autonomy to conclude an agreement on this matter, previous to litigation. In particular, it has to be highlighted that, for this very reason, contingency fees agreements cannot be concluded in class action cases. However, the application of the common fund doctrine shares many similarities with this scheme.[227] In both cases, the principle of 'no win no pay' applies. Similarly, the attorney is paid out of the parties' recovery.

In this section dedicated to financial aspects of class actions, a word should be said about punitive damages, which 'provide plaintiffs in civil procedures with additional monetary relief beyond the value of the harm incurred'.[228] This type of remedy is available where substantive law permits it. Typically, in personal injury cases, punitive damages are allowed. Their primary objective is to deter potential wrongdoers from violating the law.[229] Conversely to what people usually think, the combination of class actions and punitive damages is not so common and US courts try to limit them.[230]

V. Conclusion

The first chapter of this research project has described the structure of the US class action, as well as the specific environment surrounding this device. In particular, class actions impose a certification stage that the class must win in order to proceed as such; the process relies on two main actors, ie the representative plaintiff and the class counsel; the device is opt-out based; the system encourages parties to settle; and strong financial incentives have been adopted in order to foster the private enforcement of collective rights. It has to be highlighted that the modern structure of the American class action is the result of a long process of procedural adaptations. Indeed, the scope of Rule 23 has been successively expanded and restricted over decades, depending on social needs.

[225] Klonoff (n 57) 277–78; McLaughlin (n 26) para 6:24; Rubenstein (n 26) paras 15:38, 15:50–51.

[226] JR Macey and GP Miller, 'The Plaintiffs' Attorney's Role in Class Action and Derivative Litigation: Economic Analysis and Recommendations for Reform' (1991) 58(1) *The University of Chicago Law Review* 1, 50–55; Klonoff (n 57) 276–77; Rubenstein (n 26) para 15:83.

[227] JC Alexander, 'Contingent Fees and Class Actions' (1998) 47(2) *DePaul Law Review* 347, 349–50.

[228] C Vanleenhove, *Punitive Damages in Private International Law: Lessons for the European Union* (Intersentia, 2016) 10.

[229] SB Scheuerman, 'Two Worlds Collide: How the Supreme Court's Recent Punitive Damages Decisions Affect Class Actions' (2008) 60(3) *Baylor Law Review* 880, 886–92.

[230] FE McGovern, 'Punitive Damages and Class Actions' (2010) 70 *Louisiana Law Review* 435, 436–38; Rubenstein (n 26) para 12:1.

Sometimes considered as a shining knight,[231] its ability to offer a form of relief for the 'smaller guys'[232] has been welcomed. For example, the class action's potential for access to justice was particularly valued at the time of the 1966 reform. At other times, the class action device has been depicted as a 'Frankenstein monster'[233] because of the abuses that it generated. For example, it has been said that class actions expose businesses to excessive economic pressure. Coupled with mass tort cases, the device has dangerously overburdened courts with cases unfit to proceed as classes. This situation encouraged the legislator to 'jump in'. As a result, Rule 23(f) on interlocutory appeals was enacted. Furthermore, the entry into force of CAFA regulated coupon settlements, which had triggered collusive behaviours in the past. Finally, historical judgments also deterred the abuse of class actions like the famous *Wal-Mart* case.

As explained in chapter 2, most EU collective redress schemes possess a relatively different structure. The analysis in chapter 1 highlights and explains those differences.

Furthermore, this chapter has put the spotlight on the jurisdictional complexities that class actions generated. The first fundamental question that US courts had to deal with was the extension of their jurisdictional power over absent class members. This question was solved by the Supreme Court in *Shutts*.[234] Then, although the centralisation of class actions in a single forum – for example in the state of incorporation of the defendant – is possible, parallel litigation governs in practice. Indeed, forum shopping and duplicative proceedings are consequences of federalism. In this context, courts have developed flexible coordination tools in order to bring coherence to the legal system without attacking states' sovereignty. Additionally, this chapter highlighted that inter-state class actions generate jurisdictional issues too. Specifically, when a class action starts in a state with no general jurisdictional power, it might be difficult for the courts of that state to centralise claims of plaintiffs whose damage occurred in another state.

The US experience regarding jurisdictional issues will inspire the construction of the proposal in chapter 4.

[231] This wording was used by Professor Miller in one of his influential papers (see above n 43). However, the author mentions that the 'paternity' of this term must be attributed to Chief Judge Lumbard in the *Eisen v. Carlisle & Jacquelin* decision (391 F.2d 555, 572 [2d Cir 1968], CJ Lumbard dissenting).

[232] This wording was used by Benjamin Kaplan, quoted by ME Frankel, 'Amended Rule 23 From a Judge's Point of View' (1966) 32 *Antitrust Law Journal* 295, 299.

[233] See n 43.

[234] *Phillips Petroleum* (n 81).

2

Collective Redress Mechanisms in the EU

Collective redress schemes in Europe take different shapes and assume distinct functions. Early on, Member States allowed certified entities, such as representative consumer associations, to bring actions for the protection of consumers' general interests. Thereafter, this type of instrument crystallised in Directive 2009/22/EC on injunctions for the protection of consumers' interests (hereafter, Directive 2009/22/EC, or the Injunctions Directive).[1] Subsequently, the rise of globalisation increased the international traffic and simultaneously created a fertile ground for widespread violations. At that time, Member States primarily perceived collective redress as an interesting management tool capable of tackling large-scale damages.

At the EU level, collective redress is perceived as a potential candidate to improve access to justice. As a result, the EU has tried to boost its implementation in Member States. Nevertheless, the prospective intervention of the EU in this matter is challenged: on the one hand, its competence to regulate collective redress pursuant to the Treaty on the Functioning of the European Union[2] (TFEU) is contested. On the other hand, according to collective redress opponents, the EU has not demonstrated that this instrument is indispensable in order to ensure private enforcement. Similarly, collective redress also defies EU private international law rules. It is interesting to note that few cross-border collective claims have been registered until today. Unfortunately, this question has not received much attention from the EU.

In light of this, chapter 2 is divided into two sections: the first section investigates the development of collective redress schemes in the Member States (I.). The structure of EU collective redress mechanisms is analysed in comparison with the US class action. Although these mechanisms vary greatly from one Member State to another, it is possible to categorise them according to their common features. As a result, collective redress instruments are organised into

[1] Council Directive 2009/22/EC of 23 April 2009 on injunctions for the protection of consumers' interests (codified version) [2009] OJ L110/30. Note that a former version of this Directive was adopted in 1998: Council Directive 98/27/EC of 19 May 1998 on injunctions for the protection of consumers' interests [1998] OJ L166/51.

[2] Consolidated version of the Treaty on the Functioning of the European Union [2012] OJ C326/47.

four representative categories. These categories will guide the private international law analysis in chapter 3. The second section of this chapter provides an overview of the work that has been carried out by the EU institutions in this field (II.). As explained below, the lack of political consensus and the procedural complexities that collective redress generates deterred an incisive legislative measure. Moreover, it is not clear whether the EU has the competence to legislate and whether any intervention is desirable at all. In this sense, opponents of collective redress believe that ADR alone should be a sufficient dispute resolution mechanism. These questions are analysed thoroughly below.

I. Developments of National Collective Redress Mechanisms

This section starts with general aspects of collective redress, namely the definition of the concept, its purposes and functions (B. and C.). Then, common structural characteristics of national collective redress mechanisms are presented (D.). This could be achieved by way of an exhaustive timeline listing all the collective redress instruments so far adopted by national legislators (A.). The results of this comparative law exercise demonstrates that even though these instruments are heterogeneous, they share significant similarities too. This section eventually classifies collective redress instruments into four categories, on which chapter 3 relies.

A. Chronological Overview

A look at all the collective redress mechanisms adopted by Member States so far shows that the law-making activities regarding this procedural tool have been relatively constant since the end of the 1970s. Besides, the following timeline reveals that Member States usually possess various instruments of collective redress. Although these legislative efforts are certainly positive, many national collective redress tools remain defective. In order to remedy these deficiencies, different reform processes have taken place since 2012. Interestingly, those reforms often follow similar patterns: for example, they usually extend the scope of application of collective redress,[3] include ADR mechanisms[4] and increasingly rely

[3] eg this is the case of the French *action de groupe*, whose scope was broadened in 2016 in order to encompass actions related to health, discrimination, environment and data protection. Interestingly, a reform was commenced in Italy in 2015, whose purpose is to introduce the class action (*azione di classe*) in the Italian Code of Civil Procedure (Arts 840-bis and ff.).

[4] This is the case with the French *action de groupe*, which is coupled with a mediation process and the Belgian *action en réparation collective*, which includes a negotiation phase.

on opt-out-based systems.[5] Furthermore, national legislators often engage in a comparative law exercise in order to improve their own mechanism.[6]

Based on Table 1, the following comparative analysis has been undertaken: to begin with, national collective redress instruments of Table 1 are compared with the US class action – comparison ad extra. Then, collective redress instruments are compared with each other – comparison ad intra. This exercise achieves three goals: it defines collective redress as clearly as possible; it establishes its essential features; and it builds up the four predominant collective redress categories mentioned below.

Table 1 List of Collective Redress Mechanisms Organised in a Chronological Order[7]

Entry into Force	Mechanism	Member State
1975	*Action exercée dans l'intérêt collectif des consommateurs*	(FR)
1978	Group action for the protection of general interests	(FI)
1979	*Verbandsklage*	(AT)
1983	§ 227 Austrian Code of Civil Procedure	(AT)
1989	*Acção popular*	(PT)
1992	*Action en représentation conjointe*	(FR)
1994	Collective action	(NL)
1999	*Verbandsklage* (enactment of § 28a *KSchG*)	(AT)
2000	GLO and representative action	(GB)

(continued)

[5] Typically, the Dutch WCAM procedure. Additionally, some Member States have recently adopted hybrid systems of participation combining opt-out and opt-in mechanisms. This is the case with Belgium and the United Kingdom. The later adopted a collective action for competition law infringements (s 47B of the Competition Act).

[6] eg in Belgium, one of the proposals to introduce collective redress was based on the Dutch WCAM (S Voet, 'Consumer Collective Redress in Belgium: Class Actions to the Rescue?' (2015) 16 *European Business Organization Law Review* 121, 124).

[7] Table 1 only encompasses collective redress instruments that are still in force today. In addition, Table 1 takes into account the last codified version of the provisions or laws that enact such instruments. eg although the *action en cessation* was available in Belgium before 2014, Table 1 refers to its last codification in the Economic Code. Furthermore, Table 1 does not take into account unaccomplished collective redress reforms. In this context, it should be highlighted that the entry into force of the Regulation (EU) 2016/679 of 27 April 2016 on the protection of natural persons with regard to the processing of personal data and on the free movement of such data generated the extension of the scope of many collective redress instruments. This was, eg, the case in Germany and France. When a collective redress instrument was the object of many legislative modifications, which did not significantly alter its substance (such as the German *Verbandsklage*), it was not mentioned in Table 1, since it would be burdensome and would not provide relevant information regarding the evolution of the collective redress mechanism in question. For more information regarding the methodology used, see the explanations provided in Annex II.

Table 1 ***(Continued)***

Entry into Force	Mechanism	Member State
2001	*Acción colectiva para la defensa de derechos e intereses de los consumidores y usuarios*	(ES)
2002	*Verbandsklage*	(DE)
2003	Action for the protection of general consumer interests	(GB)
2003	Group proceedings	(SE)
2005	*WCAM*	(NL)
2005	Action to protect consumers' interests	(IT)
2005	*KapMuG*	(DE)
2007	Class Action	(FI)
2008	Class Action	(BG)
2008	Legal Services Act	(DE)
2009	§ 502 Austrian Code of Civil Procedure	(AT)
2010	*Azione di classe*	(IT)
2010	Group proceedings	(PL)
2012	Amendment of the *Azione di classe*	(IT)
2012	Reform of the *KapMuG*	(DE)
2013	Reform of the *WCAM*	(NL)
2014	Reform of the *Acción colectiva*	(ES)
2014	*Action en cessation*	(BE)
2014	*Action en réparation collective*	(BE)
2014	*Action de groupe*	(FR)
2016	*Action de groupe* (scope extended)	(FR)

B. Collective Redress: A Concept with Fuzzy Boundaries

Logically, this chapter should start by defining collective redress. However, collective redress is a concept whose boundaries are fuzzy. Both, scholars[8] and EU institutions, have given different meanings and shapes to this device.

[8] eg D Fairgrieve and G Howells, 'Collective Redress Procedures: European Debates' in D Fairgrieve and E Lein (eds), *Extraterritoriality and Collective Redress* (Oxford University Press, 2012) 17–18 reserve the term 'class action' for the US device and distinguish between group actions and collective redress depending on their function: while the first is a mere management tool, the second possesses regulatory powers. As for C Hodges, *The Reform of Class and Representative Actions in European Legal Systems*, Studies of the Oxford Institute of European and Comparative Law, vol 8 (Hart Publishing, 2008) 3, he includes ADR mechanisms within the concept of 'collective redress'; CI Nagy, 'Comparative

In particular, the EU's definition of collective redress has been evolving over time. In a public consultation paper of 2011,[9] the Commission primarily adopted a relatively broad definition of collective redress, which included very different models. According to this document, collective redress is a

> broad concept encompassing any mechanism that may accomplish the cessation or prevention of unlawful business practices which affect a multitude of claimants or the compensation for the harm caused by such practices. There are two main forms of collective redress: by way of injunctive relief, claimants seek to stop the continuation of illegal behaviour; by way of compensatory relief, they seek damages for the harm caused. Collective redress procedures can take a variety of forms, including out-of-court mechanisms for dispute resolution or, the entrustment of public or other representative entities with the enforcement of collective claims.[10]

According to Hess, this 'umbrella definition' covers many different types of collective redress instruments like group litigation, model case-litigation, actions brought by ombudsmen or consumer organisations, collective settlement based on opt-out mechanisms, skimming-off actions and injunctions against unlawful practices.[11]

Two years later, however, the Commission released its Recommendations on common principles for injunctive and compensatory collective redress mechanisms in the Member States concerning violations of rights granted under EU law.[12] In this document, it sharpened its previous definition of collective redress by excluding some mechanisms from its scope.[13] Interestingly, Hodges noted a change of terms since the start of debates regarding collective redress: indeed, the EU would have purposely embraced the notion of collective redress in order to distinguish this procedural tool from US class actions.[14]

As for Member States, they have often implemented collective redress mechanisms under imprecise labels. This certainly adds greater difficulties to this already

Collective Redress from a Law and Economics Perspective: Without Risk There is no Reward!' (2013) 19(3) *Columbia Journal of European Law* 469, 470 uses the terms 'class action', 'group proceedings', 'collective proceedings or actions' and 'collective redress' interchangeably; finally, A Nuyts, 'The Consolidation of Collective Claims Under Brussels I' in A Nuyts and NE Hatzimihail (eds), *Cross-Border Class Actions: The European Way* (Sellier European Law Publishers, 2014) 69 draws a distinction between 'group actions', whereby a number of claimants aggregate their claims in one proceedings, 'representative actions' that involve the intervention of a representative entity and the 'class action' model where a claimant acts on behalf of a group of victims.

[9] Commission, Public Consultation: Towards a Coherent European Approach to Collective Redress SEC (2011) 173 final.

[10] ibid 3.

[11] B Hess, 'Collective Redress and the Jurisdictional Model of the Brussels I Regulation' in Nuyts and Hatzimihail, *Cross-Border Class Actions* (n 8) 59.

[12] Commission, Recommendation of 11 June 2013 on common principles for injunctive and compensatory collective redress mechanisms in the Member States concerning violations of rights granted under Union Law [2013] OJ L201/60.

[13] This point is discussed in detail later in this chapter (II.B.ii.b.).

[14] C Hodges, 'Collective Redress: A Breakthrough or a Damp Squib?' (2014) 37 *Journal of Consumer Policy* 67, 72.

complex landscape: for example, the Spanish legislator created a collective redress system named class actions (*acciones colectivas*) but this mechanism does not permit one claimant to sue on behalf of a group like in the US class action. Similarly, the French group action (*action de groupe*) does not allow a group of victims to sue on behalf of similarly situated persons. In fact, only accredited associations have standing to sue under this scheme.

In case the EU plans to regulate collective redress, a clearer frame would have to be adopted for this concept, depending on the scheme(s) it wishes to promote. The recent Proposal for a Directive on representative actions[15] for the protection of the collective interests of consumers – in its current form – seems to opt for a specific collective redress model, which involves the representation of collective interests by qualified entities (Article 3(3) of the Proposal).

The objective of this section is to provide an exhaustive overview of the existing collective redress mechanisms in the EU. This justifies the adoption of a broad definition. Accordingly, this work covers all instruments which aim at bundling various individual and homogeneous rights, as well as tools which permit the defence of general interests. Furthermore, this concept embraces both claims for injunctive and compensatory relief. This notion will be more strictly delimited once the analysis of national instruments is done. Such delineation is carried out in chapter 4 (II.).

C. Goals and Functions of Collective Redress

As mentioned earlier in this work, the modern version of the US class action was adopted for both management and access to justice considerations. Its objective is to offer compensation and deter prospective unlawful behaviours. Chapter 1 also highlighted that these goals and functions are not static: they might vary according to policy objectives or the nature of the actions brought (chapter 1, I.B.i.). In the EU, although the categories representing the goals and functions of collective redress are essentially the same, the landscape is sketchier.

To start with, the reliance on litigation as an enforcement tool is not uniform among the Member States. Some of them rely much more on public authorities in order to protect certain interests, which transcend the mere individual sphere.[16] In those states, the necessity of collective redress instruments is called into question.[17] However, some influential scholars have demonstrated that private and

[15] Proposal for a Directive on representative actions for the protection of the collective interests of consumers, and repealing Directive 2009/22/EC, COM (2018) 184 final.

[16] This is the case of Nordic states for example.

[17] C Hodges, 'Collectivism: Evaluating the Effectiveness of Public and Private Models for Regulating Consumer Protection' in WH van Boom and M Loos (eds), *Collective Enforcement of Consumer Law: Securing Compliance in Europe through Private Group Action and Public Authority Intervention* (Groningen, Europa Law Publishing, 2007) 218–19.

public enforcement are useful complements rather than alternatives. For the sake of this research project, and since this debate is not closed yet, it is assumed that the development of both disciplines is not mutually exclusive.

Turning to the function of collective redress instruments in the EU, it often consists in providing access to justice. This trend is also reflected at the EU level. For example, in a Communication of 2013, the EU Commission acknowledged that

> whereas it is the core task of public enforcement to apply EU law in the public interest and impose sanctions on infringers to punish them and to deter them from committing future infringements, private collective redress is seen primarily as an instrument to provide those affected by infringements with access to justice.[18]

In other words, the Commission attributes different policy goals to public and private enforcement. This situation differs from the US, where the class action is able to generate access to justice and deterrence at the same time.

At the national level, from the 1970s until the 1990s, Member States essentially drafted collective redress mechanisms that were capable of protecting consumer interests at large. These interests, referred to as 'general interests' for the sake of this research project, cannot be individualised.[19] The procedural tools drafted by Member States mainly consisted in actions for injunctive relief and standing to sue was mainly attributed to either consumer associations or public bodies.[20] According to Garth and Cappelletti, the enactment of such instruments was part of a movement towards access to justice.[21] Today, access to justice is still an argument that motivates national legislators to adopt collective redress instruments. This is especially true where small-value claims are involved.[22]

Thereafter, however, many Member States adopted collective redress actions for damages in order to tackle the rise of mass damages. For example in Germany,

[18] Commission, Communication: Towards a European Horizontal Framework for Collective Redress COM (2013) 401 final 10.

[19] Usually, literature distinguishes between various types of interests, although using a different terminology: on the one hand, there are interests that pertain to a given collectivity – or the public in general – but which cannot be held by individuals. eg a harm to the environment or the widespread use of unfair terms on the market. For the sake of this research project, these are called 'general interests'. On the other hand, there are interests which affect individual members of a group. Typically, unlawful overcharges imposed by telecom companies will individually affect a group of consumers. These interests are referred to as 'collective interests'. For more information on this dichotomy, see Art 1 of the Latin American Model Code on Class Actions mentioned below (ch 2, I.D.); S Corominas Bach, 'La legitimación en la futura regulación europea de las acciones colectivas de consumo' and MP Sánchez González, 'Los interéses difusos bajo la óptica del derecho civil' both in E Carbonell Porras and R Cabrera Mercado (eds), *Intereses Colectivos y Legitimación Activa* (Thomson Reuters, 2014) 137–61, 531–33; P Gutiérrez de Cabiedes and H de Caviedes, *La Tutela Jurisdiccional de los Intereses Supraindividuales: Colectivos y Difusos* (Aranzadi, 1999) 99–113.

[20] Hodges, *The Reform of Class and Representative Actions in European Legal Systems* (n 8) 9–10.

[21] BG Garth and M Cappelletti, 'Access to Justice: The Newest Wave in the Worldwide Movement to Make Rights Effective' (1978) 27 *Buffalo Law Review* 181, 209–22.

[22] Hodges (n 8) 188.

the *KapMuG* was adopted after the *Telekom* case;[23] the Spanish collective redress scheme followed the rapeseed oil scandal;[24] the Italian class action appeared after the *Parmalat* case;[25] and the *DES* case is at the origin of the adoption of an out-of-court collective redress procedure in the Netherlands.[26] Therefore, it appears that collective redress actions for damages were primarily considered as a case-management tool and access to justice seems to have played a secondary role, at least in those Member States.

As regards the goals of national collective redress mechanisms, they depend on the protected interests. For example, an instrument that aims at protecting the general interests of consumers at large – such as air pollution or the presence of unfair terms in a trader's terms and conditions – would probably pursue an objective of deterrence more than compensation. This is easily understandable since in those cases the harm can hardly ever be individualised. However, the Evaluation Study on the effectiveness and efficiency of collective redress mechanisms in the EU[27] acknowledges that the potential deterrent effect of collective redress actions is limited, especially where instruments lack efficiency or where damages awarded do not correspond to the illegal gain obtained by a given wrongdoer.

Therefore, some mechanisms aim at compensating victims for their damage. The English Group Litigation Order (GLO) and the German *KapMuG* should fall under this category. Both instruments allow individual claimants to record their claims in a register. Then, a court rules on the common issues that those cases entail. Once this task is done, individual proceedings continue independently. Nevertheless, it is hard to delineate clearly whether a given mechanism pursues one goal or the other, given that nothing impedes collective redress schemes from pursuing both objectives simultaneously.

D. Structural Aspects

This sub-section studies the structural characteristics of national collective redress mechanisms in Europe pursuant to the following parameters: participation (i.), standing to sue (ii.), certification criteria (iii.), costs and financing (iv.) and the role of ADR (v.). The EU structure of collective redress is compared to the US class

[23] M Bakowitz, 'The German Experience with Group Action' in V Harsági and CH van Rhee (eds), *Multi-Party Redress Mechanisms in Europe: Squeaking Mice?* (Intersentia, 2014) 157.

[24] P Gutiérrez de Cabiedes Hidalgo, Group Litigation in Spain, National Report, para 2, available at globalclassactions.stanford.edu.

[25] E Silvestri, 'Class Actions in Italy: Great Expectations, Big Disappointment' in Harsági and van Rhee, *Multi-Party Redress Mechanisms in Europe: Squeaking Mice?* (n 23) 197.

[26] T Arons and WH van Boom, 'Beyond Tulips and Cheese: Exporting Mass Securities Claim Settlements from The Netherlands' (2010) *European Business Law Review* 857, 866.

[27] Commission, 'Evaluation of the Effectiveness and Efficiency of Collective Redress Mechanisms in the European Union', final report part I (2008) 54–55, available at www.civic-consulting.de/reports/collective%20redress_study.pdf.

action. Moreover, some specific reference to the solutions provided by the Latin American Model Code on Class Actions (*Código Modelo de Procesos Colectivos para Iberoamérica*, hereafter, the Model Code), which was adopted by the Latin American Institute of Procedural Law (*Instituto Iberoamericano de Derecho Procesal*) in 2004 are included.[28] This Code gathers existing or improved rules and principles on collective proceedings adopted by Latin American states, but also serves as a model for future reforms.

As this research project shows, collective redress neither resembles the US class action nor the Model Code. Most of the time, Member States have equipped their device with structural features, which are poles apart from their American counterpart. Unfortunately, these choices have led to efficiency problems that national legislators gradually solve through reforms. In this sense, the process of evaluation and corrections of collective redress weaknesses through reforms resembles what the American legislator has done in order to reach a certain equilibrium between access to justice and procedural efficiency, without hindering the rights of the defence.

i. Participation: Opt-In, Opt-Out and Automatic Membership

Under the opt-in system, victims have to manifest themselves if they wish to be bound by a collective decision or a settlement.[29] Despite that, opt-in participants do usually not technically become parties to the proceedings.[30] The opt-in system has the advantage of respecting parties' willingness to sue and makes the size of the collective claim foreseeable for the defendant.[31]

Nevertheless, opt-in collective actions might not include all victims and, thus, the exposure of the defendant could dramatically shrink.[32] Another negative aspect of the opt-in regime is that it implies an important investment of financial and administrative resources in order to spot potential victims and organise the group.[33] Similarly, this system creates an additional burden for courts, which have to take all individual aspects of the claims into account.[34] Besides, it is unsure that the participative attitude required by an opt-in system remains efficient where psychological and economic barriers discourage victims from manifesting

[28] The provisions of the Code are available in Spanish at www.iibdp.org/es/codigos-modelo.html.

[29] R Mulheron, *The Class Action in Common Law Legal Systems – A Comparative Perspective* (Hart Publishing, 2004) 29.

[30] ibid 30; The Study Centre for Consumer Law/Centre for European Economic Law, 'An Analysis and Evaluation of Alternative Means of Consumer Redress Other Than Redress Through Ordinary Judicial Proceedings' (Leuven, 2007) 288, available at www.eurofinas.org/uploads/documents/policies/OTHER%20POLICY%20ISSUES/comparative_report_en.pdf.

[31] R Mulheron, 'Some Difficulties with Group Litigation Orders – and Why a Class Action is Superior' (2005) 24 *Civil Justice Quarterly* 40, 50; Commission, Communication (n 18) 12.

[32] Mulheron, 'Some Difficulties with Group Litigation Orders' (n 31) 50.

[33] R Mulheron, 'The Case for an Opt-out Class Action for European Member States: A Legal and Empirical Analysis' (2009) 15(3) *Columbia Journal of European Law* 409, 428–29.

[34] ibid 428.

themselves and becoming part of the collective proceedings. In this sense, an opt-in based instrument might not sufficiently promote access to justice.[35]

The *Consumer Association v JJB Sports PLC*[36] case illustrates the shortcomings of an opt-in collective action. The facts can be summarised as follows: in 2007, the British consumer association Which? sued JJB Sports under section 47B of the Competition Act 1998. The original version of this provision states that a specified body may bring an action before the Competition Appeal Tribunal, which comprises consumer claims filed or continued on behalf of at least two individuals.[37] In order to be included in the proceedings, victims must opt in. In the case at stake, the lawsuit brought by Which? followed a sanction imposed by the Office of Fair Trading, which fined several companies that entered into price-fixing agreements. Due to this unlawful practice, the consumer association estimates that around one million replica football T-shirts were sold at an artificially high price.[38] In January 2008, judicial proceedings stalled when parties reached a settlement, whereby the defendant would pay 'damages to affected consumers of between £5 and £20 per shirt'.[39] The settlement was concluded on behalf of only 130 victims.[40] Due to the difficulties of gathering victims and the costs relating thereto, this claim was the only one that was brought under section 47B of the Competition Act 1998.[41] Today, many collective redress schemes follow the opt-in approach.

As for the automatic membership model, it establishes that members are encompassed in the collective action without any possibility to get excluded. The American experience shows that the interest of the defendant not to have to comply with potentially contradictory decisions dictates such a system. In Europe, automatic membership applies predominantly when a general interest is at stake. For example, this is typically the case when an environmental organisation initiates proceedings against an industrial company whose activities pollute the air of a given geographical area. In this context, an action seeking injunctive relief would usually not allow consumers either to opt in or to opt out.[42] However, if the organisation wins the case, all people living in the polluted area would benefit from this judgment.

[35] Mulheron (n 31) 50.

[36] *The Consumer Association v JJB Sports PLC* [2009] CAT 2 (Case No 1078/7/9/07).

[37] Until 30 September 2015, s 47B read: 'A specified body may (subject to the provisions of this Act and Tribunal rules) bring proceedings before the Tribunal which comprise consumer claims made or continued on behalf of at least two individuals'.

[38] M Murphy, 'JJB and Which? settle football shirt case' (10.01.2008) *FT.com*, available at next.ft.com/content/bd0acca2-bf08-11dc-8c61-0000779fd2ac.

[39] *The Consumer Association v JJB Sports PLC* [2009] CAT 2 (Case nº 1078/7/9/07), para 13.

[40] ibid para 7.

[41] On the deficiencies of this mechanism, see R Mulheron, 'Reform of Collective Redress in England and Wales: A Perspective of Need', Report submitted to the Civil Justice Council of England and Wales (2008) 37–46. Because the collective action could not properly tackle rational apathy, the Consumer Rights Act 2015 reformed s 47B. Henceforth, opt-out collective actions are available under said section.

[42] CI Nagy, 'The European Collective Redress Debate After the European Commission's Recommendation – One Step Forward, One Step Back?' (2015) 22(4) *Maastricht Journal of European and Comparative Law* 530, 537–38, 541.

Lastly, according to the opt-out system, people are included in a collective action, unless they manifest their intention not to be bound by the decision or the settlement. Although this system is feared by some, because of its potentially unconstitutional character and the abuses it may trigger,[43] quite a few Member States have adopted an opt-out regime, ie Bulgaria, the Netherlands and Portugal. Others have implemented an innovative solution whereby opt-in and opt-out participation schemes coexist (hybrid system). For example, in Norway, section 35–7 of the Dispute Act 2005 states that opt-out proceedings may be ordered by the court where 'amounts or interests (…) are so small that it must be assumed that a considerable majority of them would not be brought as individual actions' and the claims 'are not deemed to raise issues that need to be heard individually'. The rationale is to offer access to justice to victims when an opt-out collective action is the only available means to obtain redress. Similarly, Belgium, Denmark and Norway have adopted a hybrid system but different criteria apply in order to determine whether courts should let the action proceed under the opt-in or opt-out regime. In these states, no abusive litigation or harm to businesses has been registered.[44] This certainly demonstrates that an opt-out regime by itself cannot trigger abusive litigation. In reality, abuses stem from other elements of the legal environment such as attractive rules on costs and funding, as well as the presence of favourable substantive laws.[45]

One of the potentially problematic elements of the opt-out model is that it contradicts the right to be heard, given that absent members of a collective action would eventually be bound by a decision without having participated in the proceedings.[46] This argument is partially true: indeed, if absent victims are adequately notified and, thus, are offered an opportunity either to intervene or to get out of the collective action, then their right to be heard is preserved. In this vein, Ervo makes an interesting remark: she states that an opt-out system coupled with adequate notification better respects the right to be heard than a collective

[43] Commission, Communication (n 18) 11.

[44] Commission, 'Evaluation of the Effectiveness and Efficiency of Collective Redress' (n 27) 78–79; Nagy, 'The European Collective Redress Debate After the European Commission's Recommendation' (n 42) 545.

[45] L Ervo, 'Opt-In is Out and Opt-out is In' in B Hess et al (eds), *EU Civil Justice: Current Issues and Future Outlook*, Swedish Studies in European Law, vol 7 (Bloomsbury, 2016) 198. The author states that '[t]he possibility to abuse the system is the most traditional argument against class actions generally and especially against the opt-out system. However, this argument does not hold. Because, in such case, substantive law (…) does not change; and collective redress will not do so either. If punitive damages are not allowed according to substantive law or if the threshold for establishing negligence or liability has not been lowered, the fear of this type of negative Americanisation is amateurish. Collective redress is just a procedural tool to realise substantive law like all procedures'.

[46] Regarding this argument, see R Gaudet, 'Turning a Blind Eye: the Commission's Rejection of Opt-out Class Actions Overlooks Swedish, Norwegian, Danish and Dutch Experience' (2009) 30(3) *European Competition Law Review* 107, 107–09; J Stuyck, 'Class Actions in Europe? To Opt-In or to Opt-Out, That is the Question' (2009) 20(4) *European Business Law Review* 483, 491; DPL Tzakas, 'Effective Collective Redress in Antitrust and Consumer Protection Matters: A Panacea or a Chimera?' (2011) 48(4) *Common Market Law Review* 1125, 1144–47.

redress judgment that would only bind opt-in members but could nevertheless create a precedent or be used as evidence in future proceedings.[47] Moreover, when the conflict involves small-value claims, the opt-out nature of the system cannot take away the right to be heard, since the alternative to collective proceedings would be no day in court at all.[48]

Similarly, the opt-out regime is meant to infringe the right of disposal, given that members are dragged into collective proceedings.[49] As adequate notice and opt-out provide an 'exit door', this argument cannot be validly accepted. Taken seriously, this would also mean that automatic membership violates the right of disposal, as well as the right to be heard. However, this model is permitted in the EU.

On the positive side of the balance, an opt-out regime offers access to justice to small-value claimants and fights against rational apathy.[50] Thanks to this mechanism, victims' negotiation power is enhanced. Furthermore, opt-out collective redress allows defendants to obtain closure and avoid the cost of litigating the same cases several times in distinct locations.[51]

These participation schemes generate various issues from a civil procedure perspective: to start with, the status of absent parties is unclear. Sometimes they are considered as parties to the proceedings – this entails the respect of certain procedural rights, like the right to present evidence –, and sometimes they are not qualified as such. For example, under the Italian *azione di classe*, which is based on an opt-in system, absent members do not have the right to participate in collective proceedings or to intervene.[52] Their role is purely passive. Interestingly, in Sweden, although absent members are not parties to collective proceedings, they may de facto be considered as such under certain circumstances: for example, this will be the case for questions related to *lis pendens*, joinder – of pending cases or other related group actions –, rules on evidence, and other matters submitted to general rules of civil procedure.[53] An absent member can also intervene and exercise the right to appeal. The second issue concerns *res judicata*. In principle, *res judicata* only binds parties to the proceedings. However, in collective redress proceedings, the judgment or the settlement covers absent members, who are not parties. The American experience has shown that admitting an *ultra partes* effect challenged the traditional rules of civil procedure.

[47] Ervo, 'Opt-In is Out and Opt-out is In' (n 45) 197.

[48] Nagy (n 42) 536–37.

[49] On this question, see A Higgins and A Zuckerman, 'Class Actions come to England – More Access to Justice and More of a Compensation Culture, but they are Superior to Alternatives' (2016) 35(1) *Civil Justice Quarterly* 1, 3–5; Nagy (n 42) 536–38; Tzakas, 'Effective Collective Redress in Antitrust and Consumer Protection Matters' (n 46) 1137–39.

[50] R Mulheron, 'Justice Enhanced: Framing an Opt-Out Class Action for England' (2007) 70 *The Modern Law Review* 550, 556; AL Sibony, 'A Behavioural Perspective on Collective Redress' in E Lein et al (eds), *Collective Redress in Europe – Why and How?* (The British Institute of International and Comparative Law, 2015) 51–56.

[51] Mulheron, 'Justice Enhanced' (n 50) 556.

[52] G Cataldi, 'La nuova azione di classe' (2009) 3 *Consumatori, Diritti e Mercato* 136–37.

[53] Ervo, 'Group Actions in Sweden – A Moderate Start' in Harsági and van Rhee (n 23) 248–49.

ii. Standing to Sue

Under traditional litigation standards, the question of who should have standing to sue is relatively straightforward, since the holders of the rights and obligations usually are also the parties to the proceedings. Nowadays, however, modern society has to face new situations, which challenge the institution of standing to sue: the first case refers to violations that affect numerous victims individually, and the second one concerns harms to general interests, which affect a community and cannot be individualised. Because these types of damages go beyond a single person's harm, one may wonder who should have standing to sue in order to obtain redress. The United States and EU Member States have built up different rules on standing to sue in response to this problem.

In the United States, Rule 23 allocates standing to any party of the class who has standing to sue and adequately represents absent class members. In this case, the representative plaintiff litigates in his own name as regards his/her personal claim, but on behalf of absent class members. In some cases, when some sub-classes must be formed in order to ensure that all victims are represented, various plaintiffs can take the role of representative. On the contrary, associations only have standing to sue when they seek the enforcement of their members' rights. Notably, the Latin American Model Code adopted liberal rules regarding standing to sue. To be more specific, Article 3 of the Model Code contains a list of eight categories of actors who have standing to start collective proceedings, namely natural persons defending general interests; members of a group of victims; the Public Prosecutor's Office, the Ombudsman's Office or the Public Defender's Office; legal persons of public law; entities or organs pertaining to the public administration; trade unions; associations with one year of existence, which protect the rights promoted by the Model Code; and political parties.

The allocation of standing to sue to a great range of actors, including individuals, is a policy choice that favours access to justice. Indeed, the probability that one of these actors decides to sue is bigger than if standing is limited to a reduced group of players. This decision also hinges on the interests that are to be protected. However, as the next paragraphs show, there might be some practical obstacles to the actual exercise of standing to sue.

In many Member States in Europe – and contrary to the US –, individuals do not have standing to sue in collective redress actions. Moreover, the list of actors who have standing to sue is usually not as extensive as that provided by the Model Code. Rather, national legislation of EU Member States often imposes strict criteria on standing and reserves it to specific entities. Most of the time, these entities have not suffered any damage and, thus, do not have any claim against the defendant. However, national provisions on standing to sue are quite heterogeneous: a small number of countries allocate standing to individuals; others reserve it to specific private entities such as consumer associations; and some only make it possible for public authorities to bring collective actions. It is worth mentioning that the test case model that is described below (I.E.iii.) does not use any intermediary or representative claimant. Therefore, the comments made here are not applicable to this model, which resembles more joinder than class action. In the next paragraphs, three models that have been adopted in Member States are presented, as well as the drawbacks that each of these actors may face in practice.

First of all, some Member States have given individuals standing to sue in collective proceedings, on the model of the US class action. As mentioned earlier, this solution fosters access to justice, as any victim has the right to initiate a collective action. For example, Article 140-bis of the Italian consumer code states that consumers and users have the power to bring collective actions in order to defend homogeneous individual rights. They can also mandate an association to litigate on their behalf. In practice, however, no individual usually takes the lead to initiate collective proceedings. This can be explained by the enormous financial risks that the representative faces: in case the claimant loses at trial, the loser-pays principle will make them liable to reimburse the defendant's costs.[54]

In this context, if the representative claimant does not benefit from a financial incentive, like a risk premium, it is unlikely that he/she would litigate. Besides, because other victims prefer to free-ride on the actions of a representative claimant, then everybody may wait for others to act. This creates a situation of apathy that eventually leads to no litigation at all. This is particularly obvious in an action for injunctive relief: imagine that a neighbour initiates proceedings against an industrial firm that pollutes the air and creates a danger for people's health. If the judge condemns this firm to reduce contamination, then this is beneficial for all the neighbours who were suffering from this unlawful conduct. However, the claimant is the only one who faces the cost of litigation and the risk of losing at trial. This situation could, for example, be remedied if a financial incentive were offered to the claimant, given that his/her active attitude would benefit a large number of people.

Secondly, entities such as consumer associations play an important role for consumer protection. Hence, many Member States allocate them standing to sue in order to defend consumers' interests. For instance, consumer associations are particularly valuable actors in cases involving small-value claims, given the predominance of rational apathy.[55] However, these entities usually have to comply with strict requirements in order to benefit from standing to sue in a collective redress action. Such requirements may hinder access to court to consumer associations, but they allow the legislator to control the flow of claimants willing to start judicial proceedings. This may equally constitute a shield against abusive litigation.

For example, Article R.811-1 to 7 of the French Consumer Code (FCC) establishes the conditions that consumer associations must fulfil in order to be able to

[54] Mulheron, *The Class Action in Common Law Legal Systems* (n 29) 437–38.

[55] HW Micklitz, 'Collective Private Enforcement of Consumer Law: The Key Questions' in van Boom and Loos, *Collective Enforcement of Consumer Law: Securing Compliance in Europe through Private Group Action and Public Authority Intervention* (n 17) 23.

start collective proceedings (certified entities). According to this provision and in order to be certified, an association must have a year of existence; have no professional activity; actively defend consumer interests; and be representative – this is measured according to the number of affiliated consumers. On its website,[56] the National Institute of Consumers (*Institut National de la Consommation*) informs that currently 15 consumer associations are accredited at the national level. This number is quite low for a territory as big as France. In light of these considerations, it can be inferred that, in France, litigation is reserved to relatively big and experienced associations. In particular, ad hoc entities cannot be built up for the purpose of initiating collective proceedings, given that a year of existence is required. Some additional obstacles may indirectly influence the effective exercise of standing to sue. These obstacles are essentially financing, access to information, and gathering potential participants in an opt-in based collective action. While questions of financing are dealt with below (I.D.iv.), the next lines focus on information and gathering of participants.

Because consumer associations do not suffer any damage, victims must collaborate and provide them with relevant information about their harm. In competition law, this problem is even more serious as the information is usually retained by the alleged wrongdoer and consumer associations have limited access to evidence.[57] Therefore, the building up of arguments and gathering of evidence might be complex. As regards grouping of potential participants, the French joined representative action (*action en representation conjointe*) can be taken as an example: pursuant to Article L.622-1 to 4 of the FCC, two or more consumers can mandate an accredited association to commence proceedings on their behalf. Therefore, this specific collective action is based on the opt-in system. However, under this particular scheme, the consumer association can only attract other potential participants through the written press. No other advertising means are permitted by French law. As a result, the absence of adequate means to capture opt-in claimants is one of the causes that explains the inefficiency of the joined representative action. Some studies affirm that this procedural tool was used five times in ten years of existence.[58] In light of these considerations, the French legislator decided to adopt a group action (*action de groupe*) that aims at overcoming these difficulties.

Thirdly, some Member States give public authorities the power to bring collective redress actions. This is the case of the Nordic countries and can be explained by

[56] www.conso.net/content/les-associations-de-consommateurs.

[57] O Dayagi-Epstein, 'Representation of Consumer Interest by Consumer Associations – Salvation for the Masses?' (2007) 3(2) *The Competition Law Review* 209, 238–40.

[58] C Cerutti and M Guillaume, 'Rapport sur l'action de groupe remis le 16 décembre 2005 aux Ministres de l'économie, des finances et de l'industrie et de la justice, garde des sceaux' (2005) 24, available at www.ladocumentationfrancaise.fr/var/storage/rapports-publics/054004458.pdf; Institut National de la Consommation, 'L'action de groupe : vers une consécration ?' (20–26 June 2005) 1348 *INC Hebdo*, available at www.conso.net/sites/default/files/pdf_abonne/1348-action_groupe_255.pdf.

the traditional importance of public authorities in resolving consumer disputes.[59] In particular, section 6 of the Swedish Group Proceedings Act of 2002 enables a public authority – basically, the Consumer Ombudsman and the Environmental Protection Agency – to initiate a collective action on behalf of consumers. The mechanism is based on the opt-in system and either injunctive relief or compensatory damages can be sought. In Norway, public authorities are also attributed standing to sue on top of individuals and private organisations or associations. As regards Finland, the Consumer Ombudsman has the exclusive right to bring collective proceedings on an opt-in basis. Thanks to this restrictive scope of standing, the government wants to avoid abuses of the collective action.[60] Nevertheless, it must be highlighted that no group action has been registered in Finland. The reasons for this are unclear: while some argue that the threshold for bringing this type of action is too high, others explain that the presence of a group action within the Finnish legal order has a powerful deterrent effect, hence the absence of cases.[61] The potential problems with the attribution of standing to sue to public authorities are their lack of expertise with litigation and their possible acquaintances with political powers.[62]

iii. Certification Criteria

Generally speaking, Member States do not enjoin certification criteria to their collective redress mechanisms. Most of them are not familiar with numerosity, commonality, typicality, superiority and adequacy of representation. However, their unfamiliarity is not absolute, as, some Member States adopted certification criteria that look like those contained in Rule 23. The most striking example is perhaps the case of Nordic countries, which 'mimic' most of the certification conditions of Rule 23.[63] Article 2 of the Latin American Model Code too adopted most of the requirements imposed by Rule 23.[64] To be fair, it has to be highlighted that, although many Member States have not adopted specific certification criteria, most of them do require a certain degree of commonality between class members' claims. For example, in Italy, the legislator explicitly requires claimants to possess

[59] See L Ervo and A Persson, 'Finnish and Swedish Legislation in Light of the ADR Directive – Boards and Ombudsmen' in Lein et al, *Collective Redress in Europe* (n 50) 463–71, who highlight the important role of boards and ombudsmen in Nordic countries.

[60] Hodges (n 8) 29.

[61] Ervo and Persson, 'Finnish and Swedish Legislation in Light of the ADR Directive' (n 59) 471.

[62] M Cappelletti, 'Vindicating the Public Interest through the Courts: A Comparativist's Contribution' (1975–76) 25 *Buffalo Law Review* 643, 657–60; WH van Boom and M Loos 'Effective Enforcement of Consumer Law in Europe' in van Boom and Loos (n 17) 251.

[63] In Sweden, see s 8 of the Group Proceedings Act of 2002 and in Finland, see s 2 of the Group Action Act of 2007.

[64] In particular, the requirements of adequacy of representation and predominance must be fulfilled (Arts 2°.I and 2°.II.1°). Moreover, the wording of Art 2°.II.2°d suggests that some kind of commonality should link the members of the affected group. Finally, Art 2°.II looks like a superiority requirement.

homogeneous rights in order to proceed as a class.[65] In Germany, pursuant to the *KapMuG*, a higher court has the ability to rule on common issues of fact or law.

Then, it has to be pointed out that adequacy of representation is usually not a flexible condition. The criteria that serve to assess the representative nature of a given claimant are rather static – in the sense that it is allocated by the law, disregarding the nature of the dispute. Therefore, this result departs from the American solution. One counter-example may be found in the Netherlands, where Article 7:907(3)(f) of the Dutch Civil Law Code states that the court may call into question the validity of a collective settlement if 'the foundations or associations (…) are not sufficiently representative with regard to the interests of persons on whose behalf the agreement has been concluded'.

iv. Costs and Financing

In the previous chapter, the financial aspects surrounding the American class action device were explained. In this context, it should be highlighted that the common fund doctrine helps the class to finance class actions, given that it makes the financial burden fall back onto the class counsel. Additionally, the 'American rule' regarding costs applies. Besides, the fundamental role of judges in assessing the reasonableness of attorneys' fees was highlighted. Taken together, these factors provide significant incentives for parties to litigate. Furthermore, the litigation culture, coupled with high financial stakes, sometimes leads parties to collude.

On the other side of the Atlantic, however, things are different: to start with, there is no adversarial legalism – at least not as it stands in the US – and a large number of Member States forbid contingency fee agreements and limit third-party funding.[66] Moreover, punitive damages are not available and the loser-pays principle is the predominant rule regarding costs.[67] These legislative choices significantly limit incentives to sue and, thus, may affect the effectiveness of collective redress mechanisms. This is quite unfortunate, given that appropriate pecuniary incentives

[65] Art 140-bis(1) of the Italian Consumer Code.

[66] This statement must, however, be nuanced: in Spain, former Art 16 of the Lawyers' Code of Ethics forbade the conclusion of contingency fee agreements. In 2008, however, the Supreme Court held that such a prohibition violated national competition law norms. Specifically, it stated that the prohibition to conclude contingency fee agreements was equivalent to the establishment of minimal prices. See judgment of the Spanish Supreme Court (*Tribunal Supremo*), Administrative Chamber, case 6610/2008 rendered on 4 November 2008, as well as the explanations of C Gómez Ligüerre and CA Ruiz García, 'Honorarios de abogados, competencia y pacto de quota litis' (2009) 1 *InDret*, available at www.indret.com. Similarly, in Germany, former Art 49 of the Federal Lawyer Ordinance (*Bundesrechtsanwaltsordnung*) prohibited contingency fees. After a 2006 ruling of the Constitutional Court, which stated that the strict outlawing of contingency fees was contrary to the freedom of enterprise, Art 4a of the Law on Remuneration of Lawyers (*Gesetz über die Vergütung der Rechtsanwältinnen und Rechtsanwälte*) was adopted and allows such a financial scheme, in the event that it would offer access to justice to claimants. See the judgment of the Constitutional Court (*Bundesverfassungsgericht*), case 1 BvR 2576/04 rendered on 12 December 2006.

[67] C Hodges et al, *The Costs and Funding of Civil Litigation – A Comparative Perspective* (CH Beck/Hart, 2010) 17, 25–27.

have the power to fight rational apathy and foster access to justice.[68] In any case, it is important to strike the right balance between the protection of the defendant from blackmail or unmeritorious claims on the one hand, and proper financial incentives to sue on the other. In principle, national legislation on collective redress do not contain any provision regarding costs and funding. Hence, most of the time, general rules of civil procedure apply. This means that a large majority of collective redress schemes follow the loser-pays principle.

The loser-pays rule – also called cost-shifting or the 'English rule' – on costs is a cardinal principle of civil litigation in Europe. According to this concept, the losing party has to reimburse the recoverable costs of the winning counterpart.[69] Even though this principle represents a shield against unmeritorious claims, it may equally act as a disincentive to litigate, given that the financial risk is higher.[70] As a result, some Member States soften the loser-pays rule in specific circumstances. For example, under the Portuguese popular action scheme, the representative claimant does not bear any costs if the case is – partially – successful.[71] If the claimant loses at trial, it only bears between 10 and 50 per cent of the defendant's costs. The judge has discretionary power to rule on this matter. The Latin American Model Code goes one step further: Article 15(3) exempts claimants from paying any costs, unless they acted in bad faith.

It should be emphasised that the intermediary involved in collective proceedings is usually the only person liable to for costs.[72] In a few Member States, however, costs are divided among all the members of the collective suit.[73] This is the case for instruments which require the active participation of the members (opt-in) or their inscription in a register, like in Germany and England. Again, the solution provided by the Model Code is different and provides interesting incentives to litigate: in particular, under Article 15(2), the judge may offer a financial reward to the representative claimant, in case his/her intervention in the proceedings was influential.

Notably, in some Member States, the claimant usually has to bear the costs related to notification about the existence of collective redress proceedings, as well as the right to opt in or out. However, it is possible to recover those costs in case

[68] L Visscher and T Schepens, 'A Law and Economics Approach to Cost Shifting, Fee Arrangements, and Legal Expense Insurance' in M Tuil and L Visscher (eds), *New Trends in Financing Civil Litigation in Europe – A Legal, Empirical, and Economic Analysis* (Edward Elgar, 2010) 8–9.

[69] These costs usually encompass court costs, witness and expert related expenses, and lawyers' fees (Hodges et al, *The Costs and Funding of Civil Litigation* (n 67) 18).

[70] BEUC, 'Litigation Funding in Relation to the Establishment of a European Mechanism of Collective Redress' (2012), pt IV, available at https://www.beuc.eu/publications/2012-00074-01-e.pdf; Visscher and Schepens, 'A Law and Economics Approach to Cost Shifting, Fee Arrangements, and Legal Expense Insurance' (n 68) 13–14; S Shavell, *Foundations of Economic Analysis of Law* (The Belknap Press of Harvard University Press, 2004) 429.

[71] Art 20 of the Law nº 83/95 of 31 August.

[72] Commission, 'Evaluation of the Effectiveness and Efficiency of Collective Redress' (n 27) 65; R Mulheron, 'Costs and Funding of Collective Actions – Realities and Possibilities', Research paper for submission to the European Consumers' Organisation (BEUC) (2011) 84–89.

[73] Commission, 'Evaluation of the Effectiveness and Efficiency of Collective Redress (n 27) 65.

the claimant succeeds in court. For example, Article 695 and 696 of the French Code of Civil Procedure states that the expenses generated by the notification of acts abroad are recoverable by the winner. However, this means that in a collective redress action, the consumer association must take into account that such costs may not be covered by the defendant. Similarly, although Article 15 of the Spanish Law on Procedure does not mention it, the costs to advertise the existence of the collective redress action fall on the claimant. In this case too, costs of notification are recoverable if the claimant wins in court (Article 241(1)(2) of the Spanish Law on Civil Procedure).[74]

As far as funding is concerned, there are various methods to finance litigation in Europe – including collective suits.[75] The accessibility to these funding mechanisms may overcome restrictive rules on costs and immunise the claimant against financial risks. However, Member States seem to be reluctant to fully liberalise the market of litigation financing. Besides, they have taken different approaches towards the regulation of this particular matter. Nevertheless, the rest of this section attempts to provide a general overview of the available funding mechanisms in the EU. It must be highlighted that each of these mechanisms is not always present in all states. In the next lines, two of them are presented.

The first method to fund litigation is through contingency fee agreements. Under this scheme, lawyers assume the burden of financing judicial proceedings. In case they are successful at trial or if the dispute is eventually settled, their fees represent a percentage of the amount recovered. If they lose the case, lawyers are not entitled to get any fee – no cure, no fee.[76] Contingency fee agreements are

[74] F Gascón Inchausti, 'Acciones colectivas e inhibitorias para la protección de los consumidores en el proceso civil español: el papel de las asociaciones de consumidores' (2005) 17, available at https://eprints.ucm.es.

[75] A first pecuniary source that may finance litigation are public funds coupled with self-financing. In particular, an investment of the state in judicial proceedings may be justified when general interests are at stake. eg in Germany and Austria, consumer associations are mainly financed by public funds. Specifically, the *Verein für Konsumenteninformation* (VKI), the major consumer association in Austria, is able to fund its activities – including litigation – thanks to member fees and publications on the one hand, as well as an annual subsidy from the government on the other. Additionally, the Austrian entity is able to raise third-party funding in order to cover the costs of collective proceedings (this information is available at www.konsument.at). An alternative public means to finance litigation is legal aid. The negative aspect of this funding method is that legal aid is equally subject to budgetary constraints and is not available for organisations such as consumer associations (S Voet, 'The Crux of the Matter: Funding and Financing Collective Redress Mechanisms' in Hess et al, *EU Civil Justice: Current Issues and Future Outlook* (n 45) 214). However, legal aid may be provided to individual victims who are part of collective proceedings (see the example of the *Dexia* case in I Tzankova, 'Funding of Mass Disputes: Lessons From the Netherlands' (2012) 8 *Journal of Law Economics and Policy* 549, 579–81). In the competition law field, an interesting solution has been proposed in order to overcome scarcity of public funds: this is, allocating part of the fines imposed in case of competition law violations to entities that have standing to bring collective redress suits (BEUC, 'Litigation Funding in Relation to the Establishment of a European Mechanism of Collective Redress' (n 70) pt I). Finally, insurance can shift the financial burden of litigation on third parties. In particular, After the Event (ATE) and Before the Event (BTE) insurance can be taken out. The use of contingency fees and third-party funding is discussed in the next paragraphs.

[76] Mulheron, 'Costs and Funding of Collective Actions – Realities and Possibilities' (n 72) 92.

an interesting way to finance litigation, as claimants do not have to cover their lawyer's fees if they are unsuccessful at trial. In this sense, these agreements promote access to justice.[77] On the contrary, opponents argue that contingency fees are unethical.[78] In particular, as lawyers acquire a pecuniary interest in the dispute, a conflict of interests might develop. In light of the above, the Code of Conduct for European Lawyers, at Article 3(3), as well as a large majority of Member States, prohibit the use of contingency fees agreements.[79] Nevertheless, restrictions of budgets for legal aid and market conditions incentivised some states to mitigate this strict prohibition. An interesting example is the British Conditional Fee Agreement (CFA), which was implemented to make justice affordable.[80] Under a CFA,[81] the lawyer who succeeds at trial or reaches an agreement with the counterpart is paid an ordinary fee, which might correspond to the actual costs incurred by the lawyer or an hourly fee. Then, an uplift – or a success fee – is usually added on top of this. It might constitute a percentage of the ordinary fee. If the claim does not succeed, no fee is payable. The difference between a contingency and conditional fee agreement is that the uplift in a conditional fee agreement is not related to the amount adjudicated or settled.[82]

Another recent and interesting form of third-party funding appeared in the competition law field: the assignment of claims to special purpose vehicles (SPVs). For example, Cartel Damage Claims (CDC) is a Belgian service provider whose purpose is to enforce competition law claims.[83] More precisely, victims who have suffered a competition law offence transfer – or sell – their claims to CDC. Then, the special purpose vehicle brings proceedings against the wrongdoer. If successful, CDC returns a portion of the damage award to the victims. Thanks to the assignment of claims technique, the Belgian service provider is able to pool resources and obtain funding from third parties. As for victims, they are able to shift the burden and the risk to litigate onto CDC.[84] Although this model has been

[77] M Faure et al, 'No Cure, no Pay and Contingency Fees' in Tuil and Visscher, *New Trends in Financing Civil Litigation in Europe* (n 68) 39–41.

[78] ibid 37–39.

[79] But see the comment at n 66. According to a comprehensive study on litigation costs and funding of 2010, Estonia, Finland, Hungary and Spain allow contingency fee agreements. As for Germany, Italy, Lithuania, Slovakia and Slovenia, they either permit these agreements under certain conditions or impose several limitations. Finally, Poland and Sweden accept contingency fee agreements only in the context of collective redress actions (Hodges et al, (n 67) 132–33).

[80] SE Keske et al, 'Financing and Group Litigation' in Tuil and Visscher (n 68) 77.

[81] Mulheron, (n 72) 92; Faure et al, 'No Cure, no Pay and Contingency Fees' (n 77) 36.

[82] W Emons, 'Conditional versus Contingent Fees' (2007) 59(1) *Oxford Economics Papers* 1, 1, available at www.researchgate.net.

[83] For further information on the functioning of CDC, see SE Keske, *Group Litigation in European Competition Law – A Law and Economic Perspective* (Intersentia, 2010) 233–34; T Reher, 'Specific Issues in Cross-Border EU Competition Law Actions Brought by Multiple Claimants in a German Context' in M Danov et al (eds), *Cross-Border EU Competition Law Actions* (Hart Publishing, 2013) 161–62; and the firm's website www.carteldamageclaims.com.

[84] A Pinna, 'The Assignment and Securitization of Liability Claims' in Tuil and Visscher (n 68) 118.

relatively successful in competition law claims,[85] it is doubtful that this technique could be used for small-value claims in consumer law, for two reasons: first, the assignment of claims requires the active participation of consumers, given that they have to transfer their claims to an entity. Therefore, the usual rational apathy that characterises the attitude of small-value claimants may not be overcome. Second, the value of the claims may be too low to attract third-party funding.[86]

v. *The Role of ADR*

Parties to the American class action usually settle. As earlier mentioned, different factors may push parties to come to an agreement, the most convincing one being the financial risk that class proceedings represent. Therefore, negotiation is part of the class action system. Other ADR methods are equally available to parties but are independent from any class proceedings. It is worth underlining that class arbitration may occur in the United States. However, as further explained below (below II.C.i.a.), this possibility has been limited by recent judgments of the Supreme Court. As for the Latin American Model Code, its Article 11 mentions the possibility for parties to use various ADR mechanisms, such as mediation and conciliation within the judicial procedure. Nevertheless, the Model Code does not establish rules regarding the negotiation of agreements out of the court system.[87] In Europe, the fusion of collective redress with some kind of ADR system is increasingly common, probably due to the promotion of non-contentious means to solve conflicts at the EU level.[88] Usually, ADR schemes are implemented into the collective redress procedure.[89] Alternatively, other autonomous ADR mechanisms remain available to consumers. In order to illustrate this point, the rest of the section develops some recent examples of collective redress mechanisms, which associate an ADR scheme.

First of all, the Dutch legislator enacted an out-of-court settlement procedure, on the model of the US class action. According to this mechanism, parties negotiate an agreement that they submit to the Amsterdam Court of Appeal, which will declare its binding effect over absent parties if all legal requirements are fulfilled.

[85] In a paper of 2012, C Veljanovski found that seven follow-on cartel damages claims had been litigated up till then (C Veljanovski, 'Third-party Litigation Funding in Europe' (2012) 8 *Journal of Law, Economics & Policy* 431–33).

[86] BEUC (n 70) pt III.

[87] This has been criticised by Professor A Gidi in 'Notas Críticas Al Anteproyecto De Código Modelo De Procesos Colectivos Del Instituto Iberoamericano De Derecho Procesal' in A Gidi and E Ferrer (eds), *La Tutela de los Derechos Difusos, Colectivos e Individuales Homogéneos*, 2nd edn (Editorial Porrúa, 2014) 418–19.

[88] Proof of that fact is that the EU enacted important legislations in the field of ADR, such as Council Directive 2013/11/EU of 21 May 2013 on alternative dispute resolution for consumer disputes and amending Regulation (EC) 2006/2004 and Directive 2009/22/EC [2013] OJ L165/63; Council Regulation (EU) 524/2013 of 21 May 2013 on online dispute resolution for consumer disputes and amending Regulation (EC) 2006/2004 and Directive 2009/22/EC [2013] OJ L165/1; Council Directive 2008/52/EC of 21 May 2008 on certain aspects of mediation in civil and commercial matters [2008] OJ L136/3.

[89] Like in France and Belgium.

In other words, parties seek a declaratory action regarding the validity of their settlement. It has to be underlined that this negotiation phase is independent from any judicial proceedings. Besides, no collective redress action for damages is available in the Netherlands.

Secondly, in France, the new *action de groupe* integrates a mediation phase, pursuant to Articles L.623-22 and 23 FCC. According to those provisions, a certified consumer association can participate in a mediation process with the alleged wrongdoer. If an agreement is reached, it is submitted to the judge who has the power to make it binding. Then, the terms of such an agreement are made public to potential victims who can choose to opt in or not. It is not clear what the solution should be in case parties are not satisfied with the conditions of the agreement and would have preferred the judicial action to continue.[90]

Similarly, in Belgium, parties can negotiate an agreement out-of-court or after having filed an action in court.[91] During this negotiation phase, parties may require the start of a mediation process, but this is not mandatory. The homologation of an agreement between parties is applicable to all victims. In order for parties to exercise their right to opt in or out, the outcome of the mediation process has to be published, which is at odds with the principle of confidentiality that governs mediation.[92]

E. The Four Categories

Hereafter, a classification of the collective redress tools available in the EU is provided. In particular, these tools are reorganised into four categories: the representative model (i.); the class action model (ii.); the test case model (iii.); and the Dutch model (iv.).[93] The rationale of this classification is to facilitate the assessment of private international law questions in the next chapters of this work. In light of the above, four models of collective redress, which have different impact on international rules on jurisdiction are created. Thanks to this technique, research can be streamlined and permit a focus on predominant collective redress models.

The following methodology was applied to the categorisation of collective redress mechanisms: the structure of all instruments contained in Table 1 was

[90] L'action de groupe à la française: parachever la protection des consommateurs, Information Report (05.05.2017), available at www.senat.fr/rap/r09-499/r09-49917.html.

[91] For an interesting presentation of the Belgian mediation system in the context of collective redress, see A de Bandt, 'La négociation et la médiation dans le cadre de l'action en reparation collective' (2014) 6 *Revue de Droit Commercial Belge* 591, 591–605.

[92] ibid 604.

[93] As explained below, it has to be underlined that the representative model is clearly dominant in the EU. While the class action model has been implemented in some Member States (and often coupled with a representative model), the test case model has been adopted only in Germany and the United Kingdom. The Dutch collective redress mechanism is unique. Although the adoption of those three models has not been widespread, their practical relevance is significant enough to create additional categories for the sake of this research project.

analysed according to a template. The result of this work is available in Annex II. Collective redress mechanisms were then classified into four categories according to their common features.

i. The Representative Model

Pursuant to this model, a person other than a consumer brings collective proceedings against a wrongdoer. In particular, this person could be either a private entity, such as a consumer association, or a public authority, for instance, the Consumer Ombudsman. In any case, this person acts as a representative of a group of victims. For now, the question to know whether the representative acts in its own name and on behalf of third parties or in its own name and own behalf is set aside. Private or public bodies may seek injunctive or declaratory relief, as well as monetary compensation. Similarly, they may defend distinct interests – collective or general.[94] When the types of remedies and interests have a different impact on private international law solutions tackled in chapter 3, these are highlighted.

ii. The Class Action Model

The class action model resembles the American class action device in the sense that it enables a single individual to litigate on behalf of a group of victims. Importantly, this model only takes into account representative claimants who are considered as consumers under EU law. It has to be highlighted that private international rules on jurisdiction offer a protective forum at the place of certain consumers' domicile but not all of them. Besides, the representative claimant must have a claim against the defendant; otherwise, they fall under the scope of the representative model described above.

iii. The Test Case Model

Under the test case procedure, a court receives a multiplicity of similar claims. For procedural efficiency purposes, it usually picks up a case and solves common issues, while suspending related individual proceedings. Once the competent court rules on these common issues, individual proceedings are retaken and solved according to these findings. Sometimes the model requires all victims to bring a claim, while sometimes a subscription in a register is sufficient to manifest one's willingness to be part of the collective proceedings. Therefore, this model is based on an opt-in system. The most relevant feature of a test case procedure from a private international law perspective is that all the members of the collective action are claimants. For this reason, this model looks like a group action in which several

[94] The distinction between those interests is explained above at n 19.

claimants bring a collective suit together. As a result, the comments regarding the competence of the tribunal in a test case procedure are, mutatis mutandis, applicable to the group action. In light of the above and because the group action is not widespread among the EU, this mechanism is not further examined.

iv. The Dutch Model

The Dutch *Wet Collectieve Afwikkeling Massaschade* (*WCAM*) is a unique model and one of the most successful ones, at least as far as private international law is concerned. Even though only a handful of cases have been tried under this model, these were significant. At the same time, the Dutch *WCAM* generates fundamental questions that challenge current private international law rules on jurisdiction. Therefore, this model deserves some attention. Pursuant to this scheme, one or various consumer associations start negotiations with an alleged wrongdoer on behalf of the victims they represent. These negotiations occur outside of any court proceedings. Once parties reach a settlement, they present it to the Amsterdam Court of Appeal, which has exclusive jurisdiction over *WCAM* procedures. If the court deems that the content of the settlement is fair, it declares it binding for all represented but absent parties. These are notified of their right to opt out. The most important feature that characterises this procedure from a private international law perspective is the use of an out-of-court dispute resolution process with the subsequent petition to declare the collective settlement binding.

II. The Role of the EU

Consumer collective redress has been under the EU's scrutiny since 2007. The interest of the EU institutions – and in particular the Commission – for this procedural tool increased as the private enforcement gap enlarged. In light of this, the many reports published in this field attest to the EU's willingness to implement collective redress within its territory. Indeed, collective redress is an instrument that has the ability to improve access to justice. Yet, it seems that the lack of political consensus at the supranational level has hampered the enactment of any binding instrument on collective redress. Besides, some inconsistencies, which indicate that this device might not be fully understood, have been spotted. Impact assessments, as well as empirical data on this topic, are missing as well.

In light of these considerations, the first part of this sub-section begins with a chronological overview and a short summary of the documents released by the EU regarding collective redress (A.). The second part then analyses the EU's approach towards collective redress from 2007 until today (B.). Finally, two important arguments that opponents to collective redress make, which are the superior role of ADR in order to solve consumer disputes (B.i.) and the lack of competence for the EU to legislate (B.ii.), are examined. These critiques must be assessed because in case they hold true, they would certainly block any intervention of the EU or at least call into question its legitimacy.

A. Chronological Overview

This sub-section presents all the studies, initiatives and impact assessments published by the EU on collective redress in a chronological order. More precisely, a timeline first gives the reader a broad overview of all the above-mentioned documents, and then, a short summary is provided for each of them. Most of the work performed on the topic of collective redress has been carried out or ordered by the EU Commission. Therefore, all the documents presented below are available either on its website,[95] or on *eurlex*,[96] unless it is stated otherwise.

Important information could be extracted from those documents. To begin with, studies commissioned by the EU explains the functioning of procedural enforcement tools, as well as the behaviour of market players. Notably, they identify the obstacles to the start of proceedings abroad and the deficiencies that vitiate certain procedural tools. Then, the last documents released by the EU make clear that the main objective at the core of measures regarding collective redress is access to justice and that the regulation of private international law questions is not a priority for EU institutions. Finally, important critiques impact the adoption of collective redress mechanisms. They have the potential to deter the regulation of collective redress at the EU level in the future.

Table 2 Timeline

2007	• EU Consumer Policy Strategy 2007–2013 • Analysis and Evaluation of Alternative Means of Consumer Redress Other than Redress through Ordinary Judicial Proceedings • Leuven Brainstorming Event
2008	• Consultation on the Draft Consumer Collective Redress Benchmarks and Workshops • Study Regarding the Problems Faced by Consumers in Obtaining Redress • Evaluation of the Effectiveness and Efficiency of Collective Redress Mechanisms • Green Paper and Feedback Statement of the Green Paper

(continued)

[95] Originally, the Commission had set up a comprehensive website page with all relevant documents concerning collective redress. Nevertheless, said page has been removed and information has been redirected to the Commission's new website (ec.europa.eu/info/live-work-travel-eu/consumers/resolve-your-consumer-complaint_en). Although most documents are not stored on the new website, some are still accessible through https://archive.org. See https://web.archive.org/web/20170719073702/http://ec.europa.eu/consumers/solving_consumer_disputes/judicial_redress/index_en.htm. When an alternative source of information is available, it is mentioned in the relevant footnote.

[96] eur-lex.europa.eu/homepage.html?locale=en.

Table 2 ***(Continued)***

2009	• Directive 2009/22/EC on injunctions for the protection of consumers' interests • Qualitative Eurobarometer • Consultation Paper: Discussion on the Follow-up to the Green Paper
2011	• Consultation Paper: Towards a Coherent Approach to Collective Redress
2012	• EU Parliament Resolution: Towards a Coherent Approach to Collective Redress • EU Consumer Agenda
2013	• Recommendation of the Commission and Communication
2018	• Report Regarding the Implementation of the Recommendation • Proposal for a Directive on Representative Actions for the Protection of the Collective Interests of Consumers, and repealing Directive 2009/22/EC

The EU Consumer Policy Strategy 2007–2013 – Empowering Consumers, Enhancing their Welfare, Effectively Protecting Them.[97] In this document, the Commission acknowledges the important role that consumers play in the functioning of the internal market, as their consumption represents 58 per cent of EU's Gross Domestic Product (GDP). However, the exponential integration of retail markets and the rise of e-commerce generate a new reality that the current fragmentation of the internal market must overcome. In order for consumers to adapt to the rules of the game, their rights should be correspondingly updated. In light of the above, the Commission suggests that actions consolidating consumers' information, confidence and redress have to be undertaken. Among other aspects, the enforcement of EU law and cooperation between public authorities must continue. Regarding consumer redress, the document mentions that the EU will consider taking action on collective redress in consumer and antitrust matters.

An Analysis and Evaluation of Alternative Means of Consumer Redress Other than Redress through Ordinary Judicial Proceedings (the Leuven Study).[98] This 2007 study was commissioned by DG SANCO to the Study Centre of consumer Law/Centre for European Economic Law of the University of Leuven. The objective of the report is to investigate how alternative means of consumer redress other than individual court proceedings practically work for end-users. Specifically, five mechanisms are studied: (1) direct negotiation; (2) mediation and arbitration; (3) small claims procedures; (4) collective actions for damages; and (5) injunctive relief. For the sake of this work, chapter 5 of the report which deals with collective

[97] Commission, EU Consumer Policy Strategy 2007–13 – Empowering consumers, enhancing their welfare, effectively protecting them, Communication from the Commission to the Council, the European Parliament and the European Economic and Social Committee COM (2007) 99 final.

[98] The Study Centre for Consumer Law/Centre for European Economic Law (n 30).

redress actions for damages is key.[99] According to the Leuven Study, these actions encompass three different models: (1) the group action, according to which various victims bring their claims into a single action; (2) the representative action, whereby one representative claimant brings proceedings on behalf of other victims; (3) the test case procedure, whereby a case brought by one claimant will then serve as a landmark judgment to solve similar cases. The report puts the spotlight on an interesting fact, which is that collective redress actions, together with direct negotiation are deemed to be the most adequate mechanism for conflicts involving small-value claims. Then, chapter 5 includes the risks and benefits of collective redress actions. On the positive side of the balance, the report acknowledges that collective redress has the ability to reduce costs for all parties, foster access to justice, deter unlawful conduct and provide judicial economy. On the negative side of the balance, the Leuven Study worries about the start of unmeritorious claims, the overwhelming of courts with complex actions, and the misalignment of financial incentives that may lead to abuses. Finally, the document presents the different characteristics that collective redress action mechanisms possess. Specifically, it deals with questions regarding availability, scope of application, rules on standing, procedural features, cross-border disputes and rules on costs.

The Leuven Brainstorming Event.[100] The purpose of the Leuven event was to gather information on collective redress through a dialogue between the Commission and relevant stakeholders in order to create an adequate framework for the device. The introductory speech of Commissioner Kuneva illustrates this point:

> I feel that I need to examine how prevalent the problem of consumers still refraining from enforcing their rights is – and whether I can do anything further about it. Collective redress, both judicial and non-judicial, could be an effective means to address this problem. I must stress, however, that unless I am convinced that there is a strong and pressing case for it, I do not intend to take any action at EU level.[101]

This event is part of the Consumer Policy Strategy that aims at fostering consumer confidence in the internal market.

The feedback statement identifies two blocs of opinions: on the one hand, some – mostly consumer representatives – underline that the fragmentation of the internal market regarding methods of redress fosters the unequal protection of consumers among the EU and, thus, affects their confidence. This is particularly visible in cross-border cases where consumers are not always able to obtain redress. On the other hand, others – mostly business representatives – express their doubts regarding the need for collective redress. Besides, some stakeholders invoke the US class action in order to demonstrate that the adoption of collective

[99] The conclusion of the Leuven Study regarding injunctive relief is set aside since its content overlaps with the two reports on Council Directives 98/27/EC and 2009/22/EC, which are dealt with in different locations of this book.

[100] A summary of the Leuven brainstorming event is available at www.eurofinas.org/uploads/documents/policies/leuven_brainstorming.pdf.

[101] Speech of Commissioner Kuneva (Leuven, 29 June 2007).

redress could have disastrous effects on companies. Finally, the role of ADR was discussed and the question of funding was pointed out as one of the major problems affecting the functioning of national collective redress mechanisms.

Consultation on the Draft Consumer Collective Redress Benchmarks and Workshops. The benchmarks put in place by the Commission are general principles that any collective redress mechanisms should respect. Specifically, claimants should be able to bundle their claims thanks to an adequate information networking when individual action is not possible. Then, from a financial perspective, access to justice should be affordable for consumers. Furthermore, the monetary award has to be adequately distributed among the parties involved in collective proceedings. However, the 'loser-pays' rule and the prohibition of punitive damages should be maintained, so that the defendant is not economically overburdened. Along these lines, collective actions should have a certain deterrent effect but no unmeritorious claim should be encouraged. From a procedural perspective, the length of proceedings must be reasonable and the use of out-of-court mechanisms boosted.

Subsequently, the Commission organised a workshop in order to discuss these benchmarks with stakeholders. The results show that consumer representatives usually agree with the Commission's benchmarks. However, they often regret the too general nature of the vocabulary employed. They would have welcomed more precision on certain benchmarks. As for business representatives, they regard collective redress sceptically: they call into question its need and argue that the efficiency of current procedural instruments should first be examined. Alternatively, they advocate a collective redress model that integrates a previous mandatory out-of-court procedure. The industry considers that funding techniques have to be limited, punitive damages prohibited and the 'loser-pays' rule respected. Besides, compensation should only be paid to claimants, excluding representative bodies. Finally, safeguards must be put in place in order to prevent unmeritorious claims and skimming-off procedures should only be ordered by public authorities. Overall, legal practitioners and academics usually agree with business representatives, although they sometimes adopt a more nuanced approach.

Study Regarding the Problems Faced by Consumers in Obtaining Redress for Infringements of Consumer Protection Legislation, and the Economic Consequences of such Problems.[102] This study conducted by Civic Consulting of the Consumer Policy Evaluation Consortium (CPEC) contains two reports: the first one (the main report) assesses the issues faced by multiple consumers in obtaining redress against the same wrongdoer – referred to as mass claims/issues. The second report presents the results of discussion groups held in Austria, France, Italy and Portugal in which citizens were asked about their experience in resolving disputes through

[102] Civic Consulting of the Consumer Policy Evaluation Consortium (CPEC), Study regarding the problems faced by consumers in obtaining redress for infringements of consumer protection legislation, and the economic consequences of such problems (2008), available at www.civic-consulting.de/reports/redress%20problem_study.pdf.

either individual action, collective action or ADR procedures. Only the main report is examined as it integrates the conclusions of the discussion groups.

Overall, litigation costs are perceived as the most important barrier to obtain satisfactory redress. Additionally, when conflicts have a cross-border nature, the difficulties that consumers experience are similar to those existing at the national level but in an amplified way because of their international component. Specifically, several hurdles impede consumers from bringing collective redress proceedings: (1) the unavailability of consumer collective redress mechanism; (2) the limited standing to sue; (3) the lack of financial resources; (4) the limited – human and financial – resources of consumer organisations; (5) the lack of expertise of intermediaries; (6) the lack of expertise of judges in managing the collective action; (7) the difficulties of informing potential claimants about the collective actions; (8) the difficulties in awarding and distributing the compensation. The economic analysis points out that collective redress mechanisms, as well as ADR procedures – especially where special ADR instruments for consumers are available – are particularly fit for low or medium value claims. As for individual proceedings, they are often reserved to high-value claimants. However, it appears that both collective redress and ADR often lack incentives, which makes them less appealing.

Study on Evaluation of the Effectiveness and Efficiency of Collective Redress Mechanisms.[103] The study was elaborated by Civic Consulting in association with Oxford Economics for the Commission. It comprises three reports: the first one is the main report and summarises the overall results of the research; then, the second report assembles country studies that set forth the structure of collective redress tools in 13 Member States; as for the final report, it contains information on national case law involving collective suits. It is interesting to note that of the 326 cases gathered, only 10 per cent were of a cross-border nature.

For the sake of this work, only the results of the main report are synthesised. They can be divided into three parts. First, in order to assess the effectiveness and efficiency of collective redress, the report analyses the length of proceedings, the cost of collective redress for consumers or their representatives, as well as businesses, and the added value of such a tool in comparison with other procedural devices. The conclusions are as follows: although collective suits can slow down the litigation process – because of the complexity of the collective suit or the lack of efficiency of the judicial system –, the length of proceedings is still reasonable compared to individual litigation. Then, the costs related to collective actions are usually low or nonexistent for consumers. However, the representative claimant will often have to bear the financial risk of litigation. In this context, the report highlights that an opt-in based system increases the cost of finding the claimants and joining them together, which makes this procedure unattractive for low-value cases. The risk of having to pay the defendant's costs is a further disincentive to

[103] Commission, 'Evaluation of the Effectiveness and Efficiency of Collective Redress' (n 27).

sue for intermediaries but represents a safeguard against unmeritorious claims. Additionally, it seems that collective redress does not generate unreasonable costs on businesses. Rather, collective redress tends to decrease defendants' costs, given that they do not have to defend themselves in various individual proceedings and different courts. Besides, Member States reported that no business went bankrupt because of a collective suit. Finally, collective redress is an added value in all judicial systems in which it exists: importantly, this instrument offers access to justice to small-value claimants and generates significant media coverage that constitutes an incentive for businesses to settle.

The second part of the report examines whether consumers suffer a detriment when no collective redress mechanism is available to them. It estimates that consumers might suffer a detriment of EUR 2.1 million per annum, although this should be interpreted carefully. This figure is hypothetical as it is based on the results observed in Member States, which do have collective redress mechanisms and do not take into account a potential lack of efficiency or effectiveness. In any case, the report concludes that the consumer detriment is modest.

The last part of the main report emphasises that different approaches to collective redress do not seem to hinder cross-border commerce between Member States and do not lead to distortions of competition.

Green Paper on consumer collective redress.[104] The Green Paper starts by emphasising the lack of confidence affecting consumers within the EU market. Part of this lack of trust comes from the unavailability of efficient mechanisms to obtain redress. Indeed, according to some studies, 76 per cent of consumers say that it is important for their confidence to be able to bring a cross-border claim before their courts and applying their national law. High costs, lengthy proceedings and the risk of litigation are additional barriers that hinder consumers from obtaining compensation. Accordingly, the Special Eurobarometer on Access to Justice states that 18 per cent of consumers questioned would definitely not go to court for less than EUR 500.[105] The same proportion of consumers would go to court only for claims worth more than EUR 1,000.

In this context, the EU has already set up mechanisms to improve the enforcement of EU law: the ADR Directive fosters out-of-court settlements; the Injunctions Directive allows listed consumer associations or public authorities to bring cross-border suits seeking injunctive relief; and the Consumer Protection Cooperation Regulation consolidates public enforcement. However, it appears that these instruments are not sufficient. Specifically, collective redress mechanisms adopted so far by the Member States are only partially efficient. As a result, the Commission suggests that additional actions should be undertaken in order to help consumers to get their harm repaired. The Green Paper further specifies that no distinction between national and cross-border situations should be made,

[104] Commission, Green Paper on Consumer Collective Redress [2008] COM (2008) 794 final.

[105] Commission, European Union Citizens and Access to Justice, Special Eurobarometer 195 (Summary) (2004) 11, available at ec.europa.eu/commfrontoffice/publicopinion/index.cfm.

since national and foreign consumers are affected in the same way by illegal practices. Furthermore, any measure must provide access to justice to consumers but simultaneously protect defendants against unmeritorious claims.

There are four different options to be examined in order to address the current lack of redress within the EU: (1) the first proposal consists in maintaining the status quo, whereby the Commission would wait and see the capacity of both the Mediation Directive and the Small Claims Procedure to fill the current enforcement gap; (2) through the next suggestion, the Commission recommends Member States to cooperate. Specifically, they would be required to open up their collective redress mechanisms to foreign consumers and entities; (3) the third solution consists in a mix of different measures, namely the improvement of ADR mechanisms, coupled with the expansion of the Small Claims Procedure to collective actions in national and cross-border cases, as well as the guarantee that businesses have an efficient internal complaint-handling system. As for very low-value claimants, they are encouraged to resort to public authorities in order to enforce their rights; and (4) the last measure would ensure the existence of judicial collective redress procedure in all the Member States through a binding or non-binding instrument.

The feedback statement[106] that summarises the responses to the Green Paper on collective redress, which was carried out by the Consumer Policy Evaluation Consortium (CPEC), points out that most of the respondents are business representatives and a large majority of the responses come from Germany, the United Kingdom and France. Making a difference between stakeholders is important in order to understand the results of the paper. The core findings of the study report that business representatives usually prefer the first option of the Green Paper – this means, no action at the EU level – and strongly reject the introduction of collective redress within the EU. In fact, business representatives argue that no evidence supports the need for collective redress and challenge the competence of the EU to introduce such a mechanism. Moreover, they state that the current procedural mechanisms and EU measures are sufficient. On the contrary, consumer organisations favour option 4 and generally rejected all other options. According to these stakeholders, such option is the only one that would establish consumers' confidence in the internal market and improve access to justice. As for legal practitioners and Member States' public authorities, they are highly divided between option 1 and 4. Finally, academics generally prefer a combination of option 2, 3 and 4.

It has to be underlined that options 3 and 4 did not trigger much controversy: it is commonly accepted that cooperation between Member States is desirable and that the use of ADR should be further encouraged. Nevertheless, some issues

[106] Consumer Policy Evaluation Consortium, Assessment of the economic and social impact of the policy options to empower consumers to obtain adequate redress, Final Analytical Report on the Green Paper on Consumer Collective Redress (2009), available at kartellblog.de/wordpress/wp-content/uploads/Kommission-2009-assessement-impact-policy-options-adequate-redress.

still need to be solved: first, it is feared that the opening-up of national collective redress mechanisms to foreign consumers would suppose a great burden for courts hearing the collective action, and would trigger issues of applicable law. Additionally, this situation would certainly foster forum shopping. Second, because ADR proceedings are voluntary, stakeholders suspect that they would not be used unless a binding judicial system of collective redress were to be implemented.

Directive 2009/22/EC on injunctions for the protection of consumers' interests.[107] The Injunctions Directive – former Directive 98/27/EC – approximates national laws on actions for injunctive relief that aim at protecting consumers' general interests.[108] Qualified entities under Article 3 benefit from the principle of mutual recognition. Accordingly, entities that fulfil the requirements previously established by national law, in compliance with Directive 2009/22/EC, and are included in the list of Article 4(3)[109] have their legal capacity[110] automatically recognised in other Member States.[111] They will therefore be authorised to bring actions against violations of EU consumer laws listed in Annex I of the Injunctions Directive. It has to be emphasised that said Directive essentially applies to cross-border cases but may also apply in domestic ones. Article 2(2) and Recital 7 clarify that the Directive applies without prejudice to the private international law rules in place.

Eurobarometer on Consumer Redress in the European Union: Consumer Experiences, Perceptions and Choices.[112] This Eurobarometer is included in this sub-section because part of it is dedicated to collective redress. During April and May 2009, ten qualitative in-depth interviews were held in 27 Member States amongst specific target consumers. The study explores consumers' awareness and experiences regarding different redress mechanisms. The study starts with

[107] See n 1.

[108] Although the text of the Directive refers to collective interests, the protection of general interests appears to be the core objective of said piece of legislation. Indeed, Recital 3 of the Directive states 'collective interests means interests which do not include the cumulation of interests of individuals who have been harmed by an infringement'.

[109] Notification from the Commission concerning Article 4(3) of Directive 2009/22/EC on injunctions for the protection of consumers' interests, which codifies Directive 98/27/EC, concerning the entities qualified to bring an action under Article 2 of this Directive (Text with EEA relevance) [2016] OJ C361/1.

[110] It has to be underlined that any investigation regarding legal standing faces terminological difficulties (for an in-depth comparative law analysis on this question, see A Blomeyer, 'Types of Relief Available (Judicial Remedies)' in M Cappelletti (ed), *International Encyclopedia of Comparative Law*, vol 14, ch 4 (JCB Mohr/Martinus Nijhoff Publishers, 1982)). Because Member States usually approach procedural questions in a different fashion, some concepts are not easy to translate and transpose. Besides, they do not always have their equivalent in all EU Member States, which makes comparisons difficult. This research project distinguishes capacity to sue (*capacité pour agir*) from standing to sue (*qualité pour agir*).

[111] Although the Directive applies the principle of mutual recognition to capacity to sue, it seems to cover standing to sue too, inasmuch as it entrusts Member States with the design of the conditions that must be fulfilled in order to access the list of Art 4(3). Note that the Proposal for a Directive on representative actions (see below, this sub-section) changed this wording. This is visible in the French and Spanish versions of the text, which establish the mutual recognition of the *qualité pour agir/legitimación*.

[112] TNSqual+, Consumer Redress in the European Union: Consumer Experiences, Perceptions and Choices, Qualitative Eurobarometer (2009) available at kartellblog.de/wordpress/wp-content/uploads/Kommission-2009-Consumer-redress-aggregated-report.

an interesting fact: less confident consumers whose investment in a product or a service is low are not likely to complain at all. In principle, consumers of Western Europe would not complain to the supplier in respect of an amount below EUR 50 and would not seek further redress in case of negative response if their claim amounts to less than EUR 100. Therefore, this study confirms that very small-value claimants can be characterised by their apathy. Then, it is useful to report that very few respondents experienced any kind of cross-border redress. They explain that redress would be highly difficult to obtain as they do not know what their rights are in a foreign country, not to mention language barriers. Moreover, they would not know which body to approach in order to get some support and how to start any type of action.

Overall, consumers' awareness of collective redress mechanisms is low. The ones who knew about the existence of such procedural tool were informed by consumer associations. Incidentally, the Eurobarometer underlines the fundamental role that these associations and public authorities in giving information to consumers about their rights and the different ways of obtaining redress. In fact, many consumers admit that any process of recovery would first start by approaching a consumer association or a public authority. Then, consumers regard positively the sharing of costs, responsibility and time that collective proceedings offer. On the negative side of the balance, they mention that it would certainly be difficult to contact other claimants and that the collective action could cause a reduction of the compensation – due to the pay-outs that this kind of action implies.

The study further illustrates consumers' preferences regarding instruments of redress in relationship to a small-value claim – ie between EUR 5 and EUR 10 – and a high-value personal damage claim. In the first case, consumers would first approach a consumer association or a public authority and then start collective ADR proceedings if further redress is sought, as it is deemed to be quicker than court collective action. Regarding high-value claims, respondents show a preference for judicial collective proceedings because of their perceived authority and weight. Finally, collective actions were considered as an attractive tool to resolve cross-border disputes.

Consultation Paper: Discussion on the Follow-up to the Green Paper.[113] DG SANCO launched the Consultation Paper with the purpose to create a support document in preparation for the hearings of the 29 May 2009. This paper takes into account the responses, suggestions and critiques made to the Green Paper on consumer collective redress and, thus, redefines the boundaries of the discussion by proposing new tailored policy options.

To start with, the Consultation Paper recalls the central role of consumers' confidence for the construction of a competitive and innovative EU market. In this vein, the elaboration of effective redress mechanisms enhances consumers' trust and disciplines traders. The emergence of mass damages – increased by the

[113] Commission, Consultation paper for discussion on the follow-up to the Green Paper on consumer collective redress (2009), available at www.personaedanno.it/dA/07d446aef2/allegato/AA_014968_resource1_orig.pdf.

use of the Internet and globalisation – requires an adequate response. As a result, the EU proposes to elaborate accessible, affordable and effective redress to tackle this particular situation. Simultaneously, the rise of unmeritorious claims should be avoided. The Consultation Paper also underlines the existence of a justice gap for very low and low-value claimants who struggle to obtain compensation when their rights are violated. Moreover, claimants' opportunities to get their harm repaired greatly depend on their location as national legislations still have disparate protection regimes. The Consultation Paper insists on the importance of offering equal access to justice to consumers. This would also mean that traders are all subject to the same enforcement regime that would foster healthy competition. In this context, the paper acknowledges the insufficiency of the current instruments adopted both at the EU and national levels so far. In light of the above, collective redress is an interesting tool as it provides a reduction of costs for claimants and economies of scales. Nevertheless, the efficiency of such mechanism could still be improved: currently, collective redress suffers from lack of funding, publicity and incentives. Cross-border collective actions entail additional difficulties and consumer associations usually cannot represent foreign consumers.

For all these reasons, the Consultation Paper presents five options that aim at reinforcing the current redress system. All the suggestions are based on a mix of instruments involving ADR, self-regulation and judicial collective redress, as the responses to the Green Paper prescribed. Following the example of the Green Paper, the first option consists in maintaining the status quo. According to the second option, the Commission would, in cooperation with stakeholders, elaborate a collective ADR mechanism, as well as an internal complaint handling system to be implemented within businesses' corporate structure through a code of conduct. As for the third suggestion, it is a non-binding measure that would consist in encouraging Member States to adopt a collective ADR instrument together with a judicial collective redress tool, both opened to foreign consumers. Besides, the power to order skimming-off and compensation in case of very low-value claims would be given to public authorities. The fourth option is similar to the previous one but would be a binding measure for all Member States. Finally, the last option aims at establishing an EU-wide test case procedure. The Consultation Paper ends up with an impact assessment of all the options proposed, detailing the positive aspects as well as the drawbacks. The summary of the main trends of the public hearing on consumer collective redress on 29 May 2009 reports that, in general terms, business representatives support minimal EU involvement – this corresponds to the first and the second option – while consumer representatives favour the fourth and fifth options.

Consultation Paper: Towards a Coherent Approach to Collective Redress.[114] Although all Member States have adopted some kind of collective redress

[114] Commission, Public Consultation: Towards a Coherent Approach to Collective Redress SEC (2011)173 final.

instrument, these vary widely from one legal order to another. Therefore, the enforcement of rights is uneven across the EU. In light of this, the public consultation launched by the Commission aims at identifying the common principles underpinning collective redress and examining how these principles would apply to the different national mechanisms adopted within the EU. Finally, it investigates in which fields collective redress could have an added value. Broadly speaking, the numerous questions presented to stakeholders concern the need, added value, efficiency, structure and scope of collective redress, including the safeguards that should be built up to prevent abusive litigation. Besides, the role of ADR within the redress system is discussed. The next paragraphs provide a summary of stakeholders' responses during the hearings that took place on 5 April 2011. Said summary follows the tripartite structure adopted by the hearings.

First of all, the question of collective redress potential added value was addressed. In this case, consumer representatives insisted on the necessity for Member States to adopt efficient means of collective redress in order to fulfil the current enforcement gap. They also explained that ADR mechanisms would not be used in practice if no judicial collective redress instrument existed with the purpose to act as a 'stick'. On the contrary, business representatives questioned the need for collective redress: in their opinion, public authorities should remain the only actors in charge of the enforcement strategy. For the rest, ADR represents one of the cheapest and quickest means for consumers to obtain compensation. One business representative qualified the adoption of judicial collective redress as a 'bulldozer approach' since other efficient means of conflict resolution would be able to achieve the same objective at a cheaper cost.

Secondly, the hearings tackled the question of efficiency. In particular, participants and panellists were asked what kind of features an efficient collective redress mechanism should have. The views on this specific question greatly diverged: on the one hand, some respondents – essentially business representatives – expressed their fear of the American class action and the abuses that the use of this device may generate. On the other hand, opponents of this view stated that collective redress is a necessity and a matter of access to justice. From a structural perspective, participants' discussed the following elements: standing to sue – should it be wide or strict? –, the option between opt-in and opt-out – while the opt-in system is deemed difficult to implement because consumers cannot always be identified, opt-out is assimilated to the dangerous US class action system –, and funding – business representatives are usually against any kind of financial incentives. Furthermore, many participants mentioned that active case-management by judges is desirable and even specialised courts for collective redress would be an interesting solution.

Finally, the third hearings session was a sort of 'catch-all' discussion which dealt with other convenient common principles, the suitable approach to collective redress – horizontal or by sectors –, ADR and cross-border issues. During this session, stakeholders reiterated the importance of ADR for the redress system. However, one of the speakers called participants' attention to the fact that out-of-court collective settlements would pose some practical problems, such as the identification of other claimants, the way claimants take the decision to agree or reject a settlement and the issues regarding funding and costs. Then, it seems that stakeholders agreed on the fact that any collective redress system should be modelled according to the specific sector in which it is to be implemented. Last but not least, participants urged the Commission to facilitate the start of cross-border collective suits that currently face too many obstacles to be viable.

EU Parliament Resolution: Towards a Coherent Approach to Collective Redress.[115] In 2012, the EU Parliament adopted a Resolution on the topic of collective redress on its own initiative. The document goes back over the Commission's work and in particular its public consultation 'Towards a coherent European approach to collective redress'. In this context, the final version of the Parliament's Resolution suggests the introduction of a 'Union scheme of collective redress', which would apply horizontally and include a set of common principles. In this vein, the EU Parliament is concerned about providing uniform access to justice to EU citizens.[116]

Nevertheless, the text is not crystal-clear and some doubts about its interpretation still remain. A closer look at the proposals of amendments puts the spotlight on some important points of dissension between the members of the Parliament: first of all, while some parliamentarians agreed with the setting up of a horizontal framework as the Draft Report advocates,[117] others showed their preference for a sector-by-sector approach.[118] Accordingly, a horizontal approach would mean that the same collective redress framework would apply indifferently to the subject matter concerned. Contrarily, an application by sectors means that principles would be implemented differently in consumer protection, competition law, environmental matters, and so on. At the end of the day, a moderated approach was elected:[119] the Parliament recommends a horizontal framework for collective compensatory redress, which will be allowed only regarding certain legislation expressly listed in an Annex. Put differently, a uniform collective redress instrument should be adopted within the EU but its material scope should be limited. However, the text does not impede the adoption of sector-specific rules within the horizontal framework if that is deemed convenient.

Secondly, it seems that parliamentarians were divided on the question whether a Commission's initiative should apply to cross-border and/or national cases.[120]

[115] European Parliament, Resolution of 2 February 2012 on 'Towards a Coherent European Approach to Collective Redress' (2011/2089(INI)). The Draft Report (PE467.330, 15.07.2011) was elaborated by the Committee of Legal Affairs (*rapporteur*: Klaus-Heiner Lehne), and further amended by the members of the Parliament (PE472.305, 22.09.2011). All the documents are available at www.europarl.europa.eu/oeil/popups/ficheprocedure.do?lang=en&reference=2011/2089(INI)#documentGateway.

[116] European Parliament, Resolution (n 115) para 15.

[117] ibid para 8.

[118] See European Parliament, Amendments (n 115), Nos 11, 24, 25, 26, 30, 31, 34, 43, 46, 47, 64 and 67, which envision the possibility of a sectorial approach.

[119] European Parliament, Resolution (n 115) paras 15 and 24.

[120] See European Parliament, Amendments (n 115) Nos 14, 42, 44 and 45.

Although the final version of the document makes some references to the difficulties in obtaining redress in a cross-border context, it would be incautious to conclude that the Parliament recommends the exclusion of national disputes from the resolution's scope. Finally, it is also unclear whether the Parliament wished to introduce an EU-wide collective redress mechanism in addition to existing national instruments or, to harmonise national collective redress tools already adopted by Member States.

As far as jurisdiction is concerned, the *rapporteur* explicitly recommends the adoption of a special provision for collective redress actions.[121] In his opinion, the courts of the Member State where the defendant is domiciled should be competent in order to avoid forum shopping. However, amendment 68 reversed this solution by simply affirming that the Brussels I Regulation should be a 'starting point' in order to determine which court has jurisdiction.

EU Consumer Agenda.[122] The EU Consumer Agenda – which replaced the Consumer Policy Strategy – aims at boosting consumer trust into the EU market and tackles the new social and economic challenges of this era. Not surprisingly, collective redress is encompassed in the EU enforcement strategy. However, the commentaries and conclusions contained in the EU Consumer Agenda are quite meagre: taking into account the Consultation Paper of 2011 and the Parliament Resolution of 2012, the Commission will consider taking on further action in order to implement an EU framework for collective redress.

Recommendation of the Commission and Communication Accompanying It.[123] The Recommendation, together with the Communication, reflects the position of the Commission on collective redress. Whereas the Recommendation establishes common principles applicable to collective redress, the Communication contextualises them. It has to be highlighted that both documents designate access to justice as the principal goal of collective redress.[124]

Now turning to the non-binding common principles established by the Commission, these apply to judicial and out-of-court collective redress mechanisms. It is useful to point out that these principles are integrated into a horizontal framework, and thus, competition law, consumer protection, financial services, environmental protection, data protection and non-discrimination cases are included in the Recommendation's material scope. The Recommendation's objective is to provide uniform access to justice to consumers and victims within the EU market. First and foremost, the document of the Commission sets forth a definition of collective redress. In this context, the Commission acknowledges the existence of four different forms of redress: (1) the group action for injunctive relief; (2) the group action for damages; (3) the representative action

[121] European Parliament, Draft Report (n 115) para 16.

[122] Commission, A European Consumer Agenda – Boosting confidence and growth COM (2012) 225 final.

[123] Commission, Recommendation (n 12); Commission, Communication (n 18).

[124] Commission, Recommendation (n 12) Recital 10; Commission, Communication (n 18) 3, 7.

for injunctive relief; and (4) the representative action for damages. While in a group action, two or more claimants litigate on behalf of a larger group of victims, the representative action allows a representative entity, an ad hoc entity or a public authority to act in representation of a group of claimants. The common principles can be divided into three categories: the first one encompasses all principles applicable to both collective injunctive and compensatory relief. The second one specifically concerns principles applicable to injunctive relief and the last one deals with collective action for damages. The common principles are summarised in Table 3.

Table 3 Common Principles on Collective Redress

<table>
<tr><th>Actions for injunctive relief</th><th>Actions for damages</th></tr>
<tr><td colspan="2">– Early on in the case, the judge should assess whether all the conditions regarding admissibility are fulfilled – be they codified or left to the discretion of the judge, – so that unmeritorious claims are refrained.
– The dissemination of the information about the existence of a collective action or the intention to bring one should take various interests into account, such as the freedom of expression, the right to information and the protection of the defendant's reputation.
– Standing to sue should be limited and attributed under clear conditions of eligibility. This can be explained by the fact that consumers or victims are not parties to the proceedings, and thus, it is fundamental to guarantee that their interest is well represented.
– National rules on admissibility and standing should not impede cross-border collective redress. Moreover, representative entities entitled to bring collective proceedings in one Member State should be able to do it in others.
– The 'loser-pays' rule should apply.
– The origin of the funds that finance the collective action has to be disclosed to the court, so that conflict of interests or the insufficiency of resources can be detected.</td></tr>
<tr><td>– The action seeking injunctive relief should be tackled in an expeditious manner in order to prevent the violation of EU law.
– Adequate sanctions must be put in place for defendants who do not comply with the injunctive relief order.</td><td>– Collective redress should in principle be based on an opt-in basis.
– The use of ADR should be encouraged but remain voluntary.
– Contingency fees and punitive damages have to be prohibited.
– Third parties who finance the collective action should not obtain a reward based on the amount of the settlement or the compensation awarded.
– Any follow-on action can only start after the decision of the public authority in order to avoid procedural and substantive inconsistencies.</td></tr>
</table>

Finally, the Commission advocates the creation of national registers of collective actions. An assessment of the implementation of the Recommendation has been carried out and published in 2018.

Report on the Implementation of the Recommendation 2013.[125] In 2018, the Commission published its report, which evaluates the implementation process of the Recommendation 2013. Section 2 of the report concludes that not all Member States have adopted collective redress mechanisms for compensatory redress, despite the Recommendation of the Commission. Overall, Member States allocate standing to sue to a limited range of actors, such as consumer associations or public bodies. Therefore, the Recommendation has been respected regarding this particular point. Practice regarding the admissibility of a collective redress action diverges: while some Member States do not contain any specific provisions dealing with admissibility in collective redress cases, others require that courts rule on this question in a specific decision. Besides, the Commission notes that conditions to admit an action vary from one Member State to another. As far as information to consumers is concerned, the Commission regrets that it is not communicated early on – before proceedings. The overwhelming majority of Member States apply the loser-pays principle and thus, follow the Recommendation. As regards funding, the Commission notices that it remains largely unregulated and fears the creation of wrong incentives. Finally, the Commission notes the absence of rules regarding the recognition of representative entities outside the scope of the Injunctions Directive. As far as actions for injunctive relief are concerned, the Commission acknowledges that their efficiency could be further improved. Then, as regards actions for damages, although most Member States adopted the opt-in system, opt-out-based collective redress mechanisms have been recently implemented in some national legal orders. The possibility to conclude out-of-court settlements is available in recent collective redress mechanisms, although it is not present in a large number of Member States. Finally, the Recommendation had little effect on the regulation of lawyers' fees. It should also be highlighted that the majority of Member States do not award punitive damages.

Proposal for a Directive on Representative Actions.[126] On 11 April 2018, the Commission published its proposal for a Directive on representative actions, the aim of which is to modernise and repeal the Injunctions Directive (see above, II.A.). The Proposal allows qualified entities to bring actions for injunctive relief, as well as actions for damages, where a trader's violation of EU law – listed in Annex I of the Proposal – harmed the collective interest of consumers. Notably, the Directive should apply to both domestic and cross-border cases, but adopts no specific private international law rules. Recital 9 of the Proposal, as well as Article 2(3), make clear that the private international law regime applicable by

[125] Report on the implementation of the Commission Recommendation of 11 June 2013 on common principles for injunctive and compensatory collective redress mechanisms in the Member States concerning violations of rights granted under Union law (2013/396/EU) COM (2018) 40 final.

[126] See n 15.

default will regulate cross-border representative actions. Article 16 of the proposed Directive specifically deals with cross-border actions, ie actions brought by qualified entities in another Member State. Following the example of the Injunctions Directive, legal standing of entities encompassed within the list mentioned at Article 4 of the Proposal should be mutually recognised in all Member States. Moreover, and this appears as a novelty, Article 16(2) allows several qualified entities to join forces into a single representative action. Again, the text remains silent on potential private international law issues. The Proposal also allows one entity to act on behalf of others. Article 20(2) of the Proposal adds a coordination rule in cross-border cases, whereby a final decision that an infringement has occurred in a Member State should be treated as a rebuttable presumption in other Member States. Finally, the Proposal encourages the conclusion of out-of-court settlements (Article 8).

B. The EU's Journey Towards the Implementation of Collective Redress

As the documents released by the EU show, the implementation of collective redress has the potential to foster access to justice. Nevertheless, this policy objective might be difficult to guarantee in a cross-border context, as many obstacles still deter people from litigating in another Member State. Such obstacles are detailed below (i.). The persistence of the enforcement gap has encouraged the EU to enact or reinforce existing procedural tools. Therefore, the second part of this sub-section critically analyses the steps taken by the EU in order to implement collective redress in light of the documents presented above (ii.).

i. Empirical Evidence on Consumer Behaviour

The following discussion sheds some light on consumer behaviour in the internal market, and especially in cross-border transactions or collective redress actions. Empirical evidence presents the obstacles that consumers face in obtaining redress. Spotting those obstacles would allow the EU to offer an appropriate response to those problems. At present, however, said empirical evidence is fragmentary. In particular, data is lacking regarding the actual number of consumer cross-border cases over a given period, as well as the number of collective redress claims brought so far. Additionally, there is no clear picture on the 'size' of the enforcement gap and the impact of harmonisation measures on consumer confidence.[127]

[127] As Loos points out, 'empirical evidence that full harmonization is the most effective means of solving the perceived problems of the fragmentation of rules for the use of the internal market or of improving consumer confidence in the internal market is missing entirely'. Although this argument concerns harmonisation of substantive consumer law, it should be applicable to harmonisation of

This work relies on the studies commissioned by the EU on collective redress, as well as Eurobarometer surveys. These sources put the spotlight on the factors that affect consumers' confidence in the market and, thus, deter them from shopping across the border and eventually obtain compensation for their harm. From all these documents, three important points could be extracted.

First, empirical evidence confirms that small-value claimants are usually rationally apathetic. In particular, studies show that consumers would usually not seek redress if the amount of their damage were below EUR 500.[128] This result is approximately the same for cross-border transactions.[129] Eurobarometers also indicate that some people questioned would not go to court whatever the amount of their claim.[130] However, only a few people who tried to solve their dispute amicably could not come to a solution.[131] This tendency is also reflected in cross-border transactions.[132]

Secondly, many barriers impede consumers to seek recovery on an individual basis: the cost of taking action; the unawareness regarding the way to enforce rights; the time needed to prepare and organise the case; the risk of losing time and money if the case does not succeed; and the lack of bargaining power of consumers with respect to defendants.[133] Moreover, it has to be highlighted that consumers face additional obstacles when their conflict entails an international component. Specifically, consumers who have to cross the border in order to defend their rights state that they struggle to get in contact with the company, face language issues, as well as additional costs and are confronted with differences between national legislation.[134] So much that many of the people surveyed think that 'it is "almost impossible" to seek redress in relation to cross-border purchases'.[135] In all cases, only 2 per cent of people surveyed were involved in judicial proceedings abroad.[136] As regards collective redress, the possibility to get together appears to incentivise many consumers to go to court. For example, a Eurobarometer shows that 41 per cent of people surveyed would be willing to litigate their rights if they could join other claimants.[137] This number reached 67 per cent in a subsequent Eurobarometer.[138]

procedural laws as well (M Loos, 'Full Harmonisation as a Regulatory Concept and its Consequences for the National Legal Orders: The Example of the Consumer Rights Directive', Centre for the Study of European Contract Law Working Paper Series No 2010/03 9, available at https://papers.ssrn.com).

[128] Civic Consulting of the Consumer Policy Evaluation Consortium (CPEC), Study (n 102) 12; Commission, Special Eurobarometer 136, Les Européens et l'accès à la justice (2000) 13; Commission, Special Eurobarometer 195, Les citoyens de l'Union européenne et l'accès à la justice (2004) 27–28.

[129] Special Eurobarometer 195 (n 128) 53.

[130] Special Eurobarometer 136 (n 128) 28; Special Eurobarometer 195 (n 128) 28.

[131] Special Eurobarometer 195 (n 128) 22.

[132] Special Eurobarometer 136 (n128) 28; Special Eurobarometer 195 (n 128) 54–56.

[133] Civic Consulting of the Consumer Policy Evaluation Consortium (CPEC), Study (n 102) 4.

[134] TNSqual+ (n 112) 52; Commission, Special Eurobarometer 292, Civil Justice in the European Union (2008), 9; Commission, Special Eurobarometer 351, Civil Justice (2010) 33–37.

[135] TNSqual+ (n 112) 52.

[136] Special Eurobarometer 292 (n 134) 3, 5; Special Eurobarometer 351 (n 134) 22.

[137] Special Eurobarometer 136, above n 370, 16–17.

[138] ibid 36–40.

Finally, studies underline the importance of certain entities such as consumer associations or public entities in order to defend consumer rights. The role of lawyers should also be emphasised. According to some surveys, consumers highly trust these actors in order to defend their rights.[139] Additionally, one survey reveals that approximately 'one in ten Europeans (…) had asked for advice or assistance from a consumer association'.[140] Usually, they contact consumer associations in order to get practical information or obtain legal advice.[141] To the best of this author's knowledge, no empirical data has been gathered regarding the obstacles faced by consumer associations or public bodies when they have to start judicial proceedings abroad. However, the reports on the Injunctions Directive show that these obstacles are likely to be significant. To be more specific, the second report on the Injunctions Directive shows that either consumer associations or public authorities rarely seek injunctive relief in the courts of another Member State.[142] Instead, representative entities usually start litigation in the market in which they are active, when this is possible. The report identifies various obstacles to cross-border actions for injunctive relief, namely the costs and length of proceedings, the complexity of the procedure, the limited effects of injunctions and the difficulty in enforcing the judgment when the trader does not comply with it.[143]

In order to reinforce those findings, a specific questionnaire on obstacles to cross-border litigation and collective redress was drafted. After having distributed this questionnaire to many consumer associations and EU Consumer Centres, three answers were received – from Altroconsumo, ADICAE and DECO – which are published in Annex III. Although this result might be quite meagre and, hence, no strong conclusions can be built up, interesting results could still be extracted from those answers. Those findings are included in the relevant sections of this book.

As regards cross-border litigation, consumer associations were asked about obstacles to the start of proceedings abroad.[144] Although the answers were rather sketchy, the overall impression was that all the listed elements were potential obstacles to cross-border litigation. Out of this list, the most relevant barriers that impede consumer associations to bring actions abroad appear to be the costs of proceedings, language and differences in substantive laws. The same question was asked regarding cross-border collective redress.[145] Again, responses vary significantly and all elements seem to be problematic. Overall, main obstacles to the start

[139] Special Eurobarometer 136 (n 128) 24–25, 28–30; Special Eurobarometer 195 (n 128) 40–41, 49–51.

[140] Commission, Special Eurobarometer 130, Europeans and Consumer Associations (1999) 94.

[141] ibid 97.

[142] Report concerning the application of Directive 2009/22/EC of the European Parliament and of the Council on injunctions for the protection of consumers' interest COM (2012) 635 final, para 2.5.

[143] ibid paras 4.1–4.5.

[144] Question 3 of the questionnaire.

[145] Question 4.4 of the questionnaire.

of collective redress actions abroad include costs of proceedings, lack of financial resources, difficulties in gathering victims together and distributing compensation.

ii. The Initiative of the EU

The next paragraphs present the measures taken by the EU in order to implement collective redress and, hence, fulfil the current private enforcement gap. Special attention is given to the last documents released by the Commission, namely its Recommendation of 2013, as well as its Proposal for a Directive on representative actions. The legislative path taken by the EU regarding collective redress essentially consists in regulating its procedural aspects. However, it is doubtful whether those measures improve the attractiveness of collective redress and tackle the access to justice issues described in the last section (above II.B.i).

a. The Pre-Recommendation Landscape

Through the harmonisation of substantive consumer laws at the national level, the EU attempted to foster consumer confidence in the market. However, EU institutions soon realised that the existence of substantive rights without procedural enforcement was useless. In light of the above, the EU has explored various ways to fulfil the current enforcement gap.[146] For instance, it first enacted the Injunctions Directive, as well as the Small Claims Procedure, and then encouraged the use of ADR mechanisms. Additionally, it strengthened the cooperation of public authorities regarding consumer protection. With the same goal in mind, the Commission started to investigate collective redress in 2007. Because this instrument is able to overcome rational apathy, achieve economies of scale and reduce information asymmetries,[147] it is perceived as a serious candidate to improve access to justice.

In this context, the EU institutions examined various options to implement this procedural tool: to start with, the Green Paper on consumer collective redress presented four policy options to be considered by stakeholders: these suggestions range from simple passivity of the EU legislator to the enactment of a collective redress mechanism. However, the answers to the Green Paper show a strong opposition from business representatives who challenge the necessity of such an instrument, as well as the competence of the EU to take any legislative measure. Instead, business representatives advocate that ADR could perfectly fulfil the current enforcement gap. These considerations were taken into account by the Commission in its Consultation Paper of 2009: henceforth, judicial collective

[146] I Benöhr, *EU Consumer Law and Human Rights* (Oxford University Press, 2013) 179–81.

[147] R van den Bergh and L Visscher, 'The Preventive Function of Collective Actions for Damages in Consumer Law' (2008) 1 (2) *Erasmus Law Review* 5, 16–22; G Wagner, 'Private Law Enforcement Through ADR: Wonder Drug or Snake Oil?' (2014) 51 *Common Market Law Review* 165, 189–90.

redress is only considered as a viable alternative if complemented with ADR mechanisms.[148] In a sense, the Commission mitigated its options in order to make them more attractive to business representatives, who are the ones that should be convinced for a political consensus to be reached.

The documents published by the Commission before the publication of its Recommendation of 2013 do not establish a clear path towards the regulation of collective redress. To begin with, the Commission does not state whether it aims at covering cross-border or purely national cases. Certainly, this represents an important decision, as it conditions the EU's competence to legislate. Then, one does not know what instrument should carry out a potential legislative measure and if it should be binding or not. Besides, the proper terms of some documents, are quite vague: for instance, option 4 of the Green Paper suggests that the EU could adopt 'a non-binding or binding EU measure to ensure that a collective redress judicial mechanism exists in all Member States'.[149] However, this choice of terms makes it difficult to guess whether the EU would adopt a uniform procedure available in cross-border cases on the model of the Small Claims Procedure, whether it aims at harmonising existing national collective redress mechanisms, or whether it simply requires that all Member States have a collective redress instrument, whatever its shape. Another element that should be highlighted is that no collective redress model seems to be favoured by the EU, although in the Consultation Paper of 2009 it seems to incline towards the test case procedure.[150] Nevertheless, the document does not advance the reasons for such a choice. Finally, the same happens when the Consultation Paper suggests the combination of ADR with collective proceedings. No studies or impact assessment examine the feasibility or the desirability of such a solution. It looks like the dispute system design is 'à la carte'.

b. The Recommendation of 2013

In 2013, the Commission's Recommendation was released.[151] The Recommendation establishes strong safeguards but promote in a limited way the implementation of efficient collective redress mechanisms. Private international law questions are excluded from the Recommendation. The next lines highlight the shortcomings of the text that one might want to reconsider, should a more incisive regulation be adopted.

[148] Hodges, 'Collective Redress' (n 14) 70.

[149] Commission, Green Paper (n 104) para 48.

[150] Commission, Consultation paper (n 113) 18–19, para 62.

[151] For other critical comments of the Commission's Recommendation and Communication, see Nagy (n 42) 530–52; XE Kramer, 'Securities Collective Action and Private International Law Issues in Dutch WCAM Settlements: Global Aspirations and Regional Boundaries' (2014) 27 *Global Business & Development Law Journal* 235, 244–48; J Sorabji, 'Reflections on the Commission Communication on Collective Redress' (2014) 17(1) *Irish Journal of European Law* 62–76; A Stadler, 'The Commission's Recommendation on Common Principles of Collective Redress and Private International Law Issues' (2013) 4 *Nederlands Internationaal Privaatrecht* 483–88.

To start with, the Recommendations are restrictive in their terms. For instance, according to paragraph 3(a), the term collective redress should be understood as

> a legal mechanism that ensures a possibility to claim cessation of illegal behaviour collectively by *two or more natural or legal persons or by an entity entitled to bring a representative action* (injunctive collective redress); (ii) a legal mechanism that ensures a possibility to claim compensation collectively by *two or more natural or legal persons* claiming to have been harmed in a mass harm situation or by an *entity entitled to bring a representative action* (compensatory collective redress) (emphasis added).

Accordingly, the document offers a definition of collective redress which does not include all existing national schemes: while the Commission seems to accept the representative model, the Dutch *WCAM* seems to be excluded from the Recommendation, inasmuch as this mechanism does not involve any claim for compensation or injunctive relief. In fact, parties only request the court to make a settlement binding. Similarly, the test case model remains out of the Recommendation's scope, whereas this mechanism does not involve any representative claimant. As far as the class action model is concerned – for example as enacted in Portugal –, it is equally banned from the collective redress definition when a single person litigates on behalf of a group of victims. The adoption of such an excluding definition should be carefully pondered, as it promotes some collective redress models and rejects others. Here, it is surprising that the test case model, so much valued by the Consultation Paper of 2011, remains eventually out of the Recommendation's scope. Similarly, it is not clear whether the Dutch model is engaged by the Recommendation or not, although the promotion of ADR is an essential policy objective of the EU.

Similarly, the Recommendation defines a mass harm situation as a 'situation where two or more natural or legal persons claim to have suffered harm causing damage resulting from *the same illegal activity* (…)' (emphasis added). When the illegal activity consists in a single act, like a shipwreck or a plane crash, no major interpretative problem arises. However, one may wonder whether repeatedly similar illegal behaviours might enter the scope of this definition. For example, companies whose terms and conditions are abusive conclude different individual contracts with consumers. As a result, in case numerous consumers were to question the validity of an alleged abusive term in a collective redress action, should a court consider that their situation stems from 'the same' illegal activity?

The Recommendation uses other vague terms. For example, according to paragraph 21, an opt-in based system should be established, unless 'reasons of sound administration of justice' justify the adoption of an opt-out collective redress mechanism. Does sound administration of justice refer to manageability purposes? Or does this provision *authorise* the court or the legislator to certify or adopt an opt-out collective action when the nature of the claims – that are so small that an opt-out scheme is the only way to make them viable – commands it? Additionally, it is difficult to explain the Commission's preference for an opt-in-based collective redress mechanism. As highlighted earlier in this chapter (above I.D.i.), the opt-in system might not sufficiently foster access to justice, especially where small-value claims are involved. The well-functioning of the opt-out-based US class action further reinforces this argument. Lastly, in one of her interesting contributions, Sibony confirms that, from a behavioural perspective, the opt-out mechanism can overcome rational apathy and, hence, promote access to justice.[152]

Following this, paragraphs 25 to 28 encourage Member States to use ADR mechanisms. Nevertheless, as earlier mentioned, it is quite unfortunate that the Commission does not assess the desirability and suitability of such mechanisms for consumer disputes in case of collective harm. Specifically, the Recommendation acknowledges that parties could make use of Directive 2008/52/EC on certain aspects of mediation in civil and commercial matters.[153] However, it is arguable that mediation is an adequate dispute resolution tool for collective consumer disputes, given that many logistical problems may occur: first, how could a mediator maintain the level playing field between parties? How can a final agreement be applicable to absent parties? Who should choose the mediator and how should intervention of absent parties be managed? Can mediation adequately protect consumers' rights as judicial proceedings would? Furthermore, the Recommendation does not mention whether collective redress mechanisms should encompass an ADR process within its structure or whether ADR should be available as an independent alternative to collective redress. In this regard, the EU Parliament clarifies that ADR should be an alternative and not a pre-condition to collective redress proceedings.[154]

Then, the Recommendation establishes many safeguards that intend to control the use of collective redress: in particular, standing is allocated to representative entities and is submitted to stringent eligibility conditions; the loser-pays rule has to be maintained; third-party funding is limited; and, contingency fees, as well as punitive damages are not permitted. On the contrary, the US class action allocates standing to individuals; applies the American rule on costs; allows third-party funding; is based on a kind of contingency fees model; and permits punitive damages in certain cases. Although the American device is the target of many critiques, it is undoubtedly an efficient procedural machine. Therefore, the choice of the Commission to recommend the adoption of opposite structural features for collective redress is questionable. Accordingly, the workability of a collective redress tool that would include all these characteristics is doubtful. In an interesting and instructive paper, Hodges explains that the use of a procedural vehicle can be incentivised or disincentivised thanks to certain levers.[155] For instance, a private enforcement system that would imply no costs for the claimant; establish the

[152] Sibony, 'A Behavioural Perspective on Collective Redress' (n 50) 47–57.
[153] Council Directive 2008/52/EC (n 88).
[154] European Parliament, Resolution (n 115) para 25.
[155] C Hodges, 'Current Discussions on Consumer Redress: Collective Redress and ADR' (2012) 13 *ERA Forum* 11, 13.

loser-pays rule as a principle; provide high damages; allow contingency fees and punitive damages; accept wide discovery practices as well as jury trial and facilitate aggregation of claims, would encourage litigation.[156] On the contrary, the absence of such levers would reduce the amount of litigation in a given system. As a result, the safeguards established by the Commission in its Recommendation act as disincentives to litigate. However, the document does not offer substitution incentives that would counterbalance these limitations and foster access to justice. As Nagy states, 'the Recommendation, in essence, interdicts the risk premium devices of US law, which are rather unpopular in Europe, anyway, while it fails to offer any surrogate'.[157] Specifically, the obligation for Member States to introduce a collective redress mechanism into their legal order is not an incentive in itself because it does not guarantee the efficiency of the procedural tool. The Recommendation should achieve a certain balance between the protection of the defendant from unmeritorious claims and access to justice. In fact, the Commission's focus on safeguards is not fully justified, since Member States have enacted procedural tools that respect the rights of both parties. The proof of this fact is that no litigation 'boom' has occurred in EU legal orders, even in Portugal, where a system that looks like the US class action device was adopted.

The focus of the Recommendations on the protection of the rights of the defence demonstrates two things: first, it is arguable that the Recommendation improves access to justice because, as mentioned earlier, no incentives to litigate were introduced in the document of the Commission. In fact, uniform safeguards have the effect of guaranteeing that some minimum procedural standards are maintained in any collective redress proceedings, regardless of where the litigation takes place. Consequently, this measure probably aims at fostering mutual trust, which in turn facilitates the recognition and enforcement of judicial decisions within the EU. However, it is difficult to see how minimum standards of protection in favour of the defendant can actually motivate consumers to start litigation. Secondly, the fact that the Commission mainly focuses on the rights of the defence and imposes restrictive structural features to collective redress is probably the visible result of the lack of political consensus between consumer representatives on the one hand, and business representatives on the other. Therefore, the only possible trade-off is to encourage Member States to adopt collective redress mechanisms but under stringent conditions. This time, the Commission has not established an even playing field between the rights of claimants and defendants.

Finally, the Recommendation does not truly tackle the cross-border problems that collective redress may trigger. Paragraph 17 only clarifies that national procedural rules should not hinder parties of another Member State from initiating collective redress actions. This result is certainly unfortunate as private international law issues are numerous. This 'oversight' reveals that the EU institutions

[156] ibid.
[157] Nagy (n 42) 549.

probably do not intend to clarify private international law rules and adapt them to collective redress.

c. The Future Directive on Representative Actions

The Proposal for a Directive[158] elaborated by the Commission is a more convincing attempt to regulate procedural aspects of collective redress, although some significant limitations remain. Since this piece of legislation is currently going through the EU legislative process and, hence, will surely be the object of further modifications, only some general comments on relevant aspects of this Directive are offered. It has to be highlighted that the Directive seems to represent a sort of *lex specialis* compared to the Recommendation of 2013. In particular, the Directive states that it 'takes into account the Commission Recommendation of 11 June 2013' and that

> some procedural elements from the Recommendation are not reproduced in this proposal due to its more targeted scope, which is limited to infringements that may affect the collective interests of consumers, and the pre-existing features of the representative action model in the current Injunctions Directive.[159]

Following the example of the Injunctions Directive, the Proposal facilitates actions protecting consumers' interests[160] brought by qualified entities against violations of EU consumer law. The text significantly extended its regime: henceforth, actions for injunctive relief, as well as damages fall under the scope of the Proposal and those may be brought in a number of fields, such as data protection, financial services, travel and tourism, energy, telecommunications and environment. In cross-border cases, the mutual recognition of representative entities' legal standing applies (Article 6). Article 10 of the Proposal establishes some rules regarding the effects of final decisions. In particular, final decisions establishing that an infringement has been committed represent irrefutable proofs in subsequent proceedings before national courts. In cross-border cases, those final decisions establish a rebuttable presumption (Article 10(2)). This clarification is welcome since the effect of injunctions was relatively unclear up to now.[161] Finally, the Proposal promotes the

[158] See II.A.

[159] Proposal for a Directive (n 15) 4.

[160] It is unclear whether general interests are included in the notion of collective interests as defined by the Proposal. Note that Art 3(3) of the Proposal departs from the definition provided by the Injunctions Directive. In this context, it could have been interesting to adopt the dichotomy provided by Art 1 of the Model Code (see this chapter, I.D.).

[161] On this question, see the Evaluation Study of National Procedural Laws and Practices in Terms of their Impact on the Free Circulation of Judgments and on the Equivalence and Effectiveness of the Procedural Protection of Consumers under EU Consumer Law (Strand 2) prepared by the Consortium of European universities led by the MPI Luxembourg for Procedural Law as commissioned by the European Commission (JUST/2014/RCON/PR/CIVI/0082), ch 4, available at https://ec.europa.eu/newsroom/just/document.cfm?action=display&doc_id=49503.

conclusion of out-of-court settlements, as well as coordinated actions of representative entities in cross-border cases.

Although the above-mentioned elements are welcome, some important shortcomings have to be highlighted. To start with, the Proposal deals with funding-related issues in a limited fashion only: although Article 15(1) advises Member States to remove financial barriers hindering access to justice, Recital 4 makes clear that rules concerning the allocation of costs are not affected by the Directive. In other words, the incentives created by the Proposal are still far from the system promoted by the Model Code or the US funding system of class actions (chapter 1, IV.C. and chapter 2, I.D.iv.).

As far as rules on standing are concerned, the Directive on representative actions seems to reduce the room for manoeuvre left to national legislators. Indeed, Article 3 of the Injunctions Directive makes clear that criteria on standing should be laid down by national procedural law. Conversely, Article 4 of the Proposal seems to impose its own criteria on Member States. Accordingly, all entities complying with the requirements of the Proposal would have the right to benefit from its regime. The EU legislator offers some flexibility to Member States as regards the possibility to designate entities on an ad hoc basis for bringing specific representative actions. Additionally, entities representing consumers from different Member States may also be designated by Member States. Finally, national legislators may limit the power of qualified entities by allowing them to seek only some of the measures referred to in Articles 5 or 6.

Article 4 of the Directive is partially aligned with the General Regulation on Data Protection (GDPR).[162] Article 80 of the GDPR[163] offers representative entities the right to bring actions on behalf of data subjects[164] if they are not-for-profit, have been properly constituted in accordance with the law of a Member State, have statutory objectives that are in the public interest and are active in the data protection field. However, the Directive on representative actions has a broader scope, inasmuch as it allows qualified entities to bring actions protecting general interests.

Most importantly, the Proposal remains silent on private international law questions. As the analysis in chapter 3 demonstrates, however, the application of rules on jurisdiction remain problematic. Another, challenging situation is the recognition of out-of-court settlements in subsequent proceedings (chapter 3, II.B.iv.), since these are not regulated by the BIa. Finally, Article 16(2) of the Proposal allows entities to join forces in a unique, cross-border action. Alternatively, one qualified

[162] Council Regulation (EU) 2016/679 of 27 April 2016 on the protection of natural persons with regard to the processing of personal data and on the free movement of such data, and repealing Directive 95/46/EC [2016] OJ L119/1.

[163] For an in-depth analysis of this provision, see A Pato 'The Collective Private Enforcement of Data Protection Rights in the EU', forthcoming. This paper has been presented at the 3rd IAPL-MPI Summer School (July 2018).

[164] This right is certainly limited to the protection of collective interests.

entity may represent others in proceedings protecting consumers' interests. On the one hand, such a rule is positive because it obliges Member States to facilitate the centralisation of collective redress actions in a unique location from a procedural perspective. On the other hand, however, as explained in chapter 4 (II.A.i. and II.A.ii.), the schemes described by Article 16(2) would certainly require significant organisational efforts and hence, should not occur on a regular basis in practice.

C. Opponents' Objections to Collective Redress

i. ADR as the Only Means to Resolve Consumer Disputes

As the documents released by the EU institutions show, opponents of the adoption of collective redress argue that the necessity of such a procedural tool in the EU judicial system is far from obvious. Rather, they consider that ADR[165] is a satisfying means to address consumer disputes, and thus, that collective redress is not needed. This argument is partially valid: on the one hand, the different investigations led by the EU demonstrate that an important enforcement gap exists regarding consumer disputes. On the other hand, however, opponents rightly point out that the EU has failed in its attempt to establish the usefulness of collective redress in comparison with other extra-judicial mechanisms. For this reason, this section investigates and reveals the added value of collective redress in comparison with its direct competitor: consumer ADR. This analysis is not an exhaustive assessment, which aims at determining, in absolute terms, whether one tool is better than the other. Rather, it has to be established whether collective redress is *a priori* useless where ADR mechanisms exist, because in such a case, the debate regarding the implementation of collective redress would become worthless. Therefore, a primer on this particular topic is provided.

Beforehand, two disclaimers have to be made: in the first place, it must be recalled that collective redress takes very different forms. Therefore, the comments below could not be equally applicable to every collective redress mechanism. Consequently, and in order to facilitate the comparative assessment, the concept of collective redress will equate to the most commonly used mechanism within the EU, namely the representative model. In the second place, the debate over the suitability of ADR to consumer disputes is set aside: undeniably, consumer ADR schemes are emerging all over Europe and are here to stay.[166] Consequently, it is

[165] The terms 'ADR' and 'out-of-court or extra-judicial mechanisms' are used interchangeably.

[166] For a critique on this particular topic, see Wagner, 'Private Law Enforcement Through ADR' (n 147) 165–94; F Weber, 'Is ADR the Superior Mechanism for Consumer Contractual Disputes? – An Assessment of the Incentivizing Effects of the ADR Directive' (2015) 38 *Journal of Consumer Policy* 265–85.

pointless to question their existence. Against this backdrop, the following analysis starts by comparing the characteristics of collective redress with ADR from a structural perspective. The objective is to shed light on the comparative advantages that each instrument possesses and underline their differences (a.). Then, the specific issues that these two systems face when they are used in a cross-border context are pinpointed (h.). It is argued that the usefulness of collective redress cannot be dismissed. ADR and collective redress are complementary mechanisms as they might serve as procedural vehicles for different types of disputes and resolve distinct cross-border issues, although their coverage sometimes overlap. In this sense, the opponents' argument is not valid.

a. Consumer ADR and Collective Redress Compared …

Consumer ADR mechanisms – also called CADR or CDR – encompass any out-of-court process, which aims at resolving disputes involving consumers – the denominated B2C disputes.[167] Arbitration, conciliation and mediation are typical consumer ADR. A leading study on the use of ADR prepared by Civic Consulting observes that in 2007, over 750 CADR systems were registered across Europe.[168] A look at the structure of these mechanisms shows that important variations exist both geographically and materially: while some ADR schemes are linked to public authorities, others are private bodies; they may be financed through public or private means; their coverage could be sector-based or general; some ADR bodies apply the law, while others use an approach based on fairness; the outcome of the process might be binding or not for parties; and the adherence of businesses to an ADR scheme in a certain sector could be mandatory or not.[169] In light of the above, the ADR Directive of 2013[170] aims at improving the current system by requiring Member States to extend the coverage of their ADR schemes and building up uniform quality standards.

Even though consumer ADR mechanisms are heterogeneous, they often constitute an interesting alternative to court proceedings in terms of costs, flexibility and time:[171] as regards the financial aspect, some consumer ADR entities

[167] N Creutzfeldt, 'Alternative Dispute Resolution for Consumers' in M Stürner et al (eds), *The Role of Consumer ADR in the Administration of Justice* (Sellier European Law Publishers, 2015) 3–4.

[168] Civic Consulting, Study on the Use of Alternative Dispute Resolution in the European Union (2009) 31.

[169] For an overview of those differences in some Member States see the national reports encompassed in C Hodges et al, *Consumer ADR in Europe* (CH Beck/Hart, 2012) chs 3 to 11; P Cortes, 'The Impact of EU law in the ADR Landscape in Italy, Spain and the UK: Time for Change or Missed Opportunity' (2015) 16 *ERA Forum* 125–47.

[170] Council Directive 2013/11/EU (n 88). For a thorough analysis of this Directive, see Weber, 'Is ADR the Superior Mechanism for Consumer Contractual Disputes?' (n 166) 277–82.

[171] The Commission highlighted the positive aspects of ADR in comparison with court proceedings in its Green Paper on alternative dispute resolution in civil and commercial law COM (2002) 196 final 7–9. For a comprehensive list of ADR/ODR's advantages, see U Jeretina and A Uzelac,

offer their services to consumers for free, such as the Spanish *Sistema Arbitral de Consumo*,[172] whereas others require the payment of a modest fee. This is the case with the Dutch *Geschillencommissie*,[173] a group of sector-based complaints commissions offering different dispute resolution procedures. Depending on the sector, consumers have to pay a registration fee of approximately EUR 25 to EUR 125. These fees are refunded if the consumer wins the case. Another advantage of consumer ADR is that the procedure is often more flexible and efficient: written procedures rather than oral hearings are often preferred, legal representation is not always required, online tools are sometimes available, and the decision-making process might be based on fairness rather than law.[174] Finally, thanks to streamlined procedures, ADR is deemed to be quicker than court proceedings. In particular, the Civic Consulting study estimates that ADR entities usually issue a decision within a timeframe of 90 days.[175]

That being said, consumer ADR mechanisms equally suffer from important drawbacks: first of all, the high number of mechanisms whose coverage is limited makes it difficult for consumers and businesses to know and have access to all the existing dispute resolution tools.[176] This means that some consumer disputes might not be covered by a specific ADR scheme. Secondly, the use of ADR is voluntary. As a result, businesses that are reluctant to use out-of-court mechanisms or to comply with a non-binding decision could call into question the viability of consumer ADR.[177] Lastly, it is doubtful that all ADR instruments successfully tackle the absence of a level playing field between parties in consumer disputes: for example, traders are usually well advised and represented by lawyers. By contrast, consumers may often not hire a lawyer in order to avoid paying fees. Therefore, the preparation of the case and the development of arguments might be uneven. In the same way, mediators could experience difficulties in maintaining a certain balance between a consumer and a trader, given that mediators only empower parties to reach their own agreement and are not supposed to actively intervene in the conflict.

Now turning to the virtues and vices of collective redress in comparison with consumer ADR, various points should be made. To begin with, since the cost

'Alternative Dispute Resolution for Consumer Cases: Are Divergences and Obstacle to Effective Access to Justice?' (2014) XII(4) *International Public Administration Review* 39, 44.

[172] Art 41 of the Real Decree 231/2008 of February 15, on the Consumer Arbitration System.

[173] Hodges et al, *Consumer ADR in Europe* (n 169) 135–49.

[174] *Cf* the national reports encompassed in Hodges et al (n 169) chs 3 to 11.

[175] Civic Consulting, Study on the Use of Alternative Dispute Resolution in the European Union (n 168) 42.

[176] For more information about the characteristic of this coverage gap, see The Study Centre for Consumer Law/Centre for European Economic Law (n 30) 103–04; Civic Consulting (n 168) 56–60; Commission, 'Evaluation of the Effectiveness and Efficiency of Collective Redress' (n 27) 93.

[177] ibid 94.

of collective redress proceedings is either borne by a representative claimant or spread among all the victims, this procedure is likely to be cheap enough to fit low-value cases. This is particularly true if the collective redress mechanism is opt-out based. In this sense, collective redress could occasionally serve as a more adequate procedural vehicle than ADR mechanisms do.[178] Furthermore, collective actions could also be useful in case ADR bodies do not cover claims arising from a particular sector. Then, consumers could resort to collective redress when businesses refuse to participate in any out-of-court dispute resolution process. Finally, it must be highlighted that collective redress mostly suits small-value claims, which are numerous and widespread. Hence, contrary to ADR, this instrument is not an option when damages concern an individual consumer only. In this vein, these devices may deal with different types of disputes.

Nevertheless, some ADR entities also provide collective redress procedures, and thus, directly compete with the judicial system. In particular, the Civic Consulting Study on the use of ADR indicates that three kinds of collective redress procedures exist: the first consists in a representative process,[179] whereby a representative body 'litigates' on behalf of a number of victims. The Spanish *Sistema Arbitral de Consumo*, The Lisbon Arbitration Center, the *Service de médiation auprès du groupe SNCB* in France and the *Service de médiation pour le secteur postal* in Belgium provide such a tool. Then, some ADR service providers perform collective investigations.[180] Under this model, various cases are explored together and the decision-maker renders a subsequent single decision applicable to all claims. Finally, the collective procedure of the Scandinavian type allows an Ombudsman to initiate proceedings before an ADR body on behalf of multiple consumers.[181] There is no need for consumers to be identified or to actively manifest their desire to be bound by the decision. Although ADR entities have set up collective redress procedures, their experience remains limited.[182] In fact, according to the Study, some ADR bodies consider that courts are better equipped to deal with complex cases.[183] Indeed, it seems that consumer ADR suits simple disputes.

[178] However, Weber notes that CADR may also have the power to fight rational apathy that characterises small-value claimants, since CADR is usually cheaper than court proceedings (Weber (n 166) 271).

[179] Civic Consulting (n 168) 50.

[180] ibid 49–50.

[181] ibid 50–51.

[182] eg the Spanish consumer arbitration system allows for class arbitration (Art 56 of Royal Decree 231/2008 of 15 February, which establishes the Consumer Arbitration System). However, according to a paper written by A Montesinos García in 2014 ('Últimas tendencias en la Unión Europea sobre las acciones colectivas de consumo. La posible introducción de fórmulas de ADR' (2014) 12 *Revista electrónica del Departamento de Derecho de la Universidad de La Rioja* 87, 104) no such action has ever taken place. More generally, Radicati di Brozolo observes that Europe should see no 'waves of class action arbitrations' any time soon (LG Radicati di Brozolo, 'Class Arbitration in Europe?' in Nuyts and Hatzimihail (n 8) 219).

[183] Civic Consulting (n 168) 109.

Finally, the non-binding nature of a decision issued in an ADR process could undermine the effectiveness of collective redress.[184]

Similarly, the combination of arbitration with collective procedures – that gave rise to the concept of class arbitration[185] – have generated intense debates regarding the desirability and workability of such a cocktail in the United States: on the one hand, one may argue that nothing impedes the transplant of the class action device to arbitration.[186] In particular, the federal legislation on arbitration neither invites nor prohibits class arbitration.[187] On the other hand, and as mentioned earlier, when class actions merge with arbitration, adaptability issues may appear.[188] Besides, class arbitration engenders due process concerns:[189] specifically, since arbitration is a matter of consent, parties keep control of the design of the procedure. Therefore, the rights of absent parties in a class arbitration could be in danger.[190] In an attempt to resolve this issue, some consumer arbitration service providers solicit the intervention of courts in the class arbitration process.[191] However, this intervention may greatly complicate and slow down the pace of arbitration.[192] Some arbitration organisations such as the American Arbitration Association (AAA) have also promulgated specific procedural rules applying to this particular model or arbitration.[193]

Nevertheless, two phenomena appear to have closed this debate: first, the US Supreme Court issued two important decisions, which greatly limit the use of class actions in arbitration or litigation. To begin with, in *AT&T Mobility LLC v. Concepcion*,[194] the Supreme Court ruled that the availability of class arbitration cannot be inferred from an arbitration clause that does not tackle this particular

[184] ibid.

[185] S Strong, 'Does Class Arbitration "Change the Nature" of Arbitration? Stolt-Nielsen, AT&T, and a Return to First Principles' (2012) 17 *Harvard Negotiation Law Review* 201, 205–10.

[186] ibid 201–71. The author compares class arbitration with other multiparty arbitration proceedings and concludes that, although these devices sometimes differ, class arbitration does not 'change the nature' of arbitration. Therefore, class proceedings should not be excluded from arbitration on this ground; *Keating v. Superior Court*, 109 Cal.App.3d 784 (California Court of Appeal, 1982) 492. In this famous case, which is one of the earliest judgments dealing with class arbitration, the California Court of Appeals ruled that 'there is no insurmountable obstacle to conducting an arbitration on a class-wide basis. In an appropriate case, such a procedure undoubtedly would be the fairest and most efficient way of resolving the parties dispute'.

[187] This has been highlighted by the Supreme Court of California in *Keating v. Superior Court*, 31 Cal.3d 584 (1982) 608–14.

[188] See ch 1, II.A.

[189] J Sternlight, 'As Mandatory Binding Arbitration Meets the Class Action, Will the Class Action Surivive?' (2000) 42 *William and Mary Law Review* 1, 52–53.

[190] *AT&T Mobility LLC v. Concepcion* (563 US 333 [2011]), 348–49.

[191] MA Weston, 'Universes Colliding: The Constitutional Implications of Arbitral Class Actions' (2006) 47(5) *William and Mary Law Review* 1711, 1732–40.

[192] Sternlight, 'As Mandatory Binding Arbitration Meets the Class Action, Will the Class Action Surivive?' (n 189) 49–52.

[193] AAA, Supplementary Rules for Class Arbitration, available at www.adr.org/sites/default/files/document_repository/Supplementary%20Rules%20for%20Class%20Arbitrations.pdf.

[194] *AT&T Mobility LLC* (n 190).

question. Put differently, absent an explicit reference to class arbitration, this instrument is not available to parties. Then, traders who are willing to avoid any kind of class proceedings can insert arbitration clauses into their contracts with consumers coupled with a class action waiver.[195] The US Supreme Court recently validated that strategy in *Epic System Corp. v Levis*.[196] In that case, the Court barred access to class action litigation by enforcing a 'one-on-one arbitration' clause in employment contracts. Consequently, some argue that access to justice is substantially undermined since victims' only option is to proceed in arbitration on an individual basis.[197]

As a result, the American experience shows that class arbitration may not be the best venue to deal with consumer disputes, given that such a mix might generate important practical and due process concerns.

b. … in a Cross-Border Context

As regard cross-border disputes, the following paragraphs demonstrate that consumer ADR may not offer a better forum for consumers' complaints than collective redress. Here too, the ADR Directive should be taken into account as the text equally covers cross-border consumer disputes.

Consumers or their representatives often have to initiate collective proceedings at the domicile of the defendant. As chapter 3 further details, the general forum of Article 4 BIa – and Article 7(2) BIa to a certain extent – will usually be the only forum where collective proceedings may take place. In the same fashion, the complaint of a consumer against a trader domiciled in another Member State will likely be presented to an ADR entity based in the state in which the trader has its seat. This can be explained by the fact that, under the ADR Directive, Member States 'shall ensure that disputes covered by the Directive and which involve a trader established *on their respective territories* can be submitted to an ADR entity which complies with the requirements set out in this Directive' (emphasis added).[198] And to add: 'Member States shall ensure that ADR entities: (…) accept both

[195] A class action waiver can be defined as an arbitration provision 'that only authorizes claims brought in an individual capacity or that expressly bans representative class actions in arbitration or court' (MA Weston, 'The Death of Class Arbitration After *Concepcion*?' (2012) 60 *Kansas Law Review* 767, 767).

[196] *Epic System Corp. v Levis*, 584 US ___ (2018).

[197] In that respect, the Supreme Court of California stated that '[i]f the right to a classwide proceeding could be automatically eliminated in relationships governed by adhesion contracts through the inclusion of a provision for arbitration, the potential for undercutting these class action principles, and for chilling the effective protection of interests common to a group, would be substantial. Arbitration proceedings may well provide certain offsetting advantages through savings of time and expense; but, depending upon the nature of the issues and the evidence to be presented, it is at least doubtful that such advantages could compensate for the unfairness inherent in forcing hundreds or perhaps thousands, of individuals asserting claims involving common issues of fact and law to litigate them in separate proceedings against a party with vastly superior resources' (*Keating v. Superior Court* (n 186) 609).

[198] Art 5(1) of the ADR Directive.

domestic and cross-border disputes'.[199] In other words, the ADR Directive requires ADR service providers to accept claims lodged by consumers domiciled in a different Member State from the one in which they operate. However, the Directive does not oblige them to accept claims brought against foreign traders.[200] Exceptionally, ADR bodies sometimes cover these claims if businesses accept to be submitted to their 'jurisdiction' ('voluntary jurisdiction').[201]

In this context, the role of ECC-Net – as well as FIN-Net for financial matters – should be emphasised. Indeed, in each Member State, the EU Consumer Centres (ECC) inform consumers about their rights, assist them with their cross-border complaints and if necessary, help them to find the appropriate ADR entity where they could resolve their dispute.[202] In particular, when consumers are not able to find any amicable solution to their conflict with a trader located abroad, they can direct their complaint to the ECC of their domicile – also called the consumer ECC.[203] This Centre supports the consumer and offers translation services if needed. Then, the consumer ECC transfers the complaint to the ECC of the trader's seat – also called the trader ECC –, which in turn sends the case to the appropriate ADR scheme. The latter contacts and informs the trader about the complaint and tries to resolve the conflict. However, in practice, not many cases are actually transferred to an ADR entity: rather, ECCs usually contact the trader directly and attempt to find an amicable solution.[204] According to an ECC-Net report on cross-border dispute resolution of 2009,[205] from all complaints received in 2007, only 3.7 per cent were forwarded to an ADR body. This figure increased to 4.9 per cent for the year 2008. Furthermore, the report indicates that during these two years, ECCs resolved half of the complaints that were sent to them. It seems that the lack of available ADR schemes in many sectors is the primary cause of this result. Thanks to the adoption of the ADR Directive, which requires Member States to offer general coverage for all contractual obligations stemming from sales contracts or service contracts, this problem might partially disappear in the future.

Importantly, some empirical studies show that the use of ADR by traders remains very low, which contradicts the argument of collective redress' opponents. In particular, the Flash Eurobarometer 186[206] on business attitudes towards cross-border sales and consumer protection of December 2006 indicates that only

[199] Art 5(2)(e) of the ADR Directive.

[200] F Gascón Inchausti, 'Specific Problems of Cross-Border Consumer ADR: What Solutions?' in Stürner et al, *The Role of Consumer ADR in the Administration of Justice* (n 167) 37 and 44–48.

[201] eg the firm PayPal accepts to be submitted to the competence of the English Financial Ombudsman Service, albeit it is seated in Luxembourg (Hodges et al (n 169) 276).

[202] ECC Denmark, Cross-Border Dispute Resolution Mechanisms in Europe – Practical Reflections on the Need and Availability (2009) 10, available at dokumenter.forbrug.dk/forbrugereuropa/crossborder-dispute-resolution.

[203] For more information on the case-handling procedure, see ECC Denmark (n 202) 10–12.

[204] ibid 10–12.

[205] ibid 17 and 57.

[206] Commission, Flash Eurobarometer 186, Business attitudes towards cross-border sales and consumer protection (2006) 49.

3 per cent of the traders interviewed use ADR on a regular basis. The rest do not use out-of-court mechanisms either because they do not know of their existence (41 per cent), or because they do not need them (39 per cent). Subsequently, the Flash Eurobarometer 224[207] of January 2008, which is a follow-up to the previously-mentioned investigation, comes to the same result. As for the Flash Eurobarometer 278[208] of November 2009, it states that 8 per cent of traders did use ADR to resolve their disputes with consumers in the past two years – this figure rises to 9 per cent in 2010,[209] 10 per cent in 2011[210] and drops to 7 per cent in 2012[211] –, while 48 per cent of traders said they did not need to use ADR. To sum up, although the use of ADR has been increasing over time, the number of businesses that actually resort to out-of-court mechanisms remains low.

On the consumer side, notwithstanding the important role of the ECC-Net in facilitating the resolution of international B2C disputes, many barriers still deter them from complaining abroad. Both the Study on the use of ADR in the EU[212] and the IMCO Study on cross-border ADR[213] identify these obstacles, which sometimes overlap with those present in purely domestic cases. These include the absence of ADR schemes in certain industries or areas and the reluctance of traders to participate in an ADR procedure, and the risk of non-compliance of a non-binding decision.[214] Other issues specific to cross-border conflicts embrace language barriers, potential travel costs for the consumer and lack of awareness regarding the ADR system.[215] For example, the Financial Ombudsman Service (FOS), which deals with consumer disputes against traders located in the United Kingdom, is the most important ADR service provider in the EU. Indeed, the Ombudsman usually deals with more than 2 million inquiries and complaints a year, while other ADR schemes typically assess between 2,000 and 10,000 cases a year. It is interesting to note that between 2009 and 2014, the number of cross-border complaints presented to the FOS represented between 1 and 2 per cent of the total inquiries and complaints that the service provider dealt with.[216]

[207] Commission, Flash Eurobarometer 224, Business attitudes towards cross-border sales and consumer protection (2008) 45.

[208] Commission, Flash Eurobarometer 278, Business attitudes towards enforcement and redress in the Internal Market (2009) 69.

[209] Commission, Flash Eurobarometer 300, Retailers' attitudes towards cross-border trade and consumer protection (2011) 76.

[210] Commission, Flash Eurobarometer 331, Retailers' attitudes towards cross-border trade and consumer protection (2012) 124.

[211] Commission, Flash Eurobarometer 359, Retailers' attitudes towards cross-border trade and consumer protection (2013) 130–31.

[212] Civic Consulting (n 168) 411.

[213] European Parliament, Cross-Border Alternative Dispute Resolution in the European Union, P/A/IMCO/ST/2010-15, PE464.424 (2011), available at www.europarl.europa.eu/meetdocs/2009_2014/documents/imco/dv/adr_study_/adr_study_en.pdf.

[214] Civic Consulting (n 168) 112–15; European Parliament, Cross-Border Alternative Dispute Resolution in the European Union (n 213) 48–51.

[215] European Parliament (n 213) 48–51.

[216] *Cf* the figures presented by the FOS in its annual reports, available at www.financial-ombudsman.org.uk/publications/annual-reviews.htm.

In a cross-border context, the role of Online Dispute Resolution (ODR) should not be underestimated. Specifically, ODR is another path to consumer dispute resolution, which combines ADR with the use of technologies.[217] For instance,[218] the automated resolution system mechanism is an instrument whereby parties go through an online negotiation scheme by proposing settlement amounts. Other ODR mechanisms that are worth mentioning are online mediation and arbitration. Both instruments respect the traditional principles of ADR but introduce e-forms of communication into the dispute resolution process. The main advantage of ODR is undoubtedly its ability to reduce costs: given that face-to-face meetings are solved by the use of technologies, parties may avoid travel and accommodation expenses. Nevertheless, ODR does not resolve potential language differences and most importantly, it requires parties' consent to submit their dispute to an out-of-court system. As far as jurisdiction is concerned, the usual rules relevant for ADR schemes apply. However, technologies may circumvent jurisdictional issues if the dispute resolution process can be held entirely without the parties' physical presence in the foreign forum.

The ODR Regulation of 2013[219] aims at resolving these cross-border concerns by setting up a free-of-charge dispute resolution platform.[220] Specifically, this system deals with conflicts that arise in connection with online sales or service contracts. In order to achieve this objective, the platform allows claimants to fill out an online complaint form in one of the official languages of the EU. If necessary, the complaint is then translated and sent to the trader. As soon as the trader accepts to go through an ADR procedure, the ODR platform assists parties in searching for the appropriate ADR. This platform also serves as a forum to conduct the online resolution of the dispute. It is worth mentioning that the EU commits itself to proceed to the translation of all documents transferred via the platform. In light of these considerations, the ODR platform removes potential language barriers between the parties, as well as travelling costs.[221] These are certainly important improvements. However, the ODR Regulation is submitted to party autonomy and, thus, its effectiveness would be impaired if traders were reluctant to use ODR as a method to solve their conflict with consumers. Additionally, it must be underlined that the ODR platform has a limited coverage.

Cross-border collective redress may achieve great economies of scale in terms of costs as well. Furthermore, both the preparation and the defence of the case may be easier thanks to the representative's better expertise. Often, the representative

[217] Creutzfeldt, 'Alternative Dispute Resolution for Consumers' (n 167) 6.

[218] The following examples are extracted from S Yuthayotin, *Access to Justice in Transnational B2C E-Commerce – A Multidimensional Analysis of Consumer Protection Mechanisms* (Springer, 2015) 237–40.

[219] Council Regulation (EU) 524/2013 (n 88).

[220] This platform has been operational since 9 January 2016 and is accessible through the following link: ec.europa.eu/odr.

[221] Gascón Inchausti, 'Specific Problems of Cross-Border Consumer ADR' (n 200) 54–56.

will be assisted by a lawyer. Language issues may also be overcome for the same reason. Last but not least, it must be highlighted that judicial collective proceedings are not submitted to parties' consent: indeed, once the action is brought, the defendant will be led into the judicial machinery irrespective of consent. As far as jurisdiction is concerned, chapter 3 demonstrates that the only viable forum to litigate a collective action will usually be located at the defendant's domicile. However, this could be problematic in the absence of funding, considering that initiating judicial collective proceedings abroad is expensive. On the negative side of the balance, it should be added that collective redress instruments are not available in all fields of law and sometimes lack efficiency.

As a result, collective redress is an interesting tool that could possibly complement ADR[222] in fields that remain outside their scope. Similarly, collective redress appears to be particularly appropriate where numerous victims, who are geographically dispersed, suffer a damage that is individually low but globally huge. From an international perspective, cross-border collective redress entails as many advantages as ADR. Therefore, the choice of either instrument must be made on a case-by-case basis. The results of the questionnaire seem to confirm this fact: indeed, consumer associations believe that both ADR and collective redress are useful – with the exception of ADICAE, which believes that ADR represents a superior means to resolve disputes.[223]

Besides, collective redress may be constructed as an incentive for parties to first go through an ADR procedure, and consider collective proceedings as the *ultima ratio*. However, the development of ADR without collective redress would not give the right incentives. This has been underlined in the Netherlands, where discussions advocate the implementation of judicial collective redress in connection with the Dutch *WCAM* based on a voluntary settlement mechanism. It has been argued that the existence of a binding collective redress procedure would encourage parties to settle, as the alternative would not be 'no litigation at all' any more but go through collective redress proceedings.[224] To sum up, the added value of collective redress is evidenced and thus, the argument of opponents of this device is not viable.

ii. Competence of the EU

In 2008, the Feedback Statement on the Green Paper revealed that some industry representatives, legal experts and to a lesser extent public authorities challenge the competence of the EU to implement measures regarding collective redress. In their opinion, Articles 81, 114 and 169 TFEU, as well as the principles of subsidiarity

[222] On this argument, see also the analysis of M Stürner, 'ADR and Adjudication by State Courts: Competitors or Complements?' in Stürner et al (n 167) 11–29.

[223] Question 4.5 of the questionnaire.

[224] See the Dutch Consultation on a draft bill on Redress of Mass Damages in a Collective Action (2014), available at www.internetconsultatie.nl/motiedijksma/document/1177.

and proportionality, would limit the legislative competence of EU institutions, in particular as regards the adoption of a collective redress procedure applicable in every Member State – which corresponds to option 4 of the Green Paper.[225] They contend that further investigation is needed on this particular question before any measure is adopted. Moreover, in the Consultation Paper of 2009, some industry representatives argued that the EU would only have the power to enact provisions regarding cross-border collective redress.[226]

This argument is *a priori* valid: it is commonly acknowledged that the EU does not enjoy a general competence to legislate.[227] Rather, the institutions have to respect the principle of conferral. Besides, Member States' procedural autonomy should be preserved. Recently, however, the entry into force of the Lisbon Treaty, in combination with a relatively extensive interpretation of its wording by the CJEU, has amplified the possibility for the EU to regulate procedural questions.

As far as collective redress is concerned, two main provisions might constitute a relevant legal basis on which the EU could establish its power to legislate: Articles 81 and 114 TFEU – coupled with Article 169(2)(a) TFEU. This section voluntarily excludes other possible grounds. Specifically, Article 169(2)(b) TFEU is not examined, given that it severely limits the EU's competence.[228] Then, Article 352(1) TFEU equally remains outside the scope of this research project, as the unanimity of the Council would be required in order to implement provisions regarding collective redress. However, as earlier mentioned, the Council mainly represents Member States who do not show much enthusiasm about this new procedural tool. Finally, despite the non-negligible role of the CJEU in fostering private enforcement through the respect of the principles of equivalence and effectiveness, it does not have the power to provide national procedural rules on collective redress.

a. Article 81 TFEU

According to Article 81(1) TFEU '[t]he Union shall develop judicial cooperation in civil matters having cross-border implications, based on the principle of mutual recognition of judgments and of decisions in extrajudicial cases'. As Article 81(2) TFEU clarifies:

> [f]or the purposes of paragraph 1, the EU Parliament and the Council, acting in accordance with the ordinary legislative procedure, shall adopt measures, particularly

[225] Consumer Policy Evaluation Consortium (CPEC), Assessment of the economic and social impact of the policy options to empower consumers to obtain adequate redress – Final analytical report on the Green Paper on consumer collective redress submitted by the Consumer Policy Evaluation Consortium (2009) 9–10, available at kartellblog.de/wordpress/wp-content/uploads/Kommission-2009-assessement-impact-policy-options-adequate-redress.

[226] Commission, Feedback Statement of the Consultation Paper of 2009, 3.

[227] B Hess, *Europäisches Zivilprozessrecht: ein Lehrbuch* (CF Müller, 2010) 28.

[228] Art 169(2)(b) TFEU does not allow the EU to legislatively impose its own policy objectives. The purpose of this provision is to coordinate or reinforce existing national policies regarding consumer

> when necessary for the proper functioning of the internal market, aimed at ensuring: (…) (c) the compatibility of the rules applicable in the Member States concerning conflict of laws and of jurisdiction; (…) (f) the elimination of obstacles to the proper functioning of civil proceedings, if necessary by promoting the compatibility of the rules on civil procedure applicable in Member States.

Article 81 TFEU (ex-Article 65 TEC) is a potential legal basis on which the EU could rely in case it aims at regulating collective redress procedures in cross-border traffic. For example, the measure could consist in enacting an 'autonomous' collective procedure at the EU level on the model of the Small Claims Procedure. Similarly, Article 81 TFEU permits the promulgation of private international law rules, which would take into account the specificities of collective redress.

There are two fundamental requirements that any EU initiative based on this provision must comply with: first of all, the legislative measure has to be limited to cross-border cases. Although the interpretation of this requirement is controversial,[229] one must admit that this condition is fulfilled at least when parties are domiciled or seated in different Member States.[230] Second, the measure undertaken must concern civil matters. For the definition of this term, reference to the case law of the CJEU, which delineates this concept by reference to some EU instruments – like the BIa –, is useful.[231] Finally, it must be underlined that since the Lisbon Treaty, it is not required that the measure strictly aims at improving the functioning of the internal market.[232] Indeed, the previous version of Article 81 TFEU stated that 'measures in the field of judicial cooperation in civil matters having cross-border implications, [can] be taken (…) *in so far as necessary* for the proper functioning of the internal market' (emphasis added). Therefore, the wording of Article 65 TEC seemed to require a stronger link between this concept and the measure to be enforced. Nevertheless, strong debates arose regarding the interpretation of this provision following its elaboration: while some consider the internal market necessity as merely programmatic, others advocate for the imposition of strict competency limitations.[233] Eventually, Article 81 TFEU crystallises the earlier expansive interpretation of Article 65 TEC: henceforth, by using the

law. See DH Wendt, 'Kollektiver Rechtsschutz in Europa – Kompetenzen, Alternativen und Safeguards' (2011) 22(16) *Europaische Zeitschrift für Wirtschatsrecht* 616, 618; B Lurger, 'Art. 169 AEUV' in R Streinz (ed), *Vertrag über die Europäische Union une Vertrag über die Arbeitsweise der Europäischen Union*, 3rd edn (CH Beck, 2018) paras 32–33, available on beck-online.

[229] Hess, *Europäisches Zivilprozessrecht* (n 227) 34–36; S Peers, *EU Justice and Home Affairs Law* (Oxford University Press, 2011) 609–11.

[230] Hess (n 227) 35; S Leible, 'Art. 81 AEUV' in Streinz, *Vertrag über die Europäische Union und Vertrag über die Arbeitsweise der Europäischen Union* (n 228) para 8. This author highlights that the Commission advocates for a broad definition of the cross-border requirement. Accordingly, it considers that said requirement is fulfilled every time the case entails any international component.

[231] Leible, 'Art. 81 AEUV' (n 230) para 10; Peers, *EU Justice and Home Affairs Law* (n 22) 608.

[232] Leible (n 230) paras 11–12; Peers (n 229) 605.

[233] Hess (n 229) 33–34; E Storskrubb, *Civil Procedure and EU Law – A Policy Area Uncovered* (Oxford University Press, 2008) 43.

wording 'in particular', Article 81 TFEU does not require initiatives to be related to the internal market.

Then, Article 81(2) TFEU establishes that the measure at stake must ensure one of the goals listed in the provision. The catalogue is exhaustive.[234] Among other things, lit. (c) enables the EU to enact private international law provisions, and lit. (f) makes the adoption of measures enhancing the compatibility of Member States' civil procedural rules possible. The objective of lit. (f) consists in offering access to justice and effective legal protection.[235] Finally, lit. (g) encourages the development of ADR mechanisms.

Lastly, it is worth mentioning that Article 81 TFEU overrides the application of Article 114 TFEU,[236] which enables the EU to undertake harmonisation measures. This can be explained by the proper wording of Article 114 TFEU, which states that the provision is applicable '[s]ave where otherwise provided in the Treaties'. Where the EU shares its competence with Member States, the contemplated measure must respect the principles of subsidiarity and proportionality (Articles 5(3) and 4 TEU).

In light of these considerations, there is theoretically no obstacle to the enactment of an EU collective redress procedure that would deal with cross-border cases in conformity with Article 81(2)(f) TFEU. In case the EU were to rather enact specific private international law rules regarding collective redress and, thus, foster the interoperability of national laws in this field, then Article 81(2)(c) TFEU would be the appropriate legal basis. In any case, Article 81 TFEU is not restricted to a certain area of substantive law.[237] Therefore, a horizontal approach to collective redress would be possible under this provision.

b. Article 114 TFEU

If the EU institutions intend to harmonise[238] national procedural rules on collective redress, Article 114(1) TFEU (ex-Article 100a and 95 EC) is the relevant legal basis to examine. According to this provision, the Council, acting by qualified

[234] M Kotzur, 'Article 81 TFEU' in R Geiger et al (eds), *European Union Treaties – A Commentary* (CH Beck/Hart, 2015) 439.

[235] ibid 441.

[236] ibid 439. Against: Committee on Legal Affairs, Europeanisation of Civil Procedure: Towards Common Minimum Standards?, PE 559.499 (2015) 14–15, available at www.europarl.europa.eu/thinktank/en/document.html?reference=EPRS_IDA(2015)559499.

[237] However, the adoption of measures in the field of family law is submitted to the special legislative procedure, pursuant to Art 81(3) TFEU.

[238] In EU procedural law, this concept should be broadly interpreted. See B Hess, 'Procedural Harmonisation in a European Context' in XE Kramer and CH van Rhee (eds), *Civil Litigation in a Globalising World* (T.M.C. Asser Press, 2012) 160, who states that 'the term shall designate all kinds of the external influences to procedural systems. This approach encompasses the adaptation and reform of existing legal systems which are triggered by the competition between the national systems. (…) In European procedural law, a heterogeneous terminology is found ranging from approximation, coordination, cooperation, and harmonisation to unification'.

majority, together with the Parliament, may 'adopt the measures for the approximation of the provisions laid down by law, regulation or administrative action in Member States which have as their object the establishment and functioning of the internal market'. The content of Article 114(1) TFEU has been interpreted by the prominent *First Tobacco Advertising* case.[239] In this judgment, the CJEU ruled that the EU does not have a general and inherent competence to regulate.[240] Rather, any measure of approximation must be tightly linked to the establishment and the functioning of the internal market. Moreover, the competence that Article 114 TFEU confers on the EU has to be exercised in conformity with the principles of proportionality and subsidiarity. Exceptionally, Member States can derogate a harmonisation measure pursuant to Articles 114(4)–(9) TFEU.

Article 114(1) TFEU imposes three requirements:[241] first, there must be diverging national legislation in the particular sector that is to be the object of a harmonisation measure. Similarly, this provision is applicable when the enactment of future laws at the local level threatens the good functioning of the internal market. In this context, the CJEU clarified that the existence of differences between national laws does not automatically confer the right to harmonise. Furthermore, it is not necessary that all Member States have previously legislated in the field that is the object of the harmonisation measure. Then, these diverging national rules must constitute an obstacle to trade or threaten to act as such.[242] Therefore, this statement implies that a certain inter-state activity exists between various Member States.[243] In other words, in an integrated area, harmonisation is justified only if interaction between distinct territories is present.[244] Conversely, where all disputes remain local, no supranational act to harmonise is necessary.

Once these legislative differences are recorded, one has to verify that these lead either, to a restriction of the freedom of goods or services or to a distortion of competition. This is the second requirement necessary for the application of Article 114 TFEU.

[239] Case C-376/98 *Germany v Parliament and Council* [2000] ECR I-8419.

[240] ibid paras 83–84.

[241] Following the scheme suggested by F Geber, 'Rechtsangleichung nach Art. 114 AEUV im Spiegel der EuGH-Rechtsprechung' (2014) 1 *Juristische Schulung* 20, 22–23.

[242] I Maletić, *The Law and Policy of Harmonisation in Europe's Internal Market* (Edward Elgar, 2013) 43–45.

[243] eg in Case C-380/03 *Germany v Parliament and Council* [2006] ECR I-11573, the claimants were seeking the annulment of two provisions of Council Directive 2003/33/EC that restricted the advertising and sponsorship of tobacco products in the EU in certain types of media such as newspapers, periodicals and magazines. In this context, one of their arguments was that a large majority (99%) of the products concerned were marketed on a national basis. Therefore, according to them, the prohibition responded 'only very marginally to the supposed need to eliminate barriers to trade'. The CJEU rejected this argument by stating that the movement of newspapers, periodicals and magazines usually cross national borders and that this is even truer with the rise of Internet. Accordingly, the CJEU ruled that the harmonisation measure conformed to Art 114 TFEU.

[244] KD Kerameus, 'Procedural Harmonization in Europe' (1995) 43 *The American Journal of Comparative Law* 401, 403.

Finally, the approximation measure must aim at establishing an internal market (Article 26 TFEU). According to the case law that followed the *First Tobacco Advertising* case, it is not necessary that the measure only aims at improving the functioning of the internal market. Rather, the CJEU accepts that once it is established that the measure fulfils the requirements imposed by Article 114 TFEU, then it does not matter if this measure additionally pursues another goal – such as the protection of public health of consumers. In this case, the measure is still permitted by Article 114 TFEU.[245] In fact, it seems that a quite generous interpretation of the market-building requirement prevails, so that the link between the measure and its impact on the internal market is now loose.[246] If a measure aims at different goals at the same time, the main objective must serve as ground to set up the EU's competence.[247] As a result, harmonisation of procedure has to be based on Article 114 TFEU when it aims at improving the functioning of the internal market. If another objective is at the core of the measure, then Article 81 TFEU should be considered, but any act would be limited to international cases.[248] When the potential measure deals with harmonisation of civil procedure in a cross-border context and aims at smoothing the functioning of the internal market, Articles 81 and 114 TFEU overlap. They could both serve as a legal basis if no primary objective can be determined. However, this situation has never occurred yet.[249]

Both the Commission's Recommendation and the Proposal for a Directive on representative actions only aim to regulate the procedural aspects of collective redress. Is this technically allowed by Article 114 TFEU?

On the one hand, the mutual recognition of legal standing promoted by the Injunctions Directive and maintained by the Proposal for a Directive on representative actions certainly facilitates the start of cross-border proceedings. The attenuation of procedural differences has been welcome. Nevertheless, the reports on the Injunctions Directive, as well as the recent Fitness Check,[250] show that cross-border actions remain scarce. Therefore, one might wonder to what extent such a measure has actually contributed to the fostering of the internal market so far. In this context, the question is: is more harmonisation needed in order to stimulate cross-border litigation or is the regulation method inappropriate?

On the other hand, the harmonisation of collective redress mechanisms, as suggested by the Recommendation of 2013, is more difficult to justify for the

[245] Maletić, *The Law and Policy of Harmonisation in Europe's Internal Market* (n 242) 46–48.

[246] Maletić (n 242) 31–32, 46–48; W Frenz and C Ehlenz, 'Rechtsangleichung über Art. 114 AEUV und Grenzen gem. Art. 5 EUV nach Lissabon' (2011) 16 *Europäische Zeitschrift für Wirtschaftsrecht* 623, 624–05, who observe that once the other conditions of Art 114 TFEU are fulfilled, one can presume that there is a link between the measure and the functioning of the internal market.

[247] Case C-155/91 *Commission v Council* [1993] ECR I-00939, paras 19–21.

[248] Committee on Legal Affairs, Europeanisation of Civil Procedure: Towards Common Minimum Standards? (n 236) 13.

[249] ibid 14.

[250] Commission, Report on the Fitness check of consumer and marketing law SWD (2017) 208 final 101–05.

following reasons: to start with, this chapter has clearly shown that national legislation on collective redress are relatively heterogeneous (this chapter, I.A. to I.D.) and thus, this could theoretically justify the intervention of the EU. Nevertheless, although national differences exist, this is not sufficient for the EU to acquire a competence to harmonise pursuant to Article 114 TFEU. Additionally, these diverging national laws must create barriers to the freedom of goods or services or produce distortions of competition. However, it has not been demonstrated that the existence of diverse collective redress mechanisms among the EU actually represent such a barrier.[251] In particular, as far as consumers are concerned, it is arguable that the diversity of collective redress procedures looms large in their mind when they shop across the border.[252] So much so that the presence of a uniform collective procedure would surely not correspondingly lead to an increase of international activities because many other barriers would remain like the lack of trust to buy on the Internet, language differences, the additional cost that foreign litigation may generate, and so on.

It is true however, that the lack of uniform dispute resolution schemes in all Member States might hinder businesses when offering their products or services in other territories, as they expose themselves to different procedural systems and such a cost has to be internalised. Theoretically, the lack of uniform dispute resolution mechanism in Member States could deter EU citizens from concluding transactions in other markets as they might feel unprotected. Nevertheless, these considerations remain relatively theoretical: as far as businesses are concerned, studies show that obstacles to their international expansion are the fear of fraud, the obligation to comply with different tax laws, as well as the obligation to comply with different laws regarding consumer matters.[253] It is not clear whether this last category encompasses national procedural laws. As far as substantive law is concerned, harmonisation of consumer law must have significantly reduced the existence of this potential barrier for traders.

For now, the causal link between procedural harmonisation and the improvement of the functioning of the internal market is rather weak in the reasoning of the Commission. However, thanks to the favourable case law built up by the CJEU, regulation of collective redress pursuant to Article 114 TFEU cannot be excluded. The argument would go as follows: when consumers know that similar dispute resolution mechanisms exist in every Member State, they might trust that

[251] Wendt, 'Kollektiver Rechtsschutz in Europa' (n 228) 617–18.

[252] The same comment has been expressed by Wagner (n 147) 184 regarding ADR.

[253] See Commission, Flash Eurobarometer 186, Business attitudes towards cross-border sales and consumer protection (2006) 26–32; Flash Eurobarometer 224 (n 207) 20–27; and Flash Eurobarometer 331 (n 210) 31–48 according to which the risk of fraud or non-payment linked to cross-border transactions, as well as compliance with different tax laws and the obligation to respect different consumer protection rules represent the main barriers to the internationalisation of traders' activities. Then, Flash Eurobarometer 300, (n 209) 24–31 reveals that one-third of retailers surveyed would be interested in undertaking cross-border commerce if regulations were the same across the EU. Additionally, one-third of retailers also think that harmonisation would boost their cross-border activities.

in case of conflict, a familiar instrument will be available to vindicate their rights. Accordingly, one can argue that harmonisation fosters consumer confidence. As a result, this would increase cross-border trade and, thus, facilitate international commerce of goods or the provision of services. However, this reasoning could lead to the automatic ability to legislate under Article 114 TFUE, given that any harmonisation measure may abstractly simplify procedure in Europe and, thus, encourage citizens to shop abroad. It remains to be seen, which one of these two interpretative premises would prevail before the CJEU.

Although a literal interpretation of Article 114(1) TFEU indicates that the EU would lack competence to harmonise national procedural rules regarding collective redress, a look at practice could reverse this conclusion. Indeed, both the ADR and the Injunctions Directives have been adopted pursuant to Articles 169 and 114 TFEU and also aim at fostering access to justice.[254] Like collective redress, the harmonisation of ADR schemes among the EU do not *a priori* present any direct link with the functioning of the internal market. However, it could perfectly be argued that the harmonisation of rules regarding ADR mechanisms enhances legal certainty and encourages market players to undertake cross-border activities, as they are certain about having access to alternative means of dispute resolution abroad.

c. How Much EU Intervention is Needed?

Depending on the existence of political consensus, the EU might produce a more invasive legal instrument on collective redress in the future. Should this happen, the EU could lay down its competence on different grounds. On the one hand, Articles 81 TFEU would enable the EU either to regulate cross-border aspects of collective redress – such as jurisdiction, applicable law and recognition and enforcement – or to create an EU procedural tool available in cross-border cases – on the model of the Small Claims Procedure, for example. On the other hand, thanks to Article 114 TFEU, the EU could either approximate national legislation on collective redress or enact favourable procedural norms regarding financing, standing or costs, just to mention a few examples. In all cases, the Recommendation and of the Proposal for a Directive on representative actions show that EU institutions aim at regulating procedural aspects of collective redress, rather than adopting private international law norms.

The discussion that follows shows the benefits and shortcomings of regulating collective redress pursuant to either Article 81 or 114 TFEU. It is argued that the

[254] For an interesting critique regarding the use of these provisions, see H Eidenmüller and M Engel, 'Die Schlichtungsfalle: Verbraucherrechtsdurchsetzung nach der ADR-Richtlinie und der ODR-Verordnung der EU' (2013) 34(36) *Zeitschrift für Wirtschaftsrecht* 1704–09; G Rühl, 'Aussergerichtliche Streitbeilegung ausser Rand und Band? Zur Kompetenz des europäischen Gesetzgebers zum Erlass der Richtlinie über alternative Streitbeilegung und der Verordnung über Online-Streitbeilegung' in T Ackermann and J Köndgen (eds), *Privat- und Wirtschaftsrecht in Europa*, Festschrift für Wulf-Henning Roth zum 70. Geburtstag (CH Beck, 2015) 459–87.

benefits of an aggressive EU intervention would anyway remain limited as far as consumer matters are concerned. Alternatively, a combination of softer measures would be preferable, such as the establishment of appropriate private international law provisions regulating cross-border collective redress actions based on Article 81 TFEU, coupled with the improvement of collective redress mechanisms' efficiency and the development of ADR. In all cases, it is doubtful that ADR can exist without the 'threat' of collective redress.

Overall, regulating procedural aspects regarding collective redress through Articles 81 and 114 TFEU may have significant advantages, the most important of which is the achievement of some procedural 'uniformity' whereby parties are able to reduce the costs of litigation. Indeed, if parties presume that procedural rules are similar in every Member State, they will spend less time and effort in becoming acquainted with foreign laws. In this sense, both harmonisation and regulation of cross-border aspects of collective redress certainly bring down transactional costs.[255] As a result, this might incentivise citizens to bring their claims abroad. Moreover, the above-mentioned measures could be beneficial for traders too, as they would not have to internalise the costs of being submitted to different procedural legislation.[256] Finally, intervention of the EU in procedural matters fosters the modernisation of national procedural laws, in the sense that it establishes minimum standards. Similarly, procedural uniformity may reduce forum shopping and the race to the bottom. Although the positive aspects that convergence of national procedural laws generate should not be underestimated, the next lines reveal that any measure which attempts to modify procedural rules – either through Article 81 or 114 TFEU – might entail limited or sometimes hypothetical advantages. In other words, and without any intention to discourage the *rapprochement* between national procedural laws, it seems that the EU's initiatives have only partially fulfilled their objective, which consists in improving access to justice.

The first critique against the idea that procedural convergence may enhance cross-border litigation by reducing transaction costs is that EU legislative acts usually do not provide for exhaustive procedural rules and recourse to national provisions are often necessary.[257] Therefore, national specificities still remain, as long as fully-fledged unification is not reached. Even in this case, differences in the interpretation and the application of the legislation could materialise. A telling example is that of the EU Small Claims Procedure: according to

[255] L Visscher, 'A Law and Economics View on Harmonisation of Procedural Law' in Kramer and van Rhee, *Civil Litigation in a Globalising World* (n 238), 82; G Wagner, 'The Economics of Harmonisation: The Case for Contract Law' (2002) 39 *Common Market Law Review* 995, 1014.

[256] Although this argument originally concerns discrepancies regarding contract law, it should equally apply to civil procedure. See the Green Paper on policy options for progress towards a European Contract Law for consumers and businesses COM (2010) 348 final; likewise, Flash Eurobarometer 300 (n 209) 24 shows that '[o]ne-third of all retailers answered that they would be interested in making cross-border sales if laws regulating transactions with consumers were the same across the EU'; Wagner (n 255) 1013–14.

[257] M Tulibacka, 'Europeanization of Civil Procedures: In Search of a Coherent Approach' (2009) 46 *Common Market Law Review* 1527, 1545.

Regulation 861/2007, Member States have to provide for a procedural tool, which specifically deals with small-value claims. This procedure is optional and available for cross-border cases. However, it essentially relies on national laws, as Article 17 states. Specifically, the Regulation only establishes the procedural principles that Member States must respect and leaves the remaining questions, such as the availability of appeal, up to national legal orders. To sum up, as long as EU procedures rely on national laws, it is necessary for parties to acquire some knowledge about other legal orders if they want to appropriately bring or defend their claim. Along the same line of reasoning, some might argue that where a high degree of harmonisation exists, no private international rules are needed.[258] However, this implies that full harmonisation is possible and that it adequately tackles all cross-border issues. As mentioned earlier, this is improbable, at least for the time being.

In this context, the Injunctions Directive has illustrated the rather limited impact of harmonisation of civil procedural rules. Specifically, the two reports released regarding this Directive,[259] as well as the Fitness Check,[260] demonstrate that important barriers other than divergent procedural rules hinder entities from litigating abroad. It is true that, according to the questionnaire available in Annex III., two out of the three consumer associations interviewed would bring more collective redress actions abroad if the procedure were harmonised.[261] However, this should not constitute a 'free pass' towards a harmonisation measure. Naturally, cross-border litigation is more appealing where procedural rules are similar. But the questionnaire also highlights the presence of important obstacles to cross-border litigation that harmonisation would partially solve. In light of this, even if a certain degree of harmonisation is desirable, it cannot remove all obstacles to starting proceedings abroad.

To be more precise, the approximation of collective redress' procedural features according to Article 114 TFEU might not be able to fight all obstacles that cross-border litigation triggers, especially as regards consumer disputes, because these do not necessarily relate to the structure of collective redress: for example, how could harmonisation tackle language barriers or translation costs? Unfortunately, the costs of initiating proceedings abroad, even if minimised, would still remain too high in many cases to make litigation affordable. More importantly, perhaps, one might wonder whether the harmonisation of procedural aspects regarding collective redress would actually motivate citizens to shop abroad. In other words, it is not self-evident that procedural differences disturb the functioning of the internal market at least as far as the consumer law field is concerned.[262] To the best

[258] XE Kramer, 'Harmonisation of Civil Procedure and the Interaction with Private International Law' in Kramer and van Rhee (n 238) 124.

[259] Report from the Commission concerning the application of Directive 98/27/EC of the European Parliament and of the Council on injunctions for the protection of consumers' interest COM (2008) 756 final, paras 17–27; Report concerning the application of Directive 2009/22/EC (n 142) part 4.

[260] Fitness Check (n 250) 101–05.

[261] Question 4.7 of the questionnaire.

[262] Tulibacka, 'Europeanization of Civil Procedures: In Search of a Coherent Approach' (n 257) 1534.

of this author's knowledge, no empirical evidence shows that intra-EU trade would increase if procedural differences were erased.

In the same fashion, the ability of similar procedural rules to improve access to justice – as the Recommendation of 2013 on collective redress would like to – is questionable. Accordingly, even if collective redress procedures shared identical features, it is arguable that better accessibility to courts would be achieved. This is because access to justice hinges on the actual efficiency of the procedural tool at stake and not its similarity with sister-instruments. For instance, the test case model of collective redress would maybe perfectly work in Austria but not in Sweden, albeit these mechanisms would be one and the same. The reason for this is that procedural vehicles do not evolve in a vacuum. In fact, they are tightly linked to the judicial organisation of a given legal order, as well as to its culture and social environment. This has been demonstrated in chapter 1 regarding the US class action (chapter 1, I.A.). This is why as far as procedural law is concerned, one form does not fit all. In reality, when two collective redress mechanisms, which are structurally dissimilar, can nonetheless work efficiently, then access to justice is guaranteed.

Finally, as underlined earlier, Member States are currently undertaking important reforms regarding collective redress (this chapter, I.A.). Some latecomers are still in the process of enacting some kind of collective redress mechanism. In this context, it has been highlighted that EU legal orders often engage in a comparative law exercise in order to improve their own collective redress mechanism. As a consequence, harmonisation pursuant to Article 114 TFEU would not be an appropriate measure if systems are not 'mature' enough. Besides, the comparative law exercise undertaken by Member States may equally lead to the approximation of national legislation, with the difference that it follows a bottom-up approach and is not imposed by a supranational authority.[263] In an extreme case, a harmonisation measure might even disrupt the legislative process that takes place at the local level.[264] Besides, harmonisation might impose certain structural features to collective redress mechanisms that do not fit into a particular legal order. For example, if an EU measure imposes a mediation process as a pre-condition to the initiation of collective proceedings, this could fit in the Netherlands but not in a state where no ADR culture exists. Therefore, imposing such a process could increase parties' costs and make them lose time. In light of these considerations, national legislators are better positioned to evaluate what the relevant features of a collective redress mechanism should be according to their legal order.[265]

As regards measures adopted pursuant to Article 81 TFEU, the creation of a procedural system dealing with cross-border collective redress in parallel with

[263] Visscher, 'A Law and Economics View on Harmonisation of Procedural Law' (n 255) 78.

[264] Tulibacka (n 257) 1551; Z Vernadaki, 'Civil Procedure Harmonization in the EU: Unravelling the Policy Considerations' (2013) 9(2) *Journal of Contemporary European Research* 297, 304.

[265] Vernadaki, 'Civil Procedure Harmonization in the EU: Unravelling the Policy Considerations' (n 264) 304–05.

national provisions is not desirable. It creates complexity and increases work for national judges who are already overburdened.[266] Another problem is that this twofold system could create an important difference of treatment between parties whose disputes are purely domestic and participants to international proceedings.[267] Similarly, this discrimination problem could arise where coverage is only sector-based.

As a conclusion, although the advantages of a harmonisation measure or the creation of a cross-border procedure for collective redress are clear, these are not the best venues for the EU to act. In fact, the EU did not sufficiently prove the benefits of these measures in comparison with other alternatives. This is certainly due to the lack of clear information regarding their actual effect on the internal market. For example, it might be very hard to establish whether harmonisation has a direct impact on the rise of cross-border cases. For this reason, additional evidence should be gathered before ambitious measures such as harmonisation or the creation of a cross-border procedure are adopted. Among other aspects, it could be useful to have a clear picture about the number of international suits – including collective redress actions – brought during a certain timeframe.[268] Furthermore, more information on market players' behaviour would be welcome. In particular, it could be interesting to launch a Eurobarometer in order to measure whether the presence or the absence of collective redress modify traders' and consumers' behaviour. Finally, additional studies might further explain what incentivises people to litigate abroad and what barriers impede consumer associations and similar actors from starting collective proceedings in another Member State.

This book suggests another approach that does not condemn the above-mentioned measures but rather proposes the use of various instruments in order to foster access to justice. Such measures include the implementation of private international law rules on jurisdiction for collective redress actions in conjunction with other EU measures that aim at boosting the efficiency of national collective redress mechanisms, as well as the development of ADR. In other words, the modification of national procedures is excluded, unless it is absolutely necessary.

This approach is based on the following observations: first, the rights of the defendants do not seem to be in danger. In fact, Member States have been relatively cautious in their implementation of collective redress and, thus, there is no need for the EU to enact more safeguards for the time being. Besides, Member States'

[266] Vernadaki (n 264) 310. In a similar fashion, see also the comments of Storskrubb on the Small Claims Procedure ((n 233) 231–32).

[267] Tulibacka (n 257) 1539.

[268] See S Voet, '"Where the Wild Things Are". Reflections on the State and Future of European Collective Redress' forthcoming in M Loos and A Keirse (eds), Ius Commune Europaeum series 27–29, available at https://papers.ssrn.com, who recently collected national statistics on the number of collective redress actions brought in various Member States.

general rules of civil procedure represent a limitative framework within which any procedural vehicle should fit. In light of the above, it is doubtful that Member States would build up collective redress tools that do not respect the rights of both parties and, in particular, the rights of the defence. At least, no empirical evidence proves the contrary. Second, as explained above, states are already engaged in reforms of their collective redress mechanisms in order to improve their efficiency. Therefore, it might be preferable to let national legislators act at the local level, given their knowledge of the legal, political and social environment. In other words, the intervention of EU law into national civil procedure to maintain safeguards in collective redress cases is not justified.

From a structural perspective, this approach involves two steps: the first one consists in clarifying the private international rules regarding collective redress and in particular those regarding jurisdiction. Experience has shown that claimants – either consumers or representative bodies – struggle to bundle claims in a unique and affordable forum. It is argued that private international law has the power to resolve important cross-border barriers to access to justice. Second, measures increasing the interoperability of collective redress mechanisms – including perhaps a partial harmonisation measure – could be considered in order to resolve remaining procedural issues.

Certainly, this solution may not be the only possible approach to the question. However, it entails substantial advantages that are detailed here: first of all, the suggested solution respects the principle of subsidiarity, given that it focuses on cross-border aspects of collective redress but allows national legislators to work on the efficiency of procedural tools. In this sense, deference to subsidiarity reinforces the legitimacy of the EU's intervention. Moreover, if best practices are spotted through comparative law analysis, this can lead to the convergence of national legislation.

Second, the suggested approach brings clarity to the current landscape. As the next chapter shows, the application of private international rules on jurisdiction within the EU has been rather chaotic: because collective redress does not totally match the vision of EU private international law, the risk for forum shopping and legal uncertainty is significant. Nevertheless, private international law might not be able to tackle all cross-border obstacles.[269] Therefore, supplementary measures at the procedural law level should back up the private international law solution. A lack of coordination between these two areas could lead to undesirable consequences resulting in a waste of resources and inconsistencies. For these reasons, it is advisable to settle private international law issues first, and subsequently consider additional and more incisive measures regarding civil procedure. Naturally, this solution does not impede the development of ADR mechanisms.

[269] ibid 133.

III. Conclusion

Contrary to the US class action, collective redress is a much more colourful concept whose limits are sometimes difficult to grasp. Besides, this device aims at different goals and may assume various functions depending on the legal order. This certainly results from the great heterogeneity that characterises the numerous collective redress mechanisms adopted by Member States. As the first section of this chapter demonstrates, the structural elements of collective redress vary in terms of participation, rules on standing, certification criteria, costs and financing, availability of ADR, as well as interests and remedies. Interestingly, collective redress schemes usually possess features which are the opposite of the American class action. The unwillingness to reproduce the abuses that occurred on the other side of the Atlantic may explain this fact.

In light of such diversity, however, collective redress tools share some similarities. As a result, it was possible to come up with a classification of all existing collective redress mechanisms into four categories: the representative model, the class action model, the test case model and the Dutch model. In order to build up these categories, the structural elements that are relevant from a private international law perspective were taken into account. The objective is to facilitate the analysis in chapters 3 and 4: instead of observing how all collective redress mechanisms work in an international context, this exercise is reduced to the four above-mentioned categories.

The second part of this chapter underlines the role that the EU has played in the field of collective redress. Accordingly, an analysis of the documents released by the EU institutions is provided. This research projects puts the spotlight on important issues that may slow down the further development of an EU response to collective redress, such as the lack of political consensus and the insufficiency of empirical evidence. In this context, opponents of collective redress challenge the EU's intervention on two grounds: first of all, they argue that ADR mechanisms represent a better tool to resolve consumer disputes and thus, collective redress is not necessary. However, this work shows that collective redress has the power to reduce costs and seems to be helpful for (very) small-value claimants. Besides, opt-out-based systems are well positioned to deal with consumers' rational apathy. Finally, this device could act as an incentive for parties to settle. Besides, ADR instruments usually do not offer a better forum than collective redress in cross-border cases. Usually, victims have to either complain or litigate in the forum of the defendant's domicile. Secondly, opponents allege that the EU does not have any competence to regulate collective redress. In their opinion, either Article 81 or 114 TFEU would not constitute adequate grounds for the EU to intervene. Nevertheless, it was highlighted that both venues are potentially available.

Even though the EU could theoretically legislate on collective redress, it is fundamental to determine whether and to what extent an intervention is needed. The analysis provided above concludes that both the creation of an EU cross-border collective redress procedure or the harmonisation of national civil procedures are too invasive measures. It is not certain that they would adequately tackle all obstacles to cross-border litigation and thus, their impact on access to justice in consumer matters might very well be limited. As a result, this work suggests an alternative, which better respects the principle of conferral and subsidiarity. This approach consists in clarifying private international law rules on jurisdiction and resolving remaining cross-border issues with very limited (harmonisation) measures that would reinforce the interoperability of collective redress mechanisms. Thanks to the coordination of procedural law with private international law, synergies can be created.

3

Private International Law Analysis

The previous chapter described the characteristics that EU collective redress mechanisms usually possess. Although said mechanisms are quite heterogenous, they share important similarities, on the basis of which four main categories of collective redress could be created – the representative model, the Dutch model, the class action model and the test case model (chapter 2, I.E.).

Additionally, chapter 2 put the spotlight on the EU's desire to fulfil the current private enforcement gap. As far as collective redress is concerned, the EU could adopt a harmonisation measure or create a cross-border procedure on the model of the Small Claims Procedure. However, both initiatives have limited effects, in the sense that their capacity to improve access to justice is doubtful. In particular, their ability to resolve all cross-border litigation issues faced by consumers is uncertain.

Therefore, appropriate private international law rules on jurisdiction should be at the heart of a legislative measure regarding collective redress, since this discipline is in a good position to foster access to justice. Although collective redress actions and settlements challenge private international law in many ways, questions regarding applicable law, as well as recognition and enforcement, play a secondary role for access to justice purposes.

In light of this, the current chapter starts with a gentle reminder of the jurisdictional rules provided by the Brussels Regulation (recast) (I.), which are the ones that will usually apply to cross-border collective redress actions. Because only a primer on the Regulation is offered, references to secondary sources are less frequent than in chapter 1. Although the functioning of the Brussels provisions is well known, this reminder is instrumental to the rest of the chapter, since references to theoretical developments can be made in an organised manner and avoiding repetition. Thereafter, the second part of chapter 3 (II.) investigates how EU private international law rules apply to the four collective redress models created in chapter 2. The objective is to analyse whether current private international rules on jurisdiction offer sufficient access to justice to collective redress actions. Otherwise, an amendment of such rules should be considered in order to fulfil said policy goal. As usual, the chapter ends with a conclusion (III.).

I. Jurisdiction under the Brussels Regulation (Recast) (BIa)

Section I provides an overview of the content of the BIa. For the sake of this research project, the following analysis focuses on the rules on jurisdiction that might be used in a cross-border collective action. The objective of this section is to build up a strong theoretical background that will support section II. To be more precise, the functioning of EU private international rules on jurisdiction is first examined. Those rules will subsequently be applied to the four models of collective redress that are described in chapter 2 (I.E.).

In light of this, section A starts with an outline of the fundamental features of the Brussels Regulation (recast), including its historical roots (A.i.), its scope (A.ii.), and some general information on the type of jurisdictional rules it contains (A.iii.). Then, the present chapter explains how potentially applicable rules on jurisdiction in collective redress cases work. In particular, comments on Articles 4 and its two 'sister' provisions, Articles 7(5) and 8(1), are provided (B.). Then, Article 7(1) relating to contractual matters (C.), as well as Article 7(2), which covers matters related to tort, delict and quasi-delict (D.), and section 4 which governs consumer contracts (E.) are examined. Finally, a brief overview of the rules governing *lis pendens*, related actions (F.) and party autonomy (G.) is provided.

A. A Primer on the Brussels Regulation (Recast) (BIa)

i. *Historical Overview*

The BIa[1] is the EU legislation which codifies rules on jurisdiction, as well as recognition and enforcement of judgments in civil and commercial matters. The origin of this text can be traced back to the Brussels Convention[2] (BC), a multilateral agreement adopted in 1968 – and reformed in 1978, 1982, 1990 –[3] by the six former states of the European Economic Community, namely Belgium, France, Germany, Luxembourg, the Netherlands and Italy, pursuant to Article 220 of the Treaty of Rome.[4] The objective of the BC is to facilitate the free movement of judgments between Contracting States. Accordingly, the flexibility of the recognition and enforcement process shall only be achieved if common international rules on jurisdiction are established and followed by the participants. As a result, both elements were integrated in the BC.

[1] Council Regulation (EU) 1215/2012 of 12 December 2012 on jurisdiction and the recognition and enforcement of judgments in civil and commercial matters [2012] OJ L351/1.

[2] Brussels Convention on jurisdiction and the enforcement of judgments in civil and commercial matters (consolidated version) [1990] OJ C189/32.

[3] Convention of Accession of 9 October 1978 of the Kingdom of Denmark, of Ireland and of the United Kingdom of Great Britain and Northern Ireland to the Convention on jurisdiction and enforcement of judgments in civil and commercial matters and to the Protocol on its interpretation by the Court of Justice [1978] OJ L304/1; Convention on the accession of the Hellenic Republic to the Convention on jurisdiction and enforcement of judgments in civil and commercial matters and to the Protocol on its interpretation by the Court of Justice with the adjustments made to them by the Convention on the accession of the Kingdom of Denmark, of Ireland and of the United Kingdom of Great Britain and Northern Ireland [1982] OJ L388/1; Convention on jurisdiction and the enforcement of judgments in civil and commercial matters [1990] OJ C189/2.

[4] Treaty establishing the European Economic Community, available at eur-lex.europa.eu/legal-content/EN/TXT/?uri=celex:11957E/TXT.

In parallel, Members of the European Free Trade Association (EFTA) on the one hand, and Member States on the other, concluded the Lugano Convention in 1988, which was reformed in 2007.[5] This Convention basically mimics the Brussels regime as regards those states.[6]

With the entry into force of the Treaty of Amsterdam, the European Community acquired the power to rule on civil cooperation matters. In this context, the BC morphed into Regulation 44/2001, namely the Brussels I Regulation[7] (BI). The text of the Regulation is, however, largely inspired by the Convention. The rules on jurisdiction, as well as on recognition and enforcement contained in this Regulation, apply directly to the Member States and prevail over national laws.[8] Besides, in order to secure the correct and uniform application of its provisions, the CJEU is entrusted with their interpretation through preliminary rulings (Article 267 TFEU). On 10 January 2015, Regulation 1215/2012 entered into force and replaced Regulation 44/2001.

Since its enactment in 1968, the text of the Convention has been modified on many occasions. As a result, it is important to emphasise that the case law rendered under one version of the text is applicable to its successor where this text concurs. This principle of continuity is crystallised in Recital 34 of the BIa, which states that

> [c]ontinuity between the 1968 Brussels Convention, Regulation (EC) No 44/2001 and this Regulation should be ensured, and transitional provisions should be laid down to that end. The same need for continuity applies as regards the interpretation by the Court of Justice of the EU of the 1968 Brussels Convention and of the Regulations replacing it.

In light of these considerations, this chapter only refers to the provisions of the BIa, although the case law that is analysed below has been rendered under older versions of the text. Should textual differences between these texts exist, they will be pointed out as they arise.

It has to be highlighted that the proposal for the Brussels Regulation (recast) considered the opportunity to introduce a specific rule on the recognition and enforcement of collective redress actions at Article 37(3)(b).[9] Eventually, this idea was abandoned. According to the proposal, common rules on jurisdiction would have applied to collective redress actions.

[5] Convention on jurisdiction and the enforcement of judgments in civil and commercial matters (Lugano Convention) [1988] OJ L319/9 and [2007] OJ L339/3.

[6] See P Jenard and G Möller, Report on the Convention on jurisdiction and the enforcement of judgments in civil and commercial matters done at Lugano on 16 September 1988 [1990] OJ C189/57.

[7] Council Regulation (EC) No 44/2001 of 22 December 2000 on jurisdiction and the recognition and enforcement of judgments in civil and commercial matters [2001] OJ L012/1.

[8] Case C-25/79 *Sanicentral GmbH v René Collin* [1979] ECR 03423, para 5.

[9] See Commission, Proposal for a Regulation on jurisdiction and the recognition and enforcement of judgments in civil and commercial matters (recast) COM (2010) 748 final, as well as the comments of E Lein, 'Jurisdiction and Applicable Law in Cross-Border Mass Litigation' in F Pocar et al (eds), *Recasting Brussels I*, Studi e Pubblicazioni della Rivista di Diritto Internazionale Privato e Processuale 76 (CEDAM, 2012) 159–61.

ii. Scope of the Regulation

a. Material Scope

According to Article 1(1) BIa, the Regulation applies to civil and commercial matters whatever the nature of the court or tribunal. The concept of 'civil and commercial matters' has an autonomous meaning[10] and refers to actions of private law. Put differently, actions involving the exercise of public authority powers are not civil and commercial matters.[11] In this line, Article 1(1) BIa specifies that revenue, customs or administrative matters or the liability of the state for acts and omissions in the exercise of state authority fall outside the scope of the Regulation. Furthermore, Article 1(2) BIa explicitly excludes certain matters from its scope, namely questions regarding the status or legal capacity of natural persons (including matrimonial matters), insolvency, social security, arbitration, maintenance obligations, wills and succession.

Additionally, the Regulation applies to situations that involve various legal orders. In other words, the case at issue must have an international character for the Regulation to apply. Unfortunately, the exact meaning of this requirement has not been established either by the Court of Justice or the EU legislator. Therefore, interpretations differ regarding this concept.[12] Literature predominantly considers that the Regulation applies to claims whose components are connected to more than one Member State, whatever the nature of this element.[13] Along these lines, one might wonder whether a case which involves a Spanish citizen domiciled in Madrid, who concludes a contract with a Portuguese national domiciled in the same city, would fall under the scope of the Regulation, although the only international element is the nationality of a contractual party. This could seem far-fetched considering the fact that nationality is not a relevant connecting factor pursuant to the Regulation. However, this broad interpretation ensures a uniform application of private international law rules to cross-border cases.

b. Temporal Scope

According to Article 66 BIa, the Regulation governs legal proceedings instituted after 10 January 2015. Legal scholars suggest that the moment when proceedings are instituted should be determined by reference to Article 32 BIa regarding

[10] Case C-29/76 *LTU Lufttransportunternehmen GmbH & Co. KG v Eurocontrol* [1976] ECR 01541, para 3.

[11] Case C-814/79 *Netherlands State v Reinhold Rüffer* [1980] ECR 03807, para 8.

[12] AL Calvo Caravaca and J Carrascosa González, *Derecho Internacional Privado*, vol 1, 16th edn (Comares, 2016) 26–32; J Kropholler and J von Hein, *Europäisches Zivilprozessrecht – Kommentar zu EuGVO, Lugano-Übereinkommen 2007, EuVTVO, EuMVVO und EuGFVO*, 9th edn (Verlag Recht und Wirtschaft GmbH, 2011) 121–23.

[13] ibid 27.

lis pendens and related actions.[14] In light of this, the time when documents that institute proceedings are lodged with the court is the relevant one. This time might be slightly different in each Member State.[15] Article 66 BIa equally applies to authentic instruments registered, as well as court settlements approved or concluded after the above-mentioned date.

c. Territorial Scope

In light of Articles 68 BIa and 355 TFEU, Regulation 1215/2012 applies to all Member States except the United Kingdom, Ireland and Denmark.[16] However, since the United Kingdom and Ireland used their power to opt in, Regulation 1215/2012 applies to those territories.[17] This legislation is equally applicable to Denmark, thanks to the Agreement of 19 October 2005 between the European Community and the Kingdom of Denmark on jurisdiction and the recognition and enforcement of judgments in civil and commercial matters.[18]

iii. Types of Jurisdictional Grounds

The Brussels regime offers different types of rules on jurisdiction. To start with, the text establishes, as a general rule, that proceedings should be instituted in the defendant's domicile. This principle is outlined in Article 4 BIa. In certain circumstances, however, policy considerations dictate that courts other than the ones designated by the general regime should be given jurisdiction. For instance, consumer protection dictates that weak parties, like consumers, should be able to sue their contractual partners at the place of their domicile if they wish to. In light of the above, sections 2 to 6 BIa institute special jurisdictional rules, which exceptionally derogate from Article 4 BIa. As a consequence, the CJEU repeatedly declared that these special rules on jurisdiction should be interpreted restrictively and cannot go beyond the cases expressly envisaged by the Regulation.[19]

[14] A Briggs, *Private International Law in English Courts* (Oxford, 2014) 187; H Gaudemet-Tallon, *Compétence et exécution des jugements en Europe – Règlement 44/2001, Convention de Bruxelles (1968) et de Lugano (1988 et 2007)*, 4th edn (Lextenso éditions, 2010) 62–63.

[15] Briggs, *Private International Law in English Courts* (n 14) 187.

[16] For more detailed comments on the territorial application of the Regulation, see Calvo Caravaca and Carrascosa González, *Derecho Internacional Privado* (n 12) 203-05.

[17] See the Protocol 21 on the position of the United Kingdom and Ireland in respect of the area of freedom, security and justice annexed to the Treaty on the Functioning of the European Union and in particular its Article 3 [2012] OJ C326/295.

[18] Agreement between the European Community and the Kingdom of Denmark on jurisdiction and the recognition and enforcement of judgments in civil and commercial matters [2005] OJ L299/62; Agreement between the European Community and the Kingdom of Denmark on jurisdiction and the recognition and enforcement of judgments in civil and commercial matters [2013] OJ L79/4.

[19] See eg Case C-145/10 *Eva-Maria Painer v Standard VerlagsGmbH and Others* [ECLI:EU:C:2013:138], para 74.

Specifically, section 2 BIa provides alternative fora, whereby claimants may always choose to litigate either in the defendant's domicile or in one of the fora contained in section 2. As for sections 3 to 5 BIa, they create a protective and autonomous regime in matters relating to insurance, consumer contracts and individual contracts of employment. This means that parties whose claims fall under one of these sections cannot make use of Article 4 BIa or other jurisdictional grounds – save where otherwise provided. In other words, jurisdiction is exclusively governed by the rules of those sections. Then, section 6 gives exclusive jurisdiction to courts regarding certain matters. These courts are the only ones having jurisdiction. It has to be highlighted that the recognition and enforcement of judgments resulting from the misapplication of jurisdictional rules contained in sections 3 to 6 will be limited (Article 45.1(e) BIa). Finally, section 7 offers parties the ability to conclude their choice of court agreements to the extent that party autonomy is permitted. This ability is restricted for disputes encompassed within sections 3 to 6 BIa.

B. The Forum of the Defendant's Domicile (Article 4) and its Two Sisters (Article 7(5) and 8(1))

i. Article 4

Article 4 of the BIa (ex-Article 2 BC and BI) adopts the Roman rule *actor sequitur forum rei*,[20] which is always available unless other tribunals have an exclusive competence to rule on the dispute, or parties use their autonomy in order to submit their conflict to other courts. Specifically, this provision states that '[s]ubject to this Regulation, persons domiciled[21] in a Member State shall, whatever their nationality, be sued in the courts of that Member State'. In other words, the Regulation establishes that, as a general principle, people have to be sued in the court of their domicile, notwithstanding the application of other jurisdictional rules embraced by this text. In this regard, nationality is irrelevant. As a consequence, if a Canadian brings a lawsuit against a North American domiciled in Belgium, the courts of the latter country would have jurisdiction under Article 4 of the BIa.

[20] The first formulation of that principle is to be found in the Code of Justinian; see H Gaudemet-Tallon, *Recherches sur les origines de l'article 14 du code civil – Contribution à l'histoire de la compétence judiciaire internationale* (Presses universitaires de France, 1964) 10.

[21] The BIa determines when an individual or a legal person is domiciled in a particular territory in Arts 62 and 63 BIa. As regards individuals, the EU legislator did not adopt a uniform definition of 'domicile'. Instead, it sends this task back to Member States. As for Art 63 BIa, it opts for a different solution by providing a material definition of a legal person's domicile. In particular, this provision asserts that legal persons are domiciled at the place where they have their statutory seat, central administration, or the principal place of business. The statutory seat corresponds to the place where the legal person is formally constituted, the central administration refers to the location where the company is administered, and the principal place of business is the one where the commercial activity is undertaken.

Similarly, it must be highlighted that the domicile of the claimant is irrelevant. The courts designated by Article 4 BIa have a general competence to rule on a case, in the sense that their jurisdiction does not depend on the object of the dispute, the type of claim or the place where the factual or legal elements are located.[22] Finally, it is worth mentioning that Article 4 BIa allocates global jurisdiction to the courts of a Member State, but does not designate which one is locally competent. In order to pin down precisely the tribunal that has jurisdiction (*ratione materiae* and *ratione loci*), one has to look into the domestic law of the Member State in which the designated courts are sited.[23]

The solution provided by the Regulation fosters foreseeability and strikes a certain balance between the rights and obligations of the respective parties. Different justifications support the *actor sequitur forum rei* principle:[24] first of all, initiating proceedings at the defendant's domicile would facilitate the notification process, the gathering of evidence, as well as the recognition and enforcement of judgments or settlements, because the defendant's assets are often located there.[25] Secondly, the obligation for the claimant to litigate in another Member State generates additional costs. Therefore, this financial aspect acts as a shield against unmeritorious claims: accordingly, the claimant would only sue if the claim is valuable enough.[26] Finally, it is considered that the state of the domicile is the most appropriate to rule on the legal situation of the people located there.[27]

ii. Article 7(5)

According to Article 7(5) BIa (ex-Article 5(5) BC and BI), a defendant domiciled in a Member State can equally be sued in another Member State if he possesses a branch, an agency or another kind of establishment there.[28] This jurisdictional

[22] FJ Garcimartín Alférez, *Derecho Internacional Privado*, 3rd edn (Civitas, 2016) 91.

[23] Gaudemet-Talon, *Compétence et exécution des jugements en Europe* (n 14) 80; P Jenard, Report on the Convention on jurisdiction and the enforcement of judgments in civil and commercial matters [1979] OJ C59/18.

[24] For an interesting critique of the *actor sequitur forum rei* principle, see Calvo Caravaca and Carrascosa González (n 12) 280-83.

[25] M Virgós Soriano and FJ Garcimartín Alférez, *Derecho Procesal Civil Internacional* (Civitas, 2007) 123; D Bureau and H Muir Watt, *Droit international Privé*, vol 1, 2nd edn (Thémis Droit, 2007) 150.

[26] ibid.

[27] Virgós Soriano and Garcimartín Alférez, *Derecho Procesal Civil Internacional* (n25) 122–23; Bureau and Muir Watt, *Droit international Privé* (n 25) 150.

[28] It has to be highlighted that the concepts of 'branch, agency or other establishment' are equivalent notions and, thus, they correspond to the same reality. As a result, and for the sake of simplicity, the rest of this work only refers to the branch as a representative of the whole category. The CJEU established that, in order to qualify as a branch, an entity has to be under the control and the direction of the defendant (Case C-14/76 *A. De Bloos, SPRL v Société en commandite par actions Bouyer* [1976] ECR 01497, para 23; Case C-139/80 *Blanckaert & Willems PVBA v Luise Trost* [1981] ECR 00819, para 12). In the same fashion, it should be noted that an independent corporate entity would certainly not fulfil the dependency requirement, unless it acts as a branch on the market and third parties see it as such (Garcimartín Alférez, *Derecho Internacional Privado* (n 22) 101; Case C-218/86 *SAR Schotte*

rule is examined here because it shares important similarities with Article 4 BIa. In particular, it confers general jurisdiction on the courts designated by this norm.[29] However, these provisions differ in two significant ways: to start with, Article 7(5) BIa cannot be 'coupled with' Article 8(1) BIa, which enables the claimant to attract co-defendants in the domicile of one of them.[30] Then, contrary to Article 4 BIa, Article 7(5) BIa directly designates the tribunal that has jurisdiction at the local level, and thus there is no need to rely on national laws. Finally, only claims related to the activities of the branch may be brought pursuant to Article 7(5) BIa. In particular, these disputes might be related to the running of the entity or its relationships with third parties.[31] Both contractual and tort claims fall within the scope of this provision. Besides, it does not matter whether the execution of a certain operation occurs within the territory where the branch is seated or in another Member State.[32] Should Article 7(5) BIa be limited to this territorial scope, it would often overlap with either the forum for contractual matters (Article 7(1) BIa), or the one related to tort (Article 7(2) BIa). Hence, this provision would lose its value. Finally, yet importantly, Article 7(5) BIa remains available to consumers protected by section 4 BIa, which is analysed below (below E.).

iii. Article 8(1)

Article 8(1) BIa (ex-Article 6(1) BC and BRI) allows the claimant to sue all potential co-defendants in the domicile of one of them. Specifically, this provision states that

> [a] person domiciled in a Member State may also be sued: (1) where he is one of a number of defendants, in the courts for the place where any one of them is domiciled, provided the claims are so closely connected that it is expedient to hear and determine them together to avoid the risk of irreconcilable judgments resulting from separate proceedings.

Thanks to Article 8(1) BIa, procedural economy can be achieved, as it enables courts to rule on various but connected claims at the same time in an identical forum. However, the use of this provision is not unlimited. In particular, several restrictions, which are further detailed in the next paragraphs, circumscribe the application of Article 8(1) BIa. Therefore, even though judicial efficiency

GmbH v Parfums Rothschild SARL [1987] ECR 04905, para 15). On top of this, the branch must also have the appearance of permanency, have management and be materially equipped in order to do business with third parties (Case C-33/78 *Somafer SA v Saar-Ferngas AG* [1978] ECR 02183, para 12). In this sense, the mere presence of a letter box or a website page in a given Member State are not sufficient to establish jurisdiction.

[29] Garcimartín Alférez (n 22) 99.

[30] ibid 102.

[31] *Somafer SA* (n 28) para 13.

[32] Case C-439/93 *Lloyd's Register of Shipping v Société Campenon Bernard* [1995] ECR I-00961, para 22.

commands the accumulation of claims in the domicile of one of the defendants, this argument cannot alone justify the use of this provision.

To begin with, according to its wording, Article 8(1) BIa can only attract defendants who are domiciled within the EU. The previous version of the Regulation did not explicitly mention this condition, but this was clarified by the CJEU[33] and later codified in the recast of the Regulation. The application of this provision is only possible in the domicile of one of the defendants.[34]

Furthermore, Article 8(1) BIa clarifies that a certain connection must exist between the different claims at stake. In the words of the CJEU, the connection must be of such a kind that it is expedient to hear and determine the claims together in order to avoid the risk of irreconcilable judgments resulting from separate proceedings.[35] A glance at other language versions of the text underlines an important change of wording between the BI and the recast: it is not necessary that irreconcilable judgments could result from the non-application of Article 8(1) BIa. Today, it is sufficient that a risk of *contradictory* judgments exists.[36] In fact, the risk of contradictory judgments has to be interpreted in light of Article 29(3) BIa and the *Tatry* judgment.[37] In all cases, it is for national courts to assess the consequences that separate proceedings would have on the case at issue.[38] In this context, the CJEU clarified that it is not sufficient that there be a divergence in the outcome of the dispute. That divergence must also arise in the context of the same situation of law and fact. Such an abstract wording has triggered several requests for a preliminary ruling to the CJEU in order to shed light on the content of this concept. In particular, the Court has frequently been asked about the required degree of similarity that Article 8(1) BIa imposes between the claims at issue. For instance, the Court of Luxembourg first established that an action in delict cannot be accumulated with an action in contractual matters in the forum of the anchor defendant.[39] Later on, the CJEU introduced more flexibility in this reasoning by declaring that claims grounded on different legal bases do not automatically hinder the application of Article 8(1) BIa.[40] More than the nature of the claims,

[33] Case C-645/11 *Land Berlin v Ellen Mirjam Sapir and Others* [ECLI:EU:C:2013:228], para 55.

[34] Case C-51/97 *Réunion européenne SA and Others v Spliethoff's Bevrachtingskantoor BV and the Master of the vessel Alblasgracht V002* [1998] ECR I-06511, para 44.

[35] Case C-189/87 *Athanasios Kalfelis v Bankhaus Schröder, Münchmeyer, Hengst and Co. and Others* [1988] ECR 05565, para 12.

[36] I Heredia Cervantes, 'Artículo 8' in JP Pérez-Llorca et al (eds), *Comentario al Reglamento (UE) nº 1215/2012 relativo a la competencia judicial, el reconocimiento y la ejecución de resoluciones judiciales en materia civil y mercantil* (Thomson Reuters Aranzadi, 2016) 289–90.

[37] Case C-406/92 *The owners of the cargo lately laden on board the ship 'Tatry' v the owners of the ship 'Maciej Rataj'* [1994] ECR I-05439, para 52. In this case, the CJEU held that Art 22 BC (the predecessor of Art 30 BIa) 'cover[s] all cases where there is a risk of conflicting decisions, even if the judgments can be separately enforced and their legal consequences are not mutually exclusive'.

[38] Briggs (n 14) 288.

[39] *Réunion Européenne* (n 34) para 50.

[40] Case C-98/06 *Freeport plc v Olle Arnoldsson* [2007] ECR I-08319, para 46.

it is important to assess whether contradictory outcomes might be generated by separate proceedings.

The most recent case law rendered by the CJEU regarding patents equally illustrates that the degree of similarity between claims should not be interpreted too strictly. Initially, in *Roche Nederland*, regarding the infringement of an EU patent, the Court of Justice ruled that claims against several defendants cannot be joined under Article 8(1) BIa where these concern alleged patents infringements which are each governed by distinct national laws according to the Munich Convention.[41] Later on, however, the CJEU adopted a more flexible reasoning in a relatively similar situation: in particular, in the *Solvay* case, the Court of Luxembourg stated that Article 8(1) BIa is applicable where defendants separately committed similar infringements regarding the same products and in the same Member States, so that they infringe the same national parts of an EU patent.[42] This trend was confirmed by the case law issued in other areas of law. Said case law seems to tolerate the application of Article 8(1) BIa when distinct national laws govern the infringement at stake,[43] hence confirming the flexible approach adopted in *Solvay*.

Predictability is another limit to the application of Article 8(1) BIa. Accordingly, legal scholars consider that defendants must be previously linked by a certain relationship in order to be sued in the domicile of one of their pair.[44] As a result, Article 8(1) BIa should not be admitted in case of traffic accidents involving various responsible parties. Conversely, this provision would apply to joint guarantors, co-partners in an unlawful cartel agreement or in the context of an *action paulienne*.[45] In all cases, Article 8(1) BIa cannot be used when the purpose of the claimant is to oust the co-defendant from its natural forum.

C. Jurisdiction in Matters Related to Contracts (Article 7(1))

i. *General Aspects*

Article 7(1) BIa sets up a special forum for contractual matters. This forum represents an alternative to Article 4 BIa and assigns jurisdiction to courts that are closely connected to the contractual dispute at issue. In other words, this exception

[41] Case C-539/03 *Roche Nederland BV and Others v Frederick Primus and Milton Goldenberg* [2006] ECR I-06535, paras 26–31.

[42] Case C-616/10 *Solvay SA v Honeywell Fluorine Products Europe BV and Others* [ECLI:EU:C:2012:445], para 29.

[43] See eg *Painer* (n 19) paras 79–82 and Case C-352/13, *Cartel Damage Claims (CDC) Hydrogen Peroxide SA v Evonik Degussa GmbH and Others* [ECLI:EU:C:2015:335], paras 22–23, as well as the analysis of B Campuzano Díaz, 'El TJUE de nuevo con el foro de la pluralidad de demandados. Nota a la sentencia de 1 de diciembre de 2011 en el asunto Painer' (2012) 4(1) *Cuadernos de Derecho Transnacional* 245–55.

[44] Garcimartín Alférez (n 22) 140–41; Calvo Caravaca and Carrascosa González (n 12); Heredia Cervantes, 'Artículo 8' (n 36) 294.

[45] Heredia Cervantes (n 36) 295.

to Article 4 BIa is justified by the principle of proximity.[46] It has to be underlined that this provision allocates international jurisdiction but also designates which tribunal is locally competent. Thus, no reference to national civil procedure is needed.

In order for Article 7(1) BIa to apply, it is necessary that the case at issue enters the scope of 'matters related to contracts'. This concept has been the object of an autonomous definition.[47] In *Jakob Handte*, which concerned a dispute between a sub-buyer of goods and a manufacturer, the CJEU established that contractual matters do not cover situations in which there is no obligation freely assumed by one party towards another.[48] This means that, in cases where a single party assumes an obligation towards the other, Article 7(1) BIa may equally apply.[49] Besides, it should be emphasised that the existence of a contract between parties is not necessary for the application of this provision.

The CJEU's case law provides some illustrative examples regarding the application of this provision: in a case involving an association that claimed the payment of a sum of money to one of its members, the Court of Luxembourg admitted that this situation should be considered as a matter related to contracts. Specifically, the Court held that membership creates links between its members that are of the same kind as those which are created between parties to a contract.[50] In another judgment, the CJEU affirmed that the relationship between the payee of a promissory note and the giver of a guarantee falls within the meaning of Article 7(1) BIa, as the latter freely assumes to act as a guarantor by signing the note.[51] Finally, even though the existence of a contract is questioned, the CJEU ruled that Article 7(1) BIa is applicable. Otherwise, it would be sufficient for parties to automatically challenge the validity of the contract in order to displace the application of Article 7(1) BIa, and, thus, deprive it of its legal effect.[52] Finally, when the obligation assumed by one party arises *ex lege*, the matter should not be considered as contractual.[53]

When the case at issue is a contractual matter, the second step consists in identifying which of the three prongs of Article 7(1) BIa applies: first, Article 7(1)(a) BIa is a fallback rule that establishes jurisdiction for all types of contracts (ii.). Specifically, this provision states that the place where the obligation which forms the

[46] Case C-386/05 *Color Drack GmbH v Lexx International Vertriebs GmbH* [2007] ECR I-03699, para 22; Case C-204/08 *Peter Rehder v Air Baltic Corporation* [2009] ECR I-06073, para 32; Case C-381/08, *Car Trim GmbH v KeySafety Systems Srl* [2010] ECR I-01255, para 48; Case C-19/09, *Wood Floor Solutions Andreas Domberger GmbH v Silva Trade SA* [2010] ECR I-02121, para 22.

[47] Case C-34/82, *Martin Peters Bauunternehmung GmbH v Zuid Nederlandse Aannemers Vereniging* [1983] ECR 00987, para 10; 11; Case C-26/91, *Jakob Handte & Co. GmbH v Traitements Mécano-chimiques des Surfaces SA* [1992] I-03967, para 10; *Réunion européenne* (n 34) para 15.

[48] *Jakob Handte* (n 47) para 15.

[49] See eg Case C-27/02, *Petra Engler v Janus Versand GmbH* [2005] ECR I-00481.

[50] *Martin Peters* (n 47) para 13.

[51] Case C-419/11, *Česká spořitelna, a.s. v Gerald Feichter* [ECLI:EU:C:2013:165], paras 48–51.

[52] Case C-38/81, *Effer SpA v Hans-Joachim Kantner* [1982] ECR 00825, para 7.

[53] Case C-519/12, *OTP Bank Nyilvánosan Működő Részvénytársaság v Hochtief Solution AG* [ECLI:EU:C:2013:674], para 24.

basis of the legal proceedings is relevant to determine jurisdiction (iii.). As for the second prong, namely Article 7(1)(b) BIa, it sets forth an autonomous criterion for sales and services contracts. Accordingly, for these types of contracts, the court where the characteristic obligation is performed has jurisdiction. Finally, Article 7(1)(c) BIa explains the relationship between the first two prongs. In particular, it states that where Article 7(1)(b) does not apply, then one has to go back to the general rule of Article 7(1)(a). The transition from paragraph (b) to paragraph (a) may occur in various situations: first, when parties contractually establish that Article 7(1)(a) is applicable whatever the nature of the contract at issue is. Second, when the delivery of goods or the provision of services takes place in a third state. Third, for some authors Article 7(1)(a) should be applied when parties to a sales or services contract agree on the place of performance of the obligation to pay.[54] Fourth, certain authors consider that when the place of performance is too difficult to determine, then one should go back to Article 7(1)(a).[55]

ii. Article 7(1)(a): The Place of Performance of the Obligation in Question

Article 7(1)(a) BIa states that '[a] person domiciled in a Member State may be sued in another Member State: (1) (a) in matters relating to a contract, in the courts for the place of performance of the obligation in question'. Therefore, two steps are necessary in order to determine where claimants should litigate their contractual disputes: first, one has to find the obligation upon which the party bases the claim ('the obligation in question'). Then, the place of performance of this specific obligation has to be identified. These two elements are examined below in detail.

The term 'obligation in question' has been defined by the CJEU in *De Bloos*. As a preliminary point, it must be highlighted that this judgment was rendered under the auspices of the Brussels Convention, which sets up a forum for all types of contracts without distinction.[56] Consequently, many cases that were rendered at that time would fall under Article 7(1)(b) BIa today. Nevertheless, this case law is still useful to understanding the functioning of Article 7(1)(a) BIa. Going back to the CJEU's case law, in *De Bloos*, a Belgian firm (De Bloos) concluded an exclusive distributorship agreement with Bouyer, a business located in France. According to the contract, Bouyer transferred the exclusive right to distribute its products on various markets to De Bloos.[57] Subsequently, the latter started proceedings

[54] Garcimartín Alférez (n 22) 111. Against: AL Calvo Caravaca and J Carrascosa González, *Derecho Internacional Privado*, vol 2, 16th edn (Comares, 2016) 860; Gaudemet-Tallon, *Recherches sur les origines de l'article 14 du code civil* (n 20) 207.

[55] Gaudemet-Tallon (n 20) 204.

[56] Ex-Art 5(1) BC stated that '[a] person domiciled in a Contracting State may, in another Contracting State, be sued: (…) in matters relating to a contract, in the courts for the place of performance of the obligation in question'.

[57] *De Bloos* (n 28) Opinion of AG Reischl 1512.

in Belgium against its contractual partner, alleging a unilateral and unlawful breach of contract, without proper notice being given. Indeed, Bouyer considered that the contract had ended and, hence, entered into negotiations with another distributor.[58] On this occasion, the referring court asked the CJEU what contractual obligation(s) should be taken into account in order to anchor its jurisdictional power. The Court of Luxembourg clarified that the word 'obligation' refers to the obligation that forms the basis of the legal proceedings.[59] More precisely, this obligation corresponds to the contractual right upon which the claimant bases the action.[60] Therefore, the obligation in question does not always correspond to the characteristic performance.

The meaning of the Court's answer may first be illustrated by a simple example:[61] if a Spanish firm sues its contractual partner located in Germany for the payment of the price corresponding to a delivery of goods, the relevant obligation that determines which courts have jurisdiction is the obligation to pay. However, if the German purchaser sues the Spanish firm because the goods are defective, the obligation in question is the delivery of these goods. For distributorship agreements, such as the agreement in *De Bloos*, and similar complex contractual relationships, the answer to this question is not always straightforward. For example, should the obligation to give proper notice be the obligation in question? Instead, should the obligation not to sell products to other market players be taken into account? Or should the obligation to deliver goods, which was the principal obligation of Bouyer, be the relevant one? Unfortunately, this question was not clarified by the CJEU.

The second step of the reasoning consists in identifying the place of performance of the obligation in question.[62] In *Tessili*, the CJEU held that this place has to be understood by reference to the substantive law applicable under the private international law rules of the court before which the matter is brought.[63] To put it more simply, the court seised has to find the law applicable to the obligation in question in order to locate the place of performance. In the example mentioned

[58] ibid.

[59] *De Bloos* (n 28) para 11.

[60] ibid para 13.

[61] It is important to emphasise that today, this example would be governed by Art 7(1)(b) BIa, unless the place of delivery were located in a third state.

[62] Note that in *Shenavai*, the CJEU considered the possibility that a claim be based on various obligations. *Obiter*, it held that when more than one obligation forms the basis of legal proceedings, the courts where the principal obligation is performed have jurisdiction (Case C-266/85 *Hassan Shenavai v Klaus Kreischer* [1987] ECR 00239, para 19). This is the *accessorium sequitur principale* rule. Later on, the CJEU clarified another point: when the claim at issue is based on obligations of equal rank, then the *Shenavai* case law does not apply (Case C-420/97 *Leathertex Divisione Sintetici SpA v Bodetex BVBA* [1999] ECR I-06747, paras 39-40, 42). This means that national courts must locate the place of performance for each of the obligations concerned.

[63] Case C-12/76 *Industrie Tessili Italiana Como v Dunlop AG* [1976] ECR 01473, para 13; Case C-288/92 *Custom Made Commercial Ltd v Stawa Metallbau GmbH* [1994] ECR I-02913, para 26; Case C-440/97 *GIE Groupe Concorde and Others v The Master of the vessel 'Suhadiwarno Panjan' and Others* [1999] ECR I-06307, para 13.

in the above paragraph, which involves a Spanish and a German undertaking, if the Spanish firm seeks the payment of the price in the Spanish courts, these would have to determine what the law applicable to the obligation to pay is. Today, the law applicable to contractual obligation is regulated by the Rome I Regulation in civil and commercial matters.[64] According to this Regulation, the law applicable to the obligation to pay is the one designated by parties. In the absence of a choice of law agreement, then the law of the country where the seller has his habitual residence applies. In this example, and in case parties did not select the law applicable to their contractual relationship, Spanish law would govern the action, as it corresponds to the habitual residence of the seller.

The ultimate step is to look at Spanish substantive law in order to determine the place of performance of the obligation to pay. In this context, Article 1171 of the Spanish Civil Code establishes that, in principle, the obligation to pay is performed at the debtor's domicile, unless the parties agreed on another location. Therefore, the place of performance is Germany, given that the debtor is domiciled there. This means that Spanish courts should not accept jurisdiction under Article 7(1) BIa. Although the facts of this example seem quite simple, one quickly acknowledges the complexity of applying the *De Bloos/Tessili* case law. Consequently, the solution has been simplified since the enactment of the Brussels I Regulation for the most frequent types of commercial contract. Nevertheless, the parties can also avoid the application of this complex mechanism by locating the place of performance in the contract or concluding a choice of court agreement.[65]

iii. Article 7(1)(b): Sales and Services Contracts

Article 7(1)(b) BIa specifically deals with sale of goods and provision of services. It reads as follows:

> [a] person domiciled in a Member State may be sued in another Member State: (...) (b) for the purpose of this provision and unless otherwise agreed, the place of performance of the obligation in question shall be: – in the case of the sale of goods, the place in a Member State where, under the contract, the goods were delivered or should have been delivered, – in the case of the provision of services, the place in a Member State where, under the contract, the services were provided or should have been provided.

According to this provision, all contractual claims that derive from a sale of goods or a provision of services can be dealt with in the forum designated by Article 7(1)(b) BIa.

Article 7(1)(b) BIa directly designates the place of performance for sales of goods, as well as provision of services. Although the CJEU did not provide a

[64] Council Regulation (EC) 593/2008 of 17 June 2008 on the law applicable to contractual obligations (Rome I) [2008] OJ L177/6.

[65] While a choice of court agreement is submitted to the requirements of Art 25 BIa, an agreement on the place of performance is not (see, C-56/79, *Siegfried Zelger v Sebastiano Salinitri* [1980] ECR 00089, paras 4–5).

clear-cut definition of these two types of contracts, they should nevertheless be interpreted autonomously. One should not try to technically define the terms 'sale' or 'service' but rather identify whether the characteristic obligation could be one of a sale of goods or provision of services.[66] As a result, a contract whose characteristic obligation is the supply of goods has to be qualified as a 'sale of goods' under Article 7(1)(b) BIa. Similarly, a contract which has as its characteristic obligation the provision of services falls within the scope of services contracts.[67]

In this context, the CJEU had the opportunity to clarify that a contract whose object is to manufacture items thanks to the materials provided by the buyer and under his responsibility has to be considered as a contract for the provision of services. However, where the manufacturer provides the materials, and is responsible for the good execution of the work, then this would rather constitute a contract for the sale of goods.[68] On this occasion, the Court explained that the previous activity of manufacturing items before selling them does not affect the qualification of the contract as a sale of goods.[69] In another judgment,[70] the CJEU stated that, in complex contractual relationships covered by a distributorship agreement, although they imply the selling of goods, they are more likely to be considered as a contract for the provision of services rather than a sale of goods. According to the Court, the distributor provides a service to the grantor, by selling his products and thus, increasing his distribution. In return, the distributor earns the competitive advantage to be the sole reseller of the grantor's products in a given territorial area. Therefore, the purpose of the contract leads the Court to conclude that a distributorship contract of that kind cannot be considered as a simple collection of successive selling agreements that would qualify as a sales contract.[71]

As regards the concept of provision of services, its exact boundaries are still unclear. On the one hand, for instance, Berlioz considers that the provision of services encompasses any contract whereby a party is under the obligation to do or not to do something, for free or against remuneration, for someone's benefit.[72] The objective of such a broad meaning is to avoid falling too easily under the scope of Article 7(1)(a) BIa, and have to cope with its complexity. On the other hand, however, it has to be highlighted that some important judgments call into question the applicability of such a broad definition. For instance, in *Falco*, the CJEU

[66] Briggs (n 14) 268–69; Kropholler and von Hein, *Europäisches Zivilprozessrecht* (n 12) 173.

[67] *Car Trim* (n 46) para 32.

[68] ibid paras 40–43.

[69] ibid para 38.

[70] Case C-9/12 *Corman-Collins SA v La Maison du Whisky SA* [ECLI:EU:C:2013:860], paras 24–43.

[71] However, the CJEU acknowledged that 'a long-standing business relationship between two economic operators where that relationship is limited to successive agreements each having the object of the delivery and collection of goods' should qualify as a contract for the sale of goods. Case C-196/15 *Granarolo SpA v Ambrosi Emmi France SA* [ECLI:EU:C:2016:559], para 35.

[72] 'toute opération ayant pour finalité l'accomplissement par une personne, au profit d'une autre, d'un acte, positif ou non, à titre onéreux ou non' (P Berlioz, 'La notion de fourniture de services au sens de l'article 5-1 b) du Règlement de « Bruxelles I »' (2008) 135(3) *Journal du Droit International* 675, 717).

seems to limit the scope of services contracts in two ways: first of all, the Court states that the objectives laid down by the Regulation require Article 7(1)(b) BIa to be interpreted narrowly, as it is an exception to Article 4 BIa.[73] Secondly, the CJEU considers that in a licence agreement, whereby the owner of an intellectual property right simply commits not to challenge the use of this right by his contractual partner, no provision of services is provided. In other words, this reasoning seems to indicate that the mere abstention from one party or an obligation not to do something prevents the application of Article 7(1)(b) BIa.[74]

Overall, literature emphasises that two requirements must be fulfilled for a contract to qualify as a provision of services: an activity in exchange of a remuneration – that does not have to be monetary. For example, contracts for legal, tax or architectural services fall under the scope of this definition. Similarly, services offered by intermediaries for financial investments or by real estate agents are encompassed within the meaning of Article 7(1)(b) BIa.[75]

Furthermore, Article 7(1)(b) BIa establishes that the place of performance for sales contracts is the place where the goods are – or should have been – delivered. Similarly, as regards provision of services, the place of performance is located where the services are – or should have been – provided. In other words, this means that reference to national laws in order to determine the place of performance, as the *De Bloos*/*Tessili* case law provides, is excluded. Instead, the place of performance for these types of contract has to be interpreted in an autonomous manner, according to the origins, objectives and scheme of the Regulation.[76] Against this background, the CJEU ruled that, in a case involving a sales contract, national courts first have to ascertain whether the place of delivery is apparent from the parties' agreement.[77] In case contractual terms are silent on this particular issue, then the CJEU indicates that the final destination, where the goods were physically transferred to the purchaser, and where he obtained the actual power of disposal, is the actual place of performance.[78] The same rule is applicable mutatis mutandis to the provision of services. Nevertheless, issues could arise when the final destination of goods or services does not match the transfer of property, that is, when intermediaries are involved.[79] However, in *Car Trim*, the CJEU seems to endorse the ultimate place where goods are handled as the place of performance.[80]

[73] Case C-533/07 *Falco Privatstiftung and Thomas Rabitsch v Gisela Weller-Lindhorst* [2009] ECR I-03327, para 37.

[74] ibid para 31.

[75] Kropholler and von Hein (n 12) 169–71.

[76] *Car Trim* (n 46) para 47; *Color Drack* (n 46) paras 18, 24; *Rehder* (n 46) paras 31, 33; *Falco* (n 73) paras 20, 26.

[77] This is expressly allowed by Art 7(1)(b), which states that the place of performance corresponds to the place where services have to be provided (or should have been provided) 'under the contract' (*Car Trim* (n 46) paras 54–55). This includes Incoterms (Case C-87/10 *Electrosteel Europe SA v Edil Centro SpA* [2009] ECR I-04987, para 22).

[78] *Car Trim* (n 46) para 62.

[79] Briggs (n 14) 270.

[80] *Car Trim* (n 46) para 60.

When the contract has to be performed in various locations within a single Member State or in different Member States, the CJEU indicates that the relevant place is the one which presents the closest linking factor with the contract at issue. Most of the time, this place corresponds to the place where the main delivery of goods or provision of services is carried out, according to economic criteria.[81] This particular location has to first be inferred from the contract.[82] Alternatively, national courts have to take into account where, in fact, the majority of activities were carried out.[83] Eventually, if the principal place of performance cannot be determined, then the claimant may sue at whichever location of the delivery.[84] In this context, in a contract involving air transport services, the CJEU held that a passenger may alternatively sue the airline company, which is liable for the cancellation of his flight, at the place of departure or arrival. In the opinion of the Court, these two locations present a close linking factor with the contract.[85] On another occasion involving an agency contract, the CJEU clarified that where the place of performance cannot be inferred from the contract and no main activity can be identified, then the agent's domicile is deemed to be the place that presents the closest linking factor with the contract.[86] This result is in contrast with the previous case law of the CJEU.[87] Indeed, it seems that the Court intends to reduce the fora available to claimants when the place of performance is difficult to locate, as it establishes an alternative forum in the agent's domicile. It looks like the Court wanted to avoid the conclusion that no principal performance can be identified and, thus, allocate jurisdiction to a multiplicity of courts.

D. The Place Where the Damage Occurred (Article 7(2))

i. General Aspects

In matters relating to tort, delict or quasi-delict, a claimant may initiate proceedings 'in the courts for the place where the harmful event occurred or may occur'. For the sake of simplicity, this category is referred to as 'matters relating to tort'. Indeed, the three distinct concepts involved in Article 7(2) BIa reflect the existence of different national legal traditions and only means that this provision covers strict, as well as fault-based liability.[88] Proximity and good administration of justice

[81] *Color Drack* (n 46) para 40; *Rehder* (n 46) para 35; *Wood Floor* (n 46) para 31.
[82] *Wood Floor* (n 46) paras 38–39.
[83] ibid para 40.
[84] *Color Drack* (n 46) para 42; *Rehder* (n 46) para 44.
[85] *Rehder* (n 46) paras 43–44.
[86] *Wood Floor* (n 46) para 42.
[87] U Grušić, 'Jurisdiction in Complex Contracts under the Brussels I Regulation' (2011) 7(2) *Journal of Private International Law* 321, 328.
[88] U Magnus and P Mankowski, *Brussels I Regulation*, European Commentaries on Private International Law, 2nd edn (Sellier European Law Publishers, 2011) 234.

both command the existence of such a forum. On many occasions, the Court of Justice has stated that this special jurisdictional ground relies on 'a particularly close connecting factor between a dispute and the court which may be called upon to hear it, with a view to the efficacious conduct of the proceedings'.[89] Finally, it must be underlined that Article 7(2) BIa designates international, as well as local jurisdiction.

The type of actions encompassed within matters related to tort are not limited to actions for damages. In this sense, the text makes clear that preventive actions fall under the scope of Article 7(2) BIa, as it states that proceedings can be started at the place where the harmful event 'may' occur. Although there is no room for doubt today, it must be highlighted that the old text of the Brussels Convention did not expressly foresee this possibility. Fortunately, the CJEU came to the rescue in *Henkel*: in its judgment, the Court of Justice clarified that a preventive action brought by a consumer association in order to prohibit a German trader from using unlawful terms and conditions in his relationship with Austrian consumers fell within the scope of Article 7(2) BIa. This solution subsequently crystallised in the BI. Additionally, negative actions seeking to establish the absence of liability enter the scope of the forum for matters related to tort.[90]

ii. Matters Related to Tort

In *Kalfelis*, the CJEU established that two requirements must be met in order for a claim to be related to tort: first of all, the claim is not covered by Article 7(1) BIa on contractual matters, and secondly, the claim must aim at determining the defendant's liability.[91] In other words, the CJEU has opted for a negative and autonomous definition. Hence, in order to ascertain whether an action is a matter related to tort, it is necessary to determine first whether, in light of the EU case law, it is contractual in nature. Specifically, in *Rudolf Gabriel*, the Court of Justice established that national courts have to examine first whether Article 17 BIa applies, as it constitutes a *lex specialis* in relation to Article 7(1) BIa. Subsequently, if the case at issue is not a matter related to contracts, then national courts may envisage the application of Article 7(2) BIa. Indeed, in order for the latter to apply, the former must necessarily be discarded.[92]

[89] Case C-21/76 *Handelskwekerij G. J. Bier BV v Mines de potasse d'Alsace SA* [1976] ECR 01735, para 11. See also Case C-220/88 *Dumez France SA and Tracoba SARL v Hessische Landesbank and Others* [1990] ECR I-00049, para 17; Case C-68/93 *Fiona Shevill, Ixora Trading Inc., Chequepoint SARL and Chequepoint International Ltd v Presse Alliance SA* [1995] ECR I-00415, para 19; Case C-364/93 *Antonio Marinari v Lloyds Bank plc and Zubaidi Trading Company* [1995] ECR I-02719, para 10; *Réunion Européenne* (n 34) para 27.

[90] Case C-133/11 *Folien Fischer AG and Fofitec AG v Ritrama SpA* [ECLI:EU:C:2012:664].

[91] *Kalfelis* (n 35) para 17.

[92] Case C-96/00 *Rudolf Gabriel* [2002] ECR I-06367, paras 33–36. Confirmed by *Engler* (n 49) paras 29–32.

If Article 7(1) and 7(2) BIa are mutually exclusive, does it mean that every action which is not contractual in nature falls within the scope of matters related to tort? It seems that the answer to this question is negative. This may be illustrated by the reasoning of the CJEU in *Reichert*, a case in which a bank brought an *action paulienne* against the Reicherts for having transferred the ownership of an immovable property to their son. In its judgment, the Court of Justice stated that the action at issue was not a matter related to tort, given that it did not aim at establishing the defendant's liability. Besides, it was unlikely that this action would fall under Article 7(1) BIa, as there was no obligation freely assumed either by the bank or the Reicherts. As a result, it appeared that only Article 4 BIa was available in this case. Apart from those borderline cases, it has to be emphasised that the range of disputes covered by Article 7(2) BIa remains broad.[93]

Finally, the CJEU had the opportunity to clarify two important points: first, different actions, which are nevertheless based on a similar set of facts, cannot be accumulated in a unique forum, even though this is justified by sound administration of justice.[94] This unfortunately leads to the fragmentation of litigation.[95] Second, the CJEU held that actions related to pre-contractual negotiations fall within the scope of 'matters relating to tort'. Specifically, the Court of Justice considers that the breaking off of negotiations does not constitute the breach of an obligation freely assumed by one party towards the other. Rather, it may be a violation of a rule of law, namely the obligation to act in good faith.[96]

The abstract wording of Article 7(2) BIa has to be considered in very different kinds of situations, which might sometimes generate complexities. In light of the above, the case law of the CJEU is an important guideline to understand this provision. In the following paragraphs, some of the difficulties that have arisen in connection with the application of Article 7(2) BIa are discussed. These difficulties essentially concern the location of the place where the harmful event occurred.

iii. The Place Where the Harmful Event Occurred or May Occur

a. The Dissociation Between the Place Giving Rise to the Damage and its Materialisation

In *Mines de Potasse d'Alsace*,[97] an undertaking located in France (Mines de Potasse d'Alsace) discharged chlorides into the waters of the Rhine, which increased their

[93] Interestingly, Mankowski drafted a complete list of matters that may fall within the scope of Art 7(2) BIa. Among others, this provision may apply to antitrust matters; unfair commercial practices; copyright, patent or trade mark infringements; product liability or non-contractual liability from defective goods; environmental damage; torts committed on the capital markets; and prospectus liability (Magnus and Mankowski, *Brussels I Regulation* (n 88) 236–38).

[94] *Kalfelis* (n 35) para 21.

[95] Gaudemet-Tallon (n 20) 174–75.

[96] Case C-334/00 *Fonderie Officine Meccaniche Tacconi SpA v Heinrich Wagner Sinto Maschinenfabrik GmbH (HWS)* [2002] ECR I-07357, paras 24–25.

[97] *Mines de Potasse d'Alsace* (n 89) paras 2–6.

level of salinity. Bier, an undertaking located in the Netherlands and engaged in horticulture, waters and irrigates its seed-beds with these waters. In this context, Bier had to take costly measures in order to limit the damage that poor quality waters made to its plantations. Consequently, Bier and Stichting Reinwater, an association that promotes the improvement of the quality of the waters of the Rhine, initiated proceedings in the court of first instance of Rotterdam, alleging that the conduct of Mines de Potasse d'Alsace was illegal and caused a damage to Bier's horticultural business. The court at Rotterdam declared that it had no jurisdiction under Article 7(2) BIa. Indeed, it considered that the place where the damage occurred was located in France. As a result, the claimants lodged an appeal in the Court of Appeal in The Hague, which in turn referred to the CJEU for preliminary ruling. In particular, the referring court asked the Court of Justice whether 'the place where the damage occurred' under Article 7(2) BIa should be interpreted as the place where the damage became apparent or the place where the event having the damage as its sequel occurred.

In its judgment,[98] the CJEU held that the two above-mentioned connecting factors were of equal importance. Depending on the circumstances, they may both allocate jurisdiction to courts which are well placed for gathering of evidence or conducting proceedings. On the one hand, in case the place giving rise to the harmful event is favoured, it is likely that Article 7(2) BIa would consequently lose its effect, as this place would often coincide with the domicile of the defendant (Article 4 BIa). On the other hand, accepting the place where the damage manifested itself as the only connecting factor would impede courts that are close to the cause of the damage from having jurisdiction. As a conclusion, the CJEU considered that the claimant might initiate proceedings either in the courts of the place where the damage occurred (*Erfolgsort*), or in the courts of the place where the event giving rise to the harmful event took place (*Handlungsort*).

b. Materialisation of the Damage in Various Member States

In *Shevill*, the Court of Justice was confronted for the first time with damage which materialised in more than one Member State. In this context, the CJEU had to assist the referring court to determine where the place of the damage was. The facts of the case can be summarised as follows:[99] Press Alliance, a publisher located in France, published various press articles regarding Fiona Shevill, a national domiciled in the United Kingdom, and Chequepoint, a *bureau de change* and her former employer whose seat was in France. These press articles were published in *France-Soir*, which is essentially distributed in France. Considering that these articles were defamatory, as they implied that they had participated in drug trafficking and money laundering, Miss Shevill and Chequepoint – followed by its

[98] ibid paras 15–25.
[99] *Shevill* (n 89) paras 2–16.

sister company operating in the United Kingdom, Ixora Trading Inc, and its mother company located in Belgium – brought proceedings for damages suffered in the United Kingdom against Press Alliance in the British courts.

In the circumstances such as those in the case at issue, the Court of Justice held that the place of the event giving rise to the harmful event corresponds to the location where the publisher is established. Indeed, this is where the press article was issued and put into circulation.[100] As for the place where the damage actually materialises, it has to be located where the defamatory article was distributed and where the victim alleged to have suffered injury to his/her reputation.[101] Importantly, the CJEU pointed out that the court of the place of the event giving rise to the damage has jurisdiction to rule on the whole damage. However, the court of the place where the damage occurred has a limited territorial jurisdiction: it can only rule on the harm that took place within the state where the court seised is established.[102] In this sense, the Court of Justice departs from German law, which allows courts to order compensation for the whole damage, whatever the basis of their jurisdiction.[103] As Advocate General Darmon states, this solution would certainly encourage forum shopping. Besides, it is doubtful that the court of the place where the damage materialised has sufficient proximity with the dispute to rule on it in its entirety.[104] Nevertheless, it must be admitted that the solution of the Court of Luxembourg might trigger conflicting judgments.[105]

E. Special Jurisdiction for Consumer Matters (Section 4)

i. General Aspects

Section 4 BIa establishes a special rule on jurisdiction for certain categories of consumers, which are deemed to be weaker than their contractual partners. In order to protect them from the consequences of this uneven playing field, the EU legislator allows certain consumers to 'thwart' the general jurisdictional regime established by the Regulation.[106] The result is that these consumers can only be sued in the courts of their domicile according to Article 18(2) BIa. This objective is highlighted in Recital 18 of the Regulation and has been made explicit by the CJEU. For instance in *Shearson*, the Court affirmed that section 4

> is inspired by the concern to protect the consumer as the party deemed to be economically weaker and less experienced in legal matters than the other party to the contract, and the consumer must not therefore be discouraged from suing by being compelled to

[100] ibid para 24.
[101] ibid para 29.
[102] ibid paras 25, 30.
[103] *Shevill* (n 89) Opinion of AG Darmon, para 30.
[104] ibid paras 67, 71.
[105] ibid para 72.
[106] Jenard, Report on the Convention on jurisdiction and the enforcement of judgments in civil and commercial matters (n 23) 28.

> bring his action before the courts in the [Member] State in which the other party to the contract is domiciled.[107]

Finally, it should be reminded that the provisions of section 4 have to be interpreted in a restrictive manner, given that they constitute an exception to Article 4 BIa.

The wording of section 4 has evolved over time. Hence, case law must be analysed carefully according to the different versions of the text that have been adopted. However, where the texts concur, the case law rendered under the older versions of section 4 has to be followed. Historically, the Brussels Convention only covered a limited number of contracts. Later, section 4 was extended in order to match the growing protection that was offered to consumers under national law.[108] Finally, the text was further extended in order to encompass sales on the Internet.[109] Today, three provisions compose section 4 BIa: first of all, Article 17 sets the boundaries of the material scope of the section. Then, Article 18 clarifies the jurisdictional ground for consumer matters. Finally, Article 19 deals with party autonomy and frames the possibility for parties to conclude choice of court agreements.

As already mentioned, section 4 applies autonomously, that is, irrespective of other jurisdictional grounds. In other words, the application of section 4 is mandatory and hence, displaces the general regime established by the Regulation. There are, however, two exceptions to this rule: the first one is Article 6 BIa, which deals with defendants whose domicile is not located in a Member State. In principle, national rules of private international law apply in order to determine which court has jurisdiction over non-EU defendants. Nevertheless, the recast of the Brussels Regulation introduced an 'exception to the exception' in Article 18(1). Accordingly, it is henceforth possible for a consumer to initiate proceedings in the court of his domicile against a defendant located in a third state. It should be pointed out that this solution does not work the other way around. The second exception is materialised in Article 7(5) BIa, which enables consumers to bring their action in the courts where the branch of a company is seated. Finally, it should be underlined that section 3 relating to insurance, as well as section 6 on exclusive jurisdiction, prevail over section 4.

ii. The Notion of Consumer and the Types of Contracts Covered

As mentioned earlier, Article 17 BIa designates the types of contracts that may fall under the application of section 4. *En passant*, this provision defines

[107] Case C-89/91 *Shearson Lehmann Hutton Inc. v TVB Treuhandgesellschaft für Vermögensverwaltung und Beteiligungen mbH* [1993] ECR I-00139, para 18.

[108] P Schlosser, Report on the Convention on the Association of the Kingdom of Denmark, Ireland and the United Kingdom of Great Britain and Northern Ireland to the Convention on jurisdiction and the enforcement of judgments in civil and commercial matters and to the Protocol on its interpretation by the Court of Justice [1979] OJ C59/71.

[109] Gaudemet-Tallon (n 20) 294–95.

what a consumer is for the sake of the Regulation. Article 17 BIa reads as follows:

> 1. In matters relating to a contract concluded by a person, the consumer, for a purpose which can be regarded as being outside his trade or profession, jurisdiction shall be determined by this Section, without prejudice to Article 6 and point 5 of Article 7, if:
>
> (a) it is a contract for the sale of goods on instalment credit terms;
> (b) it is a contract for a loan repayable by instalments, or for any other form of credit, made to finance the sale of goods; or
> (c) in all other cases, the contract has been concluded with a person who pursues commercial or professional activities in the Member State of the consumer's domicile or, by any means, directs such activities to that Member State or to several States including that Member State, and the contract falls within the scope of such activities.
>
> 2. Where a consumer enters into a contract with a party who is not domiciled in a Member State but has a branch, agency or other establishment in one of the Member States, that party shall, in disputes arising out of the operations of the branch, agency or establishment, be deemed to be domiciled in that Member State.
>
> 3. This Section shall not apply to a contract of transport other than a contract which, for an inclusive price, provides for a combination of travel and accommodation.

To start with, the concept of consumer was first defined by the CJEU[110] and then crystallised in the text of the Convention, as amended in 1978. Accordingly, a consumer is a person who concludes a contract for a purpose that is not related to his trade or profession. In assessing whether a party is a consumer, national courts must take into account the position of this party in a particular contractual relationship. Hence, the subjective situation of a person is irrelevant.[111] Furthermore, the Court of Justice had the occasion to clarify that the protective forum is available to a final consumer who has not assigned his rights to another party.[112] Finally, although Article 17 does not explicitly mention it, it implies that the contractual partner of a consumer protected by section 4 has to be a professional. In other words, section 4 is not applicable to private parties, contracts between consumers and contracts between a private party and a consumer.[113]

Contrary to Article 7(1) BIa, the application of section 4 requires the actual conclusion of a contract between a consumer and a professional. This has been clarified by the CJEU in a series of judgments regarding prize notification.[114] Specifically in *Illsinger*, Schlank & Schick, a German company, sent a letter personally addressed to Ms Illsinger, domiciled in Austria, according to which she was the

[110] Case C-150/77 *Bertrand v Paul Ott KG* [1978] ECR 01431, para 21.
[111] Case C-269/95 *Francesco Benincasa v Dentalkit Srl* [1997] ECR I-03767, para 16.
[112] Case C-167/00 *Verein für Konsumenteninformation v Karl Heinz Henkel* [2002] ECR I-08111; *Shearson*, (n 107).
[113] Magnus and Mankowski (n 88) 377; Kropholler and von Hein (n 12) 327.
[114] *Rudolf Gabriel* (n 92); *Engler* (n 49); Case C-180/06 *Renate Ilsinger v Martin Dreschers* [2009] ECR I-03961.

winner of a prize. Following the instructions of the company, Ms Illsinger tore off a coupon that she joined to a 'prize claim certificate' and sent it back to Schlank & Schick with the objective to cash the prize in. Ms Illsinger argued that she simultaneously placed a trial order, but this fact was contested by the company. In any case, it should be highlighted that the obtaining of the prize did not depend on an order of goods. Subsequently, Ms Illsinger initiated proceedings in the Austrian courts against Schlank & Schick, seeking the payment of the prize. In this context, the referring court asked the CJEU whether this action was contractual in nature within the meaning of Article 17 BIa. In its answer, the Court of Justice declared that in order for section 4 to apply, a contract must be concluded between the parties. This would be the case where the professional manifests an unconditional willingness to pay the prize to consumers who accept the offer. The CJEU added that the object of this offer must be sufficiently clear and precise, as to generate a link of a contractual nature. If such a contractual link cannot be established, Article 17 BIa could apply if the consumer makes an order of goods to the professional, following the prize notification. In this case, a claim for the payment of the prize would be non-dissociable from the order and would, thus, enter the scope of this provision.[115]

There are three types of contracts contained in Article 17(1) BIa: contracts for the sale of goods on instalment credit terms (Article 17(1)(a)); contracts of loan or credit that aim at financing a purchase of goods (Article 17(1)(b)); and all other contracts that entertain a special connection with the consumer's domicile (Article 17(1)(c)).

The sale of goods on instalment credit terms is a uniform concept that has been defined by the CJEU in *Société Bertrand*. Accordingly, this concept should be defined as 'a transaction in which the price is discharged by way of several payments or which is linked to a financing contract'.[116] Besides, in *Hans-Herman Mietz*, the Court clarified that Article 17(1)(a) BIa only applies when the seller transfers the possession of the goods to the buyer before the purchase price is fully paid.[117] The object of Article 17(1)(b) BIa also encompasses sales of goods on instalment credit terms. However, it especially concerns funding operations, whose purpose is to finance sales of goods.

Article 17(1)(c) BIa covers all other contracts – except contracts of transport – concluded by a consumer with a professional, when the latter either pursues his activities in the Member State of the consumer's domicile or directs such activities to this territory. While the first option requires the trader's presence in the Member State where the consumer is domiciled, the second one suggests that the trader advertises and promotes his products or services without being physically present on this particular market. In this case, the Regulation requires the

[115] *Illsinger* (n 114) paras 54–55, 59.
[116] *Bertrand* (n 110) para 20.
[117] Case C-99/96 *Hans-Hermann Mietz v Intership Yachting Sneek BV* [1999] ECR I-02277, para 31.

contract to be in relationship with the activities directed to the Member State of the consumer domicile.

In *Rudolf Gabriel*, the Court of Justice indicated that advertising techniques may take place via press, radio, television, cinema or any other means. Additionally, more personal advertising measures are also covered by Article 17(1)(c) BIa like the sending of catalogues to the consumer or commercial offers made to him in person, in particular by an agent or door-to-door salesman.[118] The subsequent rise of the use of the Internet has produced interpretative issues concerning this provision. In particular, should one consider that the offer of products or services through a website, which is accessible from the consumer's domicile, constitutes an activity that is directed to this territory? The CJEU answered this question negatively in the joined cases *Pammer* and *Hotel Alpenhof*. Indeed, it concluded that the mere accessibility of a website is not sufficient to fulfil the requirements of Article 17(1)(c) BIa.[119] On this occasion, the Court also offered a useful non-exhaustive list of elements that may constitute evidence that the trader directed its activities to the Member State where the consumer is domiciled. These elements include:

> the international nature of the activity, mention of itineraries from other Member States for going to the place where the trader is established, use of a language or a currency other than the language or currency generally used in the Member State in which the trader is established with the possibility of making and confirming the reservation in that other language, mention of telephone numbers with an international code, outlay of expenditure on an internet referencing service in order to facilitate access to the trader's site or that of its intermediary by consumers domiciled in other Member States, use of a top-level domain name other than that of the Member State in which the trader is established, and mention of an international clientele composed of customers domiciled in various Member States.[120]

Later on, the Court of Justice added some precisions to this case law: in *Mühlleitner*, it ruled that Article 17(1)(c) BIa does not require the contract to have been concluded at a distance. In the case at issue, Ms Mühlleitner, an Austrian national, went to Germany in order to buy a car that she had previously found on a website. When she returned in Austria, she discovered that the car was defective and sued the German seller in the courts of her domicile for damages and repayment of the purchase price. In this context, the CJEU pointed out that Article 17(1)(c) BIa was applicable to the action at stake, even though Ms Mühlleitner personally went to another Member State in order to conclude the contract after having seen the offer on a website.[121] Besides, it is not necessary to establish causality between

[118] *Rudolf Gabriel* (n 92) para 44.

[119] Joined cases C-585/08 *Peter Pammer v Reederei Karl Schlüter GmbH & Co. KG* and C-144/09 *Hotel Alpenhof GesmbH v Oliver Heller* [2010] ECR I-12527, paras 69–74.

[120] ibid para 93.

[121] Case C-190/11 *Daniela Mühlleitner v Ahmad Yusufi and Wadat Yusufi* [ECLI:EU:C:2012:542] para 45.

the means used to target consumers in a given Member State and the subsequent conclusion of a contract. Indeed, in *Emrek*, a French business run by Mr Sabranovic directed its activities to Germany through its website. However, Mr Emrek, domiciled in Germany, concluded a contract with this company after having learned about its existence from acquaintances. In this case, the CJEU concluded that the application of Article 17(1)(c) BIa does not require the establishment of a causal link between the prior consultation of a website and a contract, as it would run contrary to its wording and undermine consumer protection.[122]

iii. *Protective Forum*

When an action falls within the material scope of Article 17 BIa, the consequence is that protective rules on jurisdiction apply. In particular, Article 18 BIa establishes the following:

> 1. A consumer may bring proceedings against the other party to a contract either in the courts of the Member State in which that party is domiciled or, regardless of the domicile of the other party, in the courts for the place where the consumer is domiciled.
> 2. Proceedings may be brought against a consumer by the other party to the contract only in the courts of the Member State in which the consumer is domiciled.
> 3. This Article shall not affect the right to bring a counterclaim in the court in which, in accordance with this Section, the original claim is pending.

According to this provision, two situations must be distinguished, depending on who the claimant is. In particular, consumer claimants may bring a suit against a professional domiciled in the EU, either in the courts of their own domicile or in the courts of the defendant's domicile. Since the entry into force of the BIa, consumer claimants may also start proceedings against a defendant seated in a third state in the courts of their own domicile. This amounts to a *forum actoris*.

When the claimant is the professional, then only one option is available: he must litigate in the Member State where the consumer is domiciled (Article 18(2) BIa).

F. Rules on *Lis Pendens* and Related Actions

Articles 29 and 30 BIa establish rules of coordination when two – or more – proceedings, which share a certain degree of similarity, start in the courts of different Member States. The objective of these norms is to avoid the issuance of irreconcilable judgments. According to Article 29 BIa on *lis pendens*, a second seised court located in the EU must stay proceedings if another claim 'involving the same cause of action and (…) the same parties' was first brought in the courts

[122] Case C-218/12 *Lokman Emrek v Vlado Sabranovic* [ECLI:EU:C:2013:666], paras 21, 24.

of another Member State. In this vein, the CJEU ruled that parties are identical even when their procedural position in the different proceedings diverge.[123] Additionally, the CJEU interpreted that Article 29 BIa is applicable where proceedings share a similar cause and object. On the one hand, the cause of action refers to the facts of the case and the applicable law,[124] and on the other hand, the object refers to the objective of the claim.[125] Put differently, the two proceedings must essentially relate to an identical dispute. In case the conditions of Article 29 BIa are fulfilled, the second court seised must stay proceedings. It will then decline jurisdiction in case the court first seised confirms its jurisdictional power over the dispute (Article 29(3) BIa). The only exception to the *prior tempore* rule, is contained in Article 31(2) and (3) BIa. This provision states that the court designated exclusively in a choice of court agreement shall have priority. As a result, other courts of the Member States, even if they are seised first, should stay proceedings until the designated court establishes or decline jurisdiction.[126] Finally, Article 33 BIa governs coordination between EU and extra-EU proceedings. Basically, the conditions are the same as in Article 29 BIa. If these are fulfilled, the EU court will have the possibility to stay proceedings if recognition and enforcement of the extra-EU judgment is likely and sound administration of justice commands it (Article 33(1)(a) and (b) BIa).

When two actions pending in different Member States are not identical but related, Article 30 BIa states that the second seised court may stay proceedings. In other words, there is no obligation for said court to do so, as in Article 29 BIa. At the request of one of the parties, the court may also decline jurisdiction and, thus, allow the case to be consolidated in the court first seised – assuming it has jurisdiction and that consolidation is permitted by its national procedural law. Finally, Article 30(3) BIa clarifies that actions are related when they 'are so closely connected that it is expedient to hear and determine them together to avoid the risk of irreconcilable judgments'. Therefore, the connection requirement may be fulfilled even if separate judgments with non-mutually exclusive consequences could theoretically be issued.[127]

G. Party Autonomy

According to Article 25 BIa, parties may enter into a choice of court agreement with the purpose of thwarting the general rules on jurisdiction established

[123] Case C-144/86 *Gubisch Maschinenfabrik KG v Giulio Palumbo* [1987] ECR 04861, para 19.
[124] ibid para 15; *Tatry* (n 37) para 39.
[125] ibid paras 15–17; ibid para 41.
[126] This exception thus 'corrects' the undesirable result that was generated in *Gasser* (Case C-116/02 *Erich Gasser GmbH v MISAT Srl* [2003] ECR I-14693, para 54) where the court second seised, which was also the court designated in a choice of court agreement, had to stay proceedings and wait for the decision of the first seised Italian courts.
[127] *Tatry* (n 37) para 53.

by the Brussels regime. In order to guarantee the reality of the agreement, Article 25 BIa imposes certain formal conditions. Since the BRI, consent may also be given through electronic means. For the sake of this research project, it is important to highlight that party autonomy is limited as far as consumer contracts are concerned. In particular, Article 19 BIa states that choice of court agreements are only valid if: (1) concluded after the dispute has arisen; (2) they offer additional fora where consumers may start litigation without depriving them of the ones established in section 4 BIa; (3) they designate the courts of the Member State where both parties are domiciled or habitually reside at the time the contract is concluded.

As for Article 26 BIa, it allocates jurisdiction to courts where the defendant enters an appearance and does not contest said court's jurisdictional power. The only limit to this rule is the existence of an exclusive ground of jurisdiction pursuant to Article 24 BIa. In case the defendant is the weaker party, such as a consumer, the court nonetheless has to inform him of his right to challenge jurisdiction (Article 26(2) BIa).

II. Jurisdiction and Collective Redress

A. The Representative Model

i. Outline of the Representative Model

Thanks to the enactment of Directive 2009/22/CE, all Member States have enacted a representative model of collective redress, whereby associations are entitled to protect consumer interests. However, this Directive only refers to actions for injunctive relief. In certain states, like Spain, France, Austria, Finland, Greece and Belgium, a broader range of remedies are available under the representative model. As for Portugal, Italy, Norway, Sweden, Bulgaria and Poland, the representative mechanism has been coupled with the class action model that is analysed below (C.). In other words, in those states, both representative entities and individuals may start collective redress proceedings. Although it has been shaped in different fashion, the representative model is the most widespread collective redress mechanism within the EU. This might explain the abundance of bibliographical sources regarding this model, and the corresponding literature gap with respect to others.

Basically, two scenarios are relevant for the sake of this research project: under the first, a representative body litigates on its own behalf in order to defend the interests of consumers at large. In this case, there is no transfer of an individual's claim to an intermediary. As a result, no one in particular is represented in court. Instead, a somehow abstract interest is protected. In chapter 2, these are called 'general interest' (I.C.). Usually, these actions seek injunctive – or declaratory – relief. Under the second scenario, the representative body acts on behalf of a group of victims. Therefore, it protects various aggregated individual interests. In this situation, the intermediary is the representative of a determined or determinable group of victims. Often, those actions seek monetary compensation.

In order to illustrate this point, the French system on collective redress is briefly presented, since its procedural toolkit contains both kinds of actions.[128] On the one hand, the *action exercée dans l'intérêt collectif des consommateurs* (Article L.621-6 FCC) allows any accredited consumer association to ban illegal practices, which violate EU Directives. For example, this provision enables associations to litigate against unfair terms. Because consumer associations initiate proceedings in order to protect a general interest, there is no group of victims directly represented. As one may expect, this model is usually based on automatic membership.

On the other hand, representative entities, such as consumer associations, sometimes act on behalf of identified victims. Depending on the goals of the national legislators, this specific mechanism might be opt-in or opt-out based. Typically, the French *action en représentation conjointe* (Article L.622-1 to 4 FCC) follows such a scheme. According to this procedural instrument, two or more consumers mandate an aggregated consumer association in order to defend their claims in court. Their damage must stem from the same unlawful behaviour and be committed by the same professional. In this scenario, the consumer association does not have any proper claim but assists consumers to obtain compensation. For example, the *Conseil National des Associations Familiales laïques* (Cnafal) brought an *action en représentation conjointe* against a travel agency for having sold trips to Turkey that did not actually correspond to the description in their catalogue.[129]

Taking into account these considerations, this section is structured as follows: to start with, questions surrounding the representative entity, such as its private or public nature, as well as standing to sue issues are addressed (ii.). Although the latter topic is procedural, it may have a significant impact on private international law questions. The application of private international law rules on jurisdiction to the two categories of actions described above is then analysed (iii.). The distinction between actions in the general or collective interest is important because, on the one hand, one may consider that a representative entity protecting a general interest should not benefit from the fora available to (potential) victims. On the other hand, however, this option might be open in the second scenario described above, given that the representative entity acts on behalf of a determined group of victims. Should differences exist between those actions, they will be underlined as they arise. The sub-section ends with an interim conclusion (iv.) Along the way, some emblematic cases are mentioned in order to illustrate the points made. However, because collective redress suits involving international components pursuant to

[128] For more information on the French system regarding collective redress, see Annex II.C.

[129] INC, 'L'action de groupe : vers une consécration ?' (2005) 1348 *INC Hebdo* 8, available at www.conso.net/sites/default/files/pdf_abonne/1348-action_groupe_255.pdf.

the representative model are scarce, it will unfortunately not always be possible to take a court judgment as a basis of analysis.

ii. The Representative Entity

This sub-section tackles two particular questions: the first one concerns the identification of the representative entities that fall under the scope of the Brussels regime (a.). This subject is examined in light of the judgment of the CJEU in the *Henkel* case, which was issued in 2002. As announced earlier, this leading case will also be referred to in the sub-section dedicated to questions on jurisdiction. Notably, it is not clear whether public representatives or private representatives exercising a public power could rely on the BIa for jurisdictional purposes. The second question examines standing to sue from a more general perspective by addressing the usual issues faced by representatives who wish to litigate abroad (b.). Standing to sue does not generate any fundamental issue when actions are covered by Directive 2009/22/EC. However, uncertainties arise outside the scope of said Directive, for example when actions for damages are at stake.

a. The Nature of the Representative Entity

Statement of Facts of the *Henkel* Case

The *Verein für Konsumenteninformation* (VKI) is a major Austrian consumer association domiciled in Vienna. Among other activities, the entity actively protects consumer interests in court. In this context, in 1999, the VKI brought proceedings against Mr Henkel, a trader located in Germany, in order to protect Austrian consumers.[130] According to the representative association, Mr Henkel had used or offered unfair terms in his contractual relationships with said consumers. As a result, the VKI sought injunctive relief in the Commercial Court of Vienna (*Handelsgericht Wien*) pursuant to paragraph 28 of the *Konsumenschutzgesetz* (*KSchG*), which codifies Directive 93/13/EEC on Unfair Terms.[131] The consumer association argued that the Commercial Court of Vienna had jurisdiction to hear the dispute under Article 5(3) BC, the predecessor of Article 7(2) BIa. Nevertheless, the court rejected the VKI's argument, given that no damage arose out of tort, delict or quasi-delict. In light of this, the Court found it had no jurisdiction. The court seised on appeal, namely the Higher Regional Court of Vienna (*Oberlandesgericht Wien*), overturned this decision and held that the preventive action brought by the VKI entered the scope of the BC. Subsequently, Mr Henkel brought an appeal to the Austrian Supreme Court (*Oberster Gerichtshof*), which asked the CJEU to

[130] *Henkel* (n 112).

[131] Council Directive 93/13/EEC of 5 April 1993 on unfair terms in consumer contracts [1993] OJ L095/29.

clarify whether a preventive action such as the one at issue was a matter related to tort under the Brussels regime.

In the case under analysis, the CJEU shed light on three important questions: to start with, the Court of Justice examined the potential application of section 4 BIa, as well as Articles 7(1) and (2) BIa (ex-Articles 5(1) and (3) BI) to the case at issue. Then, it ruled that preventive actions fell under the scope of Article 7(2) BIa. This solution has been accepted and codified since the entry into force of BI. In the next lines, the private or public nature of the VKI is assessed, which conditions its ability to benefit from the fora of the Brussels regime.

The Public or Private Nature of the Representative

In *Henkel*, the United Kingdom government submitted that the claim brought by the VKI did not enter the scope of the Brussels regime. In particular, it explained that the Austrian consumer association is a public entity and that the action at issue stems from the exercise of a public power. Nevertheless, the CJEU rejected this argument and concluded that the VKI was a private body. Moreover, its claim affected commercial relationships between individuals. As a consequence, the Court ruled that the action fell under the material scope of the BC. The reasoning of the CJEU has to be examined in light of Article 1 BIa, which restricts the material scope of the Regulation to 'civil and commercial matters'.

According to the CJEU's case law, the concept of 'civil and commercial matters' is the object of an autonomous definition that takes into account the objectives and the scheme of the Brussels regime. This solution has been established by the CJEU in *Eurocontrol*.[132] In this case, the claimant, namely the European organisation for the safety of air navigation (Eurocontrol), sought the payment of charges owed by a person governed by private law, for the mandatory and exclusive use of the organisation's equipment and services. In this context, the CJEU had to determine whether the action at issue was civil and commercial in nature. The Court of Luxembourg ruled that certain disputes should be excluded from the Regulation's scope, either by reason of the legal relationship between the parties to the action or the subject matter of said action.[133] In light of the above, the Court concluded that Eurocontrol was a public body that exercised a public power, given the relationship of subordination existing between such an organisation and its users.[134]

In *Ruffer*, the Court of Justice cemented its previous case law regarding Article 1 BIa.[135] This case involved a claim brought by the Netherlands against the owner of a ship for the recovery of the costs involved in the removal of a wreck in public waterways. The CJEU considered that the Netherlands acted as a body invested with public authority, as the function of policing waterways stems from

[132] *Eurocontrol* (n 10).
[133] ibid para 4.
[134] ibid para 4.
[135] *Rüffer* (n 11).

an international Treaty. The Court added that the filing of such a claim in the civil courts – and not the administrative ones – did not affect this reasoning.[136]

Conversely, for example, in *Sonntag*, the CJEU held that an action for damages brought against the teacher of a public school who caused harm to a pupil for incorrectly exercising his duty of supervision entered the scope of Article 1 BIa.[137] According to the Court, even though the parties were joined to criminal proceedings as civil parties, the action at stake had to be considered a civil claim. Furthermore, even if the teacher acted on behalf of the state, he was not invested with a public power when he supervised pupils during a school trip. In fact, he assumed the same functions as those a teacher from a private school would have.[138] The consecutive judgments that have been rendered on this matter shadow the established case law.[139]

The previously analysed case law shows that the application of the Regulation has to be rejected when two conditions are fulfilled, namely the existence of a dispute between a public authority and an individual governed by private law, and the use of public law prerogatives by said authority. As the case law highlights, however, the line separating civil and commercial relationships form public law ones is thin and sometimes difficult to establish.

Taking these considerations into account, the private or public nature of the VKI in *Henkel* is not self-evident.[140] It has to be underlined that public entities, such as the Austrian Chamber of Labour, the Austrian Labour Union Federation and the Republic of Austria, are all members of the VKI.[141] Therefore, these elements might cast some doubts regarding the private nature of this organisation. Besides, in an online document, the VKI expressly states that it litigates cases on behalf of the Austrian government.[142] This might indicate that some power is transferred from the state to the consumer association.

Along the same line of reasoning, it is difficult to conclude that the claim brought by the VKI, which consists in prohibiting a trader from using unfair terms, is of a private rather than public law nature. On the one hand, one may argue that such an action enters the scope of the Regulation, as it is founded upon Directive 93/13/EEC, which is grounded on private law. Furthermore, the power

[136] ibid paras 9-11, 13–15.

[137] Case C-172/91 *Volker Sonntag v Hans Waidmann, Elisabeth Waidmann and Stefan Waidmann* [1993] ECR I-01963, para 29.

[138] ibid paras 19–25.

[139] See eg Case C-271/00 *Gemeente Steenbergen v Luc Baten* [2002] ECR I-10489; Case C-292/05 *Eirini Lechouritou and Others v Dimosio tis Omospondiakis Dimokratias tis Germanias* [2007] ECR I-01519; *Sapir* (n 33); Case C-226/13 *Stefan Fahnenbrock and Others v Hellenische Republik* [ECLI:EU:C:2015:383].

[140] C Michailidou, 'Internationale Zuständigkeit bei vorbeugenden Verbandsklagen' (2003) 3 *Praxis des Internationalen Privat- und Verfahrensrechts* 223, 223.

[141] This information has been extracted from the VKI's documents of presentation, available at www.konsument.at/kontakt.

[142] ibid.

to challenge unfair terms under national laws is usually not restricted to certain claimants: individual consumers can equally contest the validity of a clause that governs their relationship with a trader. As a result, the object of the VKI's action is not different from a claim that would arise from a relationship governed by private law. On the other hand, however, it seems that through its action, the VKI protects interests of consumers at large and more generally, the well-functioning and the transparency of the market. In this case, the protection of Austrian consumers from the use of unfair terms in courts is a specific prerogative that no individual consumer alone is able to exercise. In fact, many Member States allocate standing to sue to a quite limited range of actors in order to guarantee that these supra-individual interests are well represented and protected.

As explained above, the representative model has been implemented in distinct ways among Member States. As a result, some national mechanisms may involve many more 'public components' than others. For these mechanisms, the application of the Brussels regime is more difficult to justify.[143] Typically, the Finnish representative action illustrates this point.[144] The Group Action Act of 2007 enables the Finnish Consumer Ombudsman, a public authority, to take a legal action in mass consumer disputes. Specifically, the Ombudsman represents consumers who opted into the proceedings and may seek usual remedies available under Finnish law. It should be highlighted that it is the only entity to have standing to sue. According to the Consumer Protection Act 34/1978, the Ombudsman may defend a general interest without consumers' consent. However, only injunctive relief is available under this model. Consumers only have a secondary right to sue, in case the public authority does not act. In both scenarios, it is not clear whether the Regulation should apply, for the following reasons: first, there is no doubt that the Finnish Consumer Ombudsman is a public authority. Second, its almost exclusive right to defend supra-individual interests indicates that this power may well have been acquired from the state.

b. Standing to Sue and Litigation Abroad

The following lines briefly present some procedural problems faced by consumer associations in cross-border collective redress cases. Specifically, national courts rule on questions regarding capacity and standing to sue in different ways. The examples below that illustrate said problems took place before the enactment of the Injunctions Directive, which sets up a system whereby capacity to sue has to be mutually recognised for certain actions. This helps to understand the significance of procedural barriers and how they could be tackled. Moreover, those barriers

[143] Along these lines, Michailidou ((n 140) 224) argues that in order for the BC (now, the BIa) to apply, one should determine whether the consumer association is entrusted with a public power or aims at controlling the fairness of given private contractual relationships. According to this reasoning, the Convention would only apply to the latter case.

[144] For more information on the Finnish system regarding collective redress, see Annex II.J.

still remain out of the scope of Directive 2009/22/EC. The next paragraphs mainly focus on procedural issues that are often faced by consumer associations, as this case is the most common.

To begin with, capacity to start proceedings relies on legal personality. Member States usually recognise an association's legal personality either according to the place of its principal establishment or the place of its incorporation.[145] In certain cases – like for public authorities –, the capacity to sue can also be established by law.[146] In the second place, standing to sue is allocated under different conditions depending on the legal order concerned and it may be examined under distinct laws. This point is illustrated by the emblematic examples presented below.

First of all, the law applicable to standing to sue in France is governed by both the *lex fori*, as well as the law under which the consumer association is constituted.[147] In France, the law limits the number of players which are able to initiate collective redress actions. In particular, consumer associations which want to start such actions have to be certified, pursuant to Article L.811-1 FCC. Among other things, these associations must have at least one year of existence and be sufficiently representative. In light of this, it is likely that French courts require foreign associations to possess such a certificate or a similar document.[148] However, certain Member States like Germany do not impose any certification process on their consumer associations. Practically, this means that German associations might not be able to litigate in France, where the Injunctions Directive does not apply.[149]

As mentioned above, French courts also take into account the law of the representative's constitution. Accordingly, if a consumer association is not able to represent certain supra-individual interests under its law of constitution, then this prohibition also applies in France.[150] Nevertheless, a German association that has standing to sue in the state of its domicile may not exercise this right in France

[145] M Fallon, 'An Essay on the Mutual Recognition of Group Actions (Governmental, Organizational, of Class Actions) in Cross-Border Consumer Conflicts within the European Community' in T Bourgoignie (ed), *Group Actions and the Defense of the Consumer Interest in the European Community* (Story, 1992) 253.

[146] JY Carlier, 'Les actions collectives transfrontières. Rapport belge' in B Stauder (ed), *Les actions collectives transfrontières des organisations de consommateurs – Droit international et droit du marché intérieur*, Actes du colloque organisé avec le Centre d'études juridiques européennes (Schultess, 1997) 47–48; Fallon, 'An Essay on the Mutual Recognition of Group Actions (n 144) 253.

[147] P Mayer and V Heuzé, *Droit international privé* (Lextenso éditions, 2010) 375–76; A Morin, 'Les actions collectives transfrontières. Rapport français' in Stauder, *Les actions collectives transfrontières des organisations de consommateurs* (n 146) 76–77.

[148] eg Belgium adopted a different solution: the requirement of a certificate is examined according to the law where the consumer association comes from. As a result, Rigaux and Fallon explain that 'l'action introduite en Belgique par une association française de consommateurs suppose que celle-ci puisse produire l'agrément octroyé conformément au droit français et qui conditionne, selon ce droit, la représentativité de l'association. Cela signifie que cette association ne doit pas, pour agir en Belgique, avoir obtenu l'agrément prévu par la droit Belge' (F Rigaux and M Fallon, *Droit international privé*, 3rd edn (Larcier, 2005) 473).

[149] JY Carlier, *Guide des litiges transfrontières* (Institut National de la Consommation, 1993) 52–55.

[150] Mayer and Heuzé, *Droit international privé* (n 147) 376.

if French associations do not possess a similar right. It would be discriminatory to allocate more rights to foreign entities than to national ones (*discrimination à rebours*).[151]

The second example concerns a case of false advertising. In 1995, the Second Instance Court of Cologne (Germany) rendered a judgment[152] in a case involving a claim brought by a German consumer association (*Verbraucherschutzverein*, VSV) – at the request of UFC-Que Choisir – against Direct Shopping, whose mailbox was located in Germany. The latter allegedly promised to sell products to French consumers against the payment of a sum of money in advance. The advertisements for this offer were sent from the Czech Republic. Consumers who accepted the trader's deal either received products whose quality did not meet the contractual standards or received no answer from their business partner at all.

In its decision,[153] the second instance court established that, according to §13 of the German competition law (*Gesetz gegen den unlauteren Wettbewerb*, UWG), a consumer association must demonstrate that its articles of association aim at protecting the interest which has been harmed. However, VSV did not encompass the protection of French consumers within its articles of association. As a result, it did not possess any *intéret à agir*. Additionally, the court mentions that §13 UWG may only be used if German law has been violated, which was doubtful in the case at issue. The decision was confirmed by the German Supreme Court (*Bundesgerichtshof*).[154]

Today, the Injunctions Directive clarifies the procedural landscape by imposing the mutual recognition of capacity to sue for most actions for injunctive relief.[155] Thanks to it, qualified entities may seek injunctive relief against a trader who has violated the text of a Directive mentioned in Annex I. Among others, the Directive on unfair terms and package travel is included in the list. Nevertheless, said Directive does not deal with what French literature calls *intérêt à agir*. On 11 April 2018, the Commission published its Proposal for a Directive on

[151] ML Niboyet and G de Geouffre de La Pradelle, *Droit international privé* (Lextenso éditions, 2011) 502–03.

[152] Judgment of the Higher Regional Court of Cologne (*Oberlandesgericht Köln*), case 6 U 25/94 rendered on 12 May 1995. The judgments of the first instance court and the German Supreme Court were not accessible but reliance was placed on the following sources: L Carballo Piñeiro, *Las acciones colectivas y su eficacia extraterritorial – Problemas de recepción y transplante de las class actions en Europa* (De conflictu legum. Estudios de Derecho Internacional Privado, 2009) 74; J Franck and P Foucher, 'Expériences concrètes de résolution de litiges transfrontières dans le domaine de la publicité' in Stauder (ed) (n 146) 83–108; HW Micklitz, 'Cross-Border Consumer Conflicts – A French-German Experience' (1993) 16 *Journal of Consumer Policy* 411, 418–34.

[153] Judgment of the Higher Regional Court of Cologne (n 152) 11–22.

[154] HW Micklitz, 'Efficacité internationale de l'action en suppression des clauses abusives: point de vue allemand' (2000) 52(4) *Revue internationale de droit comparé* 867, 874 and fn 9.

[155] This introduction was built up thanks to the following sources: D Hoffmann, 'Directive "Actions en cessation en matière de protection des intérêts des consommateurs (Dir. 98/27/CE du 19/5/98)"' (2000) 1 *European Review of Private Law* 147, 147–54; P Rott, 'The Protection of Consumers' Interests After the Implementation of the EC Injunctions Directive Into German and English Law' (2001) 24 *Journal of Consumer Policy* 399, 401–11; S Wrbka, *European Consumer Access to Justice Revisited* (Cambridge University Press, 2015) 40–53.

representative actions,[156] which should extend mutual recognition of standing to actions for damages. It remains to be seen whether the advantages of the Proposal will survive the legislative process.

To sum up, these examples show that different procedural approaches to capacity and standing to sue, as well as *intérêt à agir* in certain Member States might significantly complicate the start of proceedings abroad. Fortunately, the Injunctions Directive and the recent Proposal of the Commission should solve most of those procedural issues. However, the removal of certain procedural barriers to cross-border litigation, without offering a private international law solution as well, is likely to remain insufficient.

iii. Questions Regarding Jurisdiction

a. Section 4 BIa

As mentioned earlier, the reasoning of the CJEU in the *Henkel* case guides the analysis of jurisdictional questions. In this case, the CJEU held that a consumer association cannot benefit from the protective forum established by section 4 BIa. Another solution would run against the wording of Article 18(1) BIa, which states that

> [a] *consumer* may bring proceedings against the other party to a contract either in the courts of the Member State in which that party is domiciled or, regardless of the domicile of the other party, in the courts for the place where the consumer is domiciled (emphasis added).

Accordingly, only consumers who personally bring their claims may benefit from section 4 BIa.

Along the same line of reasoning, the following arguments support this approach: firstly, the concept of 'consumer' under section 4 BIa does not include corporations such as consumer associations. Secondly, it is doubtful that preventive actions seeking the protection of a general interest are encompassed in said section, given that its application hinges on the existence of a contract. The Court's decision in *Henkel* is also endorsed by *Shearson* where the CJEU ruled that the assignment of a consumer claim to a company (assignee) cannot be encompassed in section 4 BIa.[157] Specifically, the Court held that the Brussels regime 'protects the consumer only in so far as he personally is the plaintiff or defendant in proceedings'.[158] The strict reading of the Court significantly limits access to section 4 BIa by representative entities.

However, part of the literature underlines that a different interpretation of the Regulation is possible, at least as regards actions protecting the collective interest

[156] See ch 2, II.A.
[157] *Shearson* (n 107).
[158] ibid para 23.

of multiple individual consumers.[159] Essentially, such an interpretation advocates that the spotlight should not be put on parties in proceedings but rather on the material situation at stake.[160] Accordingly, one should not automatically reject access to section 4 BIa, when actors other than consumers go to court: when representative entities litigate on behalf of consumers who hold the substantive right for which compensation is sought, they act as mere representatives. As a result, section 4 BIa should be opened for said representatives, although they do not qualify as consumers. The representation mechanism should not change either the nature of the claim, or the reasoning regarding jurisdiction.

Besides, Article 18 BIa does not explicitly require a consumer to personally litigate his claim in court. This argument has been thoroughly developed by Danov who underlines that, pursuant to the text of the Regulation, 'consumers *may* bring proceedings' (emphasis added) in the courts listed in section 4 BIa.[161] In the author's opinion, this means that other actors are equally able to litigate in those fora.

A last argument that militates in favour of a broad interpretation of section 4 BIa is the potential application of different regimes regarding party autonomy in collective and individual actions. Supposing that representative entities would not benefit from a protective forum, Article 25 BIa would allow defendants to introduce choice of court agreements or class action waivers into their contractual relationships with consumers. Although Article 19 BIa limits the use of this kind of provision, it would not apply to a consumer who bundles his claim with others.[162] In other words, if representative entities were not included in section 4 BIa, no protective rule would regulate the use of pre-trial choice of court agreements.

Opponents of this vision may criticise this approach as it contradicts the principle, whereby provisions regarding protective fora should be interpreted restrictively. This view has to be nuanced. To start with, rather than a restrictive interpretation, the CJEU favours an interpretation that does not go beyond the cases expressly envisaged by the Regulation. For example, the CJEU regularly clarifies the scope and meaning of Article 7(2) BIa in a sense that sometimes goes beyond what a restrictive interpretation would command. In this context,

[159] M Danov, 'The Brussels I Regulation: Cross-Border Collective Redress Proceedings and Judgments' (2010) 6(2) *Journal of Private International Law* 359, 372–77; C González Beilfuss and B Añoveros Terradas, 'Compensatory Consumer Collective Redress and the Brussels I Regulation (Recast)' in A Nuyts and NE Hatzimihail (eds), *Cross-Border Class Actions: The European Way* (Sellier European Law Publishers, 2014) 248–52; P Jiménez Blanco, 'El tratamiento de las acciones colectivas en materia de consumidores en el Convenio de Brusselas' (2003) 5709 *Diario La Ley* 1573, 1574–76.

[160] Carballo, *Las acciones colectivas y su eficacia extraterritorial* (n 152) 107-08; Jiménez Blanco, 'El tratamiento de las acciones colectivas en materia de consumidores en el Convenio de Brusselas' (n 159) 1574.

[161] Danov, 'The Brussels I Regulation' (n 159) 376.

[162] Carballo (n 152) 112; González Beilfuss and Añoveros Terradas, 'Compensatory Consumer Collective Redress and the Brussels I Regulation (Recast)' (n 159) 250. DPL Tzakas, 'Effective Collective Redress in Antitrust and Consumer Protection Matters: A Panacea or a Chimera?' (2011) 48(4) *Common Market Law Review* 1125, 1166.

the CJEU occasionally 'creates' specific fora in order to deal with the emergence of complex international disputes. In this vein, the expansion of the concept of 'consumer' pursuant to Article 18 BIa in order to adapt to collective redress should not automatically run against the principle of restrictive interpretation. However, such an expansion should be supported by policy considerations. In this sense, it is arguable that the CJEU stands in a good position to assess whether section 4 BIa might be used by representative entities. Perhaps this decision should be the object of a legislative act.

Nevertheless, even if a broad interpretation were to be adopted, additional problems would remain: to start with, the categories of consumers protected by the Brussels regime are limited. As a consequence, certain categories of victims, such as investors and SMEs, are not always included into section 4 BIa. However, these actors may well be in need of more protective jurisdictional rules. In fact, the notion of 'consumer', along with the active-passive dichotomy adopted by the Regulation does not adapt to collective redress. Additionally, it has to be highlighted that general interests, in absence of any contract, remain out of said provision's scope. Finally, even though one would proceed to an extensive interpretation of Article 18 BIa, concentration of proceedings would be difficult in case consumers are domiciled in different Member States or in different locations within the same national territory: in which forum should all claims be centralised and according to which criteria?[163] On the one hand, centralising claims in the domicile of one consumer is difficult to achieve, as courts of this domicile could hardly have jurisdiction over consumers located in a different place.[164] On the other hand, bundling claims in the domicile of the representative entity is difficult to justify, as this forum is not expressly mentioned in section 4 BIa. Besides, as the analysis of the class action model highlights (below C.), the creation of a new forum in the domicile of the assignee has been rejected by the CJEU in the *Schrems* case.

b. Article 7(1) BIa

In case section 4 BIa does not apply, Articles 7(1) or 7(2) BIa could constitute an appropriate jurisdictional ground. As regards Article 7(1) BIa, one should distinguish between collective redress actions for injunctive relief that protect a general interest and actions for damages, which bundle individual consumer claims. In *Henkel*, the Austrian consumer association brought an action of the

[163] González Beilfuss and Añoveros (n 159) 252.

[164] E Lein, 'Cross-Border Collective Redress and Jurisdiction under Brussels I: A Mismatch' in D Fairgrieve and E Lein (eds), *Extraterritoriality and Collective Redress* (Oxford University Press, 2012) 135; A Nuyts, 'The Consolidation of Collective Claims Under Brussels I' in Nuyts and Hatzimihail (eds), *Cross-Border Class Actions: The European Way* (n 159) 73; M Posnow-Wurm, 'Rethinking Collective Redress, Consumer Protection and Brussels I Regulation' in Nuyts and Hatzimihail (n 159) 270. This author adds that this solution is contrary to the principle of the Regulation which consists in limiting the number of available fora.

first type against a German trader: it sought to protect the general interest of Austrian consumers, no matter the existence of potential individual contracts. In this case, the Court of Justice considered that no contract governed the relationship between the Austrian consumer association and the trader. Hence, it quickly came to the conclusion that Article 7(1) BIa could not apply to the action at issue. In its reasoning, the CJEU emphasised the nature of the claim between parties to the proceedings. However, the subject matter of the relationship between the defendant and potential victims was set aside.[165] Unfortunately, Article 7(1) BIa does not explicitly state which of these elements should be the basis of the Court's assessment.

There are some arguments for qualifying the VKI's claim as a contractual one, in the sense of Article 7(1) BIa.[166] This is justified since the use of unfair terms is always related to potential or existing contracts. Besides, the terms of this provision refer to matters *related* to contracts: this does not mean that an actual contract must exist between litigating parties.[167] In other words, the factual situation that underpins the claim could be taken into account. The fact that consumers are protected by a consumer association's judicial action should not change the nature of the claim.[168] Conversely, the interpretation of the Court means that Article 7(1) BIa would only be available for group actions, namely for actions brought by a group of victims who are contractually bound with the defendant.[169]

Now, it is not clear whether the results of the *Henkel* case law are transposable to collective actions for damages. When the representative body merely represents individual aggregated interests, it might be precipitous to conclude that, because no contractual relationship is available between the alleged wrongdoer and the consumer association, Article 7(1) BIa should not apply. Actions, whereby consumers seek monetary compensation thanks to the assistance of a representative entity, which has capacity and standing to litigate on their behalf, can be taken as an example. In this situation, because of the mere representative role of the consumer association, it might be more appropriate to focus on the subject matter of the relationship between the former parties involved in the dispute, namely the victims and the defendant. Article 7(1) BIa should cover these cases, as parties usually freely assume obligations towards each other.

Even if Article 7(1) BIa applied to both types of actions, some significant problems would still persist concerning the selection of the court where those actions

[165] ZS Tang, 'Consumer Collective Redress in European Private International Law' (2011) 7(1) *Journal of Private International Law* 101, 111; González Beilfuss and Añoveros Terradas (n 159) 253.

[166] Although they recommend the non-applicability of Art 7(1) BIa to the *Henkel* case, A Stadler and P Rémy-Corlay acknowledge the contractual nature of the VKI's claim (P Rémy-Corlay, 'Note sur l'arrêt Henkel' (2003) 4 *Revue critique de droit international privé* 690, 694; A Stadler, 'Note' (2007) 7 *Zeitschrift für Zivilprozeß International* 284, 288).

[167] Tang, 'Consumer Collective Redress in European Private International Law' (n 165) 109.

[168] Jiménez Blanco (n 159) 1576–77.

[169] Nuyts, 'The Consolidation of Collective Claims Under Brussels I' (n 164) 74.

should actually be brought. If the application of Article 7(1)(a) Bia is accepted, the obligation in question has to be pinned down. Similarly, the application of Article 7(1)(b) BIa requires the localisation of the place where goods are delivered or where services are provided.

In *Henkel*, the prohibition against using unfair terms, in relation to commercial transactions with Austrian consumers, represents the obligation in question. Yet, the place of performance of said obligation has to be located. When the action preventively seeks the prohibition of the use of unfair terms in subsequent contractual relationships, there may be various places of performance:[170] for example, the place where the contractual terms are released, which should correspond to the defendant's domicile, the place where the contract is concluded, which could be difficult to spot if the agreement takes place online, and the place where contractual terms are actually used and enforced, which would correspond to the market where the consumer association is active. All these places might be relevant locations for courts to establish jurisdiction. Nevertheless, when spotting the place of performance of the obligation in question is too hard, one may assume that the application of Article 7(1) BIa should be rejected, pursuant to the *Besix* case law.[171]

Interestingly, Stadler considers that preventive actions such as the one brought by the VKI should not benefit from the forum in contractual matters.[172] She explains that the absence of contracts impedes the proper location of the place of performance. Besides, it is doubtful that this forum could anyway entertain a close connection with the dispute. As for Rémy-Corlay, she considers that the compliance of the obligation in question cannot be located at all, given that the prohibition against using unfair terms has to be observed disregarding any location.[173] This argument is in accordance with *Besix*, whereby the CJEU rejected the application of Article 7(1) BIa to an 'obligation not to do something' without territorial limit. On the contrary, Leclerc expresses doubts over this interpretation. Instead, he suggests that the performance of the obligation can be narrowed down to the Austrian market.[174]

As regards collective redress actions for damages, some authors have examined the possibility of extending the *Color Drack* and *Wood Floor* case law to those actions.[175] In these judgments, the CJEU ruled that in the presence of various places of performance, the court where the principal one is undertaken should have jurisdiction. Could contractual claims be bundled in a single court following

[170] Rémy-Corlay, 'Note sur l'arrêt Henkel' (n 166) 694.

[171] Case C-256/00 *Besix SA v Wasserreinigungsbau Alfred Kretzschmar GmbH & Co. KG (WABAG) and Planungs- und Forschungsgesellschaft Dipl. Ing. W. Kretzschmar GmbH & KG (Plafog)* [2002] ECR I-01699.

[172] Stadler, 'Note' (n 166) 289.

[173] Rémy-Corlay (n 166) 694.

[174] F Leclerc, 'Note sur l'arrêt Henkel' (2004) 3 *Journal du droit international* 911, 915.

[175] Carballo (n 152) 119; González Beilfuss and Añoveros Terradas (n 159) 255-57; Lein, 'Cross-Border Collective Redress and Jurisdiction under Brussels I' (n 164) 137.

this case law? The answer is probably negative. The judgments only concerned one contract, two parties and various places of performance. Typically, in collective redress cases, various contracts and parties are involved, as well as multiple places of performance. Therefore, concentration of proceedings appears to be difficult, given that the place of performance of the obligation in question is likely to be located in different places in the national territory or in distinct Member States.[176]

c. Article 7(2) BIa

Again, the applicability of Article 7(2) BIa has to be assessed differently for actions protecting a general interest and actions seeking compensation for a multiplicity of individual consumers. On the one hand, the CJEU held that Article 7(2) BIa should apply to the first category of actions. In *Henkel*, the Court of Luxembourg ruled that the claim of the VKI, given that it could not be considered as a contractual matter and given that it sought to establish the defendant's liability, met the criteria of Article 7(2) BIa.[177] On the other hand, however, it is not clear whether actions defending aggregated interests would also fall under the scope of Article 7(2) BIa. In all cases, should Article 7(2) BIa apply, representative entities could litigate either at the place where the event giving rise to the damage arose or where it materialised. In both situations, the localisation of the damage might be problematic.

In *Henkel*, the CJEU did not address questions regarding territorial jurisdiction. This is rather unfortunate since the preventive character of the VKI makes the localisation of the damage particularly difficult. In the absence of any guidance from the Court of Justice and as highlighted earlier, this place could be located in many different places (this chapter, II.A.iii.b.). For example, under Spanish law,[178] it is possible to bring an action seeking the prohibition of the use of unfair terms either in the courts where the defendant has a branch or his/her domicile. Alternatively, if the defendant does not have any domicile in Spain, any qualified person may bring collective redress proceedings either in the courts where the consumer adhered to the contract (Article 52.1.14° of the Spanish Law of Civil Procedure (SLCP)), or at the domicile of the actor (Article 52.1.16° SLCP). This last sentence means that a consumer association may bring proceedings at its own domicile. It represents a good option, as it permits the localisation of the damage in a unique forum. However, this is a national legislative choice that has not been endorsed by the CJEU and, thus, other Member States may adopt a different reading of Article 7(2) BIa based on their national experience, which might disrupt a uniform interpretation.

[176] Carballo (n 152) 118-19; González Beilfuss and Añoveros Terradas, above n 691, 253; Lein (n 164) 137; Nuyts (n 164) 75; Tzakas, 'Effective Collective Redress in Antitrust and Consumer Protection Matters' (n 162) 1159.

[177] *Henkel* (n 112) para 41.

[178] This example has been extracted from Carballo (n 152) 112–13.

Furthermore, the literature has expressed its doubts on the application of Article 7(2) BIa. For example, according to Rémy-Corlay,[179] given that the consumer association in *Henkel* protects all consumers in general, the damage cannot be properly located in light of the principle of proximity. As a result, the application of Article 4 BIa should be preferred. Similarly, Kessedjian considers that Article 7(2) BIa should not be applicable to collective actions that aggregate numerous individual claims. Another solution would lead to the rise of multiple fora to the detriment of the defendant.[180]

Despite the above-mentioned interpretative difficulties, Article 7(2) BIa often offers a forum that enables representative entities to start collective actions seeking the protection of general interests in the state where they are located. At least, this is the case for actions that aim at prohibiting the use of unfair terms. For example, in 2013, a first instance court in Madrid declared the nullity of eight provisions implemented in the terms and conditions of an Irish airline company.[181] The *Organización de Consumidores y Usuarios* (OCU) – a Spanish consumer association incorporated in Madrid – started proceedings in Spain against the Irish defendant. Although the Spanish court did not state its reasoning regarding its jurisdictional power, it seems reasonable to assume that Article 7(2) BIa was the relevant basis for accepting jurisdiction.[182] In 2014, an Austrian second instance court admitted an action for injunctive relief brought by the VKI against TVP-Treuhandgesellschaft, located in Hamburg. Said court accepted jurisdiction pursuant to Article 7(2) BIa. The latter company allegedly used unfair terms and conditions in its contractual relationship with Austrian investors. The details of this case are further examined below (II.D.ii.a.). Finally, in a relatively recent judgment, the Austrian Supreme Court referred some questions to the CJEU in a case involving an action for injunctive relief brought by the VKI against Amazon – the seat of which is in Luxembourg.[183] The latter allegedly used unfair terms in its contractual relationships with Austrian consumers. Although the questions referred dealt with the applicable law, the facts show that the VKI started proceedings in Austria on the basis of Article 7(2) BIa. Since Amazon did not possess any registered office or establishment in Austria,[184] this head of jurisdiction was the only one available to start proceedings in Austrian courts.

The questionnaire drafted for the sake of this research project confirms this trend. According to the results, when consumer associations start cross-border

[179] Rémy-Corlay (n 166) 696.

[180] C Kessedjian, 'L'action en justice des associations de consommateurs et d'autres organisations représentatives d'intérêts collectifs en Europe' (1997) 2 *Rivista di diritto internazionale privato e processuale* 281, 290.

[181] Commercial Court no 5 of Madrid (*Juzgado Mercantil no 5 de Madrid*), case 113/2013 rendered on 30 September 2013.

[182] For other examples – most of which contain an international component – see the presentation prepared by BEUC, available at www.beuc.eu/publications/2013-00451-01-e.pdf.

[183] Case C-191/15 *Verein für Konsumenteninformation v Amazon EU Sàrl* [ECLI:EU:C:2016:612].

[184] ibid para 29.

litigation, they usually do so in the Member State in which they are active on the basis of Article 7(2) BIa.[185]

In case multiple aggregated interests are at stake, the representative entity may decide to initiate collective proceedings at the place where the damage arose. This alternative is interesting as it allows the representative to centralise individual claims in a single forum.[186] Besides, the court that enjoys jurisdiction has the power to rule over the whole damage. However, in certain cases, the place which gives rise to the damage may be difficult to spot. Furthermore, this place often corresponds to the defendant's domicile and significantly minimises the usefulness of Article 7(2) BIa.[187] Alternatively, a representative body might be tempted to sue the defendant at a closer location, namely the place where the damage occurred. Nevertheless, the court's jurisdiction at this particular place is territorially limited. Importantly, it can only rule on the damage that took place within its territory. This means that participation in collective redress actions initiated there would be limited and, hence, remain local.[188]

d. Other Possible Grounds for Jurisdiction

Another provision might be relevant as regards the allocation of jurisdiction for the representative model: Article 25 BIa on choice of court agreements.[189] When actions for the protection of general consumer interests are at stake, party autonomy is likely to play a minor role, since parties are usually not bound by any contractual relationship. However, a choice of court agreement can still be concluded after the dispute arises. When consumers are represented by a consumer association, the presence of choice of court agreements that bind them with the defendant should be taken into account. In those cases, such an association is usually a mere representative and does not possess any claim. Thus, choice of court agreements concluded by consumers with an alleged wrongdoer should not lose their effectiveness because of the representation scheme. The validity of ex post choice of court agreements concluded by representative entities and imposed on people represented is analysed under the Dutch model (this chapter, II.B.iv.).

[185] Questions 1.1, 1.3 and 2.1 of the questionnaire.

[186] Lein (n 164) 134; A Stadler, 'Die grenzüberschreitende Durchsetzbarkeit von Sammelklagen' in M Casper et al (eds), *Auf dem Weg zu einer europäischen Sammelklage?* (Sellier European Law Publishers, 2009) 158.

[187] Lein (n 164) 134; Nuyts (n 164) 76-77; Stadler, 'Die grenzüberschreitende Durchsetzbarkeit von Sammelklagen' (n 186) 158.

[188] Carballo (n 152) 121; Michailidou (n 140) 226-27; Nuyts (n 164) 77; Tzakas (n 162) 1162–63.

[189] Theoretically, Art 7(5) BIa represents an additional forum where collective redress claims could be brought under the representative model. According to this provision, a claimant may sue the defendant at the place where his branch is located. Sometimes, Art 7(5) BIa might offer a closer forum than the domicile of the defendant. Centralisation of all claims could be achieved at this place, just as under Art 4 BIa. Nevertheless, this forum will not always be available, as not all defendants possess branches in all EU Member States. For this reason, this provision is not further examined here.

iv. Interim Conclusion

As the *Henkel* case shows, the CJEU seems to advocate a strict interpretation of the EU private international law rules on jurisdiction, at least as regards actions protecting general interests. This is because the Court of Justice focuses only on the relationship between the litigating parties and sets aside the subject matter of the action. It remains to be seen whether this case law will equally encompass other kinds of actions, such as damages claims brought by consumer associations on behalf of victims. In the event that the interpretation of the Court in *Henkel* is maintained for all types of collective redress actions under the representative model, Article 4 BIa might well be the only viable forum where collective redress claimants seeking damages could concentrate their claims. On the positive side of the balance, the chapter shows that 7(2) BIa has been successfully used by consumer associations especially in order to fight unfair terms. In all cases, private international law rules on jurisdiction which allocate territorial jurisdiction might be problematic for the bundling of multiple individual claims. Even if a more generous and flexible interpretation were to be adopted, it is not clear whether section 4, Article 7(1) or Article 25 BIa would offer an appropriate forum where victims could alternatively concentrate their claims. This result shows the inadaptability of the Brussels regime to collective redress.

B. The Dutch Model

The Dutch model on collective redress is an innovative and relatively effective one. As a result, this model deserves to be included within this research project. Although it fosters effective administration of justice, the Dutch collective redress system challenges EU private international rules on jurisdiction. In light of this, this section first provides an outline of the Dutch model (i.). It specifically focuses on the Dutch out-of-court collective settlement procedure. Then, two cross-border cases that have been tackled by the Amsterdam Court of Appeal are studied. These examples put the spotlight on the international jurisdiction issues (ii., iii. and iv.). This section ends with a conclusion (v.).

i. Outline of the Dutch Model

The Netherlands possesses two collective redress instruments. On the one hand, Article 3:305a of the Dutch Civil Code (DCC) enables qualified associations or foundations to bring claims for injunctive or declaratory relief with the objective of protecting general interests.[190] On the other hand, the Dutch legislator

[190] In order to build up the outline of the Dutch model, the bibliographical sources listed in Annex II.A. were used.

adopted a specific procedure for mass damages claims in 2005, namely the *Wet collectieve afwikkeling van massaschades* (*WCAM*). It has to be highlighted that the Netherlands has not implemented a judicial mechanism allowing collective redress actions for damages yet. Discussions are currently ongoing at the Ministry of Justice in order to complete the procedural toolkit with such an action.[191] The following lines focus on the *WCAM* as the first instrument is part of the representative model analysed earlier in this book.

Prior to the start of the *WCAM* procedure, a representative association or foundation concludes an agreement with the alleged wrongdoer(s), on behalf of a group of victims (also called interested parties). This negotiation phase takes place out-of-court. The *WCAM* is substantially broad and usually applies to agreements whereby victims seek compensation. Since its reform in 2013, the mechanism's material scope has been enlarged and also applies to bankruptcy cases. This means that the *WCAM* procedure applies even when victims seek something other than compensation.

Once the settlement agreement is concluded, parties jointly petition the Amsterdam Court of Appeal, which has exclusive jurisdiction under the *WCAM* to make said agreement binding pursuant to Article 1013(3) of the Dutch Civil Code of Procedure (DCCP). In case petitioners were to have difficulties reaching an agreement, a pre-trial hearing in the Court of Appeal is available. As regards the substantive aspects of the settlement agreement, Article 7:907(2) DCC and Article 1013(1) DCCP enumerate a series of basic requirements that have to be fulfilled. Specifically, the agreement must contain a description of the event to which the agreement relates; a description of the group(s) of victims; the (approximate) number of persons pertaining to the mentioned group(s); the compensation that will be awarded, as well as the conditions that should be met in order to obtain redress; the procedure by which compensation will be awarded; and the name of the persons who should receive written notification. The settlement agreement has to be annexed to the request.

Subsequently, the Amsterdam Court of Appeal must assess whether the settlement agreement is fair and complies with the requirements imposed by the DCC. In order to achieve this objective, the court holds a hearing session in order to gather petitioners' arguments. At the same time, the court invites any person concerned with the agreement to appear in court and file a statement of opposition. The Amsterdam Court of Appeal shall reject the agreement in the event one of the grounds of refusal listed in Article 7:907(3) DCC arises. In particular, the most important elements examined by the court are the amount of compensation awarded to the victims on the one hand, and the representative nature of the association or foundation on the other. If the court is not entirely satisfied, it may offer petitioners the possibility to amend the settlement agreement. In case the court

[191] A bill was presented to the Dutch Parliament on 16 November 2016. An English comment was drafted by I Tzankova, available on www.collectiveredress.org/newsitem/6041, regarding this new instrument. Unfortunately, the Bill has not been translated to English yet.

considers that the contractual terms agreed upon are fair, it declares it binding on interested parties. Following the announcement of the court's decision, the group of victims on whose behalf the agreement is concluded should have an opportunity to opt out of the settlement. Accordingly, the judge sets up an appropriate timeframe of at least three months in order for people to express their desire not to be bound by the decision (Article 7:908(3) DCC). Importantly, only petitioners may jointly appeal the Amsterdam Court's decision.

Once the opt-out period is over and the decision has become binding, the compensation has to be allocated to interested parties. In light of this, people bound by the decision should present all the relevant documents that prove the existence of their claim in order to receive compensation. Usually, the procedure, the necessary documents and the distribution plan are detailed within the settlement agreement or annexed to it. In this regard, the settlement agreement may provide that the right to compensation expires after a certain period of time. This timeframe cannot be reduced to less than one year (Article 7:907(6) DCC).

The literature underlines the following positive aspects of the *WCAM*:[192] from the alleged wrongdoer's perspective, the *WCAM* is an interesting alternative to the opening of a multitude of individual proceedings. In this sense, the Dutch collective redress procedure represents a saving of costs and time. Additionally, the *WCAM* offers closure to the alleged wrongdoer, given that people encompassed in the settlement agreement lose their right to bring individual proceedings regarding the same dispute. Finally, thanks to the *WCAM*, loss of reputation can be avoided. As for interested parties, the *WCAM* allows them to centralise their claims in a single forum thanks to the help of a representative body. Here too, savings on costs and time can be achieved. On the negative side of the balance, the availability of a judicial collective redress action is missing.[193] Indeed, this kind of procedural tool would probably encourage parties to settle. Typically, this could have a significant impact on cases where negative-value claims are involved.

ii. The Shell Settlement

a. Summary of Facts

Shell is one of the most important oil and gas companies in the world. It is owned by Shell Transport and Trading Company (STT), which is seated in the United Kingdom, and Shell Petroleum N.V. (Royal Dutch), registered in the Netherlands. On 9 January 2004, the Shell group announced that it would proceed to the

[192] Government of The Netherlands, The Dutch 'Class Action Financial Settlement Act' ('WCAM'), available at www.rijksoverheid.nl/documenten/richtlijnen/2008/06/24/de-nederlandse-wet-collectieve-afwikkeling-massaschade (only available in Dutch); B Krans, 'The Dutch Act on Collective Settlement on Mass Damages' (2014) 27 *Global Business & Development Law Journal* 281, 287.

[193] On this particular point, see the interesting conclusion of JJ Kuipers, 'La loi sur le règlement collectif de dommages de masse aux Pays-Bas et ses ambitions dans l'espace judiciaire européen' (2012) 64(1) *Revue internationale de droit comparé* 213, 226–27.

re-categorisation of its 'proven' reserves, which correspond to the oil and gas reserves that the company plans to market quickly.[194] Specifically, it appears that the proven reserves of Shell had been overestimated for years because of allegedly unlawful bookkeeping practices.[195] As a result, the price of the group's shares dropped, affecting shareholders' investment all over the world.

Subsequently, some investors brought class actions in the US, claiming that Shell's disclosures regarding its actual reserves from 8 April 1999 until 2004 were misleading and thus, violated American federal securities legislation and regulations.[196] Eventually, parties to the US class action settled. Similarly, in January 2006, some EU investors brought proceedings in the United States in order to obtain redress from Shell. Nevertheless, the US courts rejected jurisdiction over non-American investors.[197] In light of these considerations, the Dutch shareholders association (VEB), alongside the Shell Reserves Compensation Foundation (the Foundation) and two pension funds on the one hand, and STT and Royal Dutch on the other, came to an agreement regarding the compensation of shareholders domiciled outside the US. On 11 April 2007, they presented a joint petition to the Amsterdam Court of Appeal under the *WCAM* procedure in order to make the agreement binding.[198] The declaration of the binding nature of the agreement was rendered on 29 May 2009. In particular, the settlement aimed at compensating shareholders – meaning natural or legal persons – who acquired shares in STT or Royal Dutch outside the US from 8 April 1999 until 18 March 2004, and who were domiciled or seated outside the US. Petitioners estimate that 500,000 investors would be covered by the agreement.[199] From these investors, 68 per cent of Royal Dutch's shareholders were domiciled or seated in Europe – in particular, the Netherlands, Switzerland, France, Germany and Belgium –, and 96 per cent of STT's shareholders had their domicile or seat in the United Kingdom.

According to the settlement agreement, the Shell companies were liable to compensate shareholders who resided outside the US, up to USD 352.6 million for the damage they suffered following the drop of the share price.[200] Yet, this

[194] B Laperche et al (eds), *Innovation, Evolution and Economic Change – New Ideas in the Tradition of Galbraith* (Edward Elgar, 2006) 179.

[195] ibid; 'Humiliation: A once Proud Firm, Brought Down by its own Flaws, Needs a Thorough Shake-up' (22.04.2014) *The Economist*, available at www.economist.com/node/2611051.

[196] Amsterdam Court of Appeal, case 106.010.887 rendered on 29 May 2009 (Shell Decision) 10. The decision is available at http://globalclassactions.stanford.edu/content/royal-dutch-shell-decision-decision-amsterdam-court-appeal-2009. Note that all the documents concerning the Shell dispute were originally available at www.shellsettlement.com/docs/, which is no longer accessible. However, most of those documents can still be consulted on archive.org.

[197] ibid 11.

[198] ibid 2.

[199] ibid 22.

[200] ibid 14. The Distribution plan is described at section II of the Shell Settlement Agreement, available at https://web.archive.org/web/20160811083710/http://shellsettlement.com/docs/Exhibit%201%20Settlement%20Agreement.pdf.

obligation did not amount to the acknowledgement of any responsibility by the Shell group. As regards shareholders, in case the settlement agreement became binding and they chose not to opt out, they would lose their right to initiate individual proceedings against the Shell companies.[201]

In its decision, the Amsterdam Court of Appeal focused on three questions: the first concerns the notification process of the binding decision and the right to opt out, the second covers international jurisdiction, and the last one consists in an assessment of the substantive aspects of the settlement agreement, notably its reasonableness. The next lines examine how the Court of Appeal established jurisdiction, but the remaining questions are set aside as they are secondary for the sake of this research project.

Figure 1 Geographic Location of Parties Involved in the Shell Settlement

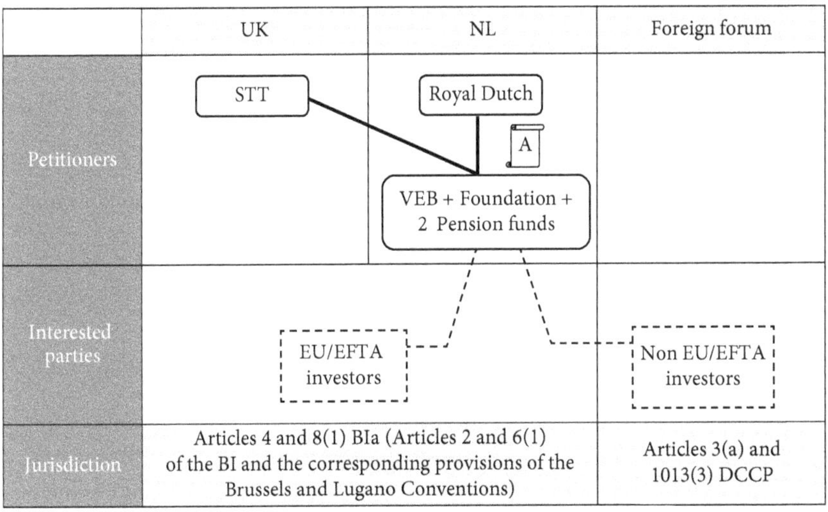

* A: Agreement.

b. Questions Regarding Jurisdiction

In order to establish its jurisdictional power, the Amsterdam Court of Appeal distinguishes between investors domiciled or seated in a Member State, and investors whose domicile or seat is located outside the EU.[202] It is useful to recall that in any case, shareholders who reside in the US are not encompassed in the settlement agreement concluded under the *WCAM* procedure. As far as other non-EU investors are concerned, the court has jurisdiction to rule on their case according

[201] Art IX of the Shell Settlement Agreement (n 200).
[202] Shell Settlement Agreement (n 200) 30–34.

to Dutch private international rules on jurisdiction. In particular, Article 3 DCCP states that

> [w]here legal proceedings are to be initiated by a petition of the petitioner or his solicitor (…), Dutch courts have jurisdiction: (a) if either the petitioner or, where there are more petitioners, one of them, or one of the interested parties mentioned in the petition has his domicile or habitual residence in the Netherlands.

As for shareholders residing within the EU, the Dutch court relied on Articles 4 and 8(1) BIa (ex-Articles 2 and 6(1) BRI), as well as the corresponding provisions of the Brussels and Lugano Convention for investors domiciled in a state covered by these laws.[203] The rest of this section explains how said court established jurisdiction under the BIa and offer a critical assessment. Other international texts on jurisdiction remain out of the scope of this research project.

Article 4 BIa

In its decision, the Amsterdam Court of Appeal explains that it has jurisdiction over investors who reside in the Netherlands according to Article 4 BIa. Curiously, the court considers that interested parties to the settlement agreement are the persons to be sued under the BIa.[204] In other words, investors have to be considered as defendants within the meaning of the Regulation. As explained in the next sub-section, the Dutch Court relies on Article 8(1) BIa in order to extend its jurisdictional power to investors located outside the Netherlands, but within the EU.[205] The same technique is applied in order to bind victims located in states submitted to the Brussels and the Lugano Conventions.

The reasoning of the Court of Appeal is questionable on various grounds. To start with, the court explains that the case at issue enters the material scope of the Regulation (Article 1 BIa).[206] Nevertheless, it does not investigate whether an international component exists,[207] although many investors, their representatives and Royal Dutch were all domiciled in the Netherlands. In case those investors acquired their shares on the Dutch market, one may wonder whether this situation actually possesses an international nature that would justify the application of the BIa.

Nevertheless, one of the parties to the negotiations, namely STT, was domiciled in another Member State. This factor may well give an international component to the *Shell* case. Additionally, a great number of investors claiming compensation

[203] Although, the Amsterdam Court of Appeal applied the provisions of the BI, reference is made to the BIa, which is the text currently in force.
[204] Shell Decision, (n 196) 31.
[205] ibid.
[206] ibid 30–31.
[207] H van Lith, *The Dutch Collective Settlements Act and Private International Law* (2010) 31, available at ec.europa.eu/competition/consultations/2011_collective_redress/saw_annex_en.pdf.

resided abroad. In the *Owusu* case,[208] the CJEU accepted the application of the Brussels regime in an action brought by a British claimant against various defendants, one of whom was domiciled in the United Kingdom, for an accident that occurred in a third state. However, one might wonder whether the solution should be the same as regards Shell investors domiciled in the Netherlands who acquired shares in Royal Dutch on the local securities market. In all cases, even though this question is interesting from a theoretical point of view, since it would clarify the 'international degree' that a dispute needs to possess in order to fall within the scope of the BIa, it appears to be secondary in this case as Dutch rules on jurisdiction alternatively open a forum in the Netherlands for a *WCAM* settlement to take place.

Furthermore, parties to the contract must bring a joint petition to the Amsterdam Court of Appeal in order to make their settlement agreement binding. In this context, it is doubtful that the presentation of a joint petition under the *WCAM* procedure can be considered as contentious proceedings,[209] since the court is seised in the absence of a present dispute.[210] Yet, one may wonder whether the filing of objections in the Court of Appeal might call into question this reasoning. Similarly, it is doubtful that petitioners seek declaratory relief. Instead, it is reasonable to conclude that the petition presented to the Amsterdam Court of Appeal triggers a non-contentious procedure.

More generally, one may wonder whether non-contentious proceedings fall within the scope of the BIa.[211] At first sight, the wording of the Regulation does not exclude them from its scope of application. In this sense, the Jenard Report explicitly states that the text applies 'irrespective of whether the proceedings are contentious or non-contentious'.[212] Along the same line of reasoning, the last version of the Regulation makes clear that the Brussels regime encompasses both out-of-court settlements validated by a court, as well as the ones concluded in the course of proceedings (Article 2(b) BIa). Finally, de Miguel Asensio confirms this interpretation in light of the *Schneider* judgment of 2013.[213] In this case, a Hungarian citizen under guardianship appealed the decision of the Sofia District Court, which denied him the authorisation to dispose of a property located in Bulgaria. The Court of Justice rejected the application of the BIa because questions

[208] Case C-281/02 *Andrew Owusu v N. B. Jackson, trading as 'Villa Holidays Bal-Inn Villas' and Others* [2005] ECR I-01383, para 35.

[209] T Bosters, *Collective Redress and Private International Law in the EU* (Springer, 2017) 121; L Perreau Saussine, 'Quelle place pour les class actions dans le règlement de Bruxelles I ?' (2011) 20 *La Semaine Juridique – Édition Générale* 992, 995.

[210] Virgós Soriano and Garcimartín Alférez (n 25) 118.

[211] Bosters, *Collective Redress and Private International Law in the EU* (n 209) 121; Perreau Saussine, 'Quelle place pour les class actions dans le règlement de Bruxelles I ?' (n 209) 995; I Tzankova and H van Lith, 'Class Actions and Class Settlements Going Global: the Netherlands' in Fairgrieve and Lein, *Extraterritoriality and Collective Redress* (n 164) 86 and fn 55.

[212] This argument is developed by van Lith (n 207) 9 citing the Jenard Report.

[213] Case C-386/12 *Proceedings brought by Siegfried János Schneider* [ECLI:EU:C:2013:633].

regarding capacity remain out of the Brussels regime's scope.[214] However, according to de Miguel Asensio this indirectly means that there is no impediment for the BIa to encompass non-contentious actions.[215]

Even assuming that this statement is correct, one cannot help but notice the unsuitability of the BIa with regard to non-contentious actions: to start with, the dichotomy between defendant and claimant that is applicable to usual contentious actions is tough to transpose to this kind of proceedings.[216] In particular, the wording used by the EU legislator regarding rules on jurisdiction, as well as recognition and enforcement do not fit non-contentious schemes. For example, by using the words 'defendant' and 'be sued' – and not 'petitioners' – in the provisions related to jurisdiction, the EU legislator seems to have contentious proceedings in mind. Then, although court settlements are explicitly included within the scope of the Regulation, the text only refers to them for enforcement purposes. In light of this, it is not clear whether rules on jurisdiction equally apply to court settlements. The exclusive application of rules regarding enforcement to settlements because of their non-contentious nature would not be especially shocking. It is well known that chapter 2 of the BIa on jurisdiction and chapter 3 on recognition and enforcement are relatively independent.[217] To such an extent that when national courts acquire jurisdiction according to their national legislation, the settlements validated by them still benefit from the EU enforcement regime.[218]

Therefore, even if one admitted that the joint petition would fall under the Brussels regime, the reason(s) that motivated the Amsterdam Court of Appeal to qualify interested parties as defendants is/are unclear. The fact that interested parties must be summoned to appear before the court seems to have constituted a relevant factor.[219] Moreover, the opportunity for interested parties to file an objection in the Court of Appeal is an additional element that supports this interpretation.[220] According to van Lith, this conception fits Dutch civil procedure but might not

[214] ibid para 31.

[215] P de Miguel Asensio, 'Ley de la Jurisdicción Voluntaria y Derecho Internacional Privado' (2016) XVI *Anuario Español de Derecho Internacional Privado* 147, 153 and fn 8.

[216] ibid 155-56; A Halfmeier, 'Recognition of a WCAM Settlement in Germany' (2012) *Nederlands Internationaal Privaatrecht* 176, 178; Kuipers, 'La loi sur le règlement collectif de dommages de masse aux Pays-Bas et ses ambitions dans l'espace judiciaire européen' (n 193) 230–31; Perreau Saussine (n 209) 995.

[217] Perreau Saussine (n 209) 996.

[218] ibid.

[219] Shell Decision (n 196) 31; R Hermans and J de B Leuveling Tjeenk, 'International Class Action Settlements in the Netherlands since *Converium*' in *The International Comparative Legal Guide to: Class & Group Actions 2016* 6, available at iclg.com. As for Kramer, she expresses doubts on the reasoning of the Amsterdam Court of Appeal (XE Kramer, 'Securities Collective Action and Private International Law Issues in Dutch WCAM Settlements: Global Aspirations and Regional Boundaries' (2014) 27 *Global Business & Development Law Journal* 235, 259).

[220] Van Lith (n 207) 38; Hermans and Leuveling Tjeenk, 'International Class Action Settlements in the Netherlands since *Converium*' (n 219) 6.

be shared by all national legal orders or the CJEU.[221] In fact, the reasoning of the Court of Appeal brings a new question to the table, namely what does 'defendant' mean within the scope of the Regulation and who should interpret it.[222] In the case at issue, the reasoning of the Court of Appeal means that it has jurisdiction if only one interested party is domiciled or seated in the Netherlands.[223] Therefore, this particular court has the power to rule on a global collective redress settlement, even if it does not have any serious connection with the case at stake.

It is difficult to qualify both petitioners as defendants,[224] since they jointly present the settlement agreement to the Court of Appeal. In light of this, neither of them is the party 'to be sued'. As regards interested parties, their position is ambiguous as in many other collective redress schemes. On the one hand, some elements indicate that they act similarly as defendants: for instance, they are able to file objections and must be summoned. On the other hand, however, they are not technically parties to the proceedings and hence, they should not acquire the status of defendant.[225] Furthermore, Halfmeier puts the spotlight on the fact that the possibility to opt out is not offered to the defendant in contentious proceedings.[226] Therefore, it is not convincing to qualify interested parties as such. Because interested parties have no right to appeal the decision of the Amsterdam Court of Appeal, Kuipers comes to the same conclusion.[227]

Taking these considerations into account, a 'fiction' might be used in order to find out who the defendant in a *WCAM* procedure is. Specifically, the status of claimant could be allocated to people who allegedly have a claim because they suffered harm, and the status of defendant to the people who are presumably responsible for said harm.[228] Accordingly, for the sake of the application of the BIa, interested parties would be qualified as claimants, and the alleged wrongdoer who contractually obliges himself to pay would be the defendant. Even though this reasoning might be fair, it is quite acrobatic. In particular, it generates two issues: the first is that the effectiveness of the *WCAM* would be negatively limited. In case this procedure is the only way for interested parties to have access to justice, this interpretation might be counterproductive. The second issue is that this reasoning

[221] Van Lith (n 207) 38.

[222] While van Lith considers that the interpretation of this procedural term should be left to Member States, Kuipers advocates a uniform interpretation (*cf* van Lith (n 207) 37 and Kuipers (n 193) 230).

[223] Kuipers (n 193), 233; Tzankova and van Lith, 'Class Actions and Class Settlements Going Global' (n 210) 84; van Lith (n 207) 39.

[224] See Bosters (n 209) 129–33, who also questions this qualification.

[225] JJ Kuipers, 'Schemes of Arrangement and Voluntary Collective Redress: A Gap in the Brussels I Regulation' (2012) 8 (2) *Journal of Private International Law* 225, 235–37; Tzankova and van Lith (n 211) 72.

[226] Halfmeier, 'Recognition of a WCAM Settlement in Germany' (n 216) 178.

[227] Kuipers (n 193) 230.

[228] According to Kuipers, the alleged wrongdoer should indeed be considered as the defendant in a WCAM procedure because he is the one accused of having committed harm and against whom compensation is sought (Kuipers (n 193) 231).

is no longer appropriate if one considers the possibility for the alleged wrongdoer to start a declaratory negative action that aims at releasing it from any liability. In such an action, the alleged wrongdoer would be the claimant and interested parties would be on the side of the defence.

To sum up, even if non-contentious actions such as joint petitions under the *WCAM* were encompassed within the Brussels regime, important mismatches would remain. Notably, the unsuitability of the defendant/claimant dichotomy to the Dutch collective redress model puts the principle of predictability into jeopardy.

Article 8(1) BIa

In the next lines, it is assumed that, according to Article 4 BIa, interested parties domiciled or seated in the Netherlands in the *Shell* case are defendants in the proceedings. In this vein, the question whether Article 8(1) BIa may constitute an appropriate ground for the Amsterdam Court of Appeal to expand its jurisdictional power and reach interested parties domiciled in other Member States has to be resolved. As explained in the previous section (I.B.iii.), Article 8(1) BIa permits the accumulation of claims in the forum of one of the defendants' domicile, when these claims are so closely connected that it is expedient to hear them together in order to avoid potentially irreconcilable – meaning contradictory – judgments. Specifically, the risk of irreconcilable judgments must stem from the similar situation of fact or law. Additionally, a previous factual link must exist between the co-defendants for Article 8(1) BIa to apply, in light of the principle of predictability.

As regards the case at issue, the Amsterdam Court of Appeal explains that Article 8(1) BIa is applicable, as claims that the Shell companies owe against interested parties are closely connected.[229] This is so, given that the alternative scenario, namely the existence of numerous individual proceedings in different Member States, would probably lead to irreconcilable judgments.[230] Moreover, the court states that the application of potentially different substantive laws does not call into question this conclusion. It particularly refers to the relationship between STT and English investors, which may be governed by English and not Dutch law.[231] In light of this, the court makes quite clear that the point of attention is the degree of similarity that Shell's claims possess under the settlement agreement.

In the event that the Court of Appeal is right to focus on the settlement agreement, it is highly likely that the claims of the Shell group arise from the same factual situation. Because the position of the Shell companies towards investors is analogous and stems from the same event,[232] the factual situation is similar.

[229] Shell Decision (n 196) 31–32.
[230] ibid.
[231] ibid 32.
[232] Van Lith (n 207), 40.

The same is true as regards the legal situation: although different national laws may apply to the substance of the case, this does not prevent the application of Article 8(1) BIa.[233] Nevertheless, this reasoning is relatively uneasy, since it is hard to determine what claims are held by the Shell group and against whom. According to the Court of Appeal, it seems that Shell's claim against investors consists in the respect of the terms of the settlement agreement.[234]

Finally, as regard the principle of predictability, it is doubtful that it is guaranteed, as there is no previous link between the co-defendants.[235] As a result, a Spanish investor who acquired shares in Royal Dutch and who was subsequently harmed by the company's conduct could be surprised to be encompassed in a Dutch collective redress scheme just because another investor – that he/she does not know – is domiciled there. This result is even more far-fetched in the *Converium* case (iii.), given that the majority of victims were located in Switzerland and only a minority resided in the Netherlands. For this particular reason, and even following the Court of Appeal's reasoning, the accumulation of claims in a single forum pursuant to Article 8(1) BIa should be rejected.

In all cases, the Amsterdam Court's decision to ground its assessment of Article 8(1) BIa on the existence of the settlement agreement rather than the underlying relationship between parties is confusing. At the time the court assessed the application of said provision, the settlement agreement was not binding. Technically, therefore, Shell did not possess any claim against investors.

If one admits that the Amsterdam Court of Appeal should rather focus on the underlying relationship binding interesting parties with the Shell Group,[236] Article 8(1) BIa could also be difficult to apply: since each relationship would have to be considered individually, differences between the investors' situation could arise. Typically, this would be the case if interested parties were divided in different groups of victims, according to the specific circumstances of their case. In this context, one might wonder whether the claims of the alleged wrongdoer would remain similar.

iii. Converium Settlement

a. Summary of Facts

On 9 July 2010, Converium, Zurich Financial Services (ZFS), the Stichting Converium Foundation (the foundation) and the VEB presented a joint petition under the *WCAM* procedure in the Amsterdam Court of Appeal in order to make

[233] *Freeport* (n 40) para 41; *Painer* (n 19) paras 79–82.
[234] Shell Decision (n 196) 32.
[235] Kuipers, 'Schemes of Arrangement and Voluntary Collective Redress' (n 225) 237–40.
[236] Kuipers seems to endorse this approach (Kuipers (n 193) 232).

their agreement binding. According to said agreement, Converium and ZFS were bound to pay USD 58,400,000 to investors who acquired shares in Converium outside the US.[237] The facts that gave rise to the damage are as follows: Converium and ZFS – the sole shareholder of Converium before December 2001 –,[238] whose domicile is in Switzerland, made repeated disclosures between January 2002 and September 2004 concerning their reserves for risks. According to the companies, these reserves were deemed insufficient and had to be adjusted.[239] This statement resulted in a drop of the share price and, thus, harmed approximately 12,000 investors. Among these investors, approximately 8,500 were located in Switzerland, about 1,500 in the United Kingdom and around 200 in the Netherlands.[240] It should also be highlighted that Converium's shares were traded on different markets including the US and Switzerland. Following these events, a group of investors domiciled in the US and who bought their shares on the American Stock Exchange brought proceedings in the District Court for the Southern District of New York. Eventually, the parties came to an agreement in December 2008.[241] However, the US District Court stated that its jurisdictional power could not reach investors domiciled outside the US and who had bought their participation on a foreign stock exchange.[242] As a result, VEB and the Foundation concluded two agreements with each of the alleged wrongdoers, on behalf of investors who purchased shares in Converium on a non-US stock exchange and who were domiciled outside the US territory.[243]

Conversely to the *Shell* case, the Amsterdam Court of Appeal dealt with the question of jurisdiction previously to the notification to interested parties about their right to opt out and before assessing the fairness of the agreement. In particular, the court affirmed that it had jurisdiction under Articles 4 and 8(1) BIa as regards investors domiciled in a Member State. The same reasoning applies mutatis mutandis to persons located in Switzerland and, hence, submitted to the Lugano Convention. Alternatively, the court ruled that it could equally have jurisdiction under Article 7(1) BIa. The reasoning of the Court of Appeal regarding the application of this provision is assessed below. Beforehand, it has to be underlined that the allocation of jurisdiction in Converium is quite arguable because the Netherlands does not entertain close connections with the case. To be more precise, both defendants, as well as the majority of investors, were located in Switzerland.

[237] See Converium and ZFS settlement agreements. All the documents concerning the Converium case are available at www.converiumsettlement.com.

[238] www.converiumsettlement.com/case-history.html.

[239] Amsterdam Court of Appeal, case 200.070.039/01 rendered on 12 November 2010 (Converium Decision) 3–4.

[240] ibid 5–6.

[241] ibid 4–5.

[242] ibid.

[243] ibid 5–6.

Figure 2 Geographic Location of Parties Involved in the Converium Settlement

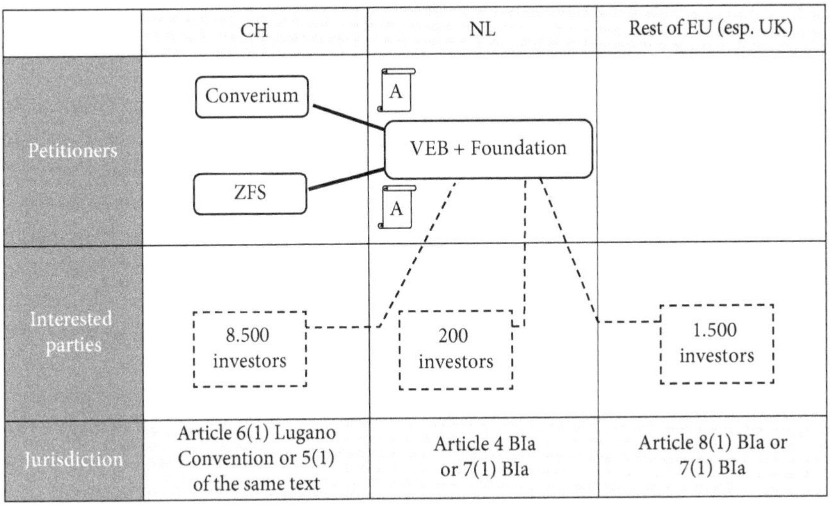

* A: Agreement.

b. Application of Article 7(1) BIa

First of all, the Amsterdam Court of Appeal explains that the validity of the settlement agreements rests upon its decision. Specifically, the court clarifies that Converium and ZFS must compensate investors who suffered harm only once the Agreements become binding.[244] Even though this contractual obligation has not come into effect yet, the Court of Appeal considers that the forum of Article 7(1) BIa – and the corresponding provision of the Lugano Convention – should be open. In order to justify its reasoning, the Court explains that the *Henkel* case regarding preventive actions may be transposed to the dispute at issue.[245] For the record, in said case, the CJEU held that preventive actions fell within the scope of Article 7(2) BIa, although the damage had not occurred yet. Secondly, the settlement agreements state that the Swiss undertakings must pay the amount of compensation to a bank account located in the Netherlands.[246] Subsequently, the Foundation will be in charge of distributing the money to the victims. As a result, the Court in Amsterdam concludes that the place where the performance of the contractual obligation shall be undertaken is the Netherlands.[247] The next lines first examine whether the joint petition is a contractual matter. In case the answer is positive,

[244] ibid 13.
[245] ibid.
[246] According to Sch A of the escrow agreement concluded between Converium and the representatives, an escrow agent is designated in order to manage the money of the settlement agreement, which has to be paid on a bank account (ABN AMRO Bank N.V. with registered office in Amsterdam). A civil law notary domiciled in The Hague will endorse the role of escrow agent. The same is applicable to ZFS.
[247] Converium Decision (n 239) 14.

the obligation in question and its place of performance must be identified. At this stage of the explanation, it is already clear that Article 7(1)(a) BIa is the relevant jurisdictional ground, since no sale of goods or provision of services took place pursuant to Article 7(1)(b) BIa.

In *Converium*, the Amsterdam Court of Appeal focuses its attention on the relationship of the parties to the proceedings (here, the petitioners). Here too, however, it is not clear whether the relationship between the petitioners or between the alleged wrongdoers and the victims should be the appropriate basis to establish jurisdiction.[248] Because the claim consists in a joint petition that refers to an agreement, it is tempting to infer that the request is contractual: indeed, petitioners conclude a contract that will benefit interested parties. In particular, the alleged wrongdoers commit themselves to pay compensation to investors, so there is at least one obligation freely assumed by one contractual party.

However, some think that the conditional nature of a settlement agreement makes the application of Article 7(1) BIa doubtful.[249] One may counter-argue that the CJEU has repeatedly held that the existence of a contract is not necessary for said provision to apply. In this sense, the conditional nature of the agreement shall not *per se* exclude a petition under the *WCAM* from the scope of 'matters related to contracts'. In this sense, the case law delivered by the CJEU regarding prize notification to consumers might help to prove this point: in *Engler*,[250] for example, the Court of Justice held that a professional who sent a letter containing a prize notification to a consumer might be a contractual matter pursuant to Article 7(1) BIa. Indeed, when a professional sends a letter on its own initiative to the consumer's domicile, which designates him/her as the winner of a prize, this may well constitute an obligation freely assumed by said professional. Only section 4 BIa would require the actual conclusion of a contract in order to apply. Along the same line of reasoning, a settlement agreement whereby an alleged wrongdoer commits himself to compensate victims may well enter the scope of Article 7(1) BIa, even though the binding effect is submitted to the subsequent approval of a Court.

Another argument that would lead to the conclusion that the matter is not contractual is that the obligation(s) freely assumed must take place *inter partes*.[251] In other words, because Converium and ZFS assume obligations towards third parties, the forum of Article 7(1) BIa would consequently not be open. However, according to Lehmann, this requirement does not mean that the claimant and the defendant must be the initial parties to the contract.[252] Rather, it 'suffices that

[248] Tzankova and van Lith (n 211) 84; van Lith (n 207) 42–45.

[249] Kramer, 'Securities Collective Action and Private International Law Issues in Dutch WCAM Settlements' (n 219) 260; Kuipers (n 193); van Lith (n 207) 43–44.

[250] *Engler* (n 49).

[251] B Allemeerschen, 'Transnational class settlements Lessons from *Converium*' in S Wrbka et al (eds), *Collective Actions: Enhancing Access to Justice and Reconciling Multilayer Interests* (Cambridge University Press, 2012) 372.

[252] M Lehmann, 'Special Jurisdiction (Article 7(1))' in A Dickinson and E Lein (eds), *The Brussels I Regulation Recast* (Oxford University Press, 2015) 145.

they have succeeded ex post to the position of one of the contractual parties'. He then mentions the assignment of claims, subrogation and succession as examples. In this vein, can one assume that interested parties succeed to the representative entities who initially concluded the settlement agreement with the alleged wrongdoer? This interpretation is rather difficult to accept since the succession of parties – supposing that it can actually be qualified as such – does not take place at the time the court is seised but only once the settlement agreement is declared binding. However, it seems reasonable to admit that interested parties must have acquired the position of contractual parties at the time the court is seised in order to benefit from the forum of Article 7(1) BIa.

Yet, supposing that the action is a contractual matter, the obligation in question has to be pinpointed and its place of performance located, according to Article 7(1)(a) BIa, as the settlement agreement does not consist in the delivery of goods or the provision of services. Although each contractual partner, as well as the beneficiaries, assumes different rights and obligations, the compensation of victims appears to be the primary obligation that justifies the petition to the Amsterdam Court of Appeal. The interested parties' waiver not to start subsequent individual proceedings is contingent on the compensation.[253]

Then, given that Converium and ZFS commit themselves to pay the due amount to a Dutch bank account, the Court of Appeal considers that the Netherlands is the place where the obligation has to be performed. On the one hand, one might consider that this contractual clause equates to an agreement on the place of performance, which displaces the *Tessili/De Bloos* case law. On the other hand, however, because the money has to be eventually carried to the victims, one might consider that the Netherlands is an intermediary location. In this case, the place of performance of the obligation in question would have to be determined. By default, the law of the habitual residence of the party required to carry out the characteristic obligation – here, the obligation to pay – applies (Article 4(2) of the Rome I Regulation), that is: Swiss law. Under that law, the obligation to pay must be held at the place of the creditor's domicile (Article 74(2)(1) of the Swiss Code of Obligations). Accordingly, the place where the obligation in question should be performed corresponds to the domicile of investors. In such a situation, Article 7(1)(a) BIa does not allow the centralisation of the *WCAM* procedure in a single forum, since investors are domiciled in different Member States.

iv. Other Possible Grounds of Jurisdiction

First of all, the application of section 4 BIa could come into play in the event that consumers protected by said section were represented.[254] Pursuant to this

[253] However, Allemeerschen (n 251) 370 thinks that those two obligations are the main ones in the Settlement Agreement.

[254] Halfmeier (n 216) 177.

provision, the domicile of the defendant seems to be the only location where the settlement agreement could be validated for all consumers. As explained in the next paragraphs, a choice of court agreement could offer an alternative forum, but it is doubtful that it can be imposed on third parties.

The application of section 4 BIa may have important consequences in the event that a consumer is entitled to obtain compensation under a *WCAM* decision, but misses the date in order to manifest him-/herself and obtain the monetary compensation. This consumer could be willing to challenge the decision of the Amsterdam Court of Appeal in subsequent individual proceedings by invoking its lack of jurisdiction. In this case, and supposing that the defendant opposes the existence of a *WCAM* settlement agreement, could consumers raise an exception to the recognition of said settlement?

First of all, it has to be emphasised that the Brussels regime does not regulate the recognition process of settlements. Therefore, it is doubtful that Article 45(1)(e)(i) BIa constitutes any ground for refusal. Rather, it is reasonable to believe that national laws govern the recognition of *WCAM* settlements agreements.[255] Therefore, the possibility to strike out the recognition of a settlement agreement depends on national laws.

Secondly, petitioners could introduce a choice of court clause pursuant to Article 25 BIa into the settlement agreement in order to dispel any doubts regarding the Dutch courts' jurisdiction. In this context, could victims actually be bound by such a clause without having expressly signed or consented to it? Some scholars answer positively to this question.[256] In order to support their approach, they argue that the *Gerling* case[257] should apply, mutatis mutandis, to cases such as *Shell* or *Converium*.

In *Gerling*, the CJEU was asked whether a choice of forum clause could apply to beneficiaries who did not agree to said clause. The Court of Justice held that a choice of court agreement, which is concluded for the benefit of people who are not parties to the contract, may be invoked by such parties. Therefore, it is not necessary that these sign the choice of forum clause.[258] According to this case law, beneficiaries of the *Shell* and *Converium* settlements should be able to invoke a choice of court agreement, which designates Dutch courts. Yet, the question remains as to whether such a clause may be imposed on them. It seems that the answer should be negative in light of the *Société financière* case,[259] where the CJEU held that a choice of court agreement cannot be relied on against a beneficiary if he has not expressly subscribed to such an agreement.

[255] Gaudemet-Tallon (n 20) 496.

[256] Tzankova and van Lith (n 211) 85-86; van Lith (n 207) 46-47. Against: Kramer (n 219) 252.

[257] Case C-201/82 *Gerling Konzern Speziale Kreditversicherungs-AG and others v Amministrazione del Tesoro dello Stato* [1983] ECR 02503.

[258] ibid 10–20.

[259] FJ Garcimartín, 'Prorogation of Jurisdiction' in Dickinson and Lein, *The Brussels I Regulation Recast* (n 252) 301 who cites the case of the CJEU C-112/03 *Société financière et industrielle du Peloux v Axa Belgium and Others* [2005] ECR I-03707, para 43.

Lastly, if the conclusion of a settlement agreement under the *WCAM* is not a contractual matter pursuant to Article 7(1) BIa, the application of Article 7(2) BIa should be examined. For this provision to apply, the action must involve the liability of the alleged wrongdoer. In this sense, the financial loss that followed the alleged wrongdoer's disclosures may justify the application of Article 7(2) BIa. However, the presentation of a settlement agreement to the Amsterdam Court of Appeal does not involve any admission of liability.[260] In this case, it is not certain that Article 7(2) BIa could apply.

v. *Interim Conclusion*

The Dutch model has been highly criticised because of its inadaptability to EU private international rules. However, this model is relatively efficient. Even though a small number of cases have been tried before the Amsterdam Court of Appeal, these cases were certainly significant. The success of the Dutch model may be explained by its flexibility and international coverage. Flexibility is achieved thanks to the Dutch system's focus on efficient administration of justice.[261] For example, Article 7:907 DCC states that associations or organisations should be sufficiently representative in order to negotiate a settlement. However, the provision does not require that all individual victims are represented and said associations or organisations can be created on an ad hoc basis. These flexible rules certainly facilitate the use of the Dutch collective redress mechanism. As regards the broad coverage of *WCAM* actions, it can be achieved thanks to the expansive interpretation of private international law rules on jurisdiction. Specifically, the application of Article 4 and 8(1) or 7(1) BIa allocates jurisdiction to the Amsterdam Court of Appeal when only one interested party is domiciled in the Netherlands.[262] Although such an interpretation fosters access to justice, it might disturb the equilibrium created by the BIa and not always respect the principle of proximity.

C. The Class Action Model

This sub-section starts with a description of the class action model (i.). Then, the emblematic *Schrems* case was selected as a basis for the private international law analysis (ii.). The facts of the case are first described and private international law questions on jurisdiction are subsequently discussed. A conclusion closes the present sub-section (iii.).

[260] In particular, see the Shell Settlement Agreement (n 200) 3–4.
[261] Kuipers (n 193) 220.
[262] Tzankova and van Lith (n 211) 84.

i. Outline of the Class Action Model

According to the class action model, a representative claimant litigates on behalf of a group of victims. Usually, this representative claimant is an individual who also has a claim against the defendant – otherwise, it falls under the representative model for the sake of this research project. In this sense, the structure of this model resembles the American class action device. However, a pure class action model has not been implemented yet in Europe, except perhaps in England where, pursuant to Rule 19.6 of the Civil Procedure Rules, only a victim with a claim can litigate on behalf of a group of individuals.[263] Specifically, this provision requires that the representative possesses an identical interest to the members of the group. Following this reasoning, individual consumers or associations cannot act as representatives when they do not have a proper claim against the defendant.[264] A majority of Member States have implemented mixed mechanisms where individuals, along with representative entities, may litigate on behalf of a group. For instance, Portugal, Italy, Norway, Sweden and Bulgaria have adopted such a system. As far as Spain is concerned, the lawmaker adopted a group action mechanism: according to the law on civil procedure,[265] a group of claimants may gather together and litigate. In this vein, it should be underlined that the class action model is not always based on a representative system. For example, in Austria, the *Österreichisches Modell der Sammelklage* (collective action of the Austrian type) allows individuals, as well as other entities such as consumer associations, to acquire claims of victims and concentrate them into one set of proceedings.[266] In such a scenario, people transfer their right to compensation to an individual, who does not technically act as a representative claimant but for himself. Article 227 of the Austrian Code of Civil Procedure (ACCP) regulates this procedure. From a private international law perspective, there is no difference between a transfer of claims to an individual and a collective redress action, whereby an individual represents the class, as long as the litigating party is a consumer with a proper claim.

ii. Schrems Case

The 'Schrems saga', is a legal dispute between an Austrian lawyer, Maximilian Schrems (Max Schrems) and Facebook which started in 2013. The *Schrems v Facebook* controversy involves various court decisions both at the national and EU levels. In particular, two different kinds of proceedings were generated by this international dispute: firstly, an administrative complaint was brought against

[263] For more information on the system of the United Kingdom regarding collective redress, see Annex II.H.

[264] PG Karlsgodt, *World Class Actions: A Guide to Group and Representative Actions around the Globe* (Oxford University Press, 2012) 589–90.

[265] In particular, see Art 11 of the SLCP. For more information on the Spanish system regarding collective redress, see Annex II. B.

[266] For more information on the Austrian system regarding collective redress, see Annex II. G.

Facebook for breach of data protection laws in 2013. Subsequently, a collective action started in Vienna. Both proceedings gave rise to requests for preliminary ruling to the CJEU. The next paragraphs offer an overview of the administrative complaint, inasmuch as it helps to understand the substance of the dispute. The rest of the section is dedicated to the Austrian cross-border collective redress action, which triggers interesting private international law questions.

As a preliminary note, it is appropriate to issue some caveats: the next lines attempt to faithfully rebuild the *Schrems v Facebook* case. Access to the decisions of the different instance courts, as well as the applications prepared by the claimant have made this possible. However, important documents are missing, such as the answers filed by Facebook against the claimant's assertions. Because of this, it was not always possible to reconstruct perfectly the arguments of the defence in detail. Furthermore, some factual aspects of the case have been fervently debated by the litigating parties and it was not always possible for the courts to establish the truth. These disputed facts are mentioned as they arise.

a. The Administrative Complaint

On 25 June 2013, Max Schrems, a lawyer domiciled in Austria, brought a complaint[267] to the Irish Data Protection Commissioner against Facebook Ireland Ltd – a daughter company of Facebook Inc.[268] Indeed, Ireland corresponds to the place where the company has its EU headquarters. In substance, Max Schrems alleges that the transfer of his data from Facebook Ireland Ltd to the US, where the mother company is located, has to be prohibited, as the latter country does not possess the same protection standards regarding personal data. To support his argument, Max Schrems makes reference to Edward Snowden's disclosures regarding the mass surveillance tactics used by the National Security Agency (NSA).[269] Thanks to a program named PRISM, the NSA has access to information gathered by social networks like Facebook. In light of this, the NSA enjoys a broad power to survey EU Facebook users.

Notwithstanding the above, the Commission's decision 2000/520/EC, adopted in accordance with the Data Protection Directive 95/46/EC,[270] states that transfer

[267] Actually, Max Schrems first brought 22 individual complaints against Facebook to the Irish Data Protection Commissioner. Later on, he brought an additional complaint whose content is analysed in the following paragraphs. Eventually, Max Schrems withdrew the 22 original complaints in 2014. All the complaints are available at europe-v-facebook.org/EN/Complaints/complaints.html.

[268] All documents regarding the administrative complaint can be found on the following website: www.europe-v-facebook.org/DE/Anzeigen/anzeigen.html.

[269] G Greenwald and E MacAskill, 'NSA Prism program taps in to user data of Apple, Google and others' (07.06.2013) *The Guardian*, available at www.theguardian.com/world/2013/jun/06/us-tech-giants-nsa-data; E Macaskill and G Dance, 'NSA Files: Decoded – What the Revelations Mean for You' (01.11.2013) *The Guardian*, available at www.theguardian.com/world/interactive/2013/nov/01/snowden-nsa-files-surveillance-revelations-decoded#section/1.

[270] Council Directive 95/46/EC of the European Parliament and of the Council of 24 October 1995 on the protection of individuals with regard to the processing of personal data and on the free movement

of personal data from the EU to the US is allowed, as long as the latter state guarantees an adequate level of protection. This level of protection has been brought into alignment thanks to the adoption of Safe Harbour principles agreed upon by the US Department of Commerce on the one hand, and the EU Commission on the other.[271] US organisations that comply with said principles are deemed to respect an adequate level of privacy protection. Nevertheless, the Safe Harbour principles do not apply to public bodies like the NSA.

In light of the positive decision of the Commission, the Irish Commissioner rejected Max Schrems' complaint. The case went to the High Court, which referred a question for preliminary ruling to the CJEU. Indeed, the referring court wondered whether the existence of a Commission's decision impedes the surveillance authority (here, the Irish Commissioner) to assess an individual's claim for breach of data protection laws. The CJEU first ruled that the existence of a Commission decision does not suppress the power of a national supervisory authority to assess an individual complaint for breach of data protection rules, as stated in Article 28(4) of the Data Protection Directive.[272]

Then, the CJEU declared the decision of 2000 invalid. The Court of Luxembourg relies on various arguments to support this statement, which essentially all underline the unfortunate limited nature of the Safe Harbour principles, and in particular their inapplicability to US public bodies. Besides, said principles may be discarded where a national security, a public interest, or a law enforcement requirement dictates it. The Court adds that there is apparently no limit to the state's intervention when such a requirement is fulfilled. In this context, general access to personal data by public authorities goes against Article 7 of the Charter of Fundamental Rights of the EU.[273]

Since the invalidation of the Safe Harbour principles, Facebook Ireland Ltd alternatively uses model contracts in order to transfer personal data from the EU to the US. The adoption of standard contractual clauses between Facebook Ireland Ltd and its mother company is allowed by a group of decisions issued by the Commission.[274] In this vein, Max Schrems reformulated his complaint – taking into account the invalidity of the Safe Harbour principles –,[275] which the

of such data [1995] OJ L281/31. This Directive approximates Member States' legislations in order to foster the free movement of personal data, but simultaneously guarantees an appropriate level of protection of individuals' fundamental rights. As of 25 May 2018, Council Directive 95/46/EC was repealed by the recently adopted Council Regulation (EU) 2016/679 of 27 April 2016 on the protection of natural persons with regard to the processing of personal data and on the free movement of such data [2016] OJ L119/1.

[271] For more information on the content of the Safe Harbour principles, see build.export.gov/main/safeharbor/eu/eg_main_018476.

[272] Case C-362/14 *Maximillian Schrems v Data Protection Commissioner* [ECLI:EU:C:2015:650], paras 53–58.

[273] ibid paras 82, 86, 88, 94.

[274] All available at ec.europa.eu/justice/data-protection/international-transfers/transfer/index_en.htm.

[275] After the Safe Harbour principles were struck down by the CJEU, the US Department of Commerce and the European Commission concluded a new agreement on the exchange of personal

Irish Commissioner accepted to assess. The latter then started proceedings against Facebook Ireland Ltd and Mr Schrems in the Irish High Court.[276] Thanks to this, the national supervisory authority wished to obtain another judgment of the CJEU, the object of which consists in determining whether transfer of data under model contracts ensures an appropriate level of protection, as required by the Data Protection Directive.[277]

Finally, Facebook has argued that the administrative complaint should trigger the application of Article 29 BIa on *lis pendens*. In other words, the Austrian court must stay the collective action – whose content is presented in the next paragraphs – because of the existence of a previous administrative complaint. The court of second instance examined this argument and concluded that the object of the administrative process was more restricted than the judicial claim. Because the object of the complaint and the claim did not coincide, *lis pendens* rules could not apply.

In all cases, it is doubtful that the administrative complaint actually represents proceedings brought in the 'court' of a Member State, according to Article 1(1) BIa. In a similar context, the CJEU has recently rejected the application of the BIa to a writ of execution issued by a notary, ruling that he could not be considered as a 'court' within the meaning of the Regulation.[278] In order to support its argument, the CJEU emphasised that in the case at issue, the issuance of the writ was not conducted *inter partes*. Similarly, the complaint brought by Schrems petitions the Irish Data Protection Commissioner to make use of its investigating power pursuant to section 10 of the Irish Data Protection Act.[279] Therefore, this procedure involves no claim, defendant or court. Instead, the complaint generates administrative measures.

b. The Collective Judicial Action

Statement of Facts

In parallel to the administrative complaint in Ireland, Max Schrems started collective redress proceedings in Austria along with seven Facebook users. While the majority of the assignors have their domicile in Austria and India, one user is

data: the EU-US Privacy Shield. This agreement imposes more stringent conditions on the level of privacy protection and prevents general access to personal data by US government bodies. For more information on this agreement, see ec.europa.eu/justice/data-protection/international-transfers/eu-us-privacy-shield/index_en.htm, and in particular the Commission Implementing Decision (EU) 2016/1250 of 12 July 2016 pursuant to Directive 95/46/EC of the European Parliament and of the Council on the adequacy of the protection provided by the EU-US Privacy Shield (notified under document C(2016) 4176) [2016] OJ L207/1.

[276] An update of this administrative procedure is available at europe-v-facebook.org/MU_HC.pdf.

[277] The judgment of the Irish High Court is available at dataprotection.ie/documents/judgements/DPCvFBSchrems.pdf.

[278] Case C-551/15 *Pula Parking d.o.o. v Sven Klaus Tederahn* [ECLI:EU:C:2017:193], paras 54–59.

[279] Available at www.irishstatutebook.ie/eli/1988/act/25/section/10/enacted/en/html#sec10.

domiciled in Germany.[280] Thanks to an ad hoc website, 25,000 users subsequently assigned their claim to Max Schrems.[281] 50,000 additional users were registered on a waiting list. Practically, the action brought by the eight claimants has been possible thanks to Article 235 ACCP – which permits an extension of the action's scope.[282] However, no tribunal has allowed the case to proceed on a class action basis – pursuant to the *Österreichisches Modell der Sammelklage*. As already explained above, thanks to this model, individuals could assign their claims to Mr Schrems, who would bundle them in a single forum. Finally, it has to be mentioned that litigation is financed by a third-party, namely ROLAND ProzessFinanz AG, located in Germany. The firm covers trial costs, as well as the attorney's fees. In case of success, it is entitled to receive a 20 per cent share of the compensation awarded.[283]

As regards the substance of the claim, Mr Schrems argues, among other allegations, that Facebook unlawfully exploits users' personal data. For this reason, he claims up to EUR 500 per victim in compensation for the damage sustained. The Regional Court (*Landesgericht*), which is the first instance court seised, rejected the litigant's claim on the ground that it did not have jurisdiction. Specifically, the Viennese Court considers that Max Schrems cannot qualify as a consumer. Besides, a class action of this size – which involves people from other Member States and even third states – is not allowed by the Austrian Civil Code of Procedure.

In light of this ruling, Max Schrems appealed to the Higher Regional Court (*Oberlandesgericht*). This court partially overturned the first instance court's decision: on the question regarding jurisdiction, the court admitted that Max Schrems is a consumer. However, it agreed with the Regional Court by establishing that EU law does not allow the bundling of 25,000 claims in the Austrian courts.

Eventually, the Supreme Court (*Oberster Gerichtshof*), to which both litigants appealed, had to adjudicate on the admissibility of a collective redress action of the Austrian type and assess the jurisdiction of the courts. In order to fulfil this task, the Supreme Court sent two questions for preliminary ruling to the CJEU.[284] To start with, the referring Court asked whether Mr Schrems is a 'consumer' pursuant to Article 15 BIa, even though he used his Facebook account to publish books, deliver lectures (sometimes against remuneration), operate websites and collect donations and claims of other data subjects. Then, the CJEU is asked to clarify whether Article 16 BIa allows Mr Schrems to invoke the claims previously assigned to him by victims located in Austria, another Member State or even a third state, in the court of his domicile.

[280] Lawsuit initially filed in the Commercial Court of Vienna in 2014, 42–45. The document is available at www.europe-v-facebook.org/sk/sk_en.pdf.

[281] For a country breakdown, see www.europe-v-facebook.org/fbclaim_pat.pdf.

[282] www.europe-v-facebook.org/sk/fs_en.pdf.

[283] www.europe-v-facebook.org/sk/rl_fs_en.pdf.

[284] Case C-498/16 *Maximilian Schrems v Facebook Ireland Limited* [ECLI:EU:C:2018:37], para 24.

In light of the above, the next lines first examine whether Max Schrems should be considered as a consumer pursuant to section 4 BIa and whether he could litigate other consumers' claims. Can assignors open proceedings in Austria on an individual basis? Could Max Schrems, as a representative, benefit from a forum, pursuant to Article 16 BIa? Could national procedural law help to overcome private international law difficulties? What role does party autonomy play as an alternative ground of jurisdiction?

Is Mr Schrems a Consumer?

On the one hand, Facebook considers that Mr Schrems cannot reasonably be defined as a consumer, pursuant to section 4 BIa.[285] The firm argues that the claimant has used his private Facebook account in order to achieve commercial objectives. It should be underlined that parties do not discuss the fact that the defendant directs its activities to Austria, pursuant to Article 15(1)(c) BIa.

According to Facebook's statement, Mr Schrems created two relevant website pages, namely 'europe-v-facebook' and 'fbclaim' in order to advertise the publication of a book (*'Kämpf um deine Daten'*) and participated in different events and conferences – in return for a small remuneration.[286]

To be more specific, the claimant created an association called 'europe-v-facebook' in 2012. A Facebook page and a website – both created in 2011– provide an update on the association's activities.[287] The goal of this association is to enforce fundamental rights of people following violations of data protection laws. Furthermore, this legal framework was used in order to finance part of the administrative proceedings in Ireland.[288] As regards 'fbclaim', this website was created in 2014 with the objective of gathering victims together in a judicial collective action.[289] Importantly, the defendant seems to consider that Mr Schrems used his Facebook private account in order to undertake all those activities.[290] Taking these considerations into account, Facebook believes that the claimant has been using his account in an unusual manner since 2011, which is not proper for a consumer.

On the other hand, in the original lawsuit filed by Mr Schrems in the Regional Court, the claimant argued that the court had jurisdiction pursuant to Article 15(1)(c) BIa.[291] This was so because Mr Schrems was a consumer and as such, he was able to sue Facebook at the place of his domicile. As the Brussels

[285] The arguments of Facebook against Mr Schrems' capacity as a consumer, which are developed in the next lines, can be found in the judgment of the Regional Court of Vienna (*Landesgericht Wien*), case 3Cg 52/14k-29 rendered on 30 June 2015, 12–14.

[286] See ibid 19-23, for a chronological overview of the claimant's activities.

[287] An overview of the Facebook page is available at https://web.archive.org/web/20130112090303/https://www.facebook.com/eversusf and the website is europe-v-facebook.org/EN/en.html.

[288] Judgment of the Regional Court (n 285) 19, 24.

[289] ibid 21, 25. The website is available at www.fbclaim.com/ui/register.

[290] ibid 13-14.

[291] Lawsuit initially filed in the Viennese commercial court (n 280) 9.

regime establishes, section 4 BIa applies to contracts concluded between a consumer and a trader, the former being a person who acts for non-professional purposes.

In this vein, Mr Schrems shows that he has been using his Facebook account for private purposes since 2008. Similarly, the website pages 'europe-v-facebook' and 'fbclaim' have been created and are managed by the claimant himself and pursue a non-professional objective. Specifically, in order to convince the different courts seised, the claimant demonstrated that most of his actions on the above-mentioned online platforms were not related to commercial activities. For example, in his appeal to the second instance court, Mr Schrems states that out of 350 writings posted on 'europe-v-facebook', only four concerned the publication of his book, nine were related to academic or political manifestations – and thus potentially followed a commercial purpose.

Two factual questions complicated national courts' assessment of Mr Schrems' status: to start with, the parties heavily discussed the details of the contractual relationship linking Mr Schrems to Facebook. In particular, the connection between Mr Schrems' Facebook account and the Facebook page is unclear. The claimant maintains that 'europe-v-facebook' is an independent website that has no link with the consumer contract, which is the object of the claim. The relevant timeframe that should be taken into account in order to examine whether Mr Schrems was a consumer or not was debated as well. The change of Facebook's terms and conditions in 2013 added complexities to this question.

On the one hand, the Regional Court agreed with Facebook and clarified that parties' contractual relationship had been governed by two different regimes:[292] indeed, on 15 November 2013, Facebook modified its terms and conditions, which were subsequently accepted by Mr Schrems. Accordingly, the previous contractual relationship between the parties was superseded by the newly concluded contract (novatio).[293] Therefore, in the court's opinion, the contractual relationship of 2013 should be the one taken into account, in order to assess whether Mr Schrems is a consumer or not. It concluded that the professional nature of the claimant's activities had been dominant at least since 2013.[294]

On the other hand, according to the Higher Regional Court of Vienna, it is not clear whether Mr Schrems has used his private Facebook account in order to build up the website or whether he created another account – and thus, concluded a second contract with Facebook. That being said, even though one accepts the fact that an entirely new contract was signed in 2013, which supersedes the previous contractual relationship of the parties, the second instance court considered that since this year, Mr Schrems had used his Facebook account in a private manner. In order to support this argument, the Higher Regional Court acknowledged that the capacity as consumer has to be assessed at the time of the conclusion

[292] Judgment of the Regional Court of Vienna (n 285) 33.
[293] ibid 33–34.
[294] ibid 33–34.

of the contract – here, in 2013.[295] However, the claimant only started using the above-mentioned website page in an objectively professional manner the day he announced the publication of his book, namely 29 May 2014. Therefore, the professional purpose of the consumer contract, if there was one, was merely incidental at that time.[296]

In his Opinion, Advocate General Bobek first dealt with the temporal evolution of the contractual relationship between Mr Schrems and Facebook. He admitted that the time of the contract's conclusion is the relevant stage for assessing parties' status.[297] However, he also acknowledged that, exceptionally, a dynamic approach might be privileged. Typically, the purpose of contracts concerning social media, the duration of which is usually long, could change over time. Accordingly, a potential change of that purpose should be taken into account. As far as the above-mentioned contractual intricacies were concerned, the Advocate General concluded that, in the event that two distinct contracts governed the Facebook account and the Facebook page, Mr Schrems should not lose his consumer status. Indeed, it has to be highlighted that '[k]nowledge, experience, civic engagement or the fact of having acquired certain renown due to litigation do not in themselves prevent someone from being a consumer'.[298] If, on the contrary, the Facebook account and webpage formed a unique contractual relationship, it should be observed whether, the professional activities of Mr Schrems (if they exist) are negligible or predominant. In case the purpose of the contractual relationship does not clearly emanate from the terms and conditions, the evolution of that purpose over time has to be inferred from the facts.[299]

The judgment of the CJEU essentially confirmed the reasoning of the Advocate General. To be more specific, the Court validated the dynamic interpretation of the notion of consumer, at least as far as contracts concerning social media are concerned.[300] The Court acknowledged that a person may 'rely on his status as a consumer only if the predominately non-professional use of those services, for which the applicant initially concluded a contract, has not subsequently become predominately professional'. In the *Schrems* case, the exact contractual relationship between the Facebook account and the Facebook page does not matter. Since the notion of consumer is an objective one, the level of expertise or knowledge does not play any role.[301] Therefore, Mr Schrems does not lose his consumer status if he publishes books, gives conferences, raises funds and gathers claims.[302] Another interpretation would run contrary to Article 169 TFEU, which preserves consumers' right to organise themselves in order to safeguard their interests.[303]

[295] Judgment of the Higher Regional Court of Vienna (*Oberlandesgericht Wien*), case 11 R 146/15v rendered on 9 October 2015 10–11.

[296] ibid 12–13.

[297] *Schrems* (n 284) Opinion of AG Bobek, para 38.

[298] ibid para 55.

[299] ibid paras 58–60.

[300] *Schrems* (n 284) paras 37–38.

[301] ibid para 39.

[302] ibid para 41.

[303] ibid para 40.

The dynamic approach suggested by the Advocate General generates significant interpretative problems: how should one examine a change of purpose? What are the relevant criteria to be applied? Should this change of purpose be preponderant and visible for the defendant? Additionally, the Advocate General considers that a consumer can, in exceptional cases, lose this status if the purpose of the contract changes. In this case, it might seem reasonable to refuse the application of section 4 BIa. However, this interpretation becomes disturbing in the opposite situation. For example, two traders conclude a selling agreement but one of them subsequently decides to use the acquired goods for personal purposes. If the change of purpose is taken into account, section 4 BIa should apply in case of conflict. This would mean that the defendant would be subjected to different jurisdictional rules without being aware of it. Such a result seems unreasonable and runs contrary to the principle of predictability. Therefore, the time when the contract was concluded should remain the relevant starting point for analysing Mr Schrems' status. Accordingly, it is doubtful that, when Mr Schrems concluded his contract with Facebook in 2013, he had a professional activity in mind. Therefore, at the time the contract was concluded, no professional activity existed and the claimant did not manifest his intention to use his Facebook account for professional purposes.

In all cases, and following the dynamic approach suggested by the Advocate General, Mr Schrems shall indeed be treated as a consumer. In particular, the setting up of a collective redress action should not, in itself, be considered as a professional activity. Under certain circumstances, litigation may pursue a commercial purpose. For example, this might be true as regards companies like CDC,[304] which dedicates its time and money to the private enforcement of competition law claims. In the case object of analysis, however, Mr Schrems is not a businessperson whose goal is to enforce data protection rights. Unlike CDC, Mr Schrems does not bring collective redress claims on a regular basis and does not make money out of this activity. The fact that he is a lawyer should not affect this reasoning, since lawyers may also bring lawsuits outside their profession, for personal purposes.

Yet, it is true that Mr Schrems undertook three different types of activities that may involve a professional goal: first of all, the claimant created different websites in order to gather victims together and obtain financing. Secondly, Mr Schrems participated at conferences and other similar events essentially regarding the proceedings he started against Facebook. Sometimes, he received a small remuneration for his participation at said events. Last but not least, he took advantage of one of his websites in order to advertise the publication of his book '*Kämpf für deine Daten*'.

The creation of websites – linked or not to a private Facebook account –, as well as the participation in conferences and other similar manifestations should not,

[304] A description of CDC's profile and activities is available above; ch 2, I.D.iv. and corresponding footnotes.

in this case, be regarded as professional activities. Indeed, the initiation of collective proceedings always requires an investment in terms of time, money and human resources. As anyone can imagine, the management of 25,000 assigned claims is not an easy task. In this context, it does not seem reasonable to conclude that Mr Schrems is not a consumer because the creation of these websites and his participation at conferences facilitated the bundling of multiple claims. Otherwise, one should admit that all individual claimants would lose their capacity as consumers once they bring a collective action.[305] In fact, all the methods used by the claimant either helped him to handle the size of the claim or to advertise it. The fact that the claimant earned some money for those activities does not affect this reasoning, as the amount involved is almost insignificant. Finally, as regards the publication of the claimant's book, one might consider that this goes beyond the organisation and advertising of the pending dispute between Mr Schrems and Facebook. In this context, Mr Schrems used the reputation of the case in order to sell a book, which might be considered a professional activity. However, this single, marginal activity should not change the qualification of Mr Schrems as a consumer.

Can a Consumer who Represents Others Use Section 4 BIa?

As was previously explained in the statement of facts, Mr Schrems brought proceedings in the Austrian courts along with seven other claimants located in Austria, and Germany, pursuant to Article 235 ACCP. However, the claimant was willing to convert his suit into a collective redress action of the Austrian type (Article 227 ACCP) and hence, bundle claims of at least 25,000 other users dispersed around the world. In light of this, the Austrian courts had to decide whether they had jurisdiction to hear claims of the seven claimants, and whether they could extend their jurisdictional power to the rest of the victims.

The Austrian courts' jurisdictional power will be analysed in three parts, which correspond to different scenarios. First of all, can victims located in Austria, another EU Member State or a third state bring their suit in Austria under the current Brussels regime? In the event that Austrian courts have jurisdiction over (some of) the individual claims, can centralisation in a unique location occur – unless national procedural law states otherwise? Can suits be brought at the domicile of Mr Schrems? This is the question that both the Advocate General and the CJEU resolved. Finally, can national rules of civil procedure help to overcome international, jurisdictional issues?

As regards the first scenario in *CDC*,[306] where victims assigned their claims to a special purpose vehicle, the CJEU ruled that, in order to locate the place where the damage manifested itself in a case regarding artificially inflated prices induced by a cartel agreement, national courts had to identify this place 'for each alleged victim taken individually'. Therefore, it might well be that courts should not focus

[305] Judgment of the Court of Appeal, above n 832, 10.
[306] *CDC* (n 43) para 52.

on the assignee but on original claimants in order to determine whether they have jurisdiction over a whole group of consumers – like in *Schrems* – located in different states. This might often generate the fragmentation of litigation and hence, the impossibility of bringing a collective redress action, because consumers are generally domiciled in different states or in different locations within the same state.

Transposed to the *Schrems* case, this means that Austria is probably not an accessible forum for consumers located outside the country. One must distinguish between two categories of assignors: those domiciled in Austria, such as Max Schrems, and those who reside in another EU Member State.[307]

On the one hand, Austrian courts have jurisdiction to hear claims of consumers located in that state pursuant to section 4 BIa, given that they have their domicile in that location. In this context, it has to be recalled that section 4 BIa establishes international, as well as local jurisdiction when consumers wish to initiate proceedings against the trader in the forum of their domicile. Therefore, the centralisation of claims might be impeded if these consumers are domiciled in different parts of the country.[308]

On the other hand, section 4 BIa only allows consumers domiciled in a Member State other than Austria to litigate in the forum of their domicile or in the Member State where the defendant is seated – here, Ireland. As a result, these consumers can only rely on a choice of court agreement in order to litigate in Austria. The consent of the defendant would be necessary for such a forum to be open. In the case at issue, however, Facebook fervently fought the jurisdiction of the Austrian courts. In light of this, the Regional Court can only acquire jurisdiction if either Article 7(1) or 7(2) BIa is available. Nevertheless, it is doubtful that these provisions apply, inasmuch as Facebook users surely are consumers. Hence, for them, jurisdiction is exhaustively regulated by section 4 BIa.

To conclude, Austrian courts only possess jurisdiction over consumers domiciled in Austria, pursuant to section 4 BIa.

Can a new forum be inferred from the text of Article 18 BIa? This question corresponds to the second scenario.

According to the claimant,[309] when the assignee is himself a consumer, then EU, as well as Austrian case law, does not restrict access to courts pursuant to

[307] Leaving aside jurisdictional questions regarding assignors domiciled in a third state, since they do not fall under s 4 BIa. According to Art 18 BIa, consumers have the possibility to bring their claim 'in the courts of the Member State in which [they are] domiciled'. Therefore, it can be inferred that only consumers located in a Member State may be protected by this section. Conversely, foreign assignors might try to rely on another forum. The Advocate General comes to a similar conclusion. See *Schrems* (n 284), Opinion of AG Bobek, para 107.

[308] The Advocate General highlights that particular point. See *Schrems* (n 284), Opinion of AG Bobek, paras 114–16.

[309] The arguments of the claimants have been extracted from the following sources: Appeal filed by Maximilian Schrems to the Austrian Supreme Court (*Oberster Gerichtshof*) GZ 3 Cg 52/14k on 2 November 2015, 10–15; Appeal filed by Maximilian Schrems to the Higher Regional Court on 14 July 2015, 17–18; and the written submissions of Mr Schrems to the CJEU, 15–22, available at www.europe-v-facebook.org/sk/EuGH-Stellungnahme.pdf.

section 4 BIa or its national equivalent. In light of this, Mr Schrems refers to the *Shearson* case – among others – in order to demonstrate that the CJEU only prevents the use of section 4 by claimants that represent a group of consumers but are not themselves bound to the defendant by a consumer contract. The claimant comes to the same conclusion when he looks at the national case law rendered by the Austrian Supreme Court. Then, Mr Schrems argues that the text of the BIa does not impose any '*Personenidentität*'. In other words, it does not require the consumer to be the claimant. Another interpretation would strengthen the conditions of section 4 BIa, and this approach is not defendable. Along the same line of reasoning, the claimant explains that the Brussels' provisions regarding consumer contracts protect weak parties in an abstract manner. Therefore, the consumer who assigns his/her claims remain protected by section 4 BIa, even though he/she is not a party to the proceedings. Such an interpretation is in line with the function of the internal market, which consists in promoting consumers' cross-border activities, without undermining their protection.

Nevertheless, the Advocate General concluded differently. In his opinion, the wording of Article 18 BIa clearly limits the protective forum to the specific contractual parties, namely the consumer and the professional.[310] Indeed, the use of an indefinite article in the first sentence of Article 18 does not change this reasoning. This can be explained by the fact that the word 'consumer' is used for the first time in the provision.[311]

Then, a systematic interpretation of Article 18 BIa shows that the text is more precise and limited than Article 7(1) BIa, which does not refer to the identity of contractual parties. This militates in favour of a restrictive interpretation of the protective forum.[312] Moreover, the claims based on Article 18 BIa must previously fulfil the conditions established by Article 17 BIa, which requires the conclusion of a contract between a consumer and a professional. Therefore, it would be rather illogical to allow a consumer to bring a claim based on contracts concluded by others, since this is not aligned with the wording of Article 17 BIa.[313]

Finally, the teleological interpretation of Article 18 BIa leads to the same conclusion. The EU case law has already rejected the possibility for a person who is not the contractual party to benefit from section 4 BIa.[314] This situation must be distinguished from the case law concerning insurance matters (section 3 BIa), which establishes a broader head of jurisdiction than section 4 BIa.[315] As far as predictability is concerned, the Advocate General believes that the interpretation of Mr Schrems could foster forum shopping, inasmuch as claimants could concentrate their claims in the most favourable forum, by assigning those claims

[310] *Schrems* (n 284) Opinion of AG Bobek, paras 79–82.
[311] ibid para 80.
[312] ibid paras 87–88.
[313] ibid paras 84–85.
[314] ibid para 90, where the AG refers to the *Shearson* and *Henkel* cases.
[315] ibid paras 97–98.

to a consumer located there. Such an interpretation contradicts the principle of predictability.[316]

In light of the above, the Advocate General concludes that Article 18 BIa does not permit the creation of a new forum at the domicile of the assignee.

The CJEU essentially agreed with the Opinion of the Advocate General. According to EU case law, the Court recalled that only consumers who are parties to the proceedings may benefit from the forum of section 4 BIa.[317] Moreover, the assignment of claims does not modify the jurisdictional assessment.[318] As a result, the CJEU concludes that the bundling of claims cannot take place in the forum of Article 18 BIa.[319]

The inability for claimants to bundle their claims in the forum of Article 18 BIa triggers another question: can national procedural law overcome private international law difficulties? As far as consumers domiciled in Austria are concerned, the Advocate General explained that, since Article 18 BIa designates the court, which has territorial jurisdiction, it should not be possible to use Article 227 ACCP in order to modify that result. However, he admitted that although Article 18 BIa 'does *not* establish a new special jurisdiction [this] does not mean (…) that it would *prevent* it if it were internally provided for by national law'.[320] Does this statement mean that national procedural law may provide a new forum where the assignee would bundle all claims assigned to him/her, on top of EU rules on jurisdiction? If yes, it has to be highlighted that this scheme would nevertheless be limited to consumers domiciled in the same Member State.

Unfortunately, the *Österreichisches Modell der Sammelklage* (Article 227 ACCP), which states that claimants can bundle their claims in a single action against the same defendant when the court has jurisdiction over all claims and the same type of procedure applies to them,[321] does not create a new head of jurisdiction. However, a look at the state of affairs in other Member States generates some doubts regarding the interpretation of the Advocate General. For example, where national law designates a unique tribunal for collective redress matters, such as Belgian law, does this represent a new, special head of jurisdiction? Or, is it necessary to elaborate a black letter rule of law creating a new forum? Finally, does section 4 BIa actually leave some room for national procedure to intervene when the claim in question falls within its scope? This last question must be answered in the negative.

[316] ibid para 105.

[317] *Schrems* (n 284) para 44.

[318] ibid para 48.

[319] ibid para 49.

[320] *Schrems* (n 284), Opinion of AG Bobek, para 117.

[321] '(1) Mehrere Ansprüche des Klägers gegen denselben Beklagten können, auch wenn sie nicht zusammenzurechnen sind (§ 55 JN), in derselben Klage geltend gemacht werden, wenn für sämtliche Ansprüche (1) das Prozeßgericht zuständig und (2) dieselbe Art des Verfahrens zulässig ist'. The full article, along with the corresponding case law of the Supreme Court, is available at www.jusline.at/227_ZPO.html.

Other Grounds on Jurisdiction: The Role of Party Autonomy

Under the class action model, parties may conclude a choice of court agreement before or after the dispute arises. In the *Schrems* case, an ex ante choice of court agreement bound Facebook with its users. Therefore, the validity of such a clause is examined in the next paragraphs. Furthermore, the question whether Mr Schrems could alternatively present the claims he acquired in the Austrian courts thanks to the conclusion of an ex post choice of court agreement is analysed.

In his lawsuit, the claimant puts the spotlight on the existence of a choice of court agreement contained in Facebook's terms and conditions – also called Statement of Rights and Responsibilities. According to this agreement, Facebook users accept to litigate their disputes in the Californian courts. In its most recent version, Facebook's terms and conditions state the following:

> You will resolve any claim, cause of action or dispute (claim) you have with us arising out of or relating to this Statement or Facebook exclusively in the US District Court for the Northern District of California or a state court located in San Mateo County, and you agree to submit to the personal jurisdiction of such courts for the purpose of litigating all such claims. The laws of the State of California will govern this Statement, as well as any claim that might arise between you and us, without regard to conflict of law provisions.[322]

However, the claimant correctly argues that a choice of court clause concluded before the dispute arose, and which does not allow consumers covered by the Brussels regime to litigate in the fora provided by Article 18(1) BIa, cannot be valid pursuant to Article 19 BIa. Such a clause might nevertheless be valid for assignors domiciled in third states, given that they are not covered by section 4 BIa.

Supposing that the choice of court agreement were to respect section 4 BIa, it remains to be seen whether it would bind Mr Schrems as the assignee of consumer claims. The recent *CDC* case[323] sheds light on the power of choice of court agreements when victims assign their claims to a special purpose vehicle. In this case, the Court of Justice first clarified that in order for CDC to be bound by choice of court agreements, it should have succeeded in the rights and obligations of the original parties. This has to be established by the national substantive law designated by the private international law rules of the court seised.[324] If this is the case, then CDC would be bound by the choice of court agreements. This case law should equally apply to the *Schrems* case.

As far as ex post choice of courts agreements are concerned, there are no obstacles for Mr Schrems to agree on the jurisdiction of the Austrian courts after he becomes the sole holder of victims' claims. Nevertheless, the conclusion of a choice of court agreement requires the consent of the defendant. In this case, however, Facebook fiercely contests the jurisdictional power of Austrian courts. Therefore, this option seems to be excluded.

[322] See no 15 of Facebook's Terms and Conditions, available at www.facebook.com/legal/terms.
[323] *CDC* (n 43).
[324] ibid paras 64–65.

iii. Interim Conclusion

The dispute between Max Schrems and Facebook puts the spotlight on the difficulty for assignees or representatives to bundle consumer claims in a single forum. The CJEU concluded that Max Schrems was a consumer but that Article 18 BIa did not allow him to present claims of other consumers in the protective forum related to consumer contracts. Even though such a judgment is bad news for collective redress and access to justice, the protective effect of section 4 BIa, in its current wording, is unfortunately limited: consumers cannot unilaterally decide to litigate in different fora than the ones provided in said section without the defendant's consent. Furthermore, the individualistic approach of the Brussels regime does not allow national courts to rule over victims' claims arguing that they trigger common questions of fact or law. The Regulation requires that said courts establish jurisdiction over each individual claim.

However, both the Opinion of the Advocate General and the judgment of the CJEU left some questions open. In particular, Advocate General Bobek seemed to admit that national procedural law could overcome private international law difficulties, as far as consumers domiciled in the same Member State are concerned. To be more specific, he considered that assignors' claims could be bundled in a unique, special head of jurisdiction offered by national law. However, the CJEU did not clarify whether such a possibility exists or not.

D. The Test Case Model

The test case model that is presented in this sub-section has been adopted, both in Germany and in the United Kingdom, although other collective redress mechanisms have also been implemented in these states. Through the test case model procedure, claims sharing common issues of fact or law are usually listed in a register. Then, a 'pilot' case is selected, whose questions are resolved by a higher court. This case subsequently serves as an example to solve similar registered claims. In Germany, the *Gesetz über Musterverfahren in kapitalmarktrechtlichen Streitigkeiten* (*KapMuG*) adopted the test case procedure.[325] In the United Kingdom, the Group Litigation Order (GLO) was implemented in Part 19 III of the Civil Procedure Rules.[326] However, the latter mechanism does not always provide a test case procedure. Sometimes, it is used like a usual joinder.

The test case model has been included in this research project because of its increasing relevance, at least at the national level. For example, in Germany, while in '2015, the register received 17 entries, in the first half of 2016, the number of

[325] For a comprehensive description of this procedure, see below, Annex II.F.
[326] For a comprehensive description of this procedure, see below, Annex II.H.

new entries had already doubled to 34'.[327] As for the English GLO, not less than 94 cases have been tried under this mechanism from its entry into force until July 2015.[328] Because of globalisation and the increasing integration of markets, test case proceedings may involve cross-border elements with more frequency. The rest of this sub-section is dedicated to the German test case model for two reasons: first, two significant cases involving international components are currently going through this procedure. Second, the *KapMuG* essentially aims at enforcing investors' claims, who often are the weaker parties in judicial proceedings. Even though not all investors are consumers under the Brussels regime, it is interesting to take this category of victims into account, since they are potential 'clients' of the collective redress procedure.

This sub-section starts with an outline of the German test case model. Specifically, the structure of this model, the procedural requirements it imposes, as well as the advantages and drawbacks that it entails are described (i.). Following this, two recent international cases that started under the *KapMuG* procedure, namely the *MPC-Fonds* case and the *Volkswagen* scandal, are examined (ii.). Once the statement of facts of both cases is clarified, questions regarding international jurisdiction are assessed. German courts relied on Article 4 BIa in order to establish jurisdiction in both disputes (iii.). However, parallel claims, whose content is detailed in the next lines, have been triggered pursuant to other grounds of jurisdiction (iii.). This section ends with an interim conclusion (iv.).

i. Outline of the Test Case Model

In 2005, the German legislator adopted the *KapMuG*.[329] At that time, this legislation was considered as a 'pilot-project', but it was eventually amended in 2012 and prolonged until 2020.[330] The material scope of the *KapMuG* mainly encompasses securities – or shareholder – disputes. In particular, § 1 *KapMuG* states that claims regarding prospectus liability can be litigated under this Act. Moreover, disputes concerning the offer or use of false, misleading, or omitted capital market information are also included within the legislation's scope. Finally, the lack of communication of said information to investors is also mentioned in § 1 *KapMuG*. While prospectus liability protects the primary capital market, liability rules on false, misleading, or omitted capital market information safeguard transactions on the secondary market.

[327] B Schneider and H Heppner, 'Germany' in *The International Comparative Legal Guide to Class and Group Actions* (2017), available at iclg.com.

[328] A list of those cases is available at www.gov.uk/guidance/group-litigation-orders.

[329] Note that a legislative project is in the pipeline. It consists in extending the test case model to representative entities, such as consumer associations. The text of the bill is available at www.bmjv.de/SharedDocs/Gesetzgebungsverfahren/Dokumente/DiskE_Musterfeststellungsklage.pdf?__blob=publicationFile&v=3.

[330] In order to build up the outline of the German test case model, the bibliographical sources cited in Annex II.F. were used.

To sum up, the *KapMuG* only applies to a limited sector. Historical reasons may explain this fact. Indeed, said legislation was enacted following the *Deutsche Telekom* case, which invaded the German dockets a few years ago.[331] To be more precise, between 2000 and 2001, approximately, the share price of *Deutsche Telekom* dropped, causing significant damage to its investors. In particular, victims alleged that the German trader's prospectus, released at the time of the initial public offerings, contained incorrect information regarding, *inter alia*, the value of the company's real estate. As a result, around 17,000 claims massively assaulted Frankfurt's dockets, which did not possess any procedural instrument able to manage such a number of claims. As a consequence of this case, the German legislator drafted a test case model for collective cases related to securities disputes.

From a structural perspective, the test case model is a three-tier procedure. To begin with, either the claimant or the defendant brings a petition (*Musterverfahrensantrag*) to the first instance court (§ 2 (1) *KapMuG*), seeking the start of the test case proceedings. At the national level, the court that has jurisdiction is the one where the company has its registered office (Article 32b of the German Civil Code of Procedure (hereafter, GCCP)). The applicant must convince the court that the case at issue generates questions of law or fact that are common to other claims (§ 2 (3) *KapMuG*). If this is so, the court publishes the petition for a test case procedure into a specific electronic register, namely the *Klageregister*, which is available on the website of the German Official Journal (*Bundesanzeiger*).[332] Six months after the publication date, at least nine other claimants (*Beigeladenen*) must present their claim for test proceedings to start (§ 6 (1) *KapMuG*). These claims should not necessarily be presented in the same lower court.[333] Notably, the inscription in the register interrupts the prescription period. These elements show that the first phase of the model is based on the opt-in system.

Supposing that the required quorum is reached after six months, the lower court refers the case to the Higher Regional Court (*Oberlandesgericht*). To be more precise, the court which published the first petition for the initiation of a test case procedure has jurisdiction to make the order for reference (*Vorlagebeschluss*), pursuant to § 6 (1) and (2) *KapMuG*. Once the order for reference is made public, all pending claims depending on the resolution of the common issues presented

[331] For an overview of the *Deutsche Telekom* case, see A Halfmeier, 'Litigation Without an End? The *Deutsche Telekom* Case and the German Approach to Private Enforcement of Securities Law' in D Hensler et al (eds), *Class Actions in Context – How Culture, Economics and Politics Shape Collective Litigation* (Edward Elgar, 2016) 279–98; A Stadler, 'A Test Case in Germany: 16 000 Private Investors vs. Deutsche Telekom' (2009) 10(1) *ERA Forum* 37, 37–50; AW Tilp and TA Roth, 'The German Capital Market Model Proceedings Act as Illustrated by the Example of the Frankfurt Deutsche Telekom Claims' in WH van Boom and G Wagner (eds), *Mass Torts in Europe: Cases and Reflections* (Walter de Gruyter GmbH, 2014) 131–42.

[332] www.bundesanzeiger.de/ebanzwww/wexsservlet?&global_data.designmode=eb&genericsearch_param.fulltext=Klageregister%20&genericsearch_param.part_id=5&%28page.navid%3Dto_quicksearchlist%29=Suchen.

[333] As explained below (iii.a.), thanks to § 32b GCCP, domestic disputes should be centralised at the registered office of the issuer. However, in international cases, the application of the BIa may lead claimants to file their actions in different locations.

to the Higher Regional Court will be stayed and automatically included in the test case proceedings (§ 8 *KapMuG*). This phase of the model is based on the system of automatic membership. Indeed, the efficient administration of justice commands the curtailment of the parties' individual rights.

In the second phase of the test case proceedings, the Higher Regional Court must rule on the common questions of the dispute. In order to achieve this objective, said court selects one leading claimant (*Musterkläger*), whose case will serve as a model to resolve the remaining claims (§ 9 *KapMuG*). This information is published in the register. The rest of claimants are not parties to the test case proceedings. However, they are allowed to intervene, as long as their participation is not inconsistent with the lead claimant's action (§ 14 *KapMuG*). Their right to extend the object of the test case proceedings is equally noteworthy (§ 15 *KapMuG*). Within six months after the publication, other similarly-situated claimants may declare themselves to the Higher Regional Court. These claimants do not become parties to the test model proceedings either. However, after the model case decision is issued, registered claimants will be able to start proceedings and benefit from the test case decision.

Finally, the test case procedure may end up either with a decision of the Higher Regional Court or with a settlement. In the first case, that court sends its decision back to lower courts, which will continue the proceedings on an individual basis. Among other things, these courts will rule on issues regarding causation and the potential amount of damages to be allocated to the claimant in case of successful trial. The test case decision issued by the Higher Court binds all claimants whose proceedings were stayed according to § 8 (1) *KapMuG*. Any claimant or defendant can file an appeal against this decision (§ 20 *KapMuG*). In the second case, the lead claimant and the defendant can submit a written agreement to the court in order to put an end to the dispute (§ 17 *KapMuG*). The court can also make proposals in view of a settlement. In any case, the authorisation of said court is required for the agreement to be binding (§ 18 *KapMuG*). It has to be highlighted that no appeal is available against this authorisation. However, claimants are offered the opportunity to manifest their intention not to be bound by the settlement within a month of its notification to them (§ 19 *KapMuG*). This settlement remains valid, unless more than 30 per cent of victims withdraw from it (§ 17 (1) *KapMuG*). In other words, the settlement phase of the *KapMuG* is based on an opt-out system.

Although the German test case model offers investors a chance to bundle their claims and thus, achieve economies of scale, this system remains criticisable.[334]

[334] Among others, see E Feess and A Halfmeier, 'The German Capital Markets Model Case Act (KapMuG) – A European Role Model for Increasing the Efficiency of Capital Market? Analysis and Suggestions for Reform' 26–27, available at papers.ssrn.com; C Geiger, *Kollektiver Rechtsschutz im Zivilprozess – Die Gruppenklage zur Durchsetzung von Massenschäden und ihre Auswirkungen* (Mohr Siebeck, 2015) 66–70; B Haar, 'Investors Protection Through Model Case Procedures – Implementing Collective Goals and Individual Rights Under the 2012 Amendment to the German Capital Markets Model Case Act (KapMuG)' (2014) 15 *European Business Organization Law Review* 83, 96–103; B Heil and B Lee, 'The Role of Private Litigation' *Comparative Corporate Governance and Financial Regulation*, Paper 7, 9–16, available at scholarship.law.upenn.edu/fisch_2016/7; HW Micklitz and A Stadler,

The following critiques have been raised against the *KapMuG*: to start with, the test case model does not really depart from the two-party paradigm. This means that each claimant still enjoys an individual treatment to a certain extent. For instance, this explains why claimants conserve the right to intervene or to appeal, as well as filing a motion to extend the scope of the test case proceedings. However, the individualisation of claims restricts the collectivisation process and thus, may create delays and inefficiencies.

Additionally, the coming and going of the test case file between the first and the second instance courts significantly slows down proceedings. For example, the resolution of the *Deutsche Telekom* case lasted more than a decade until the German Supreme Court issued its final say.[335] Of course, it will take some more time until individual proceedings are definitely closed.

Last but not least, because the costs incurred by the test case procedure become part of the first instance proceedings, only claimants are liable for them. In other words, this means that registered claimants do not bear any cost. This might create a free-riding effect, given that victims could simply register their claim – instead of initiating proceedings – and use the decision of the Higher Regional Court at no cost.

ii. Recent International Cases Following the KapMuG *Procedure*

Two significant and international cases are now described. The statement of facts serves as a basis for the subsequent analysis of private international law questions regarding jurisdiction.

a. The MPC-Fonds Scandal

From 2002, MPC Münchmeyer & Petersen Capital AG (MPC) offered Austrian citizens, the opportunity to participate in various investment funds (MPC-Fonds), whose purpose was to pool financial resources and acquire real estate, ships and life insurances. Those funds, which are structured as closed-end funds, issue a certain number of shares on the market through an initial public offering (IPO).[336] On this occasion, a prospectus is distributed among interested investors. After the targeted amount is reached, the fund closes. Practically, this means that 'latecomers' can no longer invest in the fund.

'The Development of Collective Legal Actions in Europe, Especially in German Civil Procedure' (2006) 17(5) *European Business Law Review* 1473, 1487–88; HW Micklitz, 'Collective Private Enforcement of Consumer Law: The Key Questions in WH van Boom and M Loos (eds), *Collective Enforcement of Consumer Law: Securing Compliance in Europe through Private Group Action and Public Authority Intervention* (Europa Law Publishing, 2007) 16.

[335] Supreme Court (*Bundesgerichtshof*), case XI ZB 12/12 rendered on 21 October 2014.

[336] H Domash, *Mutual Fund and Closed-End Fund Investing: What You Need to Know* (FT Press, 2011), ch IV (only available online at proquest.safaribooksonline.com/9780132782036). A more precise definition is available on the CFE Connect website, available at www.cefconnect.com/closed-end-funds-definition.

In the *MPC-Fonds* case, MPC published a prospectus that was directed at Austrian consumers, offering them the opportunity to invest in closed-end funds – like Holland 47.[337] Those funds mainly aimed at financing the acquisition of Dutch real estate. It has to be highlighted that the offer was promoted by intermediary banks and financial consultants. The MPC-Fonds were structured on the basis of limited liability partnerships, as is usual in Germany.[338] Consequently, because investors became limited partners of those funds, they assumed far greater risks than investors who trade securities in the usual way.[339] Yet, the corporate and investment structure of the MPC-Fonds was not clearly described by the available sources of information. Suffice it to say that investors in closed-end funds usually invest either directly in the fund or indirectly through a trustee. A mixed structure is also possible.[340] In the case at issue, it seems that Austrian investors were at least offered the choice to invest via TVP-Treuhandgesellschaft, a trustee located in Germany.[341]

Following improper management activities, Austrian citizens lost a great part of their investment. As a result, 13 investors started proceedings in Germany under the *KapMuG*, with the VKI's support. In substance, they alleged that the prospectuses regarding investments in the closed-end funds were misleading. Therefore, they sought compensation for their loss against MPC, its Austrian daughter company (CPM Anlagen Vertriebs GmbH) and TVP-Treuhandgesellschaft. In 2016, the Regional Court of Hamburg (*Landgericht Hamburg*) issued a decision for the start of test case proceedings to the second instance court, regarding the MPC-Fonds scandal.

b. The Volkswagen Case

Volkswagen is an automobile manufacturer, whose seat is located in Wolfsburg (Germany).[342] Throughout the year 2007, the German firm started the construction

[337] For an overview of all the funds involved in the scandal, see verbraucherrecht.at/cms/index.php?id=2220.

[338] A Holher, 'Open-End and Closed-End Funds and Real Estate Investment Trusts' in M Mütze et al (eds), *Real Estate Investments in Germany – Transactions and Development* (Springer, 2007) 280.

[339] A notable issue is that banks, which helped finance the acquisition of Dutch real estate, could sell the properties in order to reimburse their investment. Additionally, they could ask investors to repay the distribution of money they received in the past, out of the benefits of the funds. For more information on this question, see verbraucherrecht.at/cms/index.php?id=2255.

[340] C Just, 'Legal Framework for Real Estate Asset Classes' in T Just and W Maennig (eds), *Understanding German Real Estate Markets*, 2nd edn (Springer, 2016) 129.

[341] verbraucherrecht.at/cms/index.php?id=2254.

[342] Along with the judgment of the Regional Court of Braunschweig (*Landgericht Braunschweig*), case 5 OH 62/16 rendered on 5 August 2016, the following sources have been used in order to build up the statement of facts: G Gates et al, 'How Volkswagen Is Grappling With Its Diesel Scandal' (18.11.2016) *New York Times*, available at www.nytimes.com/interactive/2015/business/international/vw-diesel-emissions-scandal-explained.html; JC Yung and SB 'Alison' Park, 'Volkswagen's Diesel Emissions Scandal' (25.10.2016) *Thunderbird International Business Review*, available at onlinelibrary.wiley.com/doi/10.1002/tie.21876/full.

of new diesel engines. Said engines were implemented in about eleven million vehicles around the globe. In May 2014, a study held by the International Council on Clean Transportation (ICCT) on the one hand, and the Center for Alternative Fuels Engines and Emissions of West Virginia University on the other, revealed that the above-mentioned Diesel engines exceeded the permitted gas emissions level – in particular, nitrogen oxides – during on-road tests. Indeed, Volkswagen implemented a 'defeat device', namely software, whose purpose was to reduce gas emission during laboratory tests. In particular, said software has the ability to recognise when a vehicle is being tested and consequently starts disguising emissions levels.

In this context, discussions started between Volkswagen and the US administration, namely the Environmental Protection Agency (EPA) and the California Air Resources Board (CARB). In December 2014, the manufacturer proceeded to a product recall, but was not able to resolve the car emissions problem. As a result, in September 2015, Volkswagen acknowledged that it had manipulated the software regulating car emissions in order to comply with regulatory standards. An article published by the *New York Times* in September 2016 estimated that the Regional Court of Braunschweig (*Landgericht Braunschweig*), which is located at Volkswagen's seat, received approximately 1,400 claims from deceived shareholders, representing a total and cataclysmic amount of EUR 8.2 billion. Both domestic and foreign, as well as private and institutional investors were suing.

Some administrative bodies in Germany equally brought a lawsuit against the manufacturer. Basically, they argue that Volkswagen should have disclosed the information regarding nitrogen emissions. By not doing so, Volkswagen is charged with insider trading.

iii. Questions Regarding Jurisdiction

Both in the *MPC-Fonds* and the *Volkswagen* cases, German courts acquired jurisdiction pursuant to Article 4 BIa (a.). However, parallel proceedings arose in other states regarding the same disputes (b.).

a. Article 4 BIa

In the *Volkswagen* case, investors started proceedings in the Regional Court of Braunschweig, which corresponds to the location where the defendant has its headquarters, pursuant to Article 4 BIa. This information can be deduced from the statement of facts established by the Regional Court, as well as press releases mentioned above. However, this question has not been explicitly tackled by said court. In the *MPC-Fonds* case, the Regional Court of Hamburg clearly set forth its reasoning regarding jurisdiction. Thanks to the similarities that the international disputes analysed above share, the remarks regarding the *MPC-Fonds* case are applicable mutatis mutandis to the *Volkswagen* scandal.

In *MPC-Fonds*, the Court of Hamburg considered that it had jurisdiction over the German trader and the trustee pursuant to Articles 4 and 63(1)(a) BIa.[343] Additionally, the court established that it equally had jurisdiction over claims directed to the Austrian daughter company, thanks to Article 8(1) BIa. Local jurisdiction is determined by § 32b GCCP. According to such provision,

> For complaints in which: 1. The compensation of damages caused by false or misleading public capital market disclosures, or caused by the failure to make such disclosure, or 2. The compensation of damages caused by the use of false or misleading public capital market disclosures, or caused by the failure to inform the public that such public capital market disclosures are false or misleading, (…) is being asserted, that court shall have exclusive jurisdiction that is located at the registered seat of the issuer concerned, (…) where said registered seat is situate[d] within Germany.[344]

Thanks to § 32b GCCP, disputes litigated under the *KapMuG* should normally be centralised in the court where the issuer has its registered seat.[345] At least, this is the case for purely domestic disputes. As far as international disputes are concerned, § 32b GCCP applies insofar as private international rules on jurisdiction – such as Article 4 BIa – do not designate the court that possesses local jurisdiction. Where claimants rely on Article 7(2) and section 4 BIa in order to litigate in Germany, national provisions regarding jurisdiction are discarded.[346]

The forum contained in Article 4 BIa is certainly advantageous for a number of reasons. First of all, the notification of the judicial action to the defendant is facilitated, inasmuch as it does not trigger the application of international texts or EU Regulations.[347] As long as the procedure is based on an opt-in system, notification of the Higher Regional Court's decision to potential foreign claimants should not pose particular problems, as they are clearly identified. The publication of important information in the register further smooths the communication between all parties concerned by the test case proceedings. Secondly, although the Injunctions Directive should usually not apply to claims in test case proceedings,[348] the initiation of proceedings by foreign claimants in Germany does not generate issues regarding recognition and standing to sue. This can be explained by the

[343] Regional Court of Hambourg (*Landgericht Hamburg*), case 327 O 279/15 rendered on 2 February 2016 4–5.

[344] An English version of this provision is available on the website of the Ministry of Justice and Consumer Protection (www.gesetze-im-internet.de/englisch_zpo/englisch_zpo.html).

[345] B Hess, 'Der Regierungsentwurf für ein Kapitalanlegermusterverfahrensgesetz – eine kritische Bestandsaufnahme' (2004) 48 *Zeitschrift für Wirtschafts- und Bankrecht – Wertpapiermitteilungen Teil IV* 2329, 2331; Micklitz and Stadler, 'The Development of Collective Legal Actions in Europe, Especially in German Civil Procedure' (n 334) 1486.

[346] Geiger, *Kollektiver Rechtsschutz im Zivilprozess* (n 334)62; C Heinrich, '§ 32b' in HJ Musielak (ed), *Kommentar zur Zivilprozessordnung*, 7th edn (Verlag Franz Vahlen, 2009) 172.

[347] For an overview of the notification process in cross-border collective redress proceedings see Carballo (n 152) 141–85.

[348] Indeed, the Directive only covers actions for injunctive relief brought by certified bodies – and not individuals –, whose name is published in the Official Journal of the EU.

fact that the *KapMuG* is not established on a representative model. Moreover, no consumer association may start test case proceedings if it does not have any proper claim. Thirdly, no process of recognition and execution should be triggered, as the assets of the defendant are usually located at his/her domicile. Finally, as specifically concerns the *MPC-Fonds* case, Austrian investors did not have to face any language issue. As a result, the remaining obstacles to the start of proceedings in Germany could be the lack of financing or the potential structural inefficiencies of the *KapMuG*, such as delays and costs.

b. Other Grounds of Jurisdiction

Theoretically, test case proceedings could certainly start in Germany by relying on a provision other than Article 4 BIa. To the best of this author's knowledge, however, this is not usual. In practice, this means that in most test case proceedings, claimants domiciled abroad usually have to move to the defendant's domicile in order to litigate under the German test case model. The *MPC-Fonds* and the *Volkswagen* cases illustrate this point. However, in both cases, parallel claims arose, along with *KapMuG* proceedings. This fragmentation of litigation may indicate the presence of a loophole in the collective private enforcement system of Member States. In particular, parallel litigation may be the result of the limited efficiency of collective redress model in Europe. Besides, this could also be a reflection of the complexity and cost of litigating abroad. Finally, the fragmentation of proceedings may simply be the result of diverse litigation strategies. As many victims are usually involved in large-scale disputes, the emergence of multiple proceedings in different locations should not be surprising.

Taking into account these considerations, the next lines deal with the parallel proceedings which have arisen both in the *MPC-Fonds* and the *Volkswagen* cases. Some considerations regarding *lis pendens* and related actions between multiple collective redress cases are provided.

MPC-Fonds Case

Along with the German test case procedure, additional collective redress proceedings took place in Austria.[349]

In 2014, the VKI brought three collective actions (*Sammelklage*) in the Commercial Court of Vienna against the Austrian branch of MPC (CPM Anlagen Vertriebs GmbH) and an Austrian bank (Hypo Steiermark) who acted as an intermediary. In these collective suits, the VKI represented 33 investors who claimed compensation – up to EUR 2.5 million – for the damage caused by wrong investment advice.[350] These suits are financed by FORIS AG, located in

[349] This sub-section does not comment on the various criminal proceedings which started against MPC, its Austrian daughter company, as well as TVP.

[350] '„Geschlossene MPC-Fonds" – VKI bringt 3. Sammelklage ein' (31.05.2016), available at www.konsument.at/presse/geschlossene-mpc-fonds-vki-bringt-3-sammelklage-ein-31-05-2016.

Germany.[351] Until now, judgments have condemned the defendants but without giving explanations as regards their jurisdictional power.[352]

In parallel, the VKI started proceedings in Vienna against TVP-Treuhandgesellschaft, whose seat is situated in Hamburg. The consumer association argues that the trustee used unfair terms and conditions in the contracts which governed its relationship with Austrian investors (*Treuhandvertrag*).[353] As a result, the VKI asked the Viennese court to declare the prohibition to use unlawful contractual clauses, pursuant to § 28 of the Austrian Consumer Law (*Konsumentenschutz Gesetz*, KSchG), as well as the publication of the judgment. The VKI had standing to bring an action for injunctive relief according to § 29 of said law. The Commercial Court of Vienna based its jurisdiction on Article 7(2) BIa.[354] As explained earlier, this technique was validated by the CJEU in the *Henkel* case.[355] This court had material jurisdiction over the dispute pursuant to § 51(2)(10) of the law on jurisdiction (*Juridiktionsnorm*).[356]

To sum up, all the parallel proceedings mentioned above took place in Austria. One may wonder whether section 4 or Article 7(2) BIa would have been available in the *MPC-Fonds* case in order to centralise all claims in Austria. On the one hand, although scant information exists on the type of investors who sustained damages in the MPC scandal, it seems that most of them could probably qualify as consumers pursuant to the Brussels regime. This might be inferred from the information released by the VKI on its website.[357] However, it is not clear whether Austrian investors actually concluded a contract with MPC. If this is the case, the use of section 4 BIa should not be excluded for individual consumer claims. In any case, it would be relatively difficult to gather all claims in a single jurisdiction, through the intervention of the VKI. In such a context, the Chief of the VKI's legal department, Dr Peter Kolba, explained that the start of proceedings in Germany was necessary, as a cross-border collective redress suit through the assignment of claims to the VKI was not possible in Austria. Moreover, he stated that because of

[351] 'Sammelklagen des VKI gegen den AWD Österreich werden fortgesetzt' (21.03.2013), available at www.foris.com/presse/detail/sammelklagen-des-vki-gegen-den-awd-oesterreich-werden-fortgesetzt.html.

[352] Commercial Court of Vienna (*Handelsgericht Wien*), case 16 Cg 45/14p rendered on 22 December 2016; Austrian Supreme Court (*Oberster Gerichtshof*), case 3 Ob 190/16m rendered on 26 January 2017.

[353] Claim filed by the VKI against TVP in the commercial Court of Vienna (*Handelsgericht Wien*) 3–9, available at verbraucherrecht.at/downloads/Verbandsklage_VKI_gegen_TVP_Treuhandgesellschaft.pdf.

[354] Commercial Court of Vienna (*Handelsgericht Wien*), case 53 Cg 43/13 i -10 rendered on 8 May 2014.

[355] See above, 0A0.0iii.c.

[356] Claim filed by the VKI against TVP in the commercial court, above n 908, 2. The law on jurisdiction is accessible online at www.jusline.at/51_JN.html.

[357] To be more specific, the consumer association mentions the presence of small investors (www.konsument.at/cs/Satellite?pagename=Konsument/MagazinArtikel/Detail&cid=318887283694).

the assignment of claims to the VKI, the protective forum contained in section 4 BIa would probably not apply.[358]

On the other hand, Article 7(2) BIa could open a forum at the domicile of the victims, as the CJEU ruled in *Kolassa*.[359] On this occasion, the Court of Justice clarified the application of Article 7(2) BIa in a prospectus liability case. Accordingly, the victim can litigate at his/her domicile, as long as this location concurs with the place where the event giving rise to the damage or the place where the damage occurred.[360] Again, this forum could be useful for individual claimants. However, the centralisation of proceedings would be difficult because the place where the damage occurs will rarely be the same for all investors.

The Volkswagen Case

The global consequences generated by the Volkswagen scandal gave rise to numerous judicial, as well as non-judicial actions supported by consumer associations around the world.[361] Essentially, two significant initiatives should be underlined.

In Europe, the Netherlands seems to be prepared for the start of a *WCAM* procedure involving all non-US investors who suffered loss as a result of their investment in Volkswagen securities. To be more precise, the Volkswagen Investor Settlement Foundation[362] seeks compensation on behalf of EU investors who acquired shares, and public or private debt, from 23 April 2008 until 4 January 2016. These investors are encouraged to join the Foundation for free in order to foster the Foundation's representative character under Dutch law. The provisions concerning the formation of the Foundation reveal that it intends to conclude a global settlement with Volkswagen under the Dutch *WCAM* procedure.[363] Apparently, the establishment of the Foundation has been financed by an American law firm.[364]

On the other side of the Atlantic, Volkswagen recently concluded a USD 14.7 billion agreement to compensate US car owners for their loss. It must be

[358] 'Diese Vorgangsweise war notwendig, weil eine grenzüberschreitende Sammelklage durch Abtretung von Ansprüchen an den VKI nicht möglich ist. Laut Rechtsprechung des Europäischen Gerichtshofes und des Obersten Gerichtshofes in Österreich, verliert man durch Abtretung von Ansprüchen an einen Verband den Verbrauchergerichtsstand in Österreich' ('Geschlossene Fonds – deutsches Gericht lässt Klage zu' (08.02.2016), available at www.konsument.at/presse/geschlossene-fonds-deutsches-gericht-laesst-klage-zu-08-02-2016).

[359] Case C-375/13 *Harald Kolassa v Barclays Bank plc* [ECLI:EU:C:2015:37].

[360] ibid paras 49–50.

[361] For an overview of the initiatives undertaken by consumer associations in Europe, see the summary prepared by BEUC on its website: www.beuc.eu/volkswagen-emission-affairs#membersactions.

[362] For more information regarding this Foundation, see volkswageninvestorsettlement.com. It has to be underlined that other types of Foundations emerged in the Netherlands. At least two others that represent different categories of victims were found, namely the Stichting Volkswagen Investors Claim (www.stichtingvolkswageninvestorsclaim.com/en/about) and the Stichting Volkswagen Car Claim (www.stichtingvolkswagencarclaim.com/).

[363] See Art 3(1)(b) of said document, available at volkswageninvestorsettlement.com.

[364] G Moss, 'Foundation set up to pursue investor claims against VW in Dutch court' (19.02.2016) *Investment & Pensions in Europe*, available at www.ipe.com/news/esg/foundation-set-up-to-pursue-investor-claims-against-vw-in-dutch-court/10011995.fullarticle.

emphasised that not investors but owners of cars modified with the defeat device were encompassed in the class. The settlement was the result of a consolidated consumer class action.[365] To be more precise, all claims pending in the US were transferred to the Northern District of California and consolidated for the resolution of pre-trial questions, following the decision of a panel on multi-district litigation.[366] Supporting the jurisdiction of the Californian Courts is the fact that 'California is the State with the most affected vehicles and dealers, where significant testing of affected vehicles occurred, and the home of the California Air Resources Board, which played an important initial role in investigating and, ultimately, revealing VW's use of the defeat devices'.[367] In any case, said courts have jurisdiction pursuant to the CAFA.[368] It remains to be seen whether this astronomic settlement will serve as roadmap for EU collective redress initiatives or not.

Overlap of Proceedings, *Lis Pendens* and Related Actions

The emergence of multiple proceedings in different states gives rise to potential 'overlaps' between the different actions. This represents a fertile ground for waste of judicial resources, inconsistent judgments, as well as overcompensation. In this context, it has to be examined whether rules on *lis pendens* or related actions could and should coordinate these actions. This question is examined here in an EU context, since there is no evidence that US proceedings overlapped with EU collective redress actions in the case examined above.

In principle, EU private international law rules on *lis pendens* rarely constitute any obstacle to the rise of parallel collective redress proceedings. Specifically, Article 29 BIa obliges the second seised court of a Member State to stay proceedings in case an action involving the same cause, as well as the same parties, is already pending in another court located in the EU. It is said that parties must be identical or at least share an indissociable interest.[369] Besides, two parallel actions must have the same object and the same cause.[370]

Usually, parallel collective redress proceedings will not involve the same parties, at least when they are represented by different entities.[371] This can be explained by the fact that original claimants are often not considered as parties to the proceedings. Rather, representative consumer associations or public bodies bring the collective suit and are considered the actual parties. In the *Volkswagen* case, for

[365] Consolidated Complaint, available on the website of the Northern District Court of California (www.cand.uscourts.gov/crb/vwmdl).

[366] Transfer Order from Judicial Panel on Multidistrict Litigation, available on the website of the Northern District Court of California (www.cand.uscourts.gov/crb/vwmdl).

[367] ibid 2.

[368] Consolidated Complaint (n 365) 5–6. For more information on the conditions imposed by the CAFA, see ch 1, II.B.iii.

[369] Case C-351/96 *Drouot assurances SA v Consolidated metallurgical industries (CMI industrial sites)* [1998] ECR I-03075, para 23.

[370] *Tatry* (n 37) paras 38, 40.

[371] JN Stefanelli, 'Parallel Litigation and Cross-Border Collective Actions' in Fairgrieve and Lein (n 164) 150; Tang (n 165) 125–27.

example, a risk of overlap actually existed since both the investors involved in the *KapMuG* procedure and the Dutch *WCAM* could be the same. However, Article 29 BIa should not apply for two reasons: first of all, while investors bring their individual claims under the *KapMuG*, they must be represented by an association under the Dutch collective settlement mechanism. Therefore, the condition regarding the similarity of parties is not fulfilled. Moreover, it is doubtful that the procedure under the *WCAM* qualifies as 'proceedings' in the sense of Article 29 BIa. For the record, such a procedure does not involve any judicial action, but the mere declaration by the Amsterdam Court of Appeal of the binding effect of an out-of-court settlement. Therefore, one might wonder whether Article 29 BIa encompasses such a constellation. If not, then one should conclude that the distinct structure of collective redress instruments could defeat the application of Article 29 BIa.

As regards Article 30 BIa, it enables the court of a Member State to stay proceedings where a related action is pending in another court of the EU. In other words, the second seised court is given the possibility to stay proceedings but is not obliged to do so. The concept of 'related actions' implies that these 'are so closely related that it is expedient to hear them together' (Article 30(3) BIa). Moreover, Article 30(2) BIa offers a possibility to consolidate distinct actions. According to Stefanelli, collective actions typically represent related actions. However, she mentions that the discretionary nature of Article 30 BIa would often give rise to the duplication of claims.[372] In *MPC-Fonds* for example, Article 30 BIa might have been used by Austrian Commercial Court in Vienna in order to stay collective proceedings against CPM Anlagen Vertriebs GmbH, and wait for the German court's decision on the defendant's liability. Taking into account the notable delays characterising the German test case procedure, it is unlikely that the Austrian Court would do so. Moreover, the claim of the VKI may contain different arguments and theories regarding the liability of the Austrian daughter company, which could perfectly be solved independently from the German sister-proceedings.

To sum up, the *lis pendens* and related actions regime of the BIa is unlikely to apply to collective redress. Therefore, distinct collective proceedings could overlap. However, because collective suits often involve large-scale and dispersed damages, as well as multiple defendants and numerous victims, one may wonder whether rules on *lis pendens* and related actions should actually apply.[373] In other words, the high degree of heterogeneity regarding the types of claims, the actors involved, and the structure of the procedural tools used could make the application of the Brussels *lis pendens* and related actions regime complicated and hence, inefficient. These considerations will be taken into account in the construction of the proposal in chapter 4 (below II.B.).

[372] Stefanelli, 'Parallel Litigation and Cross-Border Collective Actions' (n 371) 150–51.

[373] On the desirability to apply *lis pendens* to collective redress claims, see also B Hess, 'Cross-Border Collective Litigation and the Regulation Brussels I' (2010) 2 *Praxis des Internationalen Privat- und Verfahrensrechts* 116, 119–20.

iv. Interim Conclusion

The *KapMuG* is a collective redress system through which securities disputes may be litigated. It is therefore substantially limited and its structure is still tightly linked to the two-party procedural paradigm. Ultimately, two significant international disputes, namely the *MPC-Fonds* and the *Volkswagen* cases, have been tried in Germany under the test case model. Both times, the German courts relied on Article 4 BIa in order to establish jurisdiction at the defendant's domicile. This particular forum enjoys notable advantages. For some reason, however, parallel collective suits emerged in both cases. This may be due to the limited efficiency of collective redress instruments in Europe, or be part of a procedural strategy. In any case, the materialisation of multiple proceedings within the EU could create undesirable overlaps. The above paragraphs demonstrate that the Brussels *lis pendens* and related actions regime has difficulties in tackling collective redress.

III. Conclusion

Ideally, cross-border collective redress proceedings should take place in a single forum of the EU. Additionally, it should achieve high levels of efficiency, include all victims, generate economies of scale for all parties involved, and preserve judicial resources. Nevertheless, this collective-redress-wonderland remains a daydream for the time being. In fact, many different factors disturb the achievement of this ultimate situation: some of them are of a procedural nature and have already been highlighted in chapter 2 (II.B.i.). Others stem from the relative unsuitability of collective redress models to EU private international rules on jurisdiction and have been developed in the current chapter.

In particular, the dominant collective redress models struggle to permit the bundling of claims in a single forum. For example, the representative model appears to work quite well only when a general interest is at stake. In this situation, Article 7(2) BIa often offers a forum in the Member State where the representative body is located. Typically, this is the case when foreign traders use unfair terms and conditions with national consumers. However, when individual claims for damages are at stake, representative bodies may be charged with lack of standing in foreign courts. The opening of collective proceedings 'at home' against a foreign defendant appears to be equally difficult, given that the location designated by private international law rules on jurisdiction is often not the same for all victims.

As for the Dutch model, its success is built on an extensive interpretation of private international rules on jurisdiction. But it is not sure that the CJEU would back up this solution in the name of access to justice and efficient administration of justice.

Furthermore, the class action model can probably not benefit from the protective forum of section 4 BIa. Insofar as consumers are domiciled in different locations in the EU or dispersed within a single Member State, they should not be able to bundle their claims in the representative claimant's domicile.

Finally, the test case model usually relies on the application of Article 4 BIa. Other private international law rules on jurisdiction seem to have been irrelevant as far as this model is concerned.

Currently, only Article 4 BIa, as well as Article 7(2) BIa to a certain extent, seem to offer an interesting location to bundle individual claims or defend a general interest. However, because this result stems from the application of an unsuited regime, it does not mean that these fora are appropriate. The next chapter examines whether the private international law landscape should be modified in order to better apprehend cross-border collective redress.

4

Proposal for an Appropriate Forum Regarding Collective Redress Actions

The need for collective redress actions within the EU represents a challenge for EU private international law, which is hard to tackle. In particular, chapter 3 put the spotlight on the numerous mismatches between the Brussels Regulation on the one hand, and collective redress mechanisms on the other. To such extent that the domicile of the defendant seems to be the only available forum where both collective redress actions for injunctive relief and damages may be brought. Additionally, Article 7(2) BIa might be of use when a general interest is at stake. Although these provisions are theoretically available, it does not mean that they offer an appropriate forum for collective redress actions (I.A. and B.). In such a context, scholars, national legislators, private organisations and the EU institutions have presented some solutions in order to 'fix' the current landscape. A roadmap of their proposals for reform is provided in the first part of this chapter (I.C.).

As explained below, however, the provisions of the BIa do not provide accessible fora for collective redress actions. Additionally, the proposals presented only offer partial solutions to private international law issues regarding jurisdiction. In this context, a legislative reform is necessary in order to unequivocally welcome collective redress actions in Europe. Any change of the law will surely clarify the current confusion surrounding collective redress and bring legal certainty. In light of this, the second sub-section of this chapter deals with the elaboration of a new jurisdictional ground tailored to collective redress (II.). It ends with a conclusion (III.).

I. Appropriateness of the Current Provisions and Proposals for Reform

Chapter 3 underlined the relative unsuitability of collective redress in the current EU private international law landscape. It also mentioned the failed attempt of the Brussels regime to regulate collective redress at the time the recast was discussed (I.A.i.). As a result, only Article 4, as well as Article 7(2) BIa, to a certain extent, provide fora where litigation of collective redress actions can take place.

Nevertheless, this does not mean that these provisions offer appropriate fora. In order to evaluate their appropriateness, fundamental principles of the private international law field should be respected. Additionally, an appropriate forum for collective redress should be coherent with the policy objectives pursued by the EU (A.i. and ii.). The analysis provided below shows that both Articles 4 and 7(2) BIa are not perfectly fit for collective redress (B.). In this context, various proposals have been presented in order to solve this situation and facilitate cross-border collective redress within the EU. Some initiatives have popped up among scholars (C.i.) and a report has been drafted by the International Law Association on this particular topic (C.ii.). Furthermore, a few Member States have enacted specific rules on jurisdiction for collective redress (C.iii.). Finally, some solutions have been developed at the EU level (C.iv.).

A. Looking for an Appropriate Forum

In order to establish whether a given forum is appropriate or not, some parameters should be established first. Today, however, no manual or guidelines explain how to measure the appropriateness of a jurisdictional ground. In this research project, the term 'appropriateness' measures whether a given forum is fair and accessible for parties, as well as respectful of private international law principles.

In light of the above, what characteristic(s) should a suitable forum for collective redress possess? In a course given at The Hague Academy of Private International Law and published in 2002, Professor Arthur von Mehren successfully theorised the fundamental elements that should be considered in order to create a jurisdictional ground.[1] Although those principles essentially refer to the drafting of new jurisdictional rules, they should be equally useful for evaluating the appropriateness of existing fora. Additionally, any jurisdictional ground for collective redress – be it specific or not – should be consistent with EU policy objectives, such as consumer protection and market integration. Therefore, the theory established by Professor von Mehren is presented. Special attention is paid to the 'procedural' elements that an appropriate forum should respect. The EU policy objectives regarding consumer law, which represent the substantive aspect that any proposal should take into account, are then analysed.

i. The Theory of Arthur von Mehren

According to Professor von Mehren, various basic policy principles guide the design of a jurisdictional ground: the ease of administration, as well as predictability

[1] A von Mehren, 'Theory and Practice of Adjudicatory Authority in Private International Law: a Comparative Study of the Doctrine, Policies and Practices of Common- and Civil-Law Systems: General Course on Private International Law (1996)' in *Collected Courses of The Hague Academy of International Law*, Tome 295 (Martinus Nijhoff Publishers, 2002) 68–94.

on the one hand, and litigation fairness, whereby the particularities of a dispute are taken into account, on the other. Those principles are present within the Brussels regime. In particular, Recitals 13 and 15 of the BIa command that its fora should be highly predictable. Besides, the Regulation sets forth tailored jurisdictional rules regarding specific disputes. Most of them are based on the principle of proximity, which has been successfully theorised by Professor Paul Lagarde in a famous lecture at The Hague Academy of Private International Law in 1986.[2] He defines this principle as a connecting factor that links a legal relationship to the state with which said relationship entertains 'the closest – or at least a close – connection'.[3] The author underlines that this connecting factor is in principle not positively codified, as far as rules on jurisdiction are concerned, but rather guides the enactment of given jurisdictional grounds. It should be added that this principle is not absolute. Hence, it is sometimes in tension with other factors that compete with it, like party autonomy.[4] Kessedjian adds that the principle of proximity is further challenged by the splitting of connecting points among different states and the impossibility to link certain disputes with a territory. Typically, damages to the environment or conflicts stemming from contracts concluded on the Internet represent telling examples. Additionally, she explains that victims of human rights violations sometimes collectively defend their rights in an accessible but remote forum. Hence, this choice does not always comply with the principle of proximity. In her opinion, greater values require that said principle fades.[5]

Additionally, Professor von Mehren states that the principles of proportionality, as well as the vindication of important policies are additional factors that one should take into consideration. The first factor aims at providing enough fora for the claimant to litigate, without generating forum shopping. The second one concerns the opportunity for a given legal order to open its judicial system to disputes, which affect important national policies. Again, these factors influenced the construction of the Brussels regime. To be more precise, Recital 16 sets forth that the Regulation contains a multiplicity of jurisdictional grounds. The creation of additional fora, apart from the one of the defendant's domicile, may be justified because a close connection with the dispute exists or because considerations of sound administration of justice command it. However, exceptions to the forum of the defendant's domicile are interpreted narrowly and the uncontrolled multiplication of fora should be discouraged.[6]

[2] P Lagarde, 'Le principe de proximité dans le droit international privé contemporain; cours général de droit international privé' in *Collected Courses of The Hague Academy of International Law*, Tome 196 (Martinus Nijhoff Publishers, 1986).

[3] ibid 25–26. 'Ce principe exprime simplement l'idée du rattachement d'un rapport de droit à l'ordre juridique du pays avec lequel il présente les liens les plus étroits, du rattachement d'un litige aux tribunaux d'un Etat avec lequel il présente, sinon le lien le plus étroit, du moins un lien étroit, enfin d'une subordination de l'efficacité d'une décision à l'étroitesse des liens qui la rattachent à l'autorité qui l'a prise'.

[4] ibid 61–65.

[5] C Kessedjian, 'Le principe de proximité vingt ans après' in *Mélanges en l'honneur de Paul Lagarde – Le droit international privé: esprit et méthode* (Dalloz, 2005) 507–21.

[6] Case C-33/78 *Somafer SA v Saar-Ferngas AG* [1978] ECR 02183, para 7.

ii. EU Policy Objectives

The appropriateness of a given forum is certainly influenced by the policy objectives established by the EU. As a starting point, Article 81 TFEU mainly aims at improving the functioning of the internal market. EU institutions may enact private international law norms and legislate on ADR in the name of such objective. In particular, consumer policy is not totally independent from the market integration logic, although this specific policy possesses an autonomous existence.[7] Early on, the EU underlined the importance of consumers as market players. As chapter 2 explains, consumer activities represent more than half of the EU's GDP (II.A.). Consequently, their role is fundamental to the construction of the internal market.[8] In order to push consumers to shop abroad, confidence in such market is key. In this context, the EU undertook different measures in order to foster said confidence. In the 1990s, the EU assumed the harmonisation of national consumer laws.[9] It is believed that where legal standards are alike, consumers are sure to benefit from the same level of protection in any Member State. Therefore, this should motivate them to shop abroad. Despite harmonisation measures, EU institutions still face a significant issue: the private enforcement deficit (chapter 2, II.B.i.). The attribution and harmonisation of rights and obligations among the EU territory is senseless if no procedural mechanism exists to make them real. Therefore, EU institutions enacted a multiplicity of legislative acts aiming at fostering access to justice in consumer matters. For example, the EU enacted the Injunctions Directive, the Small Claims Procedure, and investigated the possibility to add collective redress to the toolbox (chapter 2, II.B.ii.).

[7] Before the enactment of the Treaty of Maastricht, the legislative acts of the EU institutions regarding consumer protection had to be linked to the functioning of the internal market. This constitutional constraint was required by Art 100 of the Treaty of Rome, as well as Art 100a introduced by the Single European Act of 1986. Since the entry into force of the Treaty of Maastricht, the EU acquired the competence to build up a consumer policy that is independent from the functioning of the internal market. For more explanations on the evolution of the EU consumer law policy, see I Benöhr, *EU Consumer Law and Human Rights* (Oxford University Press, 2013) chs 2 and 3; N Reich, 'Economic Law, Consumer Interests and EU Integration' in HW Micklitz et al (eds), *Understanding EU Consumer Law* (Intersentia, 2009) 9–16; S Weatherill, *EU Consumer Law and Policy* (Elgar European Law, 2005) 1–33.

[8] To take relatively recent examples, the link between consumer protection and the internal market has been highlighted in Commission, EU Consumer Policy Strategy 2007–13 – Empowering consumers, enhancing their welfare, effectively protecting them, Communication from the Commission to the Council, the European Parliament and the European Economic and Social Committee COM (2007) 99 final 2 and Commission, A European Consumer Agenda – Boosting confidence and growth COM (2012) 225 final, 1 – which replaced the Policy Strategy. In the first document, the Commission explains that consumers 'are the lifeblood of the economy as their consumption represents 58% of EU GDP. Confident, informed and empowered consumers are the motor of economic change as their choices drive innovation and efficiency'. And to conclude: 'The place of EU consumer policy will be at the heart of the next phase of the internal market'. In the second document, the Commission states that '[i]mproving consumer confidence in cross-border shopping online by taking appropriate policy action could provide a major boost to economic growth in Europe. Empowered and confident consumers can drive forward the European economy'.

[9] Weatherill, *EU Consumer Law and Policy* (n 7), 61–83.

Similarly, the use of consumer ADR was fostered, and methods of ODR were promoted.[10] As regards the Brussels regime, its private international law norms followed the protective policy implemented by the EU in consumer matters.[11] As a result, consumer protection increased along the different versions of the Convention and the Regulation. At first, the 1968 version of the Brussels Convention only protected consumers who concluded contracts for the sale of goods on instalment credit terms, or to contract loans expressly made to finance the sale of goods, by offering them a protective forum. In 1978, as national laws regarding consumer protection had developed, the revision of the Convention extended consumer protection to other types of contracts and situations. The objective was to align the Convention with national developments regarding consumer law. Then, the enactment of the first Brussels Regulation further increased consumer protection by extending the protective forum of section 4 to passive consumers every time traders intended to 'fish' them at the place of their domicile. Through this revision, the Regulation takes into account the rise of the Internet and the challenges that technologies trigger. Finally, the current version of the Brussels Regulation allows consumers to attract defendants located in third states in the forum of their domicile. Thanks to this, EU consumers may conclude contracts with any trader, disregarding its location, and benefit from the same protective private international law rules. Simultaneously, it discourages traders from relocating their business outside the EU, with the objective to escape those rules. To conclude, the Brussels regime adapted its protection regime to the new challenges that EU consumers faced over time. Despite all these efforts, chapter 2 highlights that an important private enforcement gap persists. This is even truer for the compensation of collective damages. In fact, harmonisation of substantive law, along with the enactment of procedural tools for individual consumers and the promotion of ADR insufficiently secure consumers' position on the market. Generally speaking, the Heidelberg report noticed that cross-border litigation in the EU was not any 'everyday business' in 2007.[12] As regards consumer matters and collective

[10] In particular, the EU enacted Council Directive 2013/11/EU of 21 May 2013 on alternative dispute resolution for consumer disputes and amending Regulation (EC) 2006/2004 and Directive 2009/22/EC [2013] OJ L165/63 and Council Regulation (EU) 524/2013 of 21 May 2013 on online dispute resolution for consumer disputes and amending Regulation (EC) 2006/2004 and Directive 2009/22/EC [2013] OJ L165/1; Council Directive 2008/52/EC of 21 May 2008 on certain aspects of mediation in civil and commercial matters [2008] OJ L136/3.

[11] Remarks concerning the evolution of the Brussels regime in consumer protection stem from the following sources: U Magnus and P Mankowski, *Brussels I Regulation, European Commentaries on Private International Law*, 2nd edn (Sellier European Law Publishers, 2011) 367–69; P Jenard, Report on the Convention on jurisdiction and the enforcement of judgments in civil and commercial matters [1979] OJ C59/18 28–29, 33–34; P Schlosser, Report on the Convention on the Association of the Kingdom of Denmark, Ireland and the United Kingdom of Great Britain and Northern Ireland to the Convention on jurisdiction and the enforcement of judgments in civil and commercial matters and to the Protocol on its interpretation by the Court of Justice [1979] OJ C59/71 117–20.

[12] B Hess et al, Report on the Application of Regulation Brussels I in the Member States, Study JLS/C4/2005/03 (2007) 16–20, available at ec.europa.eu/civiljustice/news/docs/study_application_brussels_1_en.pdf.

redress, the questionnaire confirms this trend. Notably, all three consumer associations questioned stated that they had never brought a cross-border action in another Member State.[13] The same is true for collective redress actions.[14] On a more positive note, both Altroconsumo and ADICAE have already started cross-border proceedings against a foreign defendant in the Member State in which they are active.[15] They usually do so on the basis of Article 7(2) BIa. However, only ADICAE has brought a collective redress action against a foreign defendant in Spain.[16] Finally, different documents released by the Commission confirm this statement. For example, the Evaluation of the effectiveness and efficiency of collective redress mechanisms in the EU, which is presented in chapter 2 (II.A.), shows that only 10 per cent of the judicial decisions gathered entailed a cross-border element. Furthermore, the mutual recognition of standing to sue thanks to the Injunctions Directive supposedly had to facilitate the start of proceedings abroad for specific entities such as consumer associations or public authorities. However, the reports of the Commission regarding the application of this Directive present disappointing results: it appears that the cost of foreign proceedings – among other factors – remains an important obstacle to cross-border litigation.[17] In light of this, chapter 2 suggests that private international law could constitute an appropriate corrective tool in order to solve the current distortion of the internal market and further support EU policy objectives (chapter 2, II.C.ii.c.). In order to find the appropriate forum for collective redress actions, the ideal case scenario is first described. Practical considerations will subsequently generate necessary adjustments.

B. Is the Current Situation Satisfactory?

i. The Ideal Forum for Collective Redress Actions

Taking into account the considerations developed above, what would an appropriate forum for collective redress look like? Ideally, this forum should be broad enough to host both actions for injunctive relief and damages. There, all individual actions should be bundled, by virtue of the principle of sound administration of justice. Moreover, this forum should be accessible for claimants or

[13] Question 2.1 of the questionnaire.
[14] Question 4.1 of the questionnaire.
[15] Questions 1.1 to 1.3 of the questionnaire.
[16] Question 4.2 of the questionnaire.
[17] Report from the Commission concerning the application of Directive 98/27/EC of the European Parliament and of the Council on injunctions for the protection of consumers' interest COM (2008) 756 final, paras 18–20; Report concerning the application of Directive 2009/22/EC of the European Parliament and of the Council on injunctions for the protection of consumers' interest COM (2012) 635 final, para 4; Commission, Report on the Fitness check of consumer and marketing law SWD (2017) 208 final 101–05, 101–05.

their representatives but respect the rights of the defence. In other words, a certain balance between access to justice and those rights would have to be achieved in order to avoid abusive litigation: on the one hand, the forum for collective redress actions should help to cover the current enforcement gap by helping consumers to obtain redress. On the other hand, however, abusive litigation should be avoided. As chapters 1 and 2 show, this fear stems from the negative experience acquired in the US regarding the class action device. As a consequence, most collective redress models were built up in a cautious manner (chapter 2, I.D.). Additionally, forum shopping has to be discouraged. Lastly, the forum for collective redress should be built up respecting the principles sustaining private international law. This means, for example, that collective proceedings should share a close connection with the forum court and be predictable.

The next paragraphs examine whether the current private international law rules on jurisdiction comply with the requirements described above. As demonstrated below, Articles 4 and 7(2) BIa, which are the only provisions practically available to bundle collective redress actions, do not offer a satisfying forum where aggregated claims or consumer general interests could be defended.

ii. Article 4 BIa

Chapter 3 concludes that, in principle, the defendant's domicile appears to be the only forum where collective redress actions could actually take place (chapter 3, III.). This is especially true as far as collective redress claims for damages are concerned. This result might appear to be positive at first sight, but it is not completely appropriate.

On the one hand, the domicile of the defendant is a forum consistent with private international law principles. Indeed, this connecting factor is the cornerstone of the Brussels regime and respects the principle of predictability. Besides, other positive elements support the centralisation of collective redress actions in the forum of Article 4 BIa: for example, the scope of this provision is not limited to a specific area – such as consumer contracts. Rather, all actions regarding civil and commercial matters can be brought there. This includes claims in competition law and for the protection of the environment. Additionally, this particular forum is opened to both actions for injunctive relief and damages. Finally, relying on the assumption that the defendant's assets are located at his domicile, no recognition and enforcement procedure would take place after a collective judgment is issued.

On the other hand, the defendant's domicile might not be the most appropriate forum to bring collective redress claims, inasmuch as it neglects some important factors: first of all, it reinforces the defendant's position who may always litigate in a 'familiar' legal environment.[18] Besides, it could voluntarily set up its seat in a

[18] A Nuyts, 'The Consolidation of Collective Claims Under Brussels I' in A Nuyts and NE Hatzimihail (eds), *Cross-Border Class Actions: The European Way* (Sellier European Law Publishers, 2014) 72.

Member State that is reluctant to facilitate access to justice for groups of victims, even though this behaviour might be rare in practice.[19] Secondly, issues regarding the recognition of representative entities might deter these from starting proceedings abroad, as far as the representative collective redress model is concerned. This has been underlined by the pre-Injunctions Directive practice (chapter 3, II.A.ii.b.). Moreover, Article 4 BIa seems to ignore the particularly high costs of cross-border litigation, especially in consumer disputes. Often, the bundling of claims does not offer sufficient leverage to claimants, who might renounce litigating in a foreign and remote forum.[20] In this sense, the option to litigate in the forum of the defendant's domicile does not back up EU policy objectives, which consist in guaranteeing consumers effective access to justice. In the above paragraphs, some barriers to cross-border litigation were highlighted (chapter 2, II.B.i.). When Article 4 BIa is the only forum where collective claims or interests could practically be defended, the private enforcement gap becomes even more visible. For example, the second report on the Injunctions Directive shows that Article 4 BIa is not always accessible for consumer associations or public authorities seeking injunctive relief and is rarely used.[21] Instead, representative entities usually start litigation in the market in which they are active, when this is possible. The questionnaire confirms this trend (chapter 3, II.A.iii.c. and chapter 4, I.A.ii.). Additionally, both the *Volkswagen* and the *MPC-Fonds* cases, which where litigated under the German *KapMuG*, gave rise to multiple parallel proceedings in different Member States. In this context, centralisation of all claims at the domicile of the defendant did not happen, although this was possible. This casts serious doubts on the attractiveness of Article 4 BIa for collective redress actions. The Proposal for a Directive on representative action did not take the chance to regulate private international law related-issues. Although, the mutual recognition of legal standing in case of actions for injunctive relief and damages should be welcomed, entities will often have to travel to another Member State in order to centralise the claims of numerous consumers.

To sum up, Article 4 BIa certainly might well be the unique forum where collective redress claims for damages might be bundled under the current EU private international law regime. Notably, this provision guarantees the sound

[19] A Stadler, 'Die grenzüberschreitende Durchsetzbarkeit von Sammelklagen' in M Casper et al (eds), *Auf dem Weg zu einer europäischen Sammelklage?* (Sellier European Law Publishers, 2009) 159.

[20] M Danov, 'The Brussels I Regulation: Cross-Border Collective Redress Proceedings and Judgments' (2010) 6(2) *Journal of Private International Law* 359, 365; L Gorywoda et al, 'Introduction: Market Regulation, Judicial Cooperation and Collective Redress' in Nuyts and Hatzimihail, *Cross-Border Class Actions* (n 18) 49; E Lein, 'Cross-Border Collective Redress and Jurisdiction under Brussels I: A Mismatch' in D Fairgrieve and E Lein (eds), *Extraterritoriality and Collective Redress* (Oxford University Press, 2012) 133; Nuyts, 'The Consolidation of Collective Claims Under Brussels I' (n 18) 72; B Añoveros Terradas, 'Consumer Collective Redress under the Brussels I Regulation Recast in the Light of the Commission's Common Principles' (2015) 11(1) *Journal of Private International* Law 143, 156; DPL Tzakas, 'Effective Collective Redress in Antitrust and Consumer Protection Matters: A Panacea or a Chimera?' (2011) 48 (4) *Common Market Law Review* 1125, 1156.

[21] Report concerning the application of Directive 2009/22/EC (n 17) para 2.5. This was confirmed by the Fitness Check (n 17) 101–05.

administration of justice and is consistent with the private international law principles listed by von Mehren. In practice, however, parties seem to prefer alternative fora. Finally, the defendant's domicile may not be the most appropriate forum in terms of access to justice. As explained in the above paragraphs, claimants rarely start litigation at this location, because of procedural barriers and the high cost associated with foreign proceedings.

iii. Article 7(2) BIa

As chapter 3 concludes, it seems that Article 7(2) BIa might represent an accessible forum for collective redress actions seeking injunctive relief (chapter 3, III.). This means that claims of consumer associations defending a general interest often can be brought in a single location, as no individual claim is at stake. In those cases, Article 7(2) BIa offers a close forum, which releases consumer associations from procedural issues. However, this supposes that the place where the damage occurred is known and identifiable. Unfortunately, it is not always the case: indeed, pinning down the exact location of a general damage might be tricky (for example, see chapter 3, II.A.ii.c.).

When collective redress actions for damages are at stake, the situation is even more troubling. In this case, claims might only be centralised at the place where the event giving rise to the damage occurred. Unfortunately, this place might coincide with the defendant's domicile and offer no real alternative forum.[22] As a result, if a representative body has to initiate a collective suit in a foreign court, similar issues to the ones concerning Article 4 BIa might appear. As regards the courts of the place where the damage materialised, their jurisdictional power is territorially limited.[23] Therefore, it is doubtful that all cross-border collective redress actions can be litigated there. To sum up, the initiation of collective proceedings in the alternative forum of Article 7(2) BIa is a partial solution. While it might represent an accessible forum for some actions seeking injunctive relief, it does not especially help the centralisation of actions for damages in a single court. In this sense, Article 7(2) BIa does not automatically support the sound administration of justice and access to justice.

C. Suggested Proposals for Reform

i. Scholars

A multiplicity of suggestions have emerged among private international law scholars that intend to offer an appropriate forum for collective redress: while some

[22] Lein, 'Cross-Border Collective Redress and Jurisdiction under Brussels I: A Mismatch' in D Fairgrieve and E Lein (eds), *Extraterritoriality and Collective Redress* (n 20) 134; Nuyts (n 18) 77.

[23] Danov, 'The Brussels I Regulation' (n 20) 691, 368; Nuyts (n 18) 77.

consider that an adapted interpretation of the provisions provided by the Brussels regime would be sufficient,[24] others think that the construction of a specific forum to deal with those claims would represent a better option. Among those who consider that an amendment of the EU private international law regime is necessary, some scholars think that the specific forum should be implemented within the Brussels Regulation,[25] while others advocate the creation of an independent instrument.[26]

Overall, three solutions that aim at facilitating cross-border collective redress could be extracted. The first one consists in opening up section 4 BIa to representative bodies claiming damages. Through the second solution, scholars advocate for the centralisation of proceedings in the market where most victims are affected or where the 'centre of gravity of the dispute' is located. Finally, the third solution concerns the bundling of claims pursuant to Article 8(1) BIa. The following paragraphs examine these proposals.

Some leading scholars consider that section 4 BIa has to be interpreted in the sense that it should cover collective redress actions started by representative bodies – and consumer associations in particular.[27] This is justified since consumers and their representatives often remain weak, even though a possibility to initiate collective proceedings exists.[28] However, they all acknowledge that the current wording of section 4 BIa makes such an interpretation difficult. In this context, a legislative reform may be needed in order to validate it. Although this solution is appealing, significant drawbacks remain: for example, the exact place where the representative body would have to bring the collective suit should be first determined:[29] could a collective suit be started at the place of the representative's domicile? Or should it be brought at the domicile of – one of – the represented consumers? Then, section 4 BIa only protects a certain type of consumer. A consumer association's power to

[24] L Carballo Piñeiro, *Las acciones colectivas y su eficacia extraterritorial – Problemas de recepción y transplante de las class actions en Europa* (De conflictu legum. Estudios de Derecho Internacional Privado, 2009) 130 rejects the idea of a specific forum, inasmuch as it would introduce a discrimination between individual and collective claimants; C Kessedjian, 'L'action en justice des associations de consommateurs et d'autres organisations représentatives d'intérêts collectifs en Europe' (1997) 2 *Rivista di diritto internazionale privato e processuale* 281, 286–91 believes that the domicile of the defendant is the forum where collective redress claims should be litigated.

[25] Gorywoda et al, 'Introduction' (n 20) 53.

[26] B Hess, 'Collective Redress and the Jurisdictional Model of the Brussels I Regulation' in Nuyts and Hatzimihail (n 18) 67.

[27] Carballo, *Las acciones colectivas y su eficacia extraterritorial* (n 24) 111–13; Danov (n 20) 376–77 considers that s 4 BIa should eg apply when a representative body combines an action for declaratory relief with claims for damages in the competition law field; P Jiménez Blanco, 'El tratamiento de las acciones colectivas en materia de consumidores en el Convenio de Brusselas' (2003) 5709 *Diario La Ley* 1574 believes that the protective forum of s 4 BIa should be available in cases where the representative body merely litigates on behalf of individual consumers.

[28] Against: Kessedjian, 'L'action en justice des associations de consommateurs et d'autres organisations représentatives d'intérêts collectifs en Europe' (n 24) 289; ZS Tang, 'Consumer Collective Redress in European Private International Law' (2011) 7(1) *Journal of Private International Law* 101, 112–14.

[29] Carballo (n 24) 112–13.

represent them in court would therefore be limited accordingly.[30] Furthermore, section 4 BIa requires the existence of a contract between a consumer and a professional. This strict criterion might not always be easily fulfilled: typically, this would be the case if a consumer association is fighting against the use of unfair terms that have not been implemented in individual contracts. Finally yet importantly, in case representative entities could not benefit from the protection of section 4 BIa, this means that they would have to respect choice of court agreements concluded between consumers and the defendant, although these agreements would have been ineffective pursuant to Article 19 BIa.[31] This would create a paradoxical situation since individual consumers would lose the protection of the latter provision every time a representative body litigates on their behalf.

Another innovative proposal has been under scrutiny, whereby the court of the market most affected would rule on the cross-border collective suit. This solution is inspired by Article 6(3) of the Rome II Regulation,[32] which regulates the law applicable to an act restricting free competition.[33] Nevertheless, as this connecting factor would be new to the Brussels regime, its interpretation is not clear.[34] For example, one may wonder whether quantitative requirements might suffice in order to pin down the market most affected by an unlawful practice. In this case, however, some scholars put the spotlight on the fact that small markets would never gain adjudicative power over cross-border collective redress cases, which might be unreasonable. Therefore, one could imagine the implementation of a proportionality rule, according to which the number of victims should be compared to the population of a given market. In case the definition of the market most affected were to rely on competition law, its interpretation would follow another scheme. Specifically, the product market, as well as the geographical market should be first delimited.[35] Whenever qualitative elements have to be taken into account, Tzakas highlights that this would equate to a *forum non conveniens* principle,[36] which is not completely in line with the Brussels philosophy. As for the 'centre of gravity of the dispute', it represents a parallel version of the market most affected.[37] According to this connecting factor, collective redress suits should be

[30] Along the same line of reasoning, Carballo (n 24, 108–09) states that 'el análisis subjetivo se hará siempre en relación con los consumidores, miembros del grupo, con independencia de que sea la asociación la que traiga la acción al litigio'.

[31] C González Beilfuss and B Añoveros Terradas, 'Compensatory Consumer Collective Redress and the Brussels I Regulation (Recast)' in Nuyts and Hatzimihail (n 18); Carballo (n 24) 112.

[32] Council Regulation (EC) 864/2007 of 11 July 2007 on the law applicable to non-contractual obligations [2007] OJ L199/40.

[33] B Hess, 'Cross-Border Collective Litigation and the Regulation Brussels I' (2010) 2 *Praxis des Internationalen Privat- und Verfahrensrechts* 118.

[34] Nuyts (n 18) 79; Tzakas, 'Effective Collective Redress in Antitrust and Consumer Protection Matters' (n 20) 1167–68.

[35] P Craig and G de Búrca, *EU Law – Text, Cases, and Materials*, 5th edn (Oxford University Press, 2011) 1012–16; Hess, 'Cross-Border Collective Litigation and the Regulation Brussels I' (n 33) 118.

[36] Tzakas (n 20) 1167–68.

[37] M Posnow-Wurm, 'Rethinking Collective Redress, Consumer Protection and Brussels I Regulation' in Nuyts and Hatzimihail (n 18) 275–76.

resolved by the courts of the place that lies at the centre of the dispute. It has been built up on the reasoning of Advocate General Cruz Villalón in the joined case *e-Date* and *Martinez*, whereby he suggested that the courts of the Member State where the 'centre of gravity of the dispute' is located should have jurisdiction in a case involving infringement of personality rights.[38] Añoveros Terradas believes that centralising claims in a single court would be discriminatory against those consumers whose domicile has not been selected as the leading forum. Besides, it is not clear whether this connecting factor should be interpreted according to the number of victims harmed or whether other considerations should be taken into account.[39]

The last proposal advocates for the application of Article 8(1) BIa to multiple claimants. As some scholars explain, however, the current wording of this provision, as well as its interpretation by the CJEU, does not allow such a reading.[40] Article 8(1) BIa should not be broadly interpreted, as it constitutes an exception to the general forum of Article 4 BIa. Supposing that multiple claimants could benefit from the forum offered by Article 8(1) BIa, important drawbacks would still make the bundling of claims difficult in practice: given that co-claimants could be attracted in the domicile of any one of them, the members of the collective redress action would likely end up litigating in a forum, which has no proximity to the case. If a representative entity litigates on behalf of victims in a foreign forum, issues regarding recognition and standing could arise, as well as financial hardship.

ii. The Paris-Rio Guidelines

As a preliminary point, it should be highlighted that some private initiatives dealing with collective redress or class actions have emerged. In Europe,[41] the European Law Institute (ELI) prepared a comment on the Commission's Recommendation of 2013, as well as the Directive governing actions for damages in the competition law field.[42] However, this initiative does not directly tackle issues regarding jurisdiction in the private international law area. To the best of this author's knowledge, the only project that deals with this question is the

[38] Joined cases C-509/09 *eDate Advertising GmbH v X* and C-161/10 *Olivier Martinez and Robert Martinez v MGN Limited* [2011] ECR I-10269, paras 55–67.

[39] Añoveros Terradas, 'Consumer Collective Redress under the Brussels I Regulation Recast in the Light of the Commission's Common Principles' (n 20) 153–54.

[40] Lein, (n 20), 138; Stadler, 'Die grenzüberschreitende Durchsetzbarkeit von Sammelklagen' (n 19) 158; Añoveros Terradas (n 20) 149, 150.

[41] On the other side of the Atlantic, the American Law Association drafted the *Principles of the Law on Aggregate Litigation*, available on WestlawNext. From a global perspective, the International Bar Association (IBA) drafted *Guidelines for Recognizing and Enforcing Foreign Judgements for Collective Redress* in 2008, which aim at fostering the free movement of collective redress decisions, available at https://marcomm.mccarthy.ca/pubs/Guidelines_for_Recognizing_and_Enforcing_Foreign_Judgments_for_Collective_Redress.pdf.

[42] Available at www.europeanlawinstitute.eu/fileadmin/user_upload/p_eli/Publications/S-5-2014_Statement_on_Collective_Redress_and_Competition_Damages_Claims.pdf.

Paris-Rio Guidelines drafted by the International Law Association. Its content is presented in the next lines. The International Law Association (ILA) is a non-governmental organisation located in Belgium. According to the provisions governing its constitution, the Association's purpose consists in studying, clarifying, developing and understanding private and public international law.[43] From 2006 until 2012, the ILA set up a Committee on International Civil Litigation & the Interests of the Public. The creation of such a committee stems from the acknowledgement that litigation is no longer reserved to sophisticated parties. More and more players are joining the litigation field, such as small businesses and consumers. Therefore, this changing landscape forces the law to evolve and adapt to this new reality. In particular, rules on jurisdiction should 'take into account the varying abilities of parties to litigate in distant fora'.[44]

On the 73rd Conference of the International Law Association (2008), the Committee presented its Report and Resolution on Transnational Group Actions (hereafter, the Report), as it considered that this device generated significant issues.[45] In its Report, the Committee drafted some guidelines or best practices in order to deal with cross-border aspects of collective redress, or 'group or collective actions' as the document states. In other words, the Report does not impose any specific model for collective redress at the national level. Rather, it deals with transnational coordination. Two objectives motivate the work of the Committee: on the one hand, it aims at identifying the general features of collective redress. On the other hand, it tackles specific transnational issues that collective actions face, such as standing, certification, jurisdiction, notification, applicable law, gathering of evidence and case management. As regards jurisdiction, the Committee considers that group and collective actions should take place at the defendant's domicile. Another court could only exceptionally have jurisdiction on the collective redress claims. In light of this, section 3 of the Report establishes the following rule:

> 3.1. A transnational group action may be brought in the defendant's forum. If the defendant is a corporation, the defendant's forum is located at any of the following three places: 1) where the corporation has its statutory seat or is incorporated, or in the state under whose law it was formed; 2) where it has its central administration; 3) where its business, or other professional activity is principally carried on.
>
> (…)
>
> 3.3. A transnational group action may also be brought in the courts of another country closely connected to the parties and the transactions, provided that trial of the action in that country is reasonably capable of serving the interests of the group and has not been selected to frustrate those interests.[46]

[43] ILA, *Constitution of the Association*, Art 3, available at www.ila-hq.org/en/committees/index.cfm/cid/1021.

[44] ILA, *Description of the ILA International Civil Litigation & the Interests of the Public Committee*, available at www.ila-hq.org/en/committees/index.cfm/cid/1021.

[45] ILA, *Conference Report Rio de Janeiro 2008*, available at www.ila-hq.org/en/committees/index.cfm/cid/1021.

[46] ibid 13.

The solution offered by the Report certainly respects EU private international rules on jurisdiction. According to its authors, this solution is justified given that claimants acquire significant leverage by gathering together.[47] Consequently, these players do not need any more protection. As mentioned earlier in this sub-section (I.B.ii.), the absence of limitation in the material scope has to be positively underlined, given that collective redress actions may be brought in a significant variety of fields such as consumer protection, competition law, environment protection and even labour law. However, one has to assess the appropriateness of the defendant's domicile differently according to the field of law, since they may involve different interests and actors. Besides, it is not sure that in all these fields, the bundling of claims truly reinforces the position of the claimants. The Report seems to turn a blind eye to the costs and procedural difficulties that entail the start of proceedings abroad. Sometimes, these issues might remain significant enough to impede the initiation of collective redress actions. As underlined above, the forum of the defendant's domicile is not ideal in terms of access to justice (I.B.ii.). Another element that should be discussed here is the choice of words made by the Committee, which talks about group and collective actions rather than collective redress. It appears that the purpose of such a terminology is to distinguish EU mechanisms allowing the bundling of claims from the US class action.[48] Due to the variety of collective redress mechanisms in Europe, a clearer delineation of the notion would be welcome. Finally, section 3.3 of the Report admits the possibility for a court other than the one of the defendant's domicile to rule on the collective redress action. Accordingly, a court that shares a close connection with the dispute could also acquire jurisdiction to rule on the collective redress case. This formulation looks like a *forum conveniens*,[49] although the Report does not expressly mention it. Additionally, the Committee clarifies that the court and not the parties should be able to decide whether another court is best placed to hear their claims. This flexible jurisdictional ground shares some similarities with the alternative fora of the BIa. However, the Brussels regime does not offer courts such a margin of discretion in order to determine whether they have jurisdiction or not. Therefore, the Report might not be in line with the Brussels regime. By drafting section 3.3, however, the ILA acknowledges that the domicile of the defendant might not be the only forum closely connected to a collective redress case.

[47] C Kessedjian, 'The ILA Rio Resolution on Transnational Group Actions' in Fairgrieve and Lein (n 20) 135–36, 238.

[48] ibid 135–36, 234 and fn 3.

[49] It is a *forum conveniens* in the sense that it allows another court than that of the defendant's domicile to exceptionally accept jurisdiction over a collective redress action. On the notion of *forum conveniens*, see M Herranz Ballesteros, *El forum non conveniens y su adaptación al ámbito europeo* (Valencia, Tirant lo blanch, 2011) 35–37.

iii. National Rules on Jurisdiction

A look at national provisions governing jurisdiction in collective redress cases might be instructive. Indeed, national solutions might be a source of inspiration for upcoming national legislation in the EU.

National rules governing jurisdiction tackle collective redress cases in a different fashion. Overall, three distinct trends could be identified: first, national legislation on collective redress remain sometimes silent as regards material and territorial jurisdiction. In other words, the ordinary system governing questions of jurisdiction applies. This is the case in Portugal, for example.

Second, other Member States allocate jurisdiction to the courts of the defendant's domicile, but simultaneously limit the number of courts that may rule on collective redress cases. For instance, in Italy, Article 140-bis (4) of the Italian Consumer Code states that collective redress claims must be submitted to the courts located in the capital of the region where the company has its registered office. France equally follows this scheme: for example, pursuant to Article R.623-2 FCC, the *Tribunal de Grande Instance* of the professional's domicile has jurisdiction to rule on the French group action.

Third, some Member States have designated a limited number of courts, which have exclusive jurisdiction to rule on collective redress actions. This solution is advantageous in the sense that it allows courts to gain expertise. Additionally, said courts are able to generate harmonised canons of interpretation. In particular, the Amsterdam Court of Appeal is the only one able to deal with a *WCAM* settlement in the Netherlands. Then, under the Belgian system, the courts and tribunals of Brussels have exclusive jurisdiction to rule on a collective suit according to Article XVII.35 of the Economic Code.

To sum up, national legislators have not developed any tailored connecting factor in order to deal with collective redress actions. Usually, the domicile of the defendant is the relevant place to bring such actions. Alternatively, Member States only allocate jurisdiction to a limited number of specific courts.

iv. Movements at the EU Level

At the EU level, institutions acknowledge the relative unsuitability of collective redress taking into account private international law rules on jurisdiction. Specifically, the Commission explained the stakeholders' position regarding various potential solutions in the Communication accompanying the Recommendations of 2013.[50] Among these stakeholders, a number of them believe that a special

[50] The different positions adopted by stakeholders are contained in the EU Commission's Communication; Commission, Communication: Towards a European Horizontal Framework for Collective Redress COM (2013) 401 final, 13–14.

forum should be created in order to tackle cross-border collective redress: for some, the courts of the Member States where the majority of claimants are located should have jurisdiction, while for others, jurisdiction over consumer contracts should extend to representative entities. Another group of stakeholders argues that the defendant's domicile is the appropriate forum where cross-border collective redress actions have to be brought. A last category of stakeholders suggests that a specific panel of the CJEU should solve those claims. Even though the Commission possesses a clear overview of the possible solutions to the jurisdictional issues generated by cross-border collective redress, none of them has been adopted yet.[51] The same is true as regards other fields of law. For example, in competition law, collective redress has been set apart from the Directive on antitrust damages actions of 2014,[52] although this topic had already been vividly discussed.[53] Along the same line of reasoning, the GDPR explicitly allows the use of collective redress but does not establish any specific forum for it. To be more precise, Article 79(2) GDPR, which deals with individual actions, states that judicial proceedings should be started 'before the courts of the Member State where the controller or processor has an establishment' (Article 79(2) GDPR). This provision recalls the wording of Article 7(5) BIa.[54] Alternatively, Article 79(2) GDPR establishes that "proceedings may be brought before the courts of the Member State where the data subject has his or her habitual residence, unless the controller or processor is a public authority of a Member State acting in the exercise of its public powers".

It is not clear, however, that such fora are available to representative entities under Article 80 GDPR.[55] On the one hand, one might argue that representative actions depend on the mandate of individuals and that entities act as mere representatives. Following this reasoning, it is tempting to conclude that the fora of Article 79(2) GDPR are equally open for representative actions. Where the first prong of Article 79(2) GDPR applies, it might offer a close forum to the victims of data protection violations, only to the extent that both actors are located in the same Member State. However, this might not always be the case. As regards the second prong of Article 79(2) GDPR, since it does not allocate territorial jurisdiction, centralisation of victims' claims habitually residing in the same Member State should be possible where national rules of civil procedure support it, ie by designating a unique court with territorial jurisdiction. On the other hand, however,

[51] An overview of all the actions undertaken by the EU is available in ch 2 (II.A. and B.)

[52] Council Directive 2014/104/EU of 26 November 2014 on certain rules governing actions for damages under national law for infringements of the competition law provisions of the Member States and of the European Union [2014] OJ L349/1. See in particular Recital 13 of said Directive.

[53] For an overview of the actions undertaken by the EU in the competition law field, see ec.europa.eu/competition/antitrust/actionsdamages/collective_redress_en.html.

[54] However, Recital 22 GDPR indicates that the notion of establishment under the GDPR is broader than Art 7(5) BIa.

[55] For a more detailed analysis of that question, see A Pato, 'The Collective Private Enforcement of Data Protection Rights in the EU', forthcoming. This paper has been presented at the 3rd IAPL-MPI Summer School (July 2018).

Article 80 GDPR does not contain an explicit reference to those specific fora, in the manner of Article 82(6) GDPR, which establishes that claims for compensation 'shall be brought before the courts competent under the law of the Member States referred to in Article 79(2)'. Therefore, assuming that the specific fora of the GDPR do not apply, the general private international law regime, ie the BIa, would come into play, with all the challenges that this piece of legislation triggers regarding collective redress.

Finally, it has to be emphasised that a proposal dealing with collective redress was presented when both the Brussels and Lugano Conventions were under reform. In 1998, an ad hoc working party was set up by the EU Council in order to revise the Brussels and Lugano Conventions. At that time, the Swedish delegation made a proposal to allow actions for injunctive relief to be brought in the interest of consumers before the courts of the state where an infringement has its effects. The proposal suggested the modification of Article 5 BC – today, Article 7 BIa – in the following way:

> A person domiciled in a Contracting State may, in another Contracting State, be sued: (…) 3. a) as regards an action for an injunction to protect the collective interests of consumers brought by a public or private entity, in the courts of the Contracting State in which the infringement has its effects.

The Swedish delegation insisted on the fact that the Convention's scope should encompass both private bodies, as well as public authorities – such as the Swedish Consumer Ombudsman, for example. This suggestion is valuable because it clarifies that public authorities should fall within the scope of the Brussels regime. Although some representative entities use this forum, for instance when they fight against unfair terms, the proposal of the Swedish delegation crystallises a certain practice. Unfortunately, said proposal does not tackle actions for damages. Eventually, the text of the Swedish delegation was rejected.[56]

II. Proposal

The first section of chapter 4 demonstrates that the current private international law rules on jurisdiction do not provide a satisfactory forum where collective redress actions could be brought. In light of this, a specific forum should be set up for those actions. However, due to the great variety of collective redress mechanisms in the EU, it would certainly be difficult to encompass all of them in a single private international law norm. Therefore, the representative model should be the foundation of any legislative proposal regarding cross-border collective redress. The reason is simple: this model is the most widespread throughout the EU territory, and it takes into account the primary role of representative entities,

[56] González Beilfuss and Añoveros Terradas, 'Compensatory Consumer Collective Redress and the Brussels I Regulation (Recast)' (n 31) 248, fn 35; Magnus and Mankowski, *Brussels I Regulation* (n 11) 233–34.

such as consumer associations, for the defence of consumer interests and the overcoming of rational apathy.

Likewise, the EU institutions seem to endorse the representative model. This is visible in the Recommendation of 2013, where the Commission reserves standing to sue to specific entities.[57] More recently, the GDPR applied the same discrimination in favour of said model. According to its Article 80, only certain bodies, organisations or associations might litigate on behalf of data subjects. Additionally, the Dutch model puts the spotlight on the virtues of out-of-court agreements: thanks to this technique, courts are not overwhelmed with thousands of claims and parties may centralise the dispute in a single forum. Private international law should consider this model too.

Conversely, although the class action model might be efficient in the United States, it is hardly ever used in Europe, because of the financial hardship it places on the representative claimant. In this vein, the *Schrems* case should be treated as an exceptional one. Therefore, the promotion of this model is not a priority. Finally, the test case model surely is a useful management tool, but it does not appear to be an efficient tool against rational apathy. Nevertheless, the structure of such a mechanism is interesting from a private international law perspective, since it allows the centralisation of common issues of fact or law in a single court, with a decentralisation system for remaining individual issues. This model may compete with the suggested proposal.

In light of those considerations, the current section starts with a description of two solutions that might facilitate cross-border collective redress actions (A.). While the first model advocates for the centralisation of collective claims in a single forum, the second one takes the German test case procedure as a basis. These options contain interesting features but do not totally support the access to justice policy. Alternatively, a suggested proposal is described in the second part of this subsection (B.).

A. The Competing Solutions

As suggested earlier, collective redress actions should ideally centralise in a single, fair and accessible forum. Furthermore, such actions should exhaustively encompass all victims who suffered harm. Therefore, this section starts with an overview of the potential benefits and drawbacks of a fully centralised model for collective redress cases, based on the representative model (i.). Alternatively, the test case model could serve as an appropriate basis to create a jurisdictional regime for collective redress. Consequently, this suggestion is also analysed below (ii.).

[57] Commission, Recommendation of 11 June 2013 on common principles for injunctive and compensatory collective redress mechanisms in the Member States concerning violations of rights granted under Union Law [2013] OJ L201/60, paras 4–7.

Beforehand, it should be noted that the models described above only focus on judicial actions. The possibility of concluding out-of-court settlements is examined in the proposal.

i. The Centralised Representative Model

The centralisation of all collective redress actions in the dockets of a single court represents an interesting option (see Figure 1). Accordingly, one or various entities representing national consumer interests would be able to start litigation in a single location, for example, in the domicile of the defendant.[58] Alternatively, it has been suggested that centralisation could be achieved in the courts of the Member State where the majority of victims are located. As mentioned earlier (I.C.i.), this criterion could give rise to important interpretative issues. In all cases, if collective redress claims can be accumulated there, significant economies of scale could be achieved. This would also help representative entities to reduce costs of proceedings.

Figure 1 Centralised Model

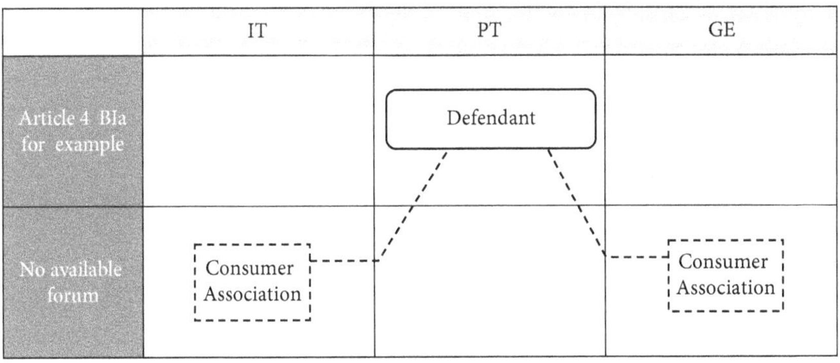

On the one hand, centralisation at the domicile of the defendant is an impeccable solution from a private international law perspective, since it follows commonly acknowledged principles of the field. Suffice it to recall that the domicile of the defendant is the cornerstone of many private international law texts, including the BIa.

On the other hand, if an alternative connecting factor is selected, such as the place where the majority of the victims are located, courts would certainly have to deal with actions which entertain no close connection with the forum. Typically, this will be the case when both the defendant and some of the victims are located

[58] Note that Art 16(2) of the Proposal for a Directive on representative actions (ch 2, I.A.) explicitly incentivises entities from different Member States to act jointly or to be represented by a single entity in case of cross-border infringement.

in Member States other than the one where litigation starts. As far as private international law is concerned, it is difficult to draft objective criteria according to which one court could have jurisdiction over foreign collective actions presenting no link with its territory. Along the same line of reasoning, removing a court's jurisdictional power in order to allocate it to another one, which possesses no connecting point with such action, is difficult to justify.[59] Similarly, a look at the American experience (chapter 1, II.B.i.) shows that state courts usually struggle to extend their jurisdictional power to out-of-state defendants and class members in multistate class actions.

Furthermore, it was already highlighted that a centralised model does not especially support access to justice, since it may trigger practical and procedural issues (I.B.ii.). In particular, supposing that a single court could be selected in order to rule on all collective redress claims, this means that the representative entity would often have to move to another state in order to litigate the case. However, it is doubtful that representative entities, which often have limited financial and human resources, would actually start proceedings in a foreign forum. Additionally, there is a risk that the prospective court in charge of the EU collective action would feel overburdened. Indeed, it is not certain that national courts possess the resources to tackle pan-EU collective redress actions. Even though certain questions are centralised and great economies of scales can be achieved, cross-border collective redress cases still place an important amount of work on national courts. This could generate important delays for parties. In light of this, it is not certain that centralisation of collective redress claims in a single court would actually support the principle of sound administration of justice.

Finally, in order for a centralised system to work, a minimal level of harmonisation of national collective redress would be needed. In particular, the existence of the representative model in each Member State would have to be guaranteed. Besides, all mechanisms would have to possess the same material scope and welcome the same types of actions – for damages and injunctive relief. Otherwise, access to and availability of a centralised system would depend on the Member State. However, as mentioned in chapter 2, harmonisation of collective redress mechanisms should be the *ultima ratio*.

Since a centralised forum may not always provide access to justice, market players might be tempted to use alternative fora when these are available, like in the *Volkswagen* and *MPC-Fonds* cases. Therefore, and in order to maintain the effectiveness of the centralisation process, a jurisdictional regime for collective redress actions should be hermetic just as section 4 BIa, for example. In other words, representative entities should not be able to use other fora apart from the one where collective redress proceedings should be centralised. In the event such a model is adopted, this means that a consumer association would not be able to litigate in the forum of Article 7(2) BIa against a trader who makes use of illegal

[59] Tang, 'Consumer Collective Redress in European Private International Law' (n 28), 118

terms and conditions as they often do. Along the same line of reasoning, a representative entity would not be able to 'short-circuit' the jurisdictional regime for collective redress by making use of Article 7(5) BIa. Such a result would significantly undermine access to justice. Therefore, a centralised system should set up additional incentives in order for representative entities to start litigation abroad.

In light of the above, the next paragraph examines a slightly different centralised system (see Figure 2) that attempts to better support access to justice. According to this model, a single consumer association – for example, one located in the domicile of the defendant – would have the power to bind consumers domiciled in other Member States, preferably on an opt-out-based system. Although this model looks simple and attractive on paper, it does not build up appropriate incentives.

Figure 2 Centralised Model *Bis*

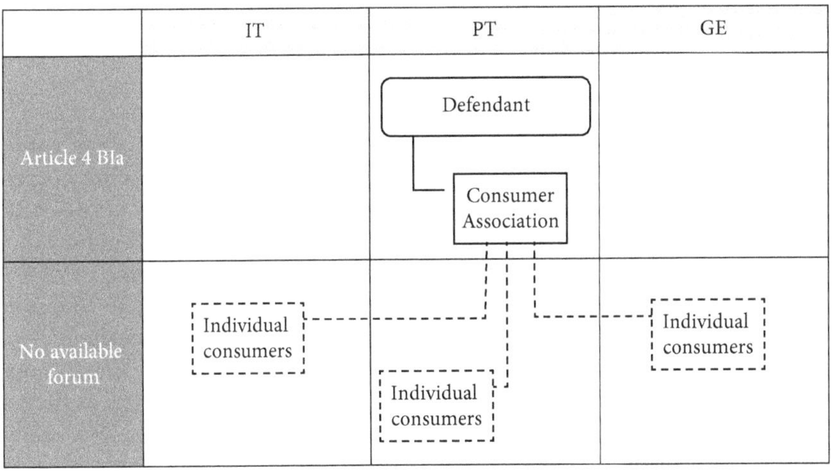

An example illustrates the functioning of the present model: DECO is a consumer association located in Portugal. This association has the power to start collective redress proceedings against a Portuguese defendant who has caused harm to numerous consumers on the EU market. In that case, it is not clear whether an EU norm could oblige DECO to represent all victims from the EU. Indeed, a consumer association has the burden of defining the 'class' and, thus, it can choose to represent only victims of the national market.

In all cases, DECO would certainly not bring a pan-EU collective redress action, even if it could. This can be explained by the additional costs that the consumer association would have to bear in case it chose to represent consumers from other Member States. Notably, DECO would have to notify them their right to opt out – probably in a different language than Portuguese – and examine whether the applicable law and the harm caused is the same everywhere. DECO would also have to deal with potential interventions and offer information to all the participants of the 'class'. As explained earlier, many costs, such as notification costs, are usually borne upfront by the claimant – here, DECO (chapter 2, I.D.iv.). In light of this, what are the incentives for a national consumer association to litigate on behalf of foreign consumers? There are probably few if any.

Certainly, such costs would decrease if an action in the defence of a general interest were brought. Most of the time, those actions are based on the automatic membership system. Hence, no notification process is necessary. However, when an injunction is sought in order to protect the general interest of consumers, its effects are usually limited to the territory of a Member State.

As a conclusion, a fully centralised model for cross-border collective redress actions is not desirable since it does not support access to justice. Rather, it obliges representative entities to figure out a way to litigate abroad, while the defendant does not assume the internationalisation of the case. Moreover, such a model requires a minimal level of harmonisation of national collective redress mechanisms.

ii. The Partial Centralisation Model

Another inspiring model is the *KapMuG* (see Figure 3). As explained earlier (chapter 3, II.D.i.), the German test case procedure centralises common questions of fact or law in the hands of a higher court. Once those issues are resolved, specific questions such as the allocation of damages take place within individual proceedings. Therefore, this model enables the 'splitting' of proceedings, which is the feature that is interesting here. It shares common features with the American MDL[60] (chapter 1, II.A.) and with the EU model on insolvency proceedings.[61]

Transposed to cross-border collective redress cases, the partial centralisation model advocates that a representative entity could open a principal collective redress procedure in the Member State where the defendant is domiciled, taking the test case model as a basis. Representative entities located in other Member States could then start territorial proceedings in order to resolve remaining issues, such as the allocation of damages. Therefore, conversely to the *KapMuG*, standing should be allocated to representative bodies in order to better fight rational apathy.

Under such a model, a single representative entity litigates the case that will serve as a test. Other bodies representing consumers from other Member States may be useful intermediaries: they can help with the notification process, determine the size of the 'class', provide additional legal support and so on. It remains to be determined whether the representative entity should bring an action in order to open territorial proceedings or whether it would be sufficient to manifest its intention to bind the consumers that it represents in the court where the

[60] See Bosters (n 61) 248–51, who considers that the MDL would be an appropriate basis to regulate cross-border collective redress actions in the EU.

[61] Council Regulation (EU) 2015/848 of 20 May 2015 on insolvency proceedings [2015] OJ L141/19 (Insolvency Regulation).

main proceedings take place. A registration system like under the *KapMuG* could perhaps be set up. In this case, one should also define how consumers might exercise their right to opt in. In order to pick up a test case, the court must first have a relatively clear picture of who the 'class' is and of the issues that are common to the claimants. Therefore, it might be better for victims to exercise their right to opt in or out before a judgment is issued. Here, the question is whether the procedural rules of the forum should be followed, or whether the modality of participation could be governed by the rules of the Member State where territorial proceedings start – on the model of Article 35 of the Insolvency Regulation. As long as rules on participation provide information on the size of the class and the nature of the claims, both options are feasible. The court may also be allocated some margin of discretion in order to establish ad hoc participation rules. A last question that should be mentioned here is the likely difficulty of dealing with potential interventions. The distance that separates the victims from the court ruling on common issues might deter interventions and, thus, undermine the right to be heard.

As far as costs are concerned, each representative would certainly have to deal with costs of notification upfront. The costs generated by the principal proceedings dealing with common issues of fact or law would also have to be shared between all representative bodies.

The connecting factor, whereby a court may open principal proceedings and the conditions to start territorial ones remain to be drafted. For example, the domicile of the defendant could be an appropriate criterion to open principal proceedings, but other options are conceivable. The court dealing with the test case would rule on common questions of fact or law. Its judgment would then serve as a basis to solve similar individual claims in territorial proceedings. Under the EU insolvency proceedings scheme, the opening of territorial, secondary proceedings is possible where the defendant has an establishment.[62] In collective redress cases, the opening of territorial proceedings could be submitted to the presence of victims or their representatives in a given Member States – through the connecting factor of their domicile or habitual residence, for example. Some requirements regarding numerosity and commonality could perhaps limit the opening of such proceedings.

Under the *KapMuG*, the declaratory judgment of the Higher Court is binding for lower courts dealing with pending similar actions. Victims who registered their claims – but did not start proceedings – are technically not bound by this judgment. In this context, how should this scheme be transposed in cross-border collective redress cases? In light of the above, it seems that the judgment issued in the test case should be recognised in Member States where territorial proceedings start. People who previously opted in would be bound by such a judgment. In this case, a facilitated regime of recognition and enforcement could be set up on the model of chapter 2 of the Insolvency Regulation. Where the defendant is reluctant to comply with an unfavourable judgment, victims may have to seek the enforcement of their judgment back in the courts of the defendant's domicile.

[62] Art 3(2) of the Insolvency Regulation.

Nevertheless, these transfers between different courts have been criticised under the *KapMuG*, since it might be quite burdensome and lengthy (chapter 3, II.D.i.).

Figure 3 The Partial Centralisation Model

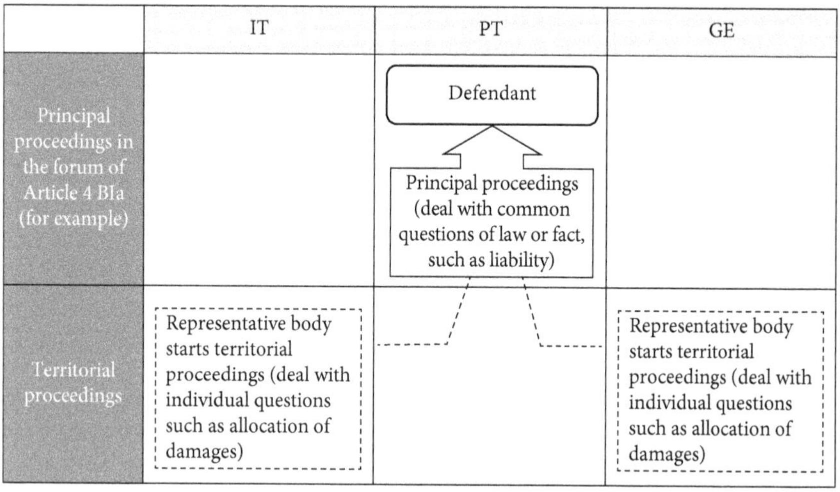

Although the benefits of such a model should be acknowledged, it is not exempted from critiques. For example, for such a model to include as many victims as possible and generate economies of scale, a proper communication channel between representative entities should be established. Otherwise, they might not even be aware of the existence of a cross-border test case procedure. Therefore, subsequent test case procedures might arise, thus wasting judicial resources. Additionally, this would surely undermine the centralisation process and offer only partial closure to the defendant. Finally, the costs related to the organisation of such coordinated proceedings should not be underestimated as the German experience demonstrates (chapter 3, II.D.i.).

Furthermore, just like the centralisation model (II.A.i.), a cross-border test case procedure would only be possible if a minimal harmonisation of collective redress mechanisms were to take place. In particular, access to justice to representative entities for both actions for damages and injunctive relief in similar areas of law should be provided. Otherwise, a test case procedure might not always be available, depending on the Member State.

Another critique that may be targeted at this model is that it offers the defendant a relatively comfortable position, in the sense that he/she knows that a cross-border collective redress will only take place at his/her domicile. Therefore, the burden of the internationalisation of the case falls on the consumer associations who have to cope with the difficulties of gathering victims together and asking for the collaboration of a colleague located in the defendant's state. In this vein, the partial centralisation model possesses a rather weak deterrent effect if any.

As a conclusion, a partial centralisation model inspired by the *KapMuG* is an interesting one since it would provide some consistency to the EU judicial area. Nevertheless, this model generates important costs, in the sense that it would require a minimal harmonisation of national procedures and setting up efficient communication channels between representative entities. Furthermore, such a model would not restore the balance between the claimant and the defendant. As a result, without rejecting outright the partial centralisation model, the following proposed model is better aligned with the EU's policy which aims at fostering access to justice.

B. The Proposal

i. Overview

The proposal offers a new, protective forum for judicial collective redress proceedings and promotes the conclusion of out-of-court agreements based on the Dutch model. To be more precise, the representative entity located in a given Member State should be able to bring collective redress actions either at its own domicile or in the domicile of the defendant. Conversely, the possibility for the defendant to bring negative actions for declaratory relief should be limited. In other words, the specific forum for collective redress should be based on the structure of section 4 BIa. Representative entities should have standing to start proceedings in the collective or general interests of consumers. Nevertheless, the representation power of those entities should be limited to the national market when they litigate in their own domicile. This would guarantee adequate representation of consumers' interests and avoid the overlap between several cross-border collective redress actions leading to concurrent judgments.

In practice, this means that a consumer association representing consumers of the national market in which it has its domicile would be able to start proceedings at this place against a defendant located in another – EU or third – state. The Member State where a given entity is situated should have the power to determine its representative nature. Despite this, the representative entity who wishes to start proceedings in the domicile of the defendant and has enough resources to do so should be able to litigate there too.[63] Thanks to this, no recognition and enforcement process will be needed if the defendant possesses his/her assets there. Additionally, leaving the forum of the defendant's domicile open offers parties a procedural choice, although the fading of procedural barriers is necessary in order to make Article 4 BIa more appealing than it currently is. This means that certain incentives have to be created. At least, mutual recognition of representative entities' standing is necessary. Just like under the modified centralised model (II.A.i.)

[63] The possibility to start proceedings in the domicile of a defendant domiciled in a third state depends on the private international law rules on jurisdiction of said state.

and Article 16(2) of the Proposal for a Directive on representative actions, these entities could be authorised by law to require the help of their colleagues domiciled in the defendant's domicile in order to start a collective redress action there, without facing procedural challenges. Naturally, representative entities requiring such help should financially support it.

Additionally, negotiation procedures on the basis of the Dutch model should be promoted. Chapter 3 highlighted that said model is relatively efficient but does not align itself with EU private international law rules (II.B.v.). The suggested proposal aims at solving this issue. This is why it is argued that the specific fora available for judicial collective proceedings should also cover out-of-court settlements. In other words, when one or various representative entities from different Member States settle with the defendant, they can make their agreement binding either in the courts of the domicile (of one of) the representative entity/ies participating in the negotiation or in the courts of the defendant's domicile. This solution is justified since the selection of the forum is consensual. Therefore, representative entities cannot force the defendant to appear in an unfavourable jurisdiction. From a structural perspective, the Dutch model represents an appropriate and efficient mechanism. The negotiation procedure is flexible and cheap. Up to now, it has proved to work well. Besides, consumers are sufficiently protected in the event that representative entities settle on their behalf and in case the courts control the validity and fairness of the agreement.

ii. Advantages

Litigating in the domicile of the defendant is justified inasmuch as parties are on a relatively equal footing. The burden of the international character of the dispute is spread among parties accordingly.[64] However, the emergence of collective harms calls into question this balance, due to the new type of damages they create – usually low and widespread – and the kind of actors they involve – multiple parties or the public in general. As a result, the previous sub-section highlighted that consumers and their representatives struggle to bring collective redress actions abroad. This means that they still face important barriers that impede them from obtaining redress. The forum of the representative entity's domicile takes into account this new reality by restoring the current uneven playing field between corporations and consumers' representatives. In this sense, the suggested proposal supports the initiatives of the EU institutions that aim at providing access to justice, by offering representative entities the possibility to protect collective and general interests in a unique and close forum, which the current private international law regime does not permit. It also exempts them from issues regarding standing to sue and costs

[64] M Virgós Soriano and FJ Garcimartín Alférez, *Derecho Procesal Civil Internacional* (Civitas, 2007) 123.

of litigation abroad. As for the possibility of concluding out-of-court settlements, this option is in alignment with EU legislative acts that encourage the use of ADR.

Additionally, it could also act as an ex ante incentive for defendants to comply with the law, as they are aware that collective redress litigation could start far from their domicile. Therefore, the suggested forum may trigger an interesting deterrent effect. Besides, it respects the rights of the defendant, in the sense that it is predictable. Conversely, the current application of private international law rules on jurisdiction creates confusion as to where collective redress actions should or could be brought. Given the absence of coordination, parallel judicial actions often arise and increase the risks of overlapping proceedings. As regards abusive litigation, it is contained thanks to the limitation of actors having standing to sue.

Another argument that supports the proposal is that the courts of the representative's domicile are often in a good position to rule on a collective redress action, given that multiple victims are located there. Indeed, the damages to individual consumers or the general interest usually materialise at this location. Moreover, this result is justified from a socio-political perspective: when multiple victims of the national market are affected by a given behaviour, courts of that state have an incentive to offer them access to justice. Even though the fora provided by the Brussels regime are technically available, practical obstacles impede their accessibility. As a result, it is common that access to courts is actually barred. The suggested proposal considers this fact.

Finally, by keeping collective proceedings national, the probability that one court has to apply many different laws to the dispute is low.[65] This reduces the workload of courts and is time-efficient. As explained below (II.B.iii.f.), such a limitation also protects the defendant from overlapping actions and, hence, overcompensation and deterrence. Eventually, it has to be underlined that this connecting factor is relatively easy to interpret, as the notion of domicile is familiar to the Brussels Regulation. In other words, it does not give rise to interpretation doubts like the connecting factor of the market most affected.

As regards declaratory actions to make collective agreements binding, the proposal certainly clarifies the present landscape. Up to now, it has not been clear whether those actions would fall under the scope of the Brussels regime (chapter 3, II.B.ii.b.). The proposal resolves this situation by establishing a specific forum for collective redress actions that covers the conclusion of collective redress settlements. This technique allows for a quick resolution of disputes without overburdening national courts. In this sense, the availability of an ADR procedure further diminishes the courts' amount of work: their role is limited to the control of the validity and fairness of the agreement. Moreover, the defendant might achieve closure. At the same time, a collective settlement involving multiple

[65] Notably, in a case such as Case C-191/15 *Verein für Konsumenteninformation v Amazon EU Sàrl* [ECLI:EU:C:2016:612], the jurisdictional rule of the suggested proposal would be coherent with the application of Art 6(1) Rome II Regulation (n 32), which designates the law of the market where the 'collective interests of consumers' are affected.

representative entities would only be possible where the defendant consents to a global settlement. Such a result is therefore respectful of his rights. As regards original claimants, they would be represented by entities, according to the respective national rules of the market where these are located.

iii. To Be Determined ...

Once the connecting factor is established, many other elements must be determined. Listed are the fundamental ones, without claiming to be exhaustive.

a. Type of Instrument

There are various ways of incorporating a specific jurisdictional ground for collective redress in the private international law network; for instance, one might consider the opportunity to create an independent instrument, such as a Directive or a Regulation. Said instrument could exclusively govern private international law questions, on the model of recent Regulations regarding family law,[66] or be part of a broader regulatory measure covering different aspects of law, like the GDPR. Alternatively, such a jurisdictional ground might be included in the Brussels regime.

On the one hand, the design of a customised legislation regarding collective redress including private international questions and possibly other aspects of law is appealing. It allows for the elaboration of an autonomous system, which might regulate coherently a specific device from the procedural and private international law perspectives. The additional aspects that should be the object of a legislative measure include the mutual recognition of capacity and standing to sue of representative entities – in case they choose to litigate in the forum of Article 4 BIa. Similarly, it could be useful to list some criteria regarding the fairness of a collective settlement and perhaps the form that such an act should possess in order to avoid potential conflicts of interests, such as those highlighted in chapter 1 (III.D.). However, the negotiation procedure should not be over-regulated, as it has to remain flexible to be effective. Finally, a specific rule on related actions could be drafted in order to coordinate parallel proceedings. The potential problems related to the emergence of parallel proceedings is examined later in this chapter (II.B.iv.b.).

On the other hand, one might consider the possibility of implementing a jurisdictional rule tailored to collective redress within the Brussels regime.

[66] eg the Council Regulation 2016/1103 of 24 June 2016 implementing enhanced cooperation in the area of jurisdiction, applicable law and the recognition and enforcement of decisions in matters of matrimonial property regime [2016] OJ L183/1, and the Council Regulation 2016/1104 of 24 June 2016 implementing enhanced cooperation in the area of jurisdiction, applicable law and the recognition and enforcement of decisions in matters of the property consequences of registered partnerships [2016] OJ L183/30.

This method makes it easier for legal professionals to work with private international law norms, as they would remain centralised in a single text. However, one has to make sure that the specific jurisdictional ground for collective redress claims is consistent with the remaining provisions of the BIa. For example, this technique permitted the introduction of a specific forum for the return of cultural objects in Article 7(4) BIa.

From a legislative perspective, both possibilities appear to be valid, although the EU legislator usually enacts private international law norms in the form of Regulations.[67] In all cases, the principle of proportionality commands the adoption of the less incisive measure (Article 5(4) TEU). Initially, the first private international law instruments adopted essentially contained rules on jurisdiction, applicable law and recognition and enforcement. Today, one may also find private international law rules in instruments with a broader coverage. For example, the GDPR essentially harmonises substantive laws of the Member States in the data protection field, but dedicates one of its chapters to private international law rules on jurisdiction.

Moreover, both Articles 81 and 114 TFEU probably enable the EU legislator to regulate collective redress to a certain extent. As far as the proposal suggested here is concerned, Article 81 TFEU seems to be the appropriate legal basis if the EU legislator wants to adopt a private international rule on jurisdiction regarding collective redress, as well as ADR. As mentioned in the above paragraphs, other legal aspects could also be the object of a legislative measure such as the mutual recognition of capacity and standing to sue. In all cases, the modification of the BIa in order to include a specific jurisdictional ground regarding collective redress seems unlikely for the time being. The Recast entered into force on 10 January 2015 and, thus, some time will probably pass before the EU considers amending this text again. Despite the numerous documents regarding collective redress that already existed at the time of the Recast, the EU institutions did not take the opportunity to regulate this topic (chapter 3, I.A.i.). Consequently, the adoption of an independent instrument might be the faster way out.

To sum up, the adoption of an independent instrument including private international law rules on collective actions for damages and injunctive relief is proposed. Additionally, some specific elements should be regulated in such an instrument, such as mutual recognition of capacity and standing to sue.

b. Nature of the Jurisdictional Rule

Jurisdictional rules have distinct natures: in particular, such rules attribute general, alternative, protective, or exclusive jurisdiction to courts within the EU.

[67] European Parliament, A European Framework for Private International Law: Current Gaps and Future Perspectives (2012) 17–21, available at www.europarl.europa.eu/document/activities/cont/2012 12/20121219ATT58300/20121219ATT58300EN.pdf.

Moreover, party autonomy plays an important role in the allocation of jurisdiction. In light of this, what is the nature of a jurisdictional rule regarding collective redress?

As pointed out above, the policy objective behind the attribution of jurisdiction to the courts of the domicile where the representative entity is located is the correction of the current imbalance between original claimants and their representatives on the one hand, and defendants on the other. Procedural considerations and policy objectives command such a measure. As a result, this rule is protective in nature. In light of this, section 4 BIa is used as a basis to draft such a rule. Representative entities should be able to bring collective redress proceedings either at their own domicile or at the domicile of the defendant. The latter should always be available since it entails significant advantages for those who can actually reach it.

c. Connecting Factor

The connecting factor for collective redress actions is the domicile of the representative entity. Nevertheless, the protective forum of the representative entity's domicile should not be available in all circumstances. For instance, it does not seem reasonable to open such a forum in cases where two French consumers bought a defective product in a local German shop while they were on holiday and, once back home, mandate a representative entity to bring an *action en représentation conjointe* in France on their behalf. One senses that it would be unreasonable to drag the defendant to the protective forum of the representative entity – supposing that the latter would litigate such a case –, since the defendant probably did not have the intention to internationalise its activities. Moreover, in the example presented above, the defendant does not seem to entertain any connection with the forum state and it did not cause any damage on that market. As a result, this connecting factor should be coupled with additional substantive conditions – on the model of section 4 BIa – in order to guarantee that the case has an appropriate connection with the forum.

In light of the above, various criteria are potentially available in order to streamline the use of collective redress procedures in the domicile of the representative entity. Nevertheless, the connecting factors contained in the BIa do not grasp the diversity of collective redress cases and, thus, do not seem to be appropriate. For example, Article 17(1)(c) BIa, which requires the trader to direct its activities to a given Member State in order for consumers to benefit from the protective forum of Article 18 BIa, essentially concerns contractual matters. Therefore, such a connecting factor would be difficult to apply to collective redress actions where no commercial activity preceded the occurrence of the damage, such as harms to the environment or mass accidents. Finally, the place where the damage occurred (*loci damni*) may constitute an interesting connecting factor. However, applied to the proposal, this means that the simple presence of two victims on the territory would allow them to sue the defendant in a close forum, even though the latter did not internationalise its activities.

In light of this, one has to find an alternative, flexible connecting criterion that is able to deal with the diversity of collective redress actions. In all cases, it would probably be wise to distinguish between actions protecting general interests on the one hand, and collective redress cases involving the collective interests of consumers on the other. As far as general interests are concerned, it was highlighted earlier that representative entities often start proceedings at the place where the damage occurred. Therefore, such a connecting factor should be maintained. Accordingly, representative entities would be able to bring an action at their own domicile if the national market or the object that they protect has been – or is about to be – damaged. By way of example, a Spanish association or organisation could start proceedings in its domicile against a company located in another – EU or third – state, if it pollutes the environment and cause damages to forests or rivers in Spain, ie the place where the damage occurred (*loci damni*). Along the same line of reasoning, such an association could litigate against a trader located in another state, if the latter used unfair terms on the local market and thus, harmed the general interest of consumers there. The advantage of such a solution – compared to Article 7(2) BIa – is that one does not struggle with pinning down the exact place where the damage occurred for the purpose of allocating territorial jurisdiction, which might be complicated when general, rather abstract interests are at stake. Ideally, procedural national law should back up this solution by allowing potential victims to join proceedings and present their individual claims.

Defining an appropriate connecting factor for actions involving the collective interests of victims is a more tricky exercise. When numerous and homogenous individual interests are at stake, the occurrence of the damage should not, in itself, allow the start of a collective redress action. Therefore, additional limitations have to shape access to such a forum. Two possibilities are: first, centralisation of numerous individual claims in the domicile of the representative entity's domicile could be submitted to the previous existence of an accessible forum for individual actions in the market concerned. Accordingly, a French consumer association could be able to litigate on behalf of victims only if those would have the ability to sue in France on an individual basis according to a head of jurisdiction – for example thanks to section 4 or 7(2) BIa. In the *Schrems* case, for example, it means that the VKI could have started proceedings in its own domicile, on behalf of Austrian consumers.[68] Such a solution fosters centralisation at the national level and is therefore in line with the suggested proposal. Additionally, it remains predictable for the defendant and does not create discrimination between individual and collective actions. In other words, there is no risk that a victim, who is part of a collective action, is more advantaged than a person suing on an individual basis. Naturally, for such a solution to work, procedural law must offer an adequate instrument for entities to sue.

[68] In this case, it is doubtful that consumers domiciled in another Member State can join the Austrian action, since no other connecting factor such as the domicile or the place where the damage occurred link them to this territory.

Alternatively, a more flexible approach could be adopted, whereby the start of collective redress actions protecting collective interests would be submitted to substantive limitations borrowed from the US class actions. For example, one could imagine that such actions would be admissible if they fulfil the numerosity (chapter 1, III.B.i.) and the superiority (chapter 1, III.C.ii.) requirements. Accordingly, cross-border actions would be admitted only if a minimum number of victims were affected on a given market. This would indirectly mean that the trader had a significant impact on the international market. Moreover, courts would have to determine whether the collective action is the most appropriate procedural tool. Among other things, the procedural balance between parties and the trader's intention to internationalise its activities could be taken into account in order to assess the admissibility of the claim. Although the superiority requirement offers flexibility and enable courts to consider the specificities of each collective redress action, it clashes with the usual mandatory nature of EU private international rules on jurisdiction, as it amounts to a kind of *forum (non) conveniens* principle. Nevertheless, in *Besix*,[69] the CJEU ruled that Article 7(1) BIa was not open to an obligation not to do with no territorial boundaries. Therefore, one must acknowledge that some flexibility in the application of the Brussels' special fora already exists and, hence, could be further exploited for the benefit of collective redress.

Finally, a combination of those alternatives is possible. For instance, the requirement concerning the availability of a previous forum for individual actions could be coupled with the numerosity requirement.

d. Terminology and Type of Action

In chapter 2, the spotlight was on the difficulties in defining the concept of 'collective redress' (chapter 2, I.B.). In this context, it has to be decided whether potential legislation on this topic should define this notion or not. In all cases, its content is more important than its 'shape'. Consequently, the inclusion of collective actions for injunctive relief, as well as collective actions for damages should be within the definition. The playing field should be levelled, given that representative entities are in a position of relative weakness when they protect either a general or a collective interest. In fact, in both actions, representative entities face similar obstacles like the cost of litigating abroad. The declaratory action to make a collective settlement binding has to be part of a private international law instrument on collective redress too.

The defendant might be tempted to bring a declaratory negative action,[70] with the objective of demonstrating his lack of liability regarding an alleged damage.

[69] Case C-256/00 *Besix SA v Wasserreinigungsbau Alfred Kretzschmar GmbH & Co. KG (WABAG) and Planungs- und Forschungsgesellschaft Dipl. Ing. W. Kretzschmar GmbH & KG (Plafog)* [2002] ECR I-01699.

[70] According to Collins '[a]n action for a negative declaration is for a declaration that the defendant has no valid claim or right against the plaintiff'. Note that in declaratory proceedings the role of parties is reversed. Therefore, consumers are defendants to the action and the trader becomes the plaintiff. See L Collins, 'Negative declarations and the Brussels Convention' (1992) 108 *Law Quarterly Review* 545, 545.

Following the suggested proposal, this means that the defendant could bring a declaratory negative action in the courts of his own domicile or in the domicile of a representative entity threatened with the initiation of collective redress proceedings. In principle, the equality of treatment of both parties commands the acceptance of the defendant's right to bring actions for negative declaratory relief in the forum of his choice. However, allowing this practice is tantamount to allowing some 'pre-emptive forum shopping',[71] whereby the defendant could secure jurisdiction in a favourable forum to the detriment of the representative entity. Therefore, this practice seriously disturbs the procedural balance between parties to litigation.[72]

In the context of the Brussels regime, the initiation of negative declaratory proceedings would not allow the subsequent start of collective redress proceedings in another Member State. Indeed, rules on *lis pendens* and related actions could bar the emergence of subsequent proceedings.[73] Nevertheless, it is not clear whether the defendant could seek negative declaratory relief against an abstract group of victims or the community. According to continental law, a negative declaratory action must take place within an existing dispute and not be intended to solve abstract legal questions.[74] Therefore, the entities and the potential group of victims they represent should be identified. However, it seems particularly tricky to determine the boundaries of the group that will be bound by a negative declaratory action in advance.

In light of those considerations, the defendant's right to start actions seeking negative declaratory relief should be limited. The protective nature of the proposed jurisdictional ground justifies this result. Thanks to this limitation, it is possible to maintain the balance between parties to the proceedings. The threat of collective proceedings abroad should incentivise parties to settle, rather than fostering negative declaratory actions that generate complex legal issues.

e. Material and Territorial Scope

A jurisdictional ground for collective redress should not be limited to certain categories of consumers and/or contracts on the model of section 4 BIa. The active-passive dichotomy and the corresponding limitation to certain contracts that this provision contains do not seem to fit collective redress actions. Indeed, the material scope of section 4 BIa appears to be particularly restrictive. For example, in the

[71] ibid 546.

[72] A Bell, 'The Negative Declaration in Transnational Litigation' (1995) 111 *Law Quarterly Review* 674, 680–83.

[73] Case C-144/86 *Gubisch Maschinenfabrik KG v Giulio Palumbo* [1987] ECR 04861; Case C-406/92 *The owners of the cargo lately laden on board the ship 'Tatry' v the owners of the ship 'Maciej Rataj'* [1994] ECR I-05439; Case C-133/11 *Folien Fischer AG and Fofitec AG v Ritrama SpA* [ECLI:EU:C:2012:664].

[74] A Blomeyer, 'Types of Relief Available (Judicial Remedies)' in M Cappelletti (ed), *International Encyclopedia of Comparative Law*, vol 14, ch 4 (JCB Mohr/Martinus Nijhoff Publishers, 1982) 43.

Volkswagen case, a majority of investors could probably qualify as consumers. Nevertheless, their access to the forum of section 4 BIa may be barred, inasmuch as no contract binds them to the defendant.[75] Along the same line of reasoning, actions seeking the prohibition of the use of unfair terms would equally fall outside the scope of section 4 BIa, since the defence of general consumer interests is not covered by this norm. As a result, the material scope of a jurisdictional norm covering collective redress claims should be wide enough to take into account the typical scenarios under which collective actions are needed.

In this context, various options are possible: on the one hand, a list of legislation, pursuant to which collective redress would be available, might be elaborated on the model of the Injunctions Directive[76] or the Insolvency Regulation. However, an exhaustive list would have to be regularly updated, and this could be a time-consuming process. For example, the Belgian legislator adopted this technique: Article XVII.36 of the Belgian Economic Code states that a collective redress claim for damages is admissible where the trader has infringed a contractual obligation or legislation listed in Article XVII.37. Said provision contains no fewer than 32 references to EU and national legislation. Notably, the list encompasses competition law, as well as intellectual property rights. On the other hand, a list of abstract fields of law could be integrated to the jurisdictional norm, such as consumer protection, shareholder disputes, and even competition law if this is deemed convenient. Although such a list offers some flexibility, it could give rise to interpretative issues. A last possibility consists in defining the actors who may litigate through a representative entity, such as consumers and investors. Thanks to this technique, any consumer or investor would be able to participate in collective proceedings, no matter the substantive area affected. The solution selected by the Belgian legislator is the most comfortable one, as it limits interpretative issues and precisely pinpoints the legislation under which collective redress actions might be needed.

As regards the territorial scope, the jurisdictional forum regarding collective redress could extend to defendants seated in third states, on the model of section 4 BIa. As a result, EU citizens would benefit from an equal treatment no matter where the defendant is domiciled.[77] This argument is at the origin of the extension of section 4 BI, during the revision process of the Brussels regime.[78] Before that, consumers willing to sue defendants domiciled in third countries had to rely on national rules on civil procedure in order to do so. However, Member States' private international law rules were highly diverse. For example, some of

[75] eg access to s 4 BIa was barred in Case C-375/13 *Harald Kolassa v Barclays Bank plc* [ECLI:EU:C:2015:37]. See also L Carballo, 'Protección de inversores, acciones colectivas y Derecho internacional privado' (2011) 37 *Revista de derecho de sociedades* 207, 219.

[76] This solution was also supported by the European Parliament, Resolution of 2 February 2012 on 'Towards a Coherent European Approach to Collective Redress' (2011/2089(INI)), paras 15, 24.

[77] Tang (n 28) 132–33.

[78] FJ Garcimartín and S Sánchez, 'El nuevo Reglamento Bruselas I: qué ha cambiado en el ámbito de la competencia judicial' (2013) 48 *Revista española de derecho europeo* 9, 13–18.

them did not offer consumers the possibility to start proceedings against foreign defendants in their own domicile. This situation generated an important market distortion: consumers located in the EU had 'more' access to justice where they sued a defendant seated in EU territory. Conversely, consumers litigating against defendants located outside the EU had no guarantee to benefit from an affordable forum. This motivated the amendment of section 4 BI.

In disputes involving a defendant located in a third state, special attention should be paid to the rise of parallel proceedings and, hence, the potential application of Articles 33 and 34 BIa. Because these provisions do not apply where protective jurisdictional norms are at stake, parallel collective redress proceedings could emerge. Where collective proceedings pending in different courts are alike, one might wonder whether the establishment of transnational rules on civil procedure could synchronise courts' work and bring legal certainty to parties. Nevertheless, it is not clear whether such a coordination is needed. For transnational rules to be adopted, it should first be confirmed that a risk of under-/overcompensation or under-/over-deterrence exists. To the best of this author's knowledge, no evidence proves this fact. For example, the comments regarding the Dutch model highlighted that American class action settlements on the one hand, and Dutch *WCAM* settlements on the other were mutually exclusive. In the particular cases examined above, no sign of overlap appeared.

In case of settlement, it remains to be seen whether representative entities from third states could participate in the negotiations. Allowing foreign representative bodies to take part in a collective settlement and make it binding in a court located in the EU seems appealing, although it might generate various issues: for example, the enforcement of such a settlement over foreign absent parties might not be guaranteed and it is doubtful that the EU has any incentive to protect foreign consumers. Additionally, negotiations can be particularly complicated if representatives are located in remote states.

f. Standing to Sue

The promotion of the representative model for collective redress automatically limits the number of players who may start collective proceedings. In principle, only certain entities, which represent consumer collective or general interests, should be able to litigate under this model. This includes at least certain consumer associations, and public authorities like ombudsmen. Should representative individuals be included within the list? This depends on one's policy objectives: when many different players have standing to sue, the chances that collective proceedings start are potentially high. Therefore, enlarging the number of actors with the ability to present collective claims fosters access to justice. However, one might be concerned to limit standing to sue in order to guarantee that original claimants' interests are well represented in court and protected. Additionally, unlimited access to courts creates the risk of overburdening them to the detriment of other valuable disputes. In all cases, the allocation of standing to sue should remain the competence of the Member States. Then, the standing of representative entities should benefit from a system of mutual recognition on the model of the Injunctions Directive.

As explained earlier, the representative power of a given entity should be limited to the national market. Various reasons justify this limitation: to start with, a limited representative power confines the definition of the 'class'. Therefore, in case parallel proceedings would arise, they should not overlap. This limitative measure aims at protecting the defendant from overcompensation and deterrence. In any case, as the analysis regarding the centralisation model shows, representative entities may lack incentive to directly represent foreign consumers because of the potentially important costs that these entities would have to assume alone.

iv. Critical Assessment

As the saying goes, nobody is perfect. Neither are jurisdictional rules. Therefore, the next paragraphs present the different critiques to which the suggested proposal could be submitted. Once again, the list is not exhaustive.

a. Fragmentation of the Internal Market

One may consider that the proposal deviates from the EU's policy, which consists in withdrawing internal barriers to the EU market. Somehow, the suggested forum acknowledges the differences that exist between Member States without trying to overcome them. Additionally, it opposes the current legislative trend towards harmonisation.

In fact, the creation of a specific forum for collective redress actions in the domicile of the representative entity contrasts with the usual top-down approach followed by the EU. However, the drawbacks that this method entails were emphasised: legislative proposals imposed from the highest level sometimes overlook practical aspects that affect their feasibility and effectiveness. Proof of this fact is the moderate success of the Injunctions Directive, as well as the EU Small Claims Procedure, to mention just those examples. Conversely, the proposal suggests that a bottom-up approach is preferable. Accordingly, this investigation project has inquired into practice and has highlighted the difficulties that may hinder access to justice. As a result, the more one tries to centralise collective redress actions in a single forum, the more distance is put between a victim and the court having jurisdiction. In such a context, access to justice is merely conceptual and hence, cannot be guaranteed in all cases. Although the creation of a specific forum for collective redress in the domicile of the representative entity may not be aligned with the current reforms that aim at reinforcing the internal market, it has the benefit of being a realistic option built upon practical observations. Additionally, the proposed solution is respectful of its environment in the sense that it does not impose harmonisation of national procedures. Moreover, it complies with EU law, as well as private international law principles. Later on, and depending on the evolution of the internal market, another, more 'centralising', solution may be adopted. Today, however, the actual guarantee of access to justice needs to be further improved. Besides, this guarantee should precede the perfection of the internal market, as the latter cannot be achieved without the former.

b. Fragmentation of Litigation

Opponents of the proposal may argue that it fosters undesirable parallel litigation. Indeed, allocating jurisdiction to the courts of the Member State where the representative entity is located and limiting its representation power to national interests creates a fertile ground for parallel proceedings. This automatically raises questions regarding coordination of collective redress actions, in order to avoid the issuance of judgments that may overlap.

The rise of various similar proceedings can take place at two different stages: on the one hand, two or more collective redress actions with a similar object and/or involving the same parties that are pending in the courts of different Member States may overlap. On the other hand, issues may equally emerge when two judgments regarding an identical dispute are to be recognised and enforced in a given Member State.

There are various weapons against the concurrence of similar actions, including *forum non conveniens*, *lis pendens*, anti-suit injunctions and clawback actions.[79] As is well known, the Brussels regime tackles parallel proceedings through its rules on *lis pendens* and related actions. As highlighted earlier (chapter 3, II.D.iii.b.), however, when concurrent collective redress actions are pending in different courts, Article 29 BIa is unlikely to apply, since those actions often technically involve different parties. In practice, 'classes' may nevertheless overlap, as the *Volkswagen* case shows. This explains why one representative entity's power should be limited to the litigation of national interests only.

On the contrary, Article 30(1) BIa on related actions has the ability to prevent the issuance of potentially inconsistent collective redress judgments. Pursuant to this provision, the courts where subsequent proceedings start could suspend them in order to adapt their decision to the firstly issued judgment. Yet, rules on related actions are not mandatory and national courts possess a discretionary power to suspend proceedings or not. Therefore, in order to guarantee the coherence of pending collective redress cases, it could be useful to oblige courts to suspend proceedings when both collective redress actions share the same object. Accordingly, the secondly seised court should be able to deviate from the first judgment only if significant differences separate the two cases.[80] Typically, this would happen

[79] GA Bermann, 'Parallel Litigation: Is Convergence Possible?' (2011) 21 *Yearbook of Private International Law* 21, 21–36.

[80] Similarly, Art 10(2) of the Proposal for a Directive on representative actions states that final decisions, such as those establishing the existence of an infringement, taken in another Member State, must be considered as 'rebuttable presumptions' that an infringement has occurred by other national courts.

where distinct substantive laws apply. This solution would maintain the coherence of the outcome for all parties.

A similar option has been adopted in the US where the centralisation of class actions in a single forum rarely happens. Rather, parallel proceedings are tolerated in the name of federalism and overlapping jurisdictional grounds (above chapter 1, II.B.ii.). In the EU, although the procedural system is not based on federalism, jurisdictional rules sometimes multiply the courts with jurisdiction over a dispute. Therefore, concurrent actions cannot be totally avoided. In such a context and in light of the US experience, an obligation to suspend proceedings and take into account the content of a first collective redress judgment is an appropriate and soft coordination measure.

Yet, when various class actions are pending in different US federal courts, pre-trial issues can be centralised through MDL. Therefore, consolidation of proceedings is possible at the federal level. In the EU, Article 30(2) BIa also states that consolidation should be allowed at the request of one party if proceedings are both pending in first instance and the court first seised has jurisdiction. In light of this, it is reasonable to wonder whether consolidation of various collective redress proceedings started in different Member States should be allowed in the courts of the domicile of a given representative entity. Unfortunately, those courts will rarely have jurisdiction to rule over collective redress actions brought in other fora, because of their lack of connection with the national territory. However, if all parties consent to it, they should be able to consolidate proceedings in the domicile of one representative entity. Settlement agreements may also be declared binding in this location. Consolidation should in any case be possible under national procedural law if representative entities are willing to litigate in the forum of the defendant's domicile.

The overlap of concurrent collective redress actions may also take place at the recognition and enforcement stage. Technically, however, the emergence of parallel collective redress proceedings should not give rise to 'irreconcilable' judgments pursuant to Article 45(1) BIa. According to this provision, judgments are irreconcilable if they involve the same parties. Unless the definition of the 'class' overlaps, this is not likely to happen. In theory, therefore, collective redress judgments, whose outcomes are different, may perfectly coexist from a private international law perspective. In practice, however, if the definition of the 'class' overlaps, overcompensation and deterrence might occur. In order to avoid such a situation, it is suggested that the representative power of a consumer association should be limited to the national market in which it is active.

c. Recognition and Enforcement

The next paragraphs examine whether one can hinder the recognition and enforcement process of collective redress judgments and thus, put into jeopardy their free movement. The same question as regards collective redress settlements is then examined.

In case a collective redress judgment is issued in the domicile of the representative entity, a potential recognition and enforcement process will probably take place in the defendant's domicile. Indeed, it is reasonable to suppose that the defendant will usually have his/her assets where he/she is domiciled. Accordingly, this means that representative entities will be forced to start recognition and enforcement proceedings abroad against reluctant defendants. This might be expensive and time-consuming. This problem has been highlighted for example by the pre-Injunctions Directive cases mentioned above (chapter 3, II.A.ii.b.). Nevertheless, this issue should tend to disappear due to the simplification of the recognition and enforcement system in the EU.

In absence of any other specific provision, the BIa should apply to collective redress judgments issued within the EU. Under the Brussels regime, the recognition and enforcement system is facilitated in civil and commercial matters, including collective redress judgments. However, it still has to be examined whether grounds for refusal may put the free movement of collective redress judgments into jeopardy. Earlier some of those grounds were examined in the EU in relationship to the recognition and enforcement of US class action judgments (chapter 1, II.B.i.). The analysis is also valid as far as collective redress judgments are concerned to a certain extent. To be more specific, some Member State courts might reject the recognition and enforcement of a collective redress judgment based on an opt-out procedure. Similarly, they can call into question the notification process that was used in light of the right of parties to be heard. However, in case the proposed forum is adopted, lack of jurisdiction – on the model of Article 45(e)(i) BIa – could not be invoked to bar recognition and/or enforcement. Finally, public order too could be used as a basis of denial.

At the time the BI was under revision, the Commission rejected the possibility of abolishing *exequatur* for collective redress judgments, since too different procedural models were implemented in Member States.[81] As for the Paris-Rio guidelines,[82] they suggest a more audacious approach, whereby rules on recognition and enforcement should prevent national courts from rejecting collective redress judgments just because they are based on an opt-out mechanism. Additionally, the guidelines state that recognition and enforcement should be promoted where the due process rights of absent claimants have been respected. The same applies where the notification process is deemed to be appropriate.

As regards collective redress settlements, they benefit from Article 59 BIa as they qualify as a 'court settlement' in the sense of Article 2(b) BIa. Accordingly, settlements that are enforceable in the Member State of origin are submitted to the enforcement regime applicable to authentic instruments. As a result, the only ground for refusal that has the ability to stop the enforcement process is public policy. Again, this gives Member States some room to reject the enforcement of

[81] Commission, Proposal for a Regulation on jurisdiction and the recognition and enforcement of judgments in civil and commercial matters COM (2010) 748 final 6.

[82] ILA, *Conference Report Rio de Janeiro 2008* (n 45) s 10.

collective redress settlements based on an opt-out basis, for example. In all cases, a specific, uniform rule dealing with the recognition of collective settlements would be welcome in order to prevent the start of subsequent overlapping individual proceedings in other Member States.

To sum up, it is not clear whether a modification of the current system is necessary, since Member States' experience regarding the recognition and enforcement of EU collective redress judgments and settlements remains limited for the time being.[83] However, the adoption of a specific rule on recognition and enforcement for collective redress judgments and settlements is conceivable. This measure would certainly facilitate and reduce the costs of the recognition and enforcement of such judgments and settlements abroad. This specific rule could be drafted according to the Paris-Rio guidelines that take an innovative approach by setting the grounds for refusal that can and cannot be invoked. Finally, said specific rule could be introduced either in the BIa or in another piece of legislation regarding collective redress.

III. Conclusion

Ideally, collective redress actions in the EU should be centralised in a single forum. This result would be perfectly in line with the principle of sound administration of justice. In practice, however, this principle is sometimes in tension with other fundamental values, policies and objectives of private international law such as the desirability of access to justice. In light of this, a solution that would comply with all these principles is rather unrealistic.

Chapter 4 of this research project highlights the difficulties of finding an appropriate forum where parties could bring collective redress actions. To start with, Article 4 BIa does not currently offer an accessible forum for consumers and their representatives. Moreover, it seems that it is hardly ever used. As regards Article 7(2) BIa, it may only be useful for the defence of general consumer interests. Then, most proposals for reform attempt to accommodate collective redress to the Brussels regime. Such attempt at reconciliation is predestined to fail: how could collective redress, which naturally involves multiple claimants or a community, fit in a legislation based on the two-party-proceedings principle? For this reason, most proposals are often partial solutions.

As a result, the creation of a new jurisdictional ground, based on the representative and the Dutch models is needed. Collective litigation should take place in the courts of the domicile of the representative entity that litigates on behalf of national consumers or their general interest. The forum of the defendant's domicile should remain open as an alternative. Moreover, the conclusion of out-of-court

[83] D Fairgrieve, 'The Impact of The Brussels I Enforcement and Recognition Rules on Collective Actions' in Fairgrieve and Lein (n 20) 178–86.

settlements should be promoted by endorsing the Dutch collective redress model. Courts of the domicile of any party – either a representative entity or the defendant – participating in the collective settlement should have jurisdiction to make it binding. On the positive side of the balance, the proposal respects the core principles of private international law and fosters access to justice.

On the negative side of the balance, however, the proposed solution does not spare judicial resources by centralising all collective actions in a single forum. Consequently, it may give rise to parallel proceedings and thus, overlapping judgments. Nevertheless, because collective redress mechanisms and actions are so different, this risk appears to be limited. Besides, the application of a rule on related actions should also participate in the limitation of such a risk. Finally, although the recognition and enforcement of collective redress judgments and settlements will often have to be started abroad, the facilitated regime established by the BIa should smooth that process. If the invocation of public policy restricts their free movement within the EU, the adoption of a specific rule dealing with the recognition and enforcement of collective redress judgments and settlements is conceivable.

Final Conclusions

The objective of the present research project consisted in facilitating cross-border collective redress actions within the EU. In order to achieve this goal, two paths could be followed. On the one hand, harmonisation of national civil procedure, which seems to be the measure that looms in the Commission's head, could be achieved pursuant to Article 114 TFEU (I.). On the other hand, the reform of EU private international law rules on jurisdiction would represent a more appropriate measure (II.). This idea stems from the belief that private international law has the ability to significantly reduce obstacles to cross-border litigation. Those measures constitute the two fundamental points around which these final conclusions are built.

I. Harmonisation of Collective Redress Mechanisms: Unity over Diversity

Collective redress mechanisms implemented by Member States are characterised by their heterogeneity. To such extent that a clear-cut definition of collective redress that would encompass all national schemes is impossible to provide (chapter 2, I.B.). Only a comparative approach facilitates the understanding of this notion. The US class action was chosen as a point of reference (chapter 1). Because of the many abuses generated by class actions, Member States primarily adopted instruments with antagonistic structural features (chapter 2, I.D.). This trend was also encouraged by the Recommendation of 2013 issued by the Commission, which requires Member States to couple their collective redress mechanisms with safeguards, but without building up the corresponding incentives to litigate (chapter 2, II.B.ii.b.). Unfortunately, these legislative choices have often affected the efficiency of collective redress mechanisms. This has encouraged national legislators to undertake different reforms with the purpose of fixing those undesirable effects (chapter 2, I.A.).

In light of the above, since 2007, the EU institutions have tried to bring some uniformity to the current landscape. Therefore, they have gathered information on collective redress mechanisms adopted by Member States and have met with representative stakeholders (chapter 2, II.A.). The EU then presented many policy options aimed at implementing collective redress. Fulfilling the private enforcement gap without affecting the rights of the defence are the main objectives pursued by the EU institutions (chapter 2, II.B.ii.).

In such a context, EU institutions may believe that harmonisation of national collective redress mechanisms and other related procedural rules is the appropriate way to regulate collective redress, pursuant to Article 114 TFEU (chapter 2, II.C.ii.b.). Indeed, procedural differences are likely to be perceived as obstacles to the internal market, which deter people from shopping abroad. This can be inferred from the documents released by the Commission. Therefore, a harmonisation measure would supposedly remove barriers in the internal market, and, thus, encourage people to engage in cross-border activities.

Nevertheless, harmonisation of collective redress mechanisms would only partially tackle obstacles in cross-border litigation (chapter 2, II.C.ii.c.). Moreover, the assumption that procedural harmonisation should encourage people to shop and litigate abroad in case of conflict remains a rhetorical argument which, to date, has not been sufficiently demonstrated. Along the same line of reasoning, Article 114 TFEU can only be used '[s]ave where otherwise provided in the Treaties'. The principles of proportionality and subsidiarity command the same approach. As a result, and since the beneficial aspects of harmonisation are not satisfactorily supported by empirical evidence, such a measure would be too intrusive. Instead, a regulation dealing with private international law aspects of collective redress represents a better option.

Although a private international law approach would be followed, the idea regarding what an appropriate measure should look like might well clash with the EU's vision. Having the construction of the internal market in mind, the latter might be tempted to suggest that collective redress actions should be centralised in a single forum – presumably the domicile of the defendant or the place where the majority of victims is located. As demonstrated in chapter 4 of this book, however, a centralisation model is predestined to fail, since it does not create sufficient incentives for consumers and their representatives to initiate proceedings in other Member States (chapter 4, II.A.i.). In other words, centralisation does not take into account the practical obstacles to cross-border litigation.

In particular, this research project has emphasised that the start of actions in another Member State, including collective redress actions, is still rare (chapter 4, II.A.ii.). The Evaluation Study on the effectiveness and efficiency of collective redress mechanisms in the EU states that only 10 per cent of the actions brought entailed an international component. Similarly, the reports on the Injunctions Directive, as well as the Fitness Check, mention that representative entities hardly ever start actions in another Member State.[1] The answers to the questionnaire used in this project confirm this fact: usually, Article 7(2) BIa is used by consumer associations in order to initiate cross-border actions 'at home' (chapter 3, II.A.iii.c.). This demonstrates that consumer associations and other similar representatives have to deal with significant barriers which deter them from initiating actions abroad.

[1] See ch 4, n 17.

II. The Proposal: Access to Justice over Unity

These considerations have led to the conclusion that a specific forum for collective redress actions which takes into account those practical problems should be created (chapter 4, II.B.). This is so, because of the patent unsuitability of BIa to collective redress. Indeed, EU private international law rules on jurisdiction mismatch the four predominant collective redress models implemented in the EU – namely the representative model (chapter 3, II.A.i.), the Dutch model (chapter 3, II.B.i.), the class action model (chapter 3, II.C.i.) and the test case procedure above (chapter 3, II.D.i.). Specifically, this research project shows that collective redress actions may only be centralised in the forum of Article 4 BIa, as well as to a certain extent Article 7(2) BIa. Nevertheless, those provisions do not always offer an accessible forum for claimants (chapter 4, I.B.). Furthermore, the analysis regarding the German test case procedure shows that even though centralisation can be achieved at the defendant's domicile, this hardly ever happens in practice. Instead, parallel and potentially overlapping proceedings often take place (chapter 3, II.D.iii.b.) Despite the above-mentioned difficulties, BIa does not contain any specific rules designed for collective redress.

In light of the above, proposals for reform have popped up essentially among scholars and private organisations. Unfortunately, those proposals often represent partial solutions and do not take into account the practical problems faced by consumers and their representatives (chapter 4, I.C.i.). This book tries to create a tailored private international law solution, which appropriately deals with cross-border collective redress.

A specific forum for collective redress actions should at least protect consumers and investors, who are often small-value claimants in need of a procedural vehicle to 'drive' their claims (chapter 4, II.B.i.). In particular, representative entities – such as consumer associations – should have standing to bring collective redress actions against defendants located abroad in the courts of their own domicile. However, the possibility to litigate in the forum of Article 4 BIa has to remain available for those who choose such a forum. The proposal offers some additional incentives in order to encourage litigation at this place, such as the mutual recognition of representatives' standing to sue, on the model of the Proposal for a Directive on representative actions (chapter 2, II.A.). Additionally, it should also be possible for parties to make their collective redress agreements binding in those fora, on the model of the Dutch *WCAM*. This scheme deserves to be promoted, since it reduces courts' workload and encourages the use of ADR.

The suggested proposal in this book represents a simple and easy to implement solution, which facilitates access to justice by re-establishing the balance between market players (chapter 4, II.B.ii.). It adopts a bottom-up approach that may not be aligned with the traditional approach followed by the EU institutions described above (chapter 4, II.B.iv.a.). However, it is realistic and feasible. It gives preference to access to justice over the achievement of the internal market, since the latter cannot survive without the first. It argues that the construction of the internal market is not mature enough for a centralisation model to be implemented. Furthermore, it follows private international law principles and respects Member States' procedural autonomy. It leaves them the responsibility to work on the efficiency of collective redress mechanisms. National legal orders are in the best position to evaluate the effectiveness of their own procedural tools and subsequently reform them if needed.

If the proposal is adopted, other elements should be determined and perfected. Among other aspects, important structural questions should be solved (chapter 4, II.B.iii.), such as the type of instrument that would crystallise the proposal – an independent legislative act or a jurisdictional rule implemented in the BIa –, the nature of the jurisdictional rule to be adopted – general, alternative, protective or exclusive –, the connecting factor, the types of actions encompassed – actions for injunctive relief and/or damages –, the material scope of the proposal – horizontal or substantially limited measure – and the allocation of standing. Similarly, the creation of a tailored forum in the domicile of the representative entity may generate private international law challenges. In particular, this means dealing with potentially concurrent actions (chapter 4, II.B.iv.b.) and making sure that Member States do not use unreasonable grounds of refusal to the recognition and enforcement of collective redress judgments and settlements (chapter 4, II.B.iv.c.). In order to avoid such issues, the representative power of an entity should be limited to national interests, so that 'classes' do not overlap. Additionally, the enactment of a specific provision dealing with recognition and enforcement of collective redress judgments and settlements is not excluded.

To sum up, hopefully the reader has been convinced that access to justice should precede the achievement of the internal market, as it is a prerequisite for trust, further integration and unity. The proposal advocates the implementation of a system that works and effectively guarantees consumers access to courts and compensation for their harm. The fact that a centralisation system was discarded does not misalign it with EU policy objectives. As the saying goes, 'all roads lead to Rome'. The proposal too will end up building up confidence in the market. It has just taken a different, more realistic, path.

ANNEXES

Annex I: United States' Most Relevant Provisions on Class Actions

Rule 23. Class Actions*

(a) Prerequisites.

One or more members of a class may sue or be sued as representative parties on behalf of all members only if:

(1) the class is so numerous that joinder of all members is impracticable;

(2) there are questions of law or fact common to the class;

(3) the claims or defenses of the representative parties are typical of the claims or defenses of the class; and

(4) the representative parties will fairly and adequately protect the interests of the class.

(b) Types of Class Actions.

A class action may be maintained if Rule 23(a) is satisfied and if:

(1) prosecuting separate actions by or against individual class members would create a risk of:

(A) inconsistent or varying adjudications with respect to individual class members that would establish incompatible standards of conduct for the party opposing the class; or

(B) adjudications with respect to individual class members that, as a practical matter, would be dispositive of the interests of the other members not parties to the individual adjudications or would substantially impair or impede their ability to protect their interests;

(2) the party opposing the class has acted or refused to act on grounds that apply generally to the class, so that final injunctive relief or corresponding declaratory relief is appropriate respecting the class as a whole; or

* The text of this provision is available in SS Gensler, *Federal Rules of Civil Procedure, Rules and Commentary*, available on WestlawNext.

(3) the court finds that the questions of law or fact common to class members predominate over any questions affecting only individual members, and that a class action is superior to other available methods for fairly and efficiently adjudicating the controversy. The matters pertinent to these findings include:

(A) the class members' interests in individually controlling the prosecution or defense of separate actions;

(B) the extent and nature of any litigation concerning the controversy already begun by or against class members;

(C) the desirability or undesirability of concentrating the litigation of the claims in the particular forum; and

(D) the likely difficulties in managing a class action.

(c) Certification Order; Notice to Class Members; Judgment; Issues Classes; Subclasses.

(1) Certification Order.

(A) Time to Issue. At an early practicable time after a person sues or is sued as a class representative, the court must determine by order whether to certify the action as a class action.

(B) Defining the Class; Appointing Class Counsel. An order that certifies a class action must define the class and the class claims, issues, or defenses, and must appoint class counsel under Rule 23(g).

(C) Altering or Amending the Order. An order that grants or denies class certification may be altered or amended before final judgment.

(2) Notice.

(A) For (b)(1) or (b)(2) Classes. For any class certified under Rule 23(b) or (b)(2), the court may direct appropriate notice to the class.

(B) For (b)(3) Classes. For any class certified under Rule 23(b)(3), the court must direct to class members the best notice that is practicable under the circumstances, including individual notice to all members who can be identified through reasonable effort. The notice must clearly and concisely state in plain, easily understood languagc:

(i) the nature of the action;

(ii) the definition of the class certified;

(iii) the class claims, issues, or defenses;

(iv) that a class member may enter an appearance through an attorney if the member so desires;

(v) that the court will exclude from the class any member who requests exclusion;

(vi) the time and manner for requesting exclusion; and

(vii) the binding effect of a class judgment on members under Rule 23(c)(3).

(3) Judgment.

Whether or not favorable to the class, the judgment in a class action must:

(A) for any class certified under Rule 23(b)(1) or (b)(2), include and describe those whom the court finds to be class members; and

(B) for any class certified under Rule 23(b)(3), include and specify or describe those to whom the Rule 23(c)(2) notice was directed, who have not requested exclusion, and whom the court finds to be class members.

(4) Particular Issues.

When appropriate, an action may be brought or maintained as a class action with respect to particular issues.

(5) Subclasses.

When appropriate, a class may be divided into subclasses that are each treated as a class under this rule.

(d) Conducting the Action.

(1) In General.

In conducting an action under this rule, the court may issue orders that:

(A) determine the course of proceedings or prescribe measures to prevent undue repetition or complication in presenting evidence or argument;

(B) require – to protect class members and fairly conduct the action – giving appropriate notice to some or all class members of:

(i) any step in the action;

(ii) the proposed extent of the judgment; or

(iii) the members' opportunity to signify whether they consider the representation fair and adequate, to intervene and present claims or defenses, or to otherwise come into the action;

(C) impose conditions on the representative parties or on intervenors;

(D) require that the pleadings be amended to eliminate allegations about representation of absent persons and that the action proceed accordingly; or

(E) deal with similar procedural matters.

(2) Combining and Amending Orders.

An order under Rule 23(d)(1) may be altered or amended from time to time and may be combined with an order under Rule 16.

(e) Settlement, Voluntary Dismissal, or Compromise.

The claims, issues, or defenses of a certified class may be settled, voluntarily dismissed, or compromised only with the court's approval. The following procedures apply to a proposed settlement, voluntary dismissal, or compromise:

(1) The court must direct notice in a reasonable manner to all class members who would be bound by the proposal.

(2) If the proposal would bind class members, the court may approve it only after a hearing and on finding that it is fair, reasonable, and adequate.

(3) The parties seeking approval must file a statement identifying any agreement made in connection with the proposal.

(4) If the class action was previously certified under Rule 23(b)(3), the court may refuse to approve a settlement unless it affords a new opportunity to request exclusion to individual class members who had an earlier opportunity to request exclusion but did not do so.

(5) Any class member may object to the proposal if it requires court approval under this subdivision (e); the objection may be withdrawn only with the court's approval.

(f) Appeals.

A court of appeals may permit an appeal from an order granting or denying class-action certification under this rule if a petition for permission to appeal is filed with the circuit clerk within 14 days after the order is entered. An appeal does not stay proceedings in the district court unless the district judge or the court of appeals so orders.

(g) Class Counsel.

(1) Appointing Class Counsel.

Unless a statute provides otherwise, a court that certifies a class must appoint class counsel. In appointing class counsel, the court:

(A) must consider:

(i) the work counsel has done in identifying or investigating potential claims in the action;

(ii) counsel's experience in handling class actions, other complex litigation, and the types of claims asserted in the action;

(iii) counsel's knowledge of the applicable law; and

(iv) the resources that counsel will commit to representing the class;

(B) may consider any other matter pertinent to counsel's ability to fairly and adequately represent the interests of the class;

(C) may order potential class counsel to provide information on any subject pertinent to the appointment and to propose terms for attorney's fees and nontaxable costs;

(D) may include in the appointing order provisions about the award of attorney's fees or nontaxable costs under Rule 23(h); and

(E) may make further orders in connection with the appointment.

(2) Standard for Appointing Class Counsel.

When one applicant seeks appointment as class counsel, the court may appoint that applicant only if the applicant is adequate under Rule 23(g)(1) and (4).

If more than one adequate applicant seeks appointment, the court must appoint the applicant best able to represent the interests of the class.

(3) Interim Counsel.

The court may designate interim counsel to act on behalf of a putative class before determining whether to certify the action as a class action.

(4) Duty of Class Counsel.

Class counsel must fairly and adequately represent the interests of the class.

(h) Attorney's Fees and Nontaxable Costs.

In a certified class action, the court may award reasonable attorney's fees and nontaxable costs that are authorized by law or by the parties' agreement. The following procedures apply:

(1) A claim for an award must be made by motion under Rule 54(d)(2), subject to the provisions of this subdivision (h), at a time the court sets. Notice of the motion must be served on all parties and, for motions by class counsel, directed to class members in a reasonable manner.

(2) A class member, or a party from whom payment is sought, may object to the motion.

(3) The court may hold a hearing and must find the facts and state its legal conclusions under Rule 52(a).

(4) The court may refer issues related to the amount of the award to a special master or a magistrate judge, as provided in Rule 54(d)(2)(D).

Annex II: Models of Collective Redress in the EU State-by-State

The comparative Table below presents the distinct collective redress mechanisms adopted by some Member States. In particular, the Table identifies the most important structural elements that characterise collective redress mechanisms: for each procedural tool, the provisions upon which it is based are provided,[1] as well as a short description of the mechanism in order to facilitate the understanding of the reader. The requirements regarding certification, the participation rule, the actors having standing to sue, the remedies available and the specific procedure that has to be followed in case there is one are described.

Although some comparative studies are already available on the market,[2] a private comparative analysis was drafted for the following reasons: to start with,

[1] Access to these legal bases are possible through the Bibliography.

[2] A Study conducted by the British Institute of International and Comparative Law was published after the conclusion of this research project. Said Study contains an overview of the collective

the studies that have been published until now often involve various national experts. Because said experts come from different legal cultures and, hence, do not use the same wording, truly comparing is a tricky exercise. Furthermore, not all above-mentioned studies are up-to-date.

The construction of this comparative table triggered several issues: to start with, some national mechanisms have not received any comment in a language understood by the author. Therefore, an exhaustive analysis could not always be provided. This is typically the case for Member States located in Eastern Europe. Additionally, because some of those instruments are relatively recent, the available information was scarce. The unavailability of academic papers or other works made this investigation particularly thorny. In any case, each procedural device is accompanied with a bibliography, thanks to which the comparative table was made.

Please note the additional comments for the following Member States:

The Netherlands. Note that no updated translation of the civil code, as well as the civil code of procedure was available in English. Therefore, comment was not possible on the new pre-trial procedure under Article 1018a DCC. Additionally, a bill on the adoption of a new collective redress action for damage is currently in the legislative pipeline. However, it is not included in the Table since no English version is available – the same applies to the Explanatory memorandum – and the text is not in force yet.

France. There is contradictory evidence as regards the availability of remedies under the joint representative action. On the one hand, the French Report prepared by Magnier and Alleweldt states that usual remedies are available. On the other hand, the Working paper written by Biard and Amaro seems to conclude that only monetary compensation is available.

Poland. The defence of general interests takes place in administrative proceedings (Title IV of the Act of 16 February 2007 on competition and consumer protection). Therefore, this mechanism is not included within the Table. The same can be said as far as complaints to the Consumer Ombudsmen are concerned in Scandinavian states.

Bulgaria. According to the Bulgarian law, some actors are able to defend the 'collective interest' of victims in courts. However, it is not clear whether this term should be understood as encompassing general interests too. Additionally, the overlap of the Code of Civil procedure with the Consumer Protection Act complicates the understanding of which law governs what.

Lithuania. An updated version of the law that regulates collective redress was not available in a language understood by the author. Moreover, bibliographical

redress instruments adopted so far in all Member States. It was used in order to update Annex II (State of Collective Redress in the EU in the Context of the Implementation of the Commission Recommendation, JUST/2016/JCOO/FW/CIVI/0099, available at www.biicl.org/documents/1881_StudyontheStateofCollectiveRedress.pdf?showdocument=1).

sources are still scarce on this instrument. These comments equally apply to *Denmark*. An exception is made for *Poland*: although the law was not available in English, the amount of bibliographical sources made the draft of a Table possible.

Hungary. Hungary does not possess any collective redress system, although the Hungarian procedural law allows the defence of consumer interests. Therefore, and in absence of more information, Hungary is excluded from this Table.

Luxembourg. There is an important bibliographical gap regarding collective redress in Luxembourg. It was therefore impossible to include it in the comparative study.

A. The Netherlands*

***Wet Collectieve Afwikkeling Massaschade* (*WCAM* procedure)**

Category	Dutch model.
Legal basis	Act on Collective Settlement of Mass Damages (*WCAM*) of 2005 and reformed in 2013. This Act materialises in Articles 7:907–7:910 of the Dutch Civil Code (DCC) and Articles 1013–1018 of the Dutch Civil Code of Procedure (DCCP).
Description	Prior to commencing a collective settlement action, a foundation or association must enter into a settlement agreement with the alleged wrongdoer. The subject matter of the agreement is not limited: since 2013, the *WCAM* procedure is no longer restricted to claims for compensation but may encompass other types of claims. Accordingly, petitioners submit the agreement to the Amsterdam Court of Appeal, which has exclusive jurisdiction to deal with the *WCAM* settlement. If all conditions are met, said court will declare the agreement binding on the entire group of victims referred to in the contract.

* **Bibliography:** T Arons and WH van Boom, 'Beyond Tulips and Cheese: Exporting Mass Securities Claim Settlements from The Netherlands' (2010) *European Business Law Review* 857–83; T Bosters, *Collective Redress and Private International Law in the EU* (Springer, 2017) 35–58; MBM Loos, 'Evaluation of the Effectiveness and Efficiency of Collective Redress Mechanisms in the European Union – Country Report The Netherlands' (2008), available at ec.europa.eu/consumers/solving_consumer_disputes/judicial_redress/index_en.htm; J Fleming and JJ Kuster, 'The Netherlands' in PG Karlsgodt (ed), *World Class Actions: A Guide to Group and Representative Actions around the Globe* (Oxford University Press, 2012) 286–300; F Gascón Inchausti, *Tutela Judicial de los Consumidores y Transacciones Colectivas* (Thomson Reuters-Civitas, 2010) 67–79; Government of The Netherlands, The Dutch 'Class Action Financial Settlement Act' ('WCAM'), available at www.rijksoverheid.nl/documenten/richtlijnen/2008/06/24/de-nederlandse-wet-collectieve-afwikkeling-massaschade; B Krans, 'The Dutch Act on Collective Settlement on Mass Damages' (2014) 27 *Global Business & Development Law Journal* 281–301; JJ Kuipers, 'La loi sur le règlement collectif de dommages de masse aux Pays-Bas et ses ambitions dans l'espace judiciaire européen' (2012) 64(1) *Revue internationale de droit comparé* 213–43; I Tzankova and H van Lith, 'Class Actions and Class Settlements Going Global: the Netherlands' in D Fairgrieve and E Lein (eds), *Extraterritoriality and Collective Redress* (Oxford University Press,

Requirements for certification	There is no regime for certification in the *WCAM* procedure. However, the DCC contains two provisions that look like requirements for certification: the first one states that the association/foundation must represent the interests of the victims according to its statutes (adequacy of representation, Articles 7:907(1) and 3:305a DCC). However, it is not necessary that the petitioner represents each victim individually. Rather, the association/foundation has to be sufficiently representative. The second one establishes that the group of affected persons must be large enough (numerosity, Article 7:907(3)(g) DCC).
Opt-in v Opt-out	Opt-out.
Standing to sue	Only 3:305a associations/foundations have the power to settle. They must sufficiently represent the persons on whose behalf the agreement is concluded.
Remedies	The only possible remedy is a court declaration that the collective settlement is binding.
Costs	Normally, parties to the settlement agreement decide who bears the costs (regarding notification, publication of the court's declaration, professional support, etc). However, the court may decide that the costs arising from the procedure have to be borne by one or more petitioners (Articles 1016.2 DCCP and 289 DCCP).
Procedure	(1) Since 2013, petitioners have been able to initiate a pre-trial hearing (Article 1018a DCC). Thanks to this procedure, parties evaluate if a potential settlement can be reached and the court assists them in formulating the main point of the dispute. (2) Settlement between the alleged liable party and an association/foundation. The agreement must fulfil the conditions set forth in Article 7:907.2 DCC. (3) Parties petition the Amsterdam Court of Appeal to declare the settlement binding (joint petition). The decision is notified to interested parties by ordinary letter (for known parties) and newspaper announcement (for unknown parties). (4) Oral hearings and evaluation of the fairness of the settlement. The petitioners can amend the agreement. As for interested parties, they have the right to appear in court and present a statement of opposition (Article 1013(5) DCCP).

2012) 67–94; I Tzankova, Class Actions in The Netherlands, Netherlands National Reports Parts 1 and 2, available at globalclassactions.stanford.edu; I Tzankova et al, 'Country Report: The Netherlands', available at www.collectiveredress.org; WH van Boom, 'Collective Settlement of Mass Claims in The Netherlands' in M Casper et al (eds), *Auf dem Weg zu einer europäischen Sammelklage?* (Sellier European Publishers, 2009) 171–92; MJ van der Heijden, 'Class Actions/les actions collectives' (2010) 14(3) *Electronic Journal of Comparative Law* 1–17, available at www.ejcl.org; CH van Rhee and I Tzankova, 'Collective Redress in The Netherlands' in V Harsági and CH van Rhee (eds), *Multi-Party Redress Mechanisms in Europe: Squeaking Mice?* (Intersentia, 2014) 209–24.

	(5) If all the conditions are fulfilled, the settlement is declared binding and made public. Injured parties are then offered an opportunity to opt out. Parties that do not make use of this power become parties to the agreement. Only petitioners can jointly appeal the decision of the Court in cassation. (6) Distribution of the compensation proceeds. Petitioners have considerable room to negotiate the plan of allocation. Sometimes, a separate administrator is entrusted with the task of distributing the settlement fund among the injured individuals.

Dutch Collective action

Category	Representation model.
Legal basis	Articles 3:305a to d DCC (introduced by the 1994 Act on Collective Action).
Description	A foundation/association may commence legal proceedings intended to protect the similar interests of third parties or a general interest. The foundation must first try to reach an agreement before suing. A claim made by a 305a foundation/association is a subsidiary claim, which does not impede individuals from commencing proceedings.
Requirements for certification	There is no requirement for certification.
Opt-in v Opt-out	Automatic membership.
Standing to sue	Standing is limited to 305a foundations/associations, which statutorily protect the interests they seek to defend. Additionally, entities put on the list referred to in Article 4.3 of the Injunctions Directive also have standing to sue (Article 3:305c DCC).
Remedies	All remedies are available apart from damages. In practice, 305a associations/foundations seek declaratory or injunctive relief judgment. Then, parties use the decision in order to obtain monetary relief through individual proceedings.
Costs	General procedural rules apply. In the Netherlands, a softened version of the 'loser-pays' principle operates: the winning party is entitled to recover part of her lawyer's and expert's fees, as well as court's fees.
Procedure	In principle, general rules of civil procedure apply. The only specificity is ruled by Article 305a.2 DCC, which states that the foundation/association must try to solve the dispute amicably before initiating judicial proceedings.

B. Spain*

***Acción colectiva para la defensa de derechos e intereses de los consumidores y usuarios* (Class action for the defence of consumer rights and interests)**

Category	Group/representation model.
Legal basis	The Spanish legislator did not create a uniform procedural regime for class action proceedings. Instead, dispersed provisions have been introduced in the *Ley de Enjuiciamiento Civil* (Spanish Law of Civil Procedure, SLCP), namely Articles 6.1.7º/8º, 7.7, 11, 15, 52.1.14º/16º, 76.2.1, 217.4/6/7, 221, 222.3, 249, 250.1.12°, 256.1.6º, 519, 711.2 and 728.3 SLCP. Furthermore, sectoral legislation completes this general system. Among others, class actions are regulated in the following sectors: consumer protection, product liability, competition law and environmental law. Notably, Article 53 of the Consumer Act (*Texto refundido de la Ley General para la Defensa de los Consumidores y Usuarios*) regulates actions for injunctive relief in fundamental areas of consumer law (unfair terms, off-premises contracts, distance sales, guarantees in the selling of goods or travel package contracts).
Description	Through the Spanish class action, claimants act to protect general interests or a plurality of homogenous individual rights. Standing to sue is restricted to a certain number of players and its allocation depends on the interests that are protected. The class action is in principle limited to consumer law (apart from contrary sectoral legislation). The SLCP provides dispersed general provisions for class actions, which are not covered by a sectoral norm. While actions for injunctive relief are usually regulated in sector-based legislation, actions for damages should in principle follow the general regime established by the SLCP.

* **Bibliography:** MJ Ariza Colmenarejo, *La acción de cesación como medio para la protección de consumidores y usuarios* (Thomson Reuters Aranzadi, 2012); T Armenta Deu, *Acciones colectivas: Reconocimiento, cosa juzgada y ejecución* (Marcial Pons, 2013); S Corominas Bach, 'La legitimación en la futura regulación europea de las acciones colectivas de consumo' in E Carbonell Porras and R Cabrera Mercado (eds), *Intereses Colectivos y Legitimación Activa* (Thomson Reuters, 2014) 137–61; J Garberí Llobregat et al, *Los Procesos Civiles*, vol 1 and 2, 2nd edn (Thomson Reuters Aranzadi, 2011); MP García Rubio and M Otero Crespo, Country Report: Spain, available at www.collectiveredress.org; MP García Rubio and M Otero Crespo, 'Rebuilding the Pillars of Collective Litigation in Light of the Commission Recommendation: The Spanish Approach to Collective Redress' in E Lein et al (eds), *Collective Redress in Europe – Why and How?* (The British Institute of International and Comparative Law, 2015) 133–51; F Gascón Inchausti, Acciones colectivas e inhibitorias para la protección de los consumidores en el proceso civil español: el papel de las asociaciones de consumidores (2005), available at eprints.ucm.es; F Gascón Inchausti, La protección de los consumidores en el proceso civil español (2005), available at eprints.ucm.es; F Gascón Inchausti, *Tutela Judicial de los Consumidores y Transacciones Colectivas* (Thomson Reuters-Civitas, 2010) 91–145; P Gutiérrez de Cabiedes Hidalgo, 'Artículo 11' in F Cordón Moreno et al (eds), *Comentarios a la Ley de Enjuiciamiento Civil*, vol 1, 2nd edn (Thomson Reuters, 2011) 185–234; P Gutiérrez de Cabiedes Hidalgo, Group Litigation in

Requirements for certification	There is no requirement for certification.
Opt-in v Opt-out	Article 222.3 SLCP states that the effect of a class action judgment reaches the absent class members, although they did not personally litigate their rights. However, the Spanish legislator did not set up any opt-out procedure. Academics disagree on the existence of this option. Notably, some of them argue that opt-out is possible through intervention. To sum up, under the Spanish collective redress model, absent members apparently can opt in but not opt out.
Standing to sue	(1) If the members of the group are identifiable, an action can be brought by consumer associations; legal entities whose purpose is to defend consumer interests – including the National Consumer Institute, the Prosecutor and listed entities pursuant to the Injunctions Directive (Article 54 of the Consumer Act); or the group of claimants, in the event that it represents the majority of the class (Article 11(2) SLCP). (2) If the members of the group are unknown, only sufficiently representative consumer associations can bring the action. As far as consumer law is concerned, these are members of the Spanish Council of Consumers (Article 24.2 of the Consumer Act), and the National Consumer Institute or the Prosecutor for class actions falling under the scope of Article 54 of the Consumer Act. Additionally, listed entities pursuant to the Injunctions Directive have standing to sue.
Remedies	Usual remedies.
Costs	The 'loser-pays' principle applies.
Procedure	The Spanish law on Civil Procedure does not provide a specific procedure for class actions. However, there are some dispersed rules on notification (Article 15 SLCP) and *res judicata* (Articles 221 and 519 SLCP). Specifically, Article 15 SLCP establishes the following rules regarding notification: (1) If the members of the group are identifiable: a notice of the intention to bring a claim, as well as a publication in the newspapers, are required.

Spain, available at globalclassactions.stanford.edu; F Malaga, 'Spain' in PG Karlsgodt (ed), *World Class Actions: A Guide to Group and Representative Actions around the Globe* (Oxford University Press, 2012) 301–11; D Marcos Francisco, 'Nuevas medidas de defensa de los consumidores en materia de acciones colectivas, asistencia jurídica gratuita, costas y tasas judiciales' (2015) 4 *InDret*, available at www.indret.com; JJ Marín López, 'Las acciones de clase en el derecho español' (2001) 3 *InDret*, available at www.indret.com; A Planchadell Gargallo, *Las 'acciones colectivas' en el ordenamiento jurídico español* (Tirant lo Blanch, 2014) 37–261; M Requejo Isidro and M Otero Crespo, 'Collective Redress in Spain: Recognition and Enforcement of Class Action Judgments and Class Settlements' in D Fairgrieve and E Lein (eds), *Extraterritoriality and Collective Redress* (Oxford University Press, 2012) 309–31.

	(2) If the members are unknown: a publication in the media is necessary to inform potential claimants about the existence of the action. Proceedings must be suspended in order to let people opt in. As far as *res judicata* is concerned, the SLCP establishes the following rules: (1) In principle (in case of action for damages or injunctive relief), the class action judgment must determine who can benefit from its effects. If no individualisation is possible, the judgment must establish the data, characteristics and requirements necessary to demand payment and, where appropriate, to request enforcement or to intervene in it. (2) If the object of the judgment consists in declaring a certain activity or behaviour unlawful, such a judgment must establish whether its effects should reach non-parties.

C. France*

***Action exercée dans l'intérêt collectif des consommateurs* (Action taken in a general interest)**

Category	Representation model.
Legal basis	Articles L.621-1 to 9 of the French Consumer Code (FCC). This action was created by the Royer Act of 27 December 1973 and its scope was broadened in 1988. Eventually, it was codified in the FCC of 1993. This type of action is also available in other sectors such as labour law, financial and environmental protection.
Description	The action taken in a collective interest may have three forms: (1) When there is a criminal violation, Article L.621-1 FCC states that associations have standing to seek civil compensation in criminal proceedings. (2) When no criminal offence has been committed, the association may intervene in individual proceedings. However, it is only possible to intervene if the responsibility of the defendant is at stake (Article L.621-9 FCC). (3) When no criminal offence has been committed, an association may start proceedings against illegal practices contravening a number of EU Directives transposed in the French legal order. In particular, associations can seek the suppression of unlawful or unfair terms (Articles L.621-7 and 8 FCC).

* **Bibliography:** S Amrani-Mekki, 'L'action de groupe du 21 siècle. Un modèle réduit et réducteur ?' (2015) 45 *La Semaine Juridique* 2029–31; A Biard and R Amaro, 'Resolving Mass Claims in France: Toolbox & Experience', Working Paper Series No 2016/5, available at www.eur.nl/sites/corporate/

Requirements for certification	There are no requirements for certification.
Opt-in v Opt-out	The association defends general interests. Therefore, there is no class/group.
Standing to sue	Technically, only accredited associations have standing to bring actions in the collective interest of consumers. Pursuant to Articles R.811-1 to 7, accreditation is subject to the following requirements: The association must (1) be declared; (2) have at least one year of existence; (3) statutorily and actively defend the interests of consumers; (4) have no professional activity, and; (5) be representative. The Ministries of Consumer Affairs and of Justice grants the approval for a period of five years with the possibility of renewal. However, the French Supreme Court has created significant confusion by allowing unaccredited consumer associations to bring actions in the general interest. Therefore, it is not clear whether accreditation is still a condition to have standing to sue to start such actions or not. Note that entities listed in the Official Journal of the EU pursuant to Article 4 of the Injunctions Directive may start an action in the collective interest under Article L.621-7.

files/Resolving_mass_claims_Amaro.pdf; L Boré, 'Les prémisses d'une consécration générale du droit d'action des associations au plan civil' (2008) 47 *Revue Lamy de Droit Civil* 17–18; J Calais-Auloy and H Temple, *Droit de la consommation*, 8th edn (Dalloz, 2010); C Cerutti and M Guillaume, Rapport sur l'action de groupe remis le 16 décembre 2005 aux Ministres de l'économie, des finances et de l'industrie et de la justice, garde des sceaux (2005), available at www.ladocumentationfrancaise.fr/var/storage/rapports-publics/054004458.pdf; A de Laforcade, 'L'évolution du droit d'agir des associations de consommateurs : vers un détachement du droit pénal de leur action en justice' (2011) 4 *Revue trimestrielle de droit commercial et de droit économique* 711–20; D Fairgrieve and A Biard, 'Country Report: France', available at www.collectiveredress.org; F Ferrand, 'Collective Litigation in France: From Distrust to Cautious Admission' in V Harsági and CH van Rhee (eds), *Multi-Party Redress Mechanisms in Europe: Squeaking Mice?* (Intersentia, 2014) 127–52; J Franck, 'Pour une véritable réparation du préjudice causé à l'intérêt collectif des consommateurs' in *Études de droit de la consommation – Liber amicorum Jean Calais-Auloy* (Dalloz, 2004) 409–19; S Guinchard et al, *Procédure civile – Droit interne et droit de l'Union européenne*, 32nd edn (Dalloz, 2014); Institut National de la Consommation, L'action de groupe : vers une consécration ? (2005) 1348 *INC Hebdo*, available at www.conso.net/sites/default/files/pdf_abonne/1348-action_groupe_255.pdf; M Leclerc, *Les class actions, du droit américain au droit européen – Propos illustrés au regard du droit de la concurrence* (Editions Larcier, 2012); V Magnier, 'Class Actions, Group Litigation & Other Forms of Collective Litigation Protocol for National Reporters – France', available at globalclassactions.stanford.edu; V Magnier and R Alleweldt, 'Evaluation of the Effectiveness and Efficiency of Collective Redress Mechanisms in the European Union – Country Report France' (2008), available at ec.europa.eu/consumers/solving_consumer_disputes/judicial_redress/index_en.htm; N Molfessis, 'L'exorbitance de l'action de groupe à la française' (2014) 16 *Recueil Dalloz* 947–53; Y Picot, *Code de la consommation commenté* (Dalloz, 2012); V Rebeyrol, 'La nouvelle action de groupe' (2014) 16 *Recueil Dalloz* 940–46; C Sportes and V Ravit, 'France' in *The International Comparative Legal Guide to Class and Group Actions* (2017), available at iclg.com.

Remedies	(1) Damages. The case law recognises that associations can receive a monetary compensation for the detriment caused to the collective interest. Often, however, this compensation is very low. (2) Ban of an illegal practice or suppression of an illicit contractual clause (Article L.621-2 and 8). (3) Publication of the judgment (Article L.621-11).
Costs	In the absence of specific legislation, the general regime on civil procedure should apply (specifically, Articles 695–700 of the French Code of Civil Procedure). Accordingly, the 'loser-pays' principle usually operates, unless the judge decides otherwise.
Procedure	The FCC does not establish specific procedural rules for the action taken in the collective interest.

Action en représentation conjointe **(Joint representative action)**

Category	Representation model.
Legal basis	Articles L.622-1 to 4 of the FCC (first enacted in 1992). The joint representative action has been extended to the financial and the environmental sectors.
Description	Two or more consumers can appoint an association to commence proceedings on their behalf. Their harm must stem from the unlawful behaviour of the same professional. Note that associations act as representatives of their clients, they do not have a claim.
Requirements for certification	(1) At least two consumers (natural persons) must have suffered individual damage. (2) The harm is caused by the same professional. (3) It has a common origin.
Opt-in v Opt-out	The system is based on the opt-in mechanism insofar as the persons having suffered the damages must duly authorise in writing the association to initiate a legal action on their behalf.
Standing to sue	(1) Only certified associations have standing to sue according to Articles R.811-1 to 7. (2) The association must be instructed to bring proceedings by two or more claimants. Note that the only available channel for associations to inform consumers about the joint action (apart from personal letters) is through the press.
Remedies	Usual remedies.
Costs	In absence of specific legislation, the general regime on civil procedure should apply (specifically, Articles 695–700 of the French Code of Civil Procedure). Accordingly, the 'loser-pays' principle usually operates, unless the judge decides otherwise.
Procedure	The FCC does not establish specific procedural rules for the action taken in the collective interest.

***Action de groupe* (group action)**

Category	Representation model.
Legal basis	Articles L.623-1 to 32 FCC govern the group action and were introduced by Law No 2014-344 of 17 of March 2014. Although the group action was originally limited to certain consumer matters, this mechanism has been introduced in the fields of health, discrimination, environment and data protection.
Description	Only certified associations can bring a group action in order to obtain compensation for losses of individuals. The group action can be brought in the following situations: (1) When the action is connected to the purchase of products or the provision of services. (2) When a competition law provision has been violated (at the national or EU level). Note that only follow-on actions are possible.
Requirements for certification	(1) Consumers must be in an identical or similar position; and (2) their harm must have been caused by the same professional and stem from the same illegal behaviour.
Opt-in v Opt-out	Opt-in.
Standing to sue	Only certified associations have standing to sue according to Articles R.811-1 to 7.
Remedies	Only actions for the compensation of financial losses stemming from material damages are available (Articles L.623-2 and 6).
Costs	In absence of specific legislation, the general regime on civil procedure should apply (specifically, Articles 695–700 of the French Code of Civil Procedure). Accordingly, the 'loser-pays' principle usually operates, unless the judge decides otherwise.
Procedure	The FCC contains a few procedural rules that are presented below. For the rest, common rules of civil procedure should apply. (1) The association brings the group action in the court that will determine whether the case is admissible. If so, said court rules on the professional's liability. In a competition law case, this step is undertaken by a competition authority. (2) The court delimits the group entitled to obtain redress and prescribes the method to publish the decision. (3) The court establishes a period of time during which consumers can adhere to the judgment (between two and six months) and, thus, be bound by it. Articles L.623-14 to 17 set up a simplified procedure: when the identity of consumers is known and their damage is of an identical amount, the court can order the defendant to compensate them directly. Although the law does not explicitly mention it, consumers should have the possibility to opt in or refuse to be bound by the outcome of the simplified procedure. Indeed, Article L.623-15 states that consumers must receive notice in order to *accept* the judgment. In all cases, a mediation procedure is available (Articles L.623-22 and 23).

D. Portugal*

***Acção Popular* (Popular action)**

Category	Representative action.
Legal basis	Article 52(3) of the Portuguese Constitution (enacted in 1989) and Law 83/95 of 31 August 1995 is the general national law that govern the Portuguese popular action. This regime is completed by some sector-based provisions (such as consumer and environmental protection). Originally, the Portuguese popular action was applicable in administrative law in order to contest public authorities' decisions. Today, this mechanism is available to private parties (horizontal application).
Description	The Portuguese system of collective redress is a representative, opt-out based mechanism. The main objective is to protect diffuse interests. However, one may file a popular action suit in order to defend collective interests (ie a multiplicity of homogeneous individual rights). Two types of suits are possible: an administrative popular action before an administrative court against the state or an administrative body; or a civil popular action.
Requirements for certification	There is no requirement for certification.
Opt-in v Opt-out	Opt-out. Note that interested claimants can participate in the proceedings and influence the outcome.
Standing to sue	(1) Any citizens in the enjoyment of their civil and political rights. (2) Any association and foundation whose goal is the protection of the rights provided for in Law 83/95, whether or not they have a direct interest in the claim. The law also requires the association/foundation to have legal personality. Besides, it cannot exercise any professional activity competing with companies and liberal professions.

* **Bibliography:** M França Gouveia and N Garoupa, 'Class Actions in Portugal' in JG Backhaus et al (eds), *The Law and Economics of Class Actions in Europe – Lessons from America* (Edward Elgar, 2012) 342–50; C Gonçalves Borges and M Serra Baptista, 'Portugal' in PG Karlsgodt (ed), *World Class Actions: A Guide to Group and Representative Actions around the Globe* (Oxford University Press, 2012) 312–22; J Pimentel and JM Judice, 'Portugal' in *The International Comparative Legal Guide to Class and Group Actions 2014*, available at www.csassociados.pt/xms/files/PUBLICACOES/CA14_Chapter-21_Portugal.pdf; P Otero, 'A acção popular: configuração e valor no actual direito português' (1999) 59 (3) *Revista da Ordem dos Advogados* 871–93; AP Pinto Monteiro and JM Judice, 'Class Actions & Arbitration in the European Union – Portugal' in *Estudos em Homenagem a Miguel Galvão Teles*, vol 2 (Coimbra, Almedina, 2012) 189–205; M Soto Maior, 'O Direito de Acção Popular na Constituição da República Portugesa' (1998) 75/76 *Documentação e Direito Comparado*, available at www.gddc.pt/actividade-editorial/pdfs-publicacoes/7576-g.pdf; H Sousa Antunes, 'Class Actions, Group Litigation & Other Forms of Collective Litigation, Portugese Report' (2007), available at globalclassactions.stanford.edu; L Tortell, 'Evaluation of the Effectiveness and Efficiency of Collective Redress Mechanisms in the European Union – Country Report Portugal' (2008), available at ec.europa.eu/consumers/solving_consumer_disputes/judicial_redress/index_en.htm; R Vale e Reis and M 'Mesquita, Country Report: Portugal', available at www.collectiveredress.org.

	(3) Local authorities also have standing when the litigation relates to interests held by people who are resident in the corresponding district. There is no requirement to ensure that the claimant is sufficiently representative. However, the Prosecutor has the power to replace the original claimant if s/he withdraws or behaves in such a manner as could put the claim at risk.
Remedies	Usual remedies.
Costs	Special rules on costs apply to the popular action: the claimant is exempt from paying court fees in case of (partial) success. In the event of total loss, the claimant will have to pay between 10 per cent and 50 per cent of the court fees in accordance with his/her economic situation and the formal or substantive grounds of the claim. Parties to the popular action bear their own attorneys' fees.
Procedure	There is no specific procedure established for popular actions. In principle, such actions must follow the rules of the Portuguese Code of Civil Procedure. However, Law 83/95 establishes the following specificities: (1) Once the popular action is submitted to the court, parties are summoned in order to join the collective proceedings, and accept to be represented. The notification takes place through media or public notice, without having to identify the claimants. (2) The final judgment is published in two newspapers that the parties are presumed to read at the expense of the losing party. Note that the public prosecutor has a general duty of reviewing the legality of the actions.

E. Italy*

Azione di classe **(class action)**

Category	Representative action.
Legal basis	Article 140-bis of the Consumer Code (ICC), introduced by Law No 244 of 24 December 2007 and replaced by a new Article 140-bis enacted by Law No 99 of 23 July 2009. Such a provision has been further amended by Article 6 of the so-called 'Decreto liberalizzazioni' enacted by Law No 27 of 24 March 2012.

* **Bibliography:** N Calcagno, '"Italian Class Action": The Beginning' (2011), available at papers.ssrn.com; Camera di comercio, industria, artigianato e agricoltura di Torino, 'Li azioni di classe' (2011), available at www.to.camcom.it/sites/default/files/regolazione-mercato/12301_CCIAATO_952011.pdf; R Caponi 'Collective Redress in Europe: Current Developments of "Class Action" Suits in Italy' (2011) 16 *Zeitschrift für Zivilprozess International* 1–17; G Cataldi, 'La nuova azione di classe' (2009)

Description	Consumers and users, as well as mandated associations, have the power to bring class action suits in the consumer field in order to protect homogeneous collective rights (*diritti individuali omogenei*) and general interests (*interessi collettivi*). The class action suit is possible only in three cases: (1) a breach of contract; (2) product or service liability; (3) unfair or anti-competitive business practices.
Requirements for certification	There are no requirements for certification.
Opt-in v Opt-out	Opt-in. However, if the representative claimant settles the case, absent members can refuse to be bound by the agreement and recover their individual right to sue.
Standing to sue	Consumers or users whose rights are homogeneous can directly sue or mandate an association to do so. However, the consumer association cannot start proceedings on its own.
Remedies	Monetary compensation only.
Costs	The 'loser-pays' rule applies in accordance with Article 91 of the Code of Civil Procedure, except if the court decides to allocate costs between parties.
Procedure	The judge has ample discretionary power to build up the class action procedure. In any case, different procedural steps can be identified: (1) During the first phase of the class action, the judge will evaluate whether the representative plaintiff has standing to sue according to the general rules of civil procedure. Then, the admissibility of the complaint is examined. In this regard,

3 *Consumatori, Diritti e Mercato* 129–42; G Cataldi, 'Le problematiche processuali dell'azione collettiva' (2008) 2 *Consumatori, Diritti e Mercato* 21–32; R Cavani and BA Fossati, 'Italy' in *The International Comparative Legal Guide to Class and Group Actions* 2017, available at iclg.com; S Enne, 'Italy' in PG Karlsgodt (ed), *World Class Actions: A Guide to Group and Representative Actions around the Globe* (Oxford University Press, 2012) 334–40; A Giussani, 'L'azione di classe aspetti processuali' (2013) 67 (1) *Rivista trimestrale di diritto e procedura civile* 341–56; M Guernelli, 'La nuova azione di classe: profili processuali' (2010) 64(3) *Rivista trimestrale di diritto e procedura civile* 917–34; MC Micklitz and C Poncibò, 'Evaluation of the Effectiveness and Efficiency of Collective Redress Mechanisms in the European Union – Country Report Italy' (2008), available at ec.europa.eu/consumers/solving_consumer_disputes/judicial_redress/index_en.htm; P Fiorio, 'L'azione di classe nel nuovo art. 140bis e gli obiettivi di deterrenza e di accesso alla giustizia dei consumatori' (2009) 172, available at www.ilcaso.it; G Principe, 'Italian Class Actions – An Update', available at globalclassactions.stanford.edu; E Rajneri and C Poncibò, 'Country Report: Italy', available at www.collectiveredress.org; P Schlesinger, 'Introduzione' in *XXV Convegni di studio 'Adolfo Beria di Argentine' Problemi attuai di diritto e procedura civile: Class action: il nuovo volto della tutela collettiva in Italia* (Giuffrè Editore, 2011) 9–22; E Silvestri, Oxford – Leuven Collective Redress Project – Italian Report (2016), available at www.law.ox.ac.uk/events/empirical-evidence-collective-redress-europe; M Taruffo, 'La tutela collettiva nell'ordinamento italiano: lineamenti generali' in *XXV Convegni di studio 'Adolfo Beria di Argentine' Problemi attuai di diritto e procedura civile: Class action: il nuovo volto della tutela collettiva in Italia* (Giuffrè Editore, 2011) 25–40.

	the action will be inadmissible if there is a conflict of interest, the representative claimant does not adequately represent the interests of the class or if consumers' or users' rights are not homogeneous. If the complaint complies with the admissibility test, the court issues a certification order that may be appealed by both the defendant and the representative plaintiff. (2) If the action is admitted, the court then establishes how other potential parties should be summoned. Regarding this particular point, the law underlines that the method for providing notice should be opportune and that the claimant should bear the costs. Besides, the court must establish the period of time during which the opt-in is possible. (3) Final decision is published and appealable. It will become enforceable after 180 days. Note that absent members of the class are not considered as parties from a procedural perspective. This means that they can neither intervene nor participate in the class proceedings.

Action to protect consumers' interests

Category	Representation model.
Legal basis	Article 140 of the ICC, introduced by Legislative Decree 206/05.
Description	Associations have the power to bring collective suits on behalf of consumers whose general interests were violated.
Requirements for certification	No requirements for certification.
Opt-in v Opt-out	Automatic membership.
Standing to sue	The consumer associations that fulfil the requirements of Article 137 ICC have standing to bring actions pursuant to Article 140 (Article 139(1) ICC). This includes entities that have standing pursuant to the Injunctions Directive (Article 139(2) ICC). Those associations may act in case of violation of interests governed by the ICC.
Remedies	The competent tribunal may be asked to: (1) stop the harmful behaviour/act; (2) adopt measures aiming at cancelling the harmful effects of a behaviour/act; (3) publish the measures adopted.
Costs	The 'loser-pays' principle applies and the consumer association bears the costs in case the case does not succeed in court.
Procedure	No specific procedural rules apply to actions pursuant to Article 140 ICC. However, parties may initiate a conciliation procedure before going to trial according to Article 140(2) ICC.

F. Germany*

***Kapitalanleger-Musterverfahrensgesetz, KapMuG* (Capital Market Model Proceedings Act)**

Category	Test case model.
Legal basis	Capital Market Model Proceedings Act (*Kapitalanleger-Musterverfahrensgesetz, KapMuG*) of 2005. In 2012, the *KapMuG* was amended and extended (until 2020). Specifically, its scope was enlarged and the procedure was modified.
Description	Through the test case procedure, the Higher Regional Court (*Oberlandesgericht*) selects a lead case that will serve as a model to resolve similar actions. The Higher Regional Court resolves issues that are common to those cases and sends its decision back to the lower courts, which will deal with the remaining individual questions such as causation and allocation of damages to the individual claimants. The *KapMuG* is applicable to claims for damages based on prospectus liability, as well as liability rules regarding inaccurate or misleading capital market information. Since 2012, the Act has also applied where the alleged wrongdoer used, or did not adequately inform investors about the content of said information.
Requirements for certification	There are no requirements for certification. However, the claimant who applies for a test case procedure under *KapMuG* must demonstrate to the court that the case shares common questions of fact or law with other claims.
Opt-in v Opt-out	In principle, the system is based on the opt-in mechanism. However, once the number of ten claimants is reached and proceedings commence, claimants who file a suit are automatically included in the test case proceedings (automatic membership). If a settlement is reached, it is binding on all involved parties unless they opt out. This settlement will be void if more than 30 per cent of claimants opt out.

* **Bibliography:** D Baegte, 'Class Actions, Group Litigation & Other Forms of Collective Litigation – Germany' (2007), available at globalclassactions.stanford.edu; M Bakowitz, 'The German Experience with Group Actions – The Verbandsklage and the Capital Markets Model Case Act (KapMuG)' in V Harsági and CH van Rhee (eds), *Multi-Party Redress Mechanisms in Europe: Squeaking Mice?* (Intersentia, 2014) 153–69; J Buchner, *Kollektiver Rechtsschutz für Verbraucher in Europa – Die grenzüberschreitende Durchsetzung des europäischen Verbraucherrechts bei Bagatellschäden*, Schriften zum Verbraucherschutz- und Wettbewerbsrecht, vol 3 (V&R unipress, 2015) 72–102; S Einhaus, *Kollektiver Rechtsschutz im englischen und deutschen Zivilprozessrecht*, Schriften zum Prozessrecht, vol 209 (Berlin, Duncker & Humblot, 2008) 315–456; E Feess and A Halfmeier, 'The German Capital Markets Model Case Act (KapMuG) – A European Role Model for Increasing the Efficiency of Capital Market? Analysis and Suggestions for Reform', available at papers.ssrn.com; C Geiger, *Kollektiver Rechtsschutz im Zivilprozess – Die Gruppenklage zur Durchsetzung von Massenschäden*

Standing to sue	There is no representation system. The court chooses one lead claimant, whose case will be used as a model in order to resolve similar claims. Any investor (individual or institutional) or defendant may petition the start of test case model proceedings.
Remedies	Declaratory judgment or settlement. Note that the declaratory judgment serves as a basis to resolve individual damages actions tried in the lower courts.
Costs	The 'loser-pays' principle applies. However, the costs of this procedure are spread among the claimants and added to the subsequent costs generated by their individual lawsuits.
Procedure	(1) Claimants bring a lawsuit at the first instance court or, the defendant makes a request for a test case proceedings. (2) The court seised publishes the request. If within six months a minimum of nine similar claims are filed, the first court seised refers the matter to the Higher Regional Court, which starts and leads the test case proceedings. Until a judgment is issued, individual proceedings are automatically stayed. (3) A lead claimant is chosen. Within six months from the publication of the identity of the lead claimant, potential claimants can notify their future claim to the Higher Regional Court in order to stop the statute of limitations (§ 10(2) *KapMuG*). However, it should be highlighted that notification does not generate participation in the model proceedings. As a result, the decision of the court or the settlement is not binding on people who notified their claims. (4) Proceedings end with a declaratory judgment or a settlement. Save where otherwise established by the *KapMuG*, ordinary rules of civil procedure apply.

und ihre Auswirkungen (Mohr Siebeck, 2015); B Haar, 'Investors Protection Through Model Case Procedures – Implementing Collective Goals and Individual Rights Under the 2012 Amendment to the German Capital Markets Model Case Act (KapMuG)' (2014) 15 *European Business Organization Law Review* 83–105; B Heil and B Lee, 'The Role of Private Litigation' *Comparative Corporate Governance and Financial Regulation*, Paper 7, available at scholarship.law.upenn.edu/fisch_2016/7; E Lein, 'Country Report: Germany', available at www.collectiveredress.org; B Hess et al, *Kölner Kommentar zum KapMuG*, 2nd edn (Carl Heymanns Verlag, 2014); B Schneider and H Heppner, 'Germany' in *The International Comparative Legal Guide to Class and Group Actions* (2017), avaiblable at iclg.com; HW Micklitz and A Stadler, 'The Development of Collective Legal Actions in Europe, Especially in German Civil Procedure' (2006) 17(5) *European Business Law Review* 1476–88; L Röckrath, 'Germany' in PG Karlsgodt (ed), *World Class Actions: A Guide to Group and Representative Actions around the Globe* (Oxford University Press, 2012) 241–51; P Rott, 'Evaluation of the Effectiveness and Efficiency of Collective Redress Mechanisms in the European Union – Country Report Germany' (2008), available at ec.europa.eu/consumers/solving_consumer_disputes/judicial_redress/index_en.htm; A Stadler, Oxford – Leuven Collective Redress Project – German Report (2016), available at www.law.ox.ac.uk/events/empirical-evidence-collective-redress-europe; M Sustmann and R Schmidt-Bendun, 'Der Referentenentwurf zur Reform des Kapitalanleger-Musterverfahrensgesetzes (KapMuG)' 2011 *Neue Zeitschrift für Gesellschaftsrecht* 1207–13.

***Verbandsklage* (Action taken by associations)**

Category	Representation model.
Legal basis	Act on Injunctive Relief for Consumer Rights and Other Violations (*Unterlassungsklagengesetz, UKlaG*), which entered into force in 2002. The Act has been amended many times and its scope extended over the years.
Description	Certain consumer associations and qualified interest groups may seek injunctive relief against wrongdoers who violate consumer laws listed in § 2 *UKlaG*.
Requirements for certification	There is no requirement for certification.
Opt-in v Opt-out	Automatic membership.
Standing to sue	A collective action can only be brought by: (1) associations representing interests of businesses; (2) Chambers of Industry and Commerce/Crafts; or (3) qualified entities that fulfil the conditions of § 4 *UKlaG*. Pursuant to this provision, four requirements must be met in order for an entity to acquire standing under the *UKlaG*: specifically, the entity must (1) possess at least three associations/organisations active in a given field or have at least 75 natural persons as members; (2) have at least one year of existence; (3) statutorily defend consumer interests and continue to effectively fulfil this task in the future. Similarly, listed entities pursuant to the Injunctions Directive have standing to sue.
Remedies	Injunctive relief. Pursuant to § 7 *UKlaG*, the claimant may also request the publication of the judgment at the expense of the defendant.
Costs	In absence of specific legislation, the general regime on civil procedure should apply – ie the 'loser-pays' principle.
Procedure	Save where the *UKlaG* otherwise states, § 12 of the Act on Unfair Competition and the general procedural rules of the German Code of Civil Procedure apply.

***Gesetz über außergerichtliche Rechtsdienstleistungen* (Legal Services Act)**

Category	Representation model.
Legal basis	*Gesetz über außergerichtliche Rechtsdienstleistungen* (Legal Services Act).
Description	The Legal Services Act allows non-lawyers to give legal advice out of court. According to § 8 of the Legal Services Act, consumer centres and other publicly funded entities may provide legal advice. Today, § 79(2)(3) of the German Code of Civil Procedure (GCCP) enable these actors to act as representative of consumers or assignee of their claims.

Requirements for certification	There is no requirement for certification.
Opt-in v Opt-out	Opt-in.
Standing to sue	Only publicly sponsored centres for consumer protection or consumer associations can represent consumers in courts. § 79(2)(3) of the Civil Code applies and states that eligible consumer associations can bring representative actions 'within their field of activity and responsibility'.
Remedies	In the absence of any mention by the law, usual remedies should be available.
Costs	The 'loser-pays' rule applies.
Procedure	The general rules of civil procedure apply.

G. Austria*

Verbandsklage (Action taken by associations)

Category	Representation model.
Legal basis	*Konsumentenschutzgesetz, KSchG* (Consumer Protection Act)
Description	Associations listed in § 29 *KSchG* have a right to file an action in the general interest of consumers. The association acts on its own behalf and actions for damages are not available. (1) Representative action against unfair and illegal clauses in general contract terms (§ 28 *KSchG*). (2) Representative action against non-compliance with consumer protection standards (§ 28a *KSchG*). (3) Representative action against violations of the Competition Law Act. Note that, pursuant to § 502(5)(3) ACCP, associations listed in § 29 *KSchG* also have the possibility to bring an assigned claim to the Supreme Court. This resulting decision will de facto be used as a precedent in similar cases by lower courts. In other words, it will serve as a guideline; it is not binding on third parties.

* **Bibliography**: J Buchner, *Kollektiver Rechtsschutz für Verbraucher in Europa – Die grenzüberschreitende Durchsetzung des europäischen Verbraucherrechts bei Bagatellschäden*, Schriften zum Verbraucherschutz- und Wettbewerbsrecht, vol 3 (V&R unipress, 2015) 111–14; K Hellbert, 'Austria' in *The International Comparative Legal Guide to Class and Group Actions* (2017), available at iclg.com; C Klausegger, 'Austria' in PG Karlsgodt (ed), *World Class Actions: A Guide to Group and Representative Actions around the Globe* (Oxford University Press, 2012) 252–63; A Klauser, 'Von der „Sammelklage nach österreichischem Recht" zur echten Gruppenklage' (2005) *Ecolex* 744–47; GE Kodek, 'Möglichkeiten zur gesetzlichen Regelung von Massenverfahren im Zivilprozess' (2005) *Ecolex* 751–54;

Requirements for certification	There are no requirements for certification.
Opt-in v Opt-out	Automatic membership.
Standing to sue	The associations mentioned in § 29(1) *KSchG*, as well as qualified entities for the purposes of the Injunctions Directive (§ 29(2) *KSchG*), can initiate a representative action.
Remedies	Injunctive relief.
Costs	The 'loser-pays' principle applies (§ 41–55 Austrian Code of Civil Procedure).
Procedure	General rules of civil procedure apply.

Österreichisches Modell der Sammelklage **(Collective redress actions of Austrian type)**

Category	Class/representation model.
Legal basis	§ 227, § 502(5)(3) of the Austrian Code of Civil Procedure (ACCP).
Description	Under this mechanism, potential claimants assign their claims to an association which then files a complaint on their behalf. This instrument is not restricted to specific areas of law.
Requirements for certification	(1) The court has jurisdiction to hear all the claims. (2) The same procedure applies to the claims. (3) The matter in dispute must be of the same nature with respect to the facts and the law.
Opt-in v Opt-out	Opt-in.
Standing to sue	Both individuals and associations can start a collective redress action, since there are no restrictions on standing to sue.
Remedies	Usual remedies.
Costs	The 'loser-pays' principle applies (§ 41–55 ACCP).
Procedure	General rules of civil procedure apply.

GE Kodek, Report: Austria, available at www.collectiveredress.org; P Kolba, 'Konsumentenschutz vor und mit der Sammelklage' (2010) *Ecolex* 864–67; P Kolba, 'Die Sammelklage nach össterreichischem Recht im Praxistext – Schadenersatz für Brech-Durchfall-Epidemie' (2009) 4 *ReiseRecht aktuell* 167–69; HW Micklitz and KP Purnhagen, 'Evaluation of the Effectiveness and Efficiency of Collective Redress Mechanisms in the European Union – Country Report Austria' (2008), available at ec.europa.eu/consumers/solving_consumer_disputes/judicial_redress/index_en.htm; B Pirker-Hörmann and P Kolba, Österreich: Von der Verbandsklage zur Sammelklage, available at verbraucherrecht.at/cms/uploads/media/Kolba_Pirker_Bamberg.pdf; WH Rechberger, 'Verbandsklagen, Musterprozesse und „Sammelklagen" -Möglichkeiten kollektiven Rechtsschutzes im österreichischen Zivilprozess' in C Fischer-Czermak et al (eds), *Festschrift Rudolf Welser zum 65. Geburtstag* (Vienna, MANZ Verlag, 2004) 871–88; E Scheuba, '„Sammelklage" – Einklang mit der ZPO erbeten' (2005) *Ecolex* 747–50.

H. United Kingdom*

Group Litigation Order (GLO)

Category	Test case model.
Legal basis	Part 19 III of Civil Procedure Rules (CPR) and Practice Direction 19B.
Description	When claims give rise to common or related issues of fact or law, the court can issue a Group Litigation Order (GLO) in order to manage those claims. The order establishes a register of claims, specifies the issues and identifies the court in charge.
Requirements for certification	Five conditions must be satisfied for a GLO to proceed: (1) There must be a number of claims (numerosity). (2) Claims give rise to common or related issues of fact or law (commonality). (3) The GLO must be consistent with the overriding objective of the CPR (the court must be able to deal with the case fairly). (4) The consent of the Lord Chief Justice, the Vice-Chancellor, or the Head of Civil Justice is needed. (5) The GLO will not proceed if consolidation or a representative action is more appropriate (superiority).
Opt-in v Opt-out	Opt-in.

* **Bibliography**: N Andrews, 'Multi-Party Litigation in England' in V Harsági and CH van Rhee (eds), *Multi-Party Redress Mechanisms in Europe: Squeaking Mice?* (Intersentia, 2014) 111–25; A Brown and I Dodds-Smith, 'England and Wales' in *The International Comparative Legal Guide to Class and Group Actions* (2017), avaiblable at iclg.com; Competition and Markets Authority, Consumer protection enforcement guidance: CMA58 (2016), available at www.gov.uk/government/publications/consumer-protection-enforcement-guidance-cma58; L Harbour and J Evans, 'United Kingdom' in PG Karlsgodt (ed), *World Class Actions: A Guide to Group and Representative Actions around the Globe* (Oxford University Press, 2012) 169–85; C Hodges, Country Report: England and Wales, available at globalclassactions.stanford.edu; C Hodges, Developments in Collective Redress in the European Union and United Kingdom (2010), available at globalclassactions.stanford.edu; C Hodges, *Multi-Party Actions* (Oxford University Press, 2001); C Hodges, Oxford – Leuven Collective Redress Project – British Report (2016), available at www.law.ox.ac.uk/events/empirical-evidence-collective-redress-europe; G Howells, Evaluation of the Effectiveness and Efficiency of Collective Redress Mechanisms in the European Union – Country Report United Kingdom (2008), available at ec.europa.eu/consumers/solving_consumer_disputes/judicial_redress/index_en.htm; R Mulheron, 'Some Difficulties with Group Litigation Orders – and why a Class Action is Superior' (2005) 24 *Civil Justice Quarterly* 40–68; V Smith and M Moeiri-Farsi, Country Report: England and Wales, available at www.collectiveredress.org; J Sorabji et al, Improving Access to Justice through Collective Actions – Developing a More Efficient and Effective Procedure for Collective Actions, Civil Justice Council (2008), available at www.ucl.ac.uk/laws/judicial-institute/files/Improving_Access_to_Justice_through_Collective_Actions_-_recommendations.pdf; A Zuckerman, *Zuckerman on Civil Procedure – Principles of Practice*, 2nd edn (Sweet & Maxwell, 2006) 508–27.

Standing to sue	In principle, the GLO does not trigger any representation mechanism and thus, all claimants are parties to the proceedings. However, if the court adopts a test case approach, then any party (defendant or claimant) can become the test claimant. (1) Any person with a claim can ask for the start of a GLO. (2) A court may discretionarily issue a GLO.
Remedies	Usual remedies.
Costs	The 'loser-pays' rule applies. Each party remains liable for its individual costs and severally for its portion of the common costs.
Procedure	(1) The claimant (or the defendant) files an application in accordance with Part 23 of the CPR. Alternatively, courts may discretionarily issue a group litigation order. (2) The GLO is published and a group register is created. Any party may apply to enter the register, as long as he/she previously brought a claim. (3) Trial and decision.

Representative Action

Category	Group/class action model.
Legal basis	Rule 19(6) of Civil Procedure Rules.
Description	A representative action can be brought against one or more persons by a representative of a group of persons having the same interest in the claim.
Requirements for certification	Two conditions must be satisfied: (1) at least one person must be associated to the claim brought by the representative (numerosity); (2) these persons share the 'same interest' (commonality). This requirement has been strictly interpreted by case law.
Opt-in v Opt-out	In principle, the representative action is based on the automatic membership system. According to the literature, however, represented persons may apply to be excluded from the represented class.
Standing to sue	Any party to the class can represent the group of claimants, provided that (s)he has a direct cause of action.
Remedies	Usual remedies (but damages are rarely sought in practice because of the restrictive interpretation of the commonality requirement).
Costs	The 'loser-pays' principle applies. The representative party bears the costs.
Procedure	General rules of civil procedure apply.

Action for the protection of general consumer interests

Category	Representation model
Legal basis	Part 8 of the Enterprise Act of 2002, as amended by the Consumer Rights Act 2015.
Description	Some qualified entities – also called enforcers – have the power to apply to the courts for an enforcement order against traders who infringed listed consumer protection laws. The enforcement order enables entities to protect the general interest of consumers.
Requirements for certification	There are no requirements for certification.
Opt-in v Opt-out	Automatic membership.
Standing to sue	According to section 213, the following persons may make an application for an enforcement order: (1) The Competition and Markets Authority (CMA) (general enforcer). (2) Other enforcers designated by the Secretary of State (designated enforcer). If they want to start civil proceedings they must first notify the CMA. (3) A qualified entity for the purposes of the Injunctions Directive (community enforcer). (4) A certain number of entities for the purposes of the CPC Regulation (CPC enforcers). While the general enforcer may make an application for an enforcement order in respect of any infringement, designated enforcers have a limited power (depending on the goal they pursue). As for community and CPC enforcers, they can only act when a community infringement has been committed (section 212).
Remedies	Injunctive relief.
Costs	The 'loser-pays' principle applies.
Procedure	Save where otherwise provided, the general rules of civil procedure apply. Note that before taking court action, an enforcer will normally attempt to stop and prevent repetition of what it considers or suspects to be an infringement by holding discussions with the trader (section 214).

I. Sweden*

Group proceedings

Category	Class/representation model.
Legal basis	Group Proceedings Act of 2002 (GPA).
Description	Private individuals or organisations (consumer associations or government-appointed authority) may initiate a group action. The procedure applies to all fields of law.
Requirements for certification	(1) Commonality (action is based on common circumstances). (2) The group proceedings must be an appropriate procedure. (3) The larger part of the claims cannot equally be pursued on an individual basis; (4) The group must be well defined. (5) The claimant is well-suited to represent the group.
Opt-in v Opt-out	Opt-in (section 14).
Standing to sue	According to sections 4 to 6, the following persons have standing to start group proceedings: (1) Natural or legal person with a claim subject to the action (private group action). (2) Not-for-profit associations that, in accordance with their rules, protect consumer or wage-earner interests (organisation action); (3) Public authority (public group action). The group representative is empowered to make settlements on behalf of the group, but any settlement must be confirmed by the court (section 26).
Remedies	Usual remedies.
Costs	The 'loser-pays' principle applies.
Procedure	Some specific rules are provided by the GPA. For the rest, general rules of civil procedure apply (section 2).

* **Bibliography**: L Ervo, 'Group Actions in Sweden – A Moderate Start' in V Harsági and CH van Rhee (eds), *Multi-Party Redress Mechanisms in Europe: Squeaking Mice?* (Intersentia, 2014) 243–59; L Ervo et al, Country Report: Sweden, available at www.collectiveredress.org; Hammarskiöld & Co, Oxford – Leuven Collective Redress Project – Swedish Report (2016), available at www.law.ox.ac.uk/events/empirical-evidence-collective-redress-europe; H Lindblom, 'Group Litigation in Scandinavia' (2009) 10(1) *ERA Forum* 7–35; H Lindblom, National Report: Group Litigation in Sweden (2007), available at globalclassactions.stanford.edu; H Lindblom, National report: Group Litigation in Sweden (2008), available at globalclassactions.stanford.edu; AH Persson, Evaluation of the Effectiveness and Efficiency of Collective Redress Mechanisms in the European Union – Country Report Sweden (2008), available at ec.europa.eu/consumers/solving_consumer_disputes/judicial_redress/index_en.htm; G Sparrman and L Göransson, 'Sweden' in PG Karlsgodt (ed), *World Class Actions: A Guide to Group and Representative Actions around the Globe* (Oxford University Press, 2012) 198–213.

J. Finland*

***Ryhmäkannelaki (444/2007)* (Class actions)**

Category	Representation model.
Legal basis	*Ryhmäkannelaki (444/2007)* (Act on Class Actions of 2007).
Description	According to the Group Action Act, the Finnish Consumer Ombudsman may take legal action and represent a specified group of consumers without an express permission of group members. The resulting judgment is binding both for and against all the members of the group. The scope of application of the Act is limited to consumer disputes only (section 1).
Requirements for certification	(1) Several persons have claims against the same defendant, based on the same or similar circumstances (commonality). (2) The hearing of the case as a class action is expedient in view of the size of the class, the subject-matter of the claims presented and the proof offered in it (superiority). (3) The class has been defined with adequate precision.
Opt-in v Opt-out	Opt-in.
Standing to sue	The Finnish Consumer Ombudsman has exclusive right to take legal action on behalf of a specified group of consumers (section 4). This means that consumer associations or individual consumers do not have even a secondary right of action in cases where the Consumer Ombudsman has decided not to start a legal proceeding.
Remedies	Usual remedies.
Costs	The 'loser-pays' principle applies (section 17).
Procedure	Save where otherwise provided by the Class Action Act, general procedural rules apply (section 1(3)).

Group action for the protection of general interests

Category	Representation model.
Legal basis	The Consumer Protection Act (34/1978), as amended.

* **Bibliography**: P Kiurunen, 'Finland' in PG Karlsgodt (ed), *World Class Actions: A Guide to Group and Representative Actions around the Globe* (Oxford University Press, 2012) 214–28; J Pråhl, Oxford – Leuven Collective Redress Project – Finnish Report (2016), available at www.law.ox.ac.uk/events/empirical-evidence-collective-redress-europe; M Välimäki, 'Introducing Class Actions in Finland – Lawmaking Without Economic Analysis' (2007), available at papers.ssrn.com; K Viitanen, Collective Litigation in Finland, available at globalclassactions.stanford.edu.

Description	The Finnish Consumer Ombudsman can take legal action against a trader for questions concerning unfair marketing practices or unfair standard contract terms in the Finnish Market Court. The purpose of these actions is solely the protection of collective consumer rights. During this procedure it is not possible to claim compensation of damages for individual consumers.
Requirements for certification	There is no requirement for certification.
Opt-in v Opt-out	Automatic membership.
Standing to sue	The Finnish Consumer Ombudsman has the exclusive right to sue. However, there is a secondary right of action for registered associations representing interests of traders, consumers or employees. The literature clarifies that entities listed in the Injunctions Directive also have the right to sue.
Remedies	Injunctive relief.
Costs	The parties – the Consumer Ombudsman and the trader – have to bear their own costs.
Procedure	The procedure is ruled by the Market Court Act (1527/2001) and the Act on Certain Proceedings before the Market Court (1528/2001).

K. Bulgaria*

Class Action

Category	Class/representation model.
Legal basis	Articles 379–388 of the Bulgarian Code of Civil Procedure (BCCP), introduced in 2008.
Description	A class action may be brought by any persons who claim to be harmed by an infringement or any organisations responsible for the protection of injured persons or for the protection of general interests. This procedural rule is available in all areas of law. When an interest covered by the Consumer Protection Act (CPA) is at stake, Articles 186–190 must be taken into account.

* **Bibliography**: V Bineva and T Goleminov, 'Evaluation of the Effectiveness and Efficiency of Collective Redress Mechanisms in the European Union – Country Report Bulgaria' (2008), available at ec.europa.eu/consumers/solving_consumer_disputes/judicial_redress/index_en.htm; A Katzarsky and G Georgiev, 'Bulgaria' in *The International Comparative Legal Guide to Class and Group Actions* (2013), avaiblable at iclg.com; Oxford – Leuven Collective Redress Project – Bulgarian Report (2016), available at www.law.ox.ac.uk/events/empirical-evidence-collective-redress-europe.

Requirements for certification	A class action may be brought on behalf of persons who are harmed by the same infringement (commonality). Additionally, the circle of persons harmed must, at least, be identifiable (if not precisely defined).
Opt-in v Opt-out	Opt-out (Article 383(2) BCCP).
Standing to sue	A person harmed by an infringement or an organisation who protects the injured persons or the general interest at stake. When an interest falling under the CPA is harmed, specific rules on standing apply. In particular, the following actors may start proceedings: (1) Consumer associations selected by the Ministry of Economy and Energy (Article 186(1) CPA). (2) Qualified entities from other Member States, provided that the infringement adversely affects the interests subject to the protection of said entities and that they are included in the list approved by the EU and published in the Official Journal – this is certainly a reference to the Injunctions Directive (Article 186a CPA). (3) Any consumer association, acting as a representative of at least two or more consumers who suffered damage (Article 188–189 CPA).
Remedies	According to Article 385 BCCP, the court may order the respondent to perform a specific act, to refrain from performing a specific act, or to pay a specific amount.
Costs	The 'loser-pays' principle applies (Article 78(1) BCCP).
Procedure	General Rules of the Bulgarian Code of Civil Procedure apply. However, chapter 33 establishes some special procedural rules for class actions that must be followed.

L. Belgium*

Action en reparation collective (Collective Action)

Category	Representation model.
Legal basis	Book XVII, title 2 of the Economic Code, introduced by the Act implementing a consumer collective redress action in the code of economic law of 28 of March 2014.

* **Bibliography:** JP Fierens and B Volders, 'Belgium' in PG Karlsgodt (ed), *World Class Actions: A Guide to Group and Representative Actions around the Globe* (Oxford University Press, 2012) 271–85; JT Nowak, 'The New Belgian Law on Consumer Collective Redress and Compliance with EU Law Requirements' in E Lein et al (eds), *Collective Redress in Europe – Why and How?* (The British

Description	Associations that fulfil the criteria set forth by Article XVII.39 can commence proceedings in order to obtain compensation for losses suffered by individuals. Alternatively, they can negotiate an agreement with the alleged wrongdoer and submit it to the court for homologation. The necessary requirements are the following: (1) Violation by a firm of a contractual obligation, an EU regulation or legislation listed on Article XVII.37. The scope is therefore, limited to consumer law. Mass accidents and shareholder disputes are not covered. (2) Standing to sue and adequacy of representation. (3) The collective action is the best procedural tool available to solve the dispute.
Requirements for certification	The representative entity must adequately represent the group of victims. The adequacy requirement is assessed by the judge and is meant to remove representatives who have conflict of interests.
Opt-in v Opt-out	If victims have their domicile in Belgium, both the opt-in and opt-out mechanisms are available. In case they do not have their domicile in Belgium or if physical or moral damages are claimed, the opt-in based collective action is the only available option. The choice to opt in or to opt out occurs after the decision of the certification or the homologation of the agreement and is irrevocable.
Standing to sue	(1) Associations (legal entities) which defend consumers' interests and which either sit on the Special Consultative Commission for Consumers or are approved by the Minister. (2) Associations (legal entities since at least three years) approved by the Minister, whose social purpose is connected to the damage suffered, and which do not pursue an economic goal. (3) The autonomous public service (Article XVI.5) is only competent to negotiate a collective settlement. Since May 2018, a group of SMEs may also be represented in a collective action.
Remedies	Monetary or in kind compensation.

Institute of International and Comparative Law, 2015) 169–201; ME Storme and E Terryn, Belgian Report on Class Actions, available at globalclassactions.stanford.edu; O Vanhulst, Country Report: Belgium, available at www.collectiveredress.org; J Verlinden and P van Mulders, 'Belgium' in *The International Comparative Legal Guide to Class and Group Actions* (2017), avaiblable at iclg.com; S Voet, Class Action Developments in Belgium (2016), available at globalclassactions.stanford.edu; S Voet, 'Consumer Collective Redress in Belgium: Class Actions to the Rescue?' (2015) 16(1) *European Business Organization Law Review* 121–43; S Voet, 'Cultural Dimensions of Group Litigation: The Belgian Case' (2013) 41 *Georgia Journal of International and Comparative Law* 433–79; S Voet, Oxford – Leuven Collective Redress Project – Belgian Report (2016), available at www.law.ox.ac.uk/events/empirical-evidence-collective-redress-europe.

Costs	The 'loser-pays' rule applies (Articles 1017–1018 of the Judicial Code).
Procedure	*Procedural steps in case of judicial action:* (1) The representative plaintiff files an application in accordance with Article XVII.42, § 1. (2) Within two months, the judge must rule on the admissibility of the application. If all the criteria are fulfilled, the decision is published in the 'Moniteur belge' and the 'SPF Economie'. The certification decision can be appealed. (3) Within a period of minimum 30 days and maximum of three months following the certification decision, members are invited to opt in or out of the collective action. (4) Then, within the time limit fixed by the judge (between three and six months, subject to renewal for a period of six months), the parties try to conclude an agreement (mandatory negotiation phase). If an agreement is reached and all the requirements are fulfilled, the judge ratifies it. The agreement is published in the 'Moniteur belge' and the 'SPF Economie'. However, if the time limit is over or no agreement has been reached, the judicial procedure continues and the judge issues a decision. (5) A claims settler is appointed in order to deal with the enforcement phase. First, the claims settler draws a provisional list of the class members that the class representative and the defendant can challenge. Then, a hearing is set up before the court in order to establish the scope of the final list. After the settlement or the decision has been enforced, the claims settler writes a final report. On this basis, the court allocates funds that were not distributed and rules on the costs and fees of the claims settler (that will be paid by the defendant). *Procedural steps for the homologation of the parties' agreement:* (1) Parties present a joint request in order to homologate their agreement according to Article XVII.42, § 2. The request must fulfil the certification criteria and the agreement must contain all the elements mentioned in Article XVII.45, § 3, 2° to 13°. (2) Within two months, the judge must rule on the admissibility of the request. If all the criteria are fulfilled, the decision is published in the 'Moniteur belge' and the 'SPF Economie'. If the judge refuses the homologation (after having offered the parties to complete the agreement), the procedure stops here. (3) The liquidation phase is the same as described under point (5) above.

***Action en cessation* (Action for Injunctive Relief)**

Category	Representation model.
Legal basis	Book XVII, title 1 of the Belgian Economic Code.
Description	This mechanism enables the President of the Commercial Tribunal to sanction the violation of one of the acts listed in Article XVII.2. Notably, this provision applies to labour law, consumer protection, advertising and intellectual property. The Tribunal can only order the termination of an illegal behaviour.
Requirements for certification	There are no requirements for certification.
Opt-in v Opt-out	Automatic membership.
Standing to sue	Only the President of the Commercial Tribunal can order the termination of an illegal behaviour. The following persons can ask the President to act: (1) Interested persons. (2) The Minister competent for the matter in question (Article XVII.8) and the director of the *Contrôle et Médiation du Service public fédéral Economie, P.M.E., Classes moyennes et Energie* in certain cases. (3) Professional groups which possess legal personality. (4) Associations which possess legal personality and whose social purpose is to protect consumers' interests. Additionally, they must be represented in the Special Consultative Commission for Consumers or be approved by the Minister. (5) Actions for injunctive relief, which aim at protecting consumer interests included in Article XVII.26, can be brought by entities listed in the Injunctions Directive. These must show that they protect the interests that have been harmed.
Remedies	Injunctive relief (termination of an illegal behaviour). Additionally, the Tribunal can also decide to publish its judgment (Article XVII.4).
Costs	The 'loser-pays' rule applies (Articles 1017–1018 of the Judicial Code).
Procedure	There is no specific procedure that governs actions for injunctive relief. In principle, they follow the rules of the Belgian Judicial Code (Article XVII.6). In particular, Articles 1034ter to 1034sexies of the Judicial Code apply. As regards actions for injunctive relief protecting consumer interests, Article XVII.32 must be taken into account.

M. Poland*

Group proceedings

Category	Group/representation model
Legal basis	Act on Pursuing Claims in Group Proceedings of 2009.
Description	The Act regulates civil court proceedings, whereby claims of the same type, based on the same or similar factual basis, are pursued by at least ten persons. The Act applies to consumer protection, product liability, and tort.
Requirements for certification	(1) The group of claimants must consist of at least ten members (numerosity). (2) All claims must arise from the same or similar facts and be of the same type (commonality). It is not necessary that all claims be based on the same legal provision. However, if the action concerns monetary claims, the amount claimed by each class member has to be made equal to the others.
Opt-in v Opt-out	Opt-in.
Standing to sue	(1) A group member who has been elected by all other group members can bring group proceedings. (2) In consumer protection cases, a group may elect a Municipal Consumer Ombudsman to fulfil the role of claimant.
Remedies	Usual remedies.
Costs	The 'loser-pays' principle applies, but discounts on court fees are available for group proceedings.
Procedure	(1) A statement of claim is filed and the tribunal renders a decision on the admissibility of the collective action on the basis of a hearing (class certification). This decision can be appealed.

* **Bibliography**: R Kos and A Trzaska, 'Poland' in *The International Comparative Legal Guide to Class and Group Actions* (2017), avaiblable at iclg.com; R Kulski, 'Polish Perspectives and Provisions on Group Proceedings' in V Harsági and CH van Rhee (eds), *Multi-Party Redress Mechanisms in Europe: Squeaking Mice?* (Intersentia, 2014) 225–41; Oxford – Leuven Collective Redress Project – Polish Report (2016), available at www.law.ox.ac.uk/events/empirical-evidence-collective-redress-europe; M Safjan et al, 'Taking the Collective Interese of Consumers Seriously: A View from Poland' in F Cafaggi and HW Micklitz (eds), *New Frontiers of Consumer Protection: The Interplay Between Private and Public Enforcement* (Intersentia, 2009) 171–206; M Sengayen, National Report for the Global Class Actions Conference at the Centre for Socio-Legal Studies (2007), available at globalclassactions.stanford.edu; M Tulibacka, Country Report: Poland, available at www.collectiveredress.org; M Tulibacka and R Goral, An Update on Class Actions and Litigation Funding in Poland, available at globalclassactions.stanford.edu.

	(2) If the statement of claim is valid, the court announces the initiation of the collective proceedings *ex officio*. The dissemination of this piece of information is usually made in the national mass media but the law does not limit the means available to the court in order to spread the information. People who would like to opt into the group proceedings must send a declaration to the representative. The latter will establish a list of persons who joined the action. The defendant can present objections to the list. (3) The tribunal examines the claims of all members and makes a decision regarding the composition of the group. This decision is appealable. No procedural rules dictate further steps for the tribunal to take a decision on the merits.

Annex III: Questionnaire on Cross-Border Litigation and Collective Redress

This questionnaire aims at gathering information on the difficulties that consumer associations (may) face in cross-border consumer litigation. The term "cross-border" designates cases whereby parties are domiciled in different Member States or, more generally, that are related to various legal orders. Section 4 specifically deals with cross-border collective redress (*acción colectiva*, *azione di classe*, *Sammelklage*, *action collective*, *acção popular*). The objective is to identify the obstacles that hinder consumer associations to use this device in international cases. The results of this inquiry will help the author to build up solutions to these problems in a future academic work.

What is the name of the consumer association that you represent in this questionnaire?

ADICAE

SECTION 1 – CROSS-BORDER LITIGATION IN A DOMESTIC COURT

1.1 Have you ever initiated proceedings against a foreign defendant in a domestic court (= in a court that is located in the State of your domicile/seat)?

☒ Yes
☐ No (*Go directly to section 2*)

1.2 What kind of relief do you usually seek in those cross-border cases?

☐ Injunctive or declaratory relief
☐ Monetary compensation
☒ Both

1.3 What legal basis do you usually use in order to establish the competence of your courts in a cross-border case?

☒ Article 5.3 of the Brussels Regulation (Regulation 44/2001) or 7.2 of its recast (Regulation 1215/2012), which corresponds to the place where the damage occurred

☐ Article 5.5 of the Brussels Regulation (Regulation 44/2001) or 7.5 of its recast (Regulation 1215/2012), which corresponds to the place in which the branch, agency or other establishment is situated

☐ Article 16 of the Brussels Regulation (Regulation 44/2001) or 18 of its recast (Regulation 1215/2012), which corresponds to the consumer's domicile

☐ I do not know

☐ I usually rely on another legal basis. Please specify: ____________________

If you would like to make additional comments in relation to this section, please write them here:

____
____
____
____

SECTION 2 – CROSS-BORDER LITIGATION IN A FOREIGN COURT

2.1 Have you ever initiated proceedings against a foreign defendant in a court that is located in a different Member State than the one of your domicile/seat?

☐ Yes

☒ No (*Go directly to section 3*)

2.2 What kind of relief do you usually seek in those cross-border cases?

☐ Injunctive or declaratory relief

☐ Monetary compensation

☐ Both

2.3 In case you sought injunctive relief, did you benefit from the application of the Injunction Directive (the Injunctions Directive 2009/22/EC aims at protecting collective interests of consumers in the internal market and enables certain entities to bring action for the cessation of infringements of consumer rights granted by EU law)

☐ Yes

☒ No

If you would like to make additional comments in relation to this section, please write them here:

____
____
____
____

SECTION 3 – BARRIERS TO CROSS-BORDER LITIGATION

3. In your experience, what are the obstacles that consumer associations face in order to start proceedings in another Member State? Please, evaluate the following factors on a scale from 0 to 3.

	0 (this is not a barrier at all)	1	2	3 (very relevant obstacle to litigation)
Costs of proceedings	☐	☐	☒	☐
Length of proceedings	☐	☐	☐	☒
Language differences	☐	☒	☐	☐
Differences in substantive laws	☐	☐	☒	☐
Differences in procedures (for example, different rules on time limits, evidence, costs, etc.)	☒	☐	☐	☐

Is there any other obstacle to cross-border litigation?

____
____
____
____

SECTION 4 – CROSS-BORDER COLLECTIVE REDRESS

4.1 Have you ever brought a collective redress claim against a foreign defendant in a court that is located in a different Member State than the one of your domicile/seat?

☐ Yes
☒ No

4.2 Have you ever brought a collective redress claim against a foreign defendant in a domestic court (= in a court that is located in the State of your domicile/seat)?

☒ Yes

☐ No, because:
- ☐ collective redress is not efficient in my country.
- ☐ courts do not have jurisdiction in this type of cases.
- ☐ it is anyway too costly to bring collective redress proceedings.
- ☐ Other difficulties. Please specify: ____________________

4.3 Would you welcome the establishment of a specific forum (by the European legislator) for cross-border collective redress claims in the Member State of your domicile/seat?

☒ Yes
☐ No
☐ It would not make any difference

4.4 In your opinion, what may impede the start of collective redress proceedings in a foreign court (supposing that this device is available there)? Please, evaluate the following factors on a scale from 0 to 3.

	0 (this is not a barrier at all)	1	2	3 (very relevant obstacle to litigation)
Costs of proceedings	☐	☐	☒	☐
Length of proceedings	☐	☐	☐	☒
Language differences	☐	☒	☐	☐
Differences in substantive laws	☐	☒	☐	☐
Differences in procedures (for example, different rules on time limits, evidence, costs, etc.)	☐	☒	☐	☐
Limited rules on standing to sue	☐	☐	☒	☐
The difficulties to bring potential victims together	☐	☐	☒	☐
Lack of financial resources	☐	☐	☐	☒
Lack of expertise	☐	☐	☒	☐
Difficulties to distribute compensation to individuals	☐	☐	☒	☐

Is there any other obstacle to cross-border collective redress?

____
____
____
____

4.5 Is collective redress a better means than Alternative Dispute Resolution (like arbitration and mediation) to solve cross-border consumer disputes?

☐ Yes
☒ No
☐ Both are useful, it depends on the case
☐ Both are useless. The most adequate tool to solve consumer disputes is:

____

4.6 Is collective redress a better means than Small Claims procedures (which deal with claims of small value) to solve cross-border consumer disputes?

☒ Yes
☐ No
☐ Both are useful, it depends on the case
☐ Both are useless. The most adequate tool to solve consumer disputes is:

____

4.7 If collective redress mechanisms were harmonised within the EU, would you bring more collective redress proceedings in courts located in different Member States?

☒ Yes
☐ No

If you would like to make additional comments in relation to this section, please write them here:

____
____
____
____

Would you allow me to publish the results of this questionnaire in my Ph.D. thesis?

☒ Yes
☐ No

Thank you very much for your valuable participation to this project.

Questionnaire on cross-border litigation and collective redress

This questionnaire aims at gathering information on the difficulties that consumer associations (may) face in cross-border consumer litigation. The term "cross-border" designates cases whereby parties are domiciled in different Member States or, more generally, that are related to various legal orders. Section 4 specifically deals with cross-border collective redress (*acción colectiva*, *azione di classe*, *Sammelklage*, *action collective*, *acção popular*). The objective is to identify the obstacles that hinder consumer associations to use this device in international cases. The results of this inquiry will help the author to build up solutions to these problems in a future academic work.

What is the name of the consumer association that you represent in this questionnaire? DECO – Associação Portuguesa para a Defesa do Consumidor.

SECTION 1 – CROSS-BORDER LITIGATION IN A DOMESTIC COURT

1.1 Have you ever initiated proceedings against a foreign defendant in a domestic court (= in a court that is located in the State of your domicile/seat)?

☐ Yes
☒ No (*Go directly to section 2*)

1.2 What kind of relief do you usually seek in those cross-border cases?

☐ Injunctive or declaratory relief
☐ Monetary compensation
☐ Both

1.3 What legal basis do you usually use in order to establish the competence of your courts in a cross-border case?

☐ Article 5.3 of the Brussels Regulation (Regulation 44/2001) or 7.2 of its recast (Regulation 1215/2012), which corresponds to the place where the damage occurred
☐ Article 5.5 of the Brussels Regulation (Regulation 44/2001) or 7.5 of its recast (Regulation 1215/2012), which corresponds to the place in which the branch, agency or other establishment is situated
☐ Article 16 of the Brussels Regulation (Regulation 44/2001) or 18 of its recast (Regulation 1215/2012), which corresponds to the consumer's domicile
☐ I do not know
☐ I usually rely on another legal basis. Please specify: ☐

If you would like to make additional comments in relation to this section, please write them here:

☐

SECTION 2 – CROSS-BORDER LITIGATION IN A FOREIGN COURT

2.1 Have you ever initiated proceedings against a foreign defendant in a court that is located in a different Member State than the one of your domicile/seat?

☐ Yes

☒ No (<u>*Go directly to section 3*</u>)

2.2 What kind of relief do you usually seek in those cross-border cases?

☐ Injunctive or declaratory relief

☐ Monetary compensation

☐ Both

2.3 In case you sought injunctive relief, did you benefit from the application of the Injunction Directive (the Injunctions Directive 2009/22/EC aims at protecting collective interests of consumers in the internal market and enables certain entities to bring action for the cessation of infringements of consumer rights granted by EU law)

☐ Yes

☐ No

If you would like to make additional comments in relation to this section, please write them here: ☐

SECTION 3 – BARRIERS TO CROSS-BORDER LITIGATION

3. In your experience, what are the obstacles that consumer associations face in order to start proceedings in another Member State? Please, evaluate the following factors on a scale from 0 to 3.

	0 (this is not a barrier at all)	1	2	3 (very relevant obstacle to litigation)
Costs of proceedings	☐	☐	☒	☐
Length of proceedings	☐	☐	☒	☐
Language differences	☐	☐	☐	☒
Differences in substantive laws	☐	☐	☐	☒
Differences in procedures (for example, different rules on time limits, evidence, costs, etc.)	☐	☐	☐	☒

Is there any other obstacle to cross-border litigation?
☐

SECTION 4 – CROSS-BORDER COLLECTIVE REDRESS

4.1 Have you ever brought a collective redress claim against a foreign defendant in a court that is located in a different Member State than the one of your domicile/seat?

☐ Yes
☒ No

4.2 Have you ever brought a collective redress claim against a foreign defendant in a domestic court (= in a court that is located in the State of your domicile/seat)?

☐ Yes

☒ No, because:
- ☐ collective redress is not efficient in my country.
- ☐ courts do not have jurisdiction in this type of cases.
- ☐ it is anyway too costly to bring collective redress proceedings.
- ☐ Other difficulties. Please specify: ☐

4.3 Would you welcome the establishment of a specific forum (by the European legislator) for cross-border collective redress claims in the Member State of your domicile/seat?

☒ Yes
☐ No
☐ It would not make any difference

4.4 In your opinion, what may impede the start of collective redress proceedings in a foreign court (supposing that this device is available there)? Please, evaluate the following factors on a scale from 0 to 3.

	0 (this is not a barrier at all)	1	2	3 (very relevant obstacle to litigation)
Costs of proceedings	☐	☐	☐	☒
Length of proceedings	☐	☐	☒	☐
Language differences	☐	☐	☐	☒

Differences in substantive laws	☐	☐	☐	☒
Differences in procedures (for example, different rules on time limits, evidence, costs, etc.)	☐	☐	☐	☒
Limited rules on standing to sue	☐	☐	☒	☐
The difficulties to bring potential victims together	☐	☐	☐	☒
Lack of financial resources	☐	☐	☒	☐
Lack of expertise	☐	☒	☐	☐
Difficulties to distribute compensation to individuals	☐	☐	☐	☒

Is there any other obstacle to cross-border collective redress?
☐

4.5 Is collective redress a better means than Alternative Dispute Resolution (like arbitration and mediation) to solve cross-border consumer disputes?

☐ Yes
☐ No
☒ Both are useful, it depends on the case
☐ Both are useless. The most adequate tool to solve consumer disputes is: ☐

4.6 Is collective redress a better means than Small Claims procedures (which deal with claims of small value) to solve cross-border consumer disputes?

☐ Yes
☐ No
☒ Both are useful, it depends on the case
☐ Both are useless. The most adequate tool to solve consumer disputes is: ☐

4.7 If collective redress mechanisms were harmonised within the EU, would you bring more collective redress proceedings in courts located in different Member States?

☒ Yes
☐ No

If you would like to make additional comments in relation to this section, please write them here:

☐

Would you allow me to publish the results of this questionnaire in my Ph.D. thesis?

☒ Yes

☐ No

Thank you very much for your valuable participation to this project.

Questionnaire on cross-border litigation and collective redress

This questionnaire aims at gathering information on the difficulties that consumer associations (may) face in cross-border consumer litigation. The term "cross-border" designates cases whereby parties are domiciled in different Member States or, more generally, that are related to various legal orders. Section 4 specifically deals with cross-border collective redress (*acción colectiva*, *azione di classe*, *Sammelklage*, *action collective*, *acção popular*). The objective is to identify the obstacles that hinder consumer associations to use this device in international cases. The results of this inquiry will help the author to build up solutions to these problems in a future academic work.

What is the name of the consumer association that you represent in this questionnaire?

ALTROCONSUMO

SECTION 1 – CROSS-BORDER LITIGATION IN A DOMESTIC COURT

1.1 Have you ever initiated proceedings against a foreign defendant in a domestic court (= in a court that is located in the State of your domicile/seat)?

☒ Yes
☐ No (*Go directly to section 2*)

1.2 What kind of relief do you usually seek in those cross-border cases?

☒ Injunctive or declaratory relief
☐ Monetary compensation
☐ Both

1.3 What legal basis do you usually use in order to establish the competence of your courts in a cross-border case?

☒ Article 5.3 of the Brussels Regulation (Regulation 44/2001) or 7.2 of its recast (Regulation 1215/2012), which corresponds to the place where the damage occurred
☐ Article 5.5 of the Brussels Regulation (Regulation 44/2001) or 7.5 of its recast (Regulation 1215/2012), which corresponds to the place in which the branch, agency or other establishment is situated
☐ Article 16 of the Brussels Regulation (Regulation 44/2001) or 18 of its recast (Regulation 1215/2012), which corresponds to the consumer's domicile
☐ I do not know
☐ I usually rely on another legal basis. Please specify: ____________________

If you would like to make additional comments in relation to this section, please write them here:

____
____
____
____

SECTION 2 – CROSS-BORDER LITIGATION IN A FOREIGN COURT

2.1 Have you ever initiated proceedings against a foreign defendant in a court that is located in a different Member State than the one of your domicile/seat?

☐ Yes

☒ No (*Go directly to section 3*)

2.2 What kind of relief do you usually seek in those cross-border cases?

☐ Injunctive or declaratory relief

☐ Monetary compensation

☐ Both

2.3 In case you sought injunctive relief, did you benefit from the application of the Injunction Directive (the Injunctions Directive 2009/22/EC aims at protecting collective interests of consumers in the internal market and enables certain entities to bring action for the cessation of infringements of consumer rights granted by EU law)

☐ Yes

☐ No

If you would like to make additional comments in relation to this section, please write them here:

____

____

____

____

SECTION 3 – BARRIERS TO CROSS-BORDER LITIGATION

3. In your experience, what are the obstacles that consumer associations face in order to start proceedings in another Member State? Please, evaluate the following factors on a scale from 0 to 3.

	0 (this is not a barrier at all)	1	2	3 (very relevant obstacle to litigation)
Costs of proceedings	☐	☐	☐	☒
Length of proceedings	☒	☐	☐	☐
Language differences	☐	☐	☐	☒
Differences in substantive laws	☐	☐	☒	☐
Differences in procedures (for example, different rules on time limits, evidence, costs, etc.)	☐	☐	☒	☐

Is there any other obstacle to cross-border litigation?

____
____
____
____

SECTION 4 – CROSS-BORDER COLLECTIVE REDRESS

4.1 Have you ever brought a collective redress claim against a foreign defendant in a court that is located in a different Member State than the one of your domicile/seat?

☐ Yes
☒ No

4.2 Have you ever brought a collective redress claim against a foreign defendant in a domestic court (= in a court that is located in the State of your domicile/seat)?

☐ Yes

☒ No, because: ☒ collective redress is not efficient in my country.
☐ courts do not have jurisdiction in this type of cases.
☐ it is anyway too costly to bring collective redress proceedings.
☐ Other difficulties. Please specify: ____________

4.3 Would you welcome the establishment of a specific forum (by the European legislator) for cross-border collective redress claims in the Member State of your domicile/seat?

☒ Yes
☐ No
☐ It would not make any difference

4.4 In your opinion, what may impede the start of collective redress proceedings in a foreign court (supposing that this device is available there)? Please, evaluate the following factors on a scale from 0 to 3.

	0 (this is not a barrier at all)	1	2	3 (very relevant obstacle to litigation)
Costs of proceedings	☐	☐	☐	☒
Length of proceedings	☒	☐	☐	☐
Language differences	☐	☐	☐	☒

Differences in substantive laws	☐	☐	☒	☐
Differences in procedures (for example, different rules on time limits, evidence, costs, etc.)	☐	☐	☒	☐
Limited rules on standing to sue	☐	☐	☐	☐
The difficulties to bring potential victims together	☐	☐	☐	☒
Lack of financial resources	☐	☐	☐	☒
Lack of expertise	☐	☐	☐	☒
Difficulties to distribute compensation to individuals	☐	☐	☐	☒

Is there any other obstacle to cross-border collective redress?

____

____

____

____

4.5 Is collective redress a better means than Alternative Dispute Resolution (like arbitration and mediation) to solve cross-border consumer disputes?

☐ Yes
☐ No
☒ Both are useful, it depends on the case
☐ Both are useless. The most adequate tool to solve consumer disputes is:

____

4.6 Is collective redress a better means than Small Claims procedures (which deal with claims of small value) to solve cross-border consumer disputes?

☐ Yes
☐ No
☒ Both are useful, it depends on the case
☐ Both are useless. The most adequate tool to solve consumer disputes is:

____

4.7 If collective redress mechanisms were harmonised within the EU, would you bring more collective redress proceedings in courts located in different Member States?

☐ Yes
☒ No

If you would like to make additional comments in relation to this section, please write them here:

____
____
____
____

Would you allow me to publish the results of this questionnaire in my Ph.D. thesis?

☒ Yes

☐ No

Thank you very much for your valuable participation to this project.

BIBLIOGRAPHY

Books and Book Chapters

Allemeerschen, B, 'Transnational Class Settlements Lessons from *Converium*' in S Wrbka et al (eds), *Collective Actions: Enhancing Access to Justice and Reconciling Multilayer Interests* (Cambridge University Press, 2012) 364–84.

Anderson, B and Trask, A, *The Class Action Playbook*, 2nd edn (Oxford University Press, 2012).

Andrews, N, 'Multi-Party Litigation in England' in V Harsági and CH van Rhee (eds), *Multi-Party Redress Mechanisms in Europe: Squeaking Mice?* (Intersentia, 2014) 111–25.

Ariza Colmenarejo, MJ, *La acción de cesación como medio para la protección de consumidores y usuarios* (Thomson Reuters Aranzadi, 2012).

Armenta Deu, T, *Acciones colectivas: Reconocimiento, cosa juzgada y ejecución* (Marcial Pons, 2013).

Bakowitz, M, 'The German Experience with Group Action' in V Harsági and CH van Rhee (eds), *Multi-Party Redress Mechanisms in Europe: Squeaking Mice?* (Intersentia, 2014) 153–69.

Bariatti, S, 'Recognition and Enforcement in the EU of Judicial Decisions Rendered Upon Class Actions: The Case of U.S. and Dutch Judgments and Settlements' in F Pocar et al (eds), *Recasting Brussels I*, Studi e Pubblicazioni della Rivista di Diritto Internazionale Privato e Processuale 76 (CEDAM, 2012) 319–39.

Benöhr, I, *EU Consumer Law and Human Rights* (Oxford University Press, 2013).

Blomeyer, A, 'Types of Relief Available (Judicial Remedies)' in M Cappelletti (ed), *International Encyclopedia of Comparative Law*, vol 14, ch 4 (JCB Mohr/Martinus Nijhoff Publishers, 1982).

van Boom, WH, 'Collective Settlement of Mass Claims in The Netherlands' in M Casper et al (eds), *Auf dem Weg zu einer europäischen Sammelklage?* (Sellier European Publishers, 2009) 171–92.

—— and Loos, M, 'Efffective Enforcement of Consumer Law in Europe' in WH van Boom and M Loos (eds), *Collective Enforcement of Consumer Law* (Groningen, Europa Law Publishing, 2007) 229–54.

Bosters, T, *Collective Redress and Private International Law in the EU* (Springer, 2017).

Briggs, A, *Private International Law in English Courts* (Oxford, 2014).

Buchner, J, 'Kollektiver Rechtsschutz für Verbraucher in Europa – Die grenzüberschreitende Durchsetzung des europäischen Verbraucherrechts bei Bagatellschäden, Schriften zum Verbraucherschutz- und Wettbewerbsrecht', vol 3 (V&R unipress, 2015).

Bureau, D and Muir Watt, H, *Droit international Privé*, vol 1, 2nd edn (Thémis Droit, 2007).

Calais-Auloy, J and Temple, H, *Droit de la consommation*, 8th edn (Dalloz, 2010).

Calvo Caravaca, AL and Carrascosa González, J, *Derecho Internacional Privado*, vol 1 and 2, 16th edn (Comares, 2016).

Cappelletti, M and Garth, B, 'Access to Justice: The Worldwide Movement to Make Rights More Effective – A General Report' in M Cappelletti and B Garth (eds), *Access to Justice – A World Survey*, vol 1 (Sijthoff and Noordhoff/Giuffrè, 1978) 1–124.

Carballo Piñeiro, L, *Las acciones colectivas y su eficacia extraterritorial – Problemas de recepción y transplante de las class actions en Europa* (De conflictu legum. Estudios de Derecho Internacional Privado, 2009).

Carlier, JY, 'Les actions collectives transfrontières. Rapport belge' in B Stauder (ed), *Les actions collectives transfrontières des organisations de consommateurs – Droit international et droit du marché intérieur*, Actes du colloque organisé avec le Centre d'études juridiques européennes (Schultess, 1997) 45–68.

—— *Guide des litiges transfrontières* (Institut National de la Consommation, 1993).

Coffee, JC, *Entrepreneurial Litigation: Its Rise, Fall, and Future* (Harvard University Press, 2015).

Corominas Bach, S, 'La legitimación en la futura regulación europea de las acciones colectivas de consumo' in E Carbonell Porras and R Cabrera Mercado (eds), *Intereses Colectivos y Legitimación Activa* (Thomson Reuters, 2014) 137–61, 525–48.

Craig, P and de Búrca, G, *EU Law – Text, Cases, and Materials*, 5th edn (Oxford University Press, 2011).

Creutzfeldt, N, 'Alternative Dispute Resolution for Consumers' in M Stürner et al (eds), *The Role of Consumer ADR in the Administration of Justice* (Sellier European Law Publishers, 2015) 3–10.

Domash, H, *Mutual Fund and Closed-End Fund Investing: What You Need to Know* (FT Press, 2011), available at proquest.safaribooksonline.com/9780132782036.

Einhaus, S, *Kollektiver Rechtsschutz im englischen und deutschen Zivilprozessrecht*, Schriften zum Prozessrecht, vol 209 (Berlin, Duncker & Humblot, 2008).

Enne, S, 'Italy' in PG Karlsgodt (ed), *World Class Actions: A Guide to Group and Representative Actions around the Globe* (Oxford University Press, 2012) 334–40.

Ervo, L, 'Group Actions in Sweden – A Moderate Start' in V Harsági and CH van Rhee (eds), *Multi-Party Redress Mechanisms in Europe: Squeaking Mice?* (Intersentia, 2014) 243–59.

—— 'Opt-In is Out and Opt-out is In' in B Hess et al (eds), *EU Civil Justice: Current Issues and Future Outlook*, Swedish Studies in European Law, vol 7 (Bloomsbury, 2016) 185–200.

—— and A Persson, 'Finnish and Swedish Legislation in Light of the ADR Directive – Boards and Ombudsmen' in E Lein et al (eds), *Collective Redress in Europe – Why and How?* (The British Institute of International and Comparative Law, 2015) 463–71.

Fairgrieve, D, 'The Impact of The Brussels I Enforcement and Recognition Rules on Collective Actions' in D Fairgrieve and E Lein (eds), *Extraterritoriality and Collective Redress* (Oxford University Press, 2012) 171–89.

—— and Howells, G, 'Collective Redress Procedures: European Debates' in D Fairgrieve and E Lein (eds), *Extraterritoriality and Collective Redress* (Oxford University Press, 2012) 15–41.

Fallon, M, 'An Essay on the Mutual Recognition of Group Actions (Governmental, Organizational, of Class Actions) in Cross-Border Consumer Conflicts within the European Community' in T Bourgoignie (ed), *Group Actions and the Defense of the Consumer Interest in the European Community* (Story, 1992) 245–61.

Faure, M et al, 'No Cure, no Pay and Contingency Fees' in M Tuil and L Visscher (eds), *New Trends in Financing Civil Litigation in Europe – A Legal, Empirical, and Economic Analysis* (Edward Elgar, 2010) 33–56.

Ferrand, F, 'Collective Litigation in France: From Distrust to Cautious Admission' in V Harsági and CH van Rhee (eds), *Multi-Party Redress Mechanisms in Europe: Squeaking Mice?* (Intersentia, 2014) 127–52.

Fierens, JP and Volders, B, 'Belgium' in PG Karlsgodt (ed), *World Class Actions: A Guide to Group and Representative Actions around the Globe* (Oxford University Press, 2012) 271–85.

Fleming, J and Hazard, GC and Leubsdorf, J, *Civil Procedure*, 5th edn (Foundation Press, 2001).

—— and Kuster, JJ, 'The Netherlands' in PG Karlsgodt (ed), *World Class Actions: A Guide to Group and Representative Actions around the Globe* (Oxford University Press, 2012) 286–300.

França Gouveia, M and Garoupa, N, 'Class Actions in Portugal' in JG Backhaus et al (eds), *The Law and Economics of Class Actions in Europe – Lessons from America* (Edward Elgar, 2012) 342–50.

Franck, J, 'Pour une véritable réparation du préjudice causé à l'intérêt collectif des consommateurs' in *Études de droit de la consommation – Liber amicorum Jean Calais-Auloy* (Dalloz, 2004) 409–19.

—— and Foucher, P, 'Expériences concrètes de résolution de litiges transfrontières dans le domaine de la publicité' in B Stauder (ed), *Les actions collectives transfrontières des organisations de consommateurs – Droit international et droit du marché intérieur*, Actes du colloque organisé avec le Centre d'études juridiques européennes (Schultess, 1997) 83–108.

Freer, RD, *Civil Procedure*, 3rd edn (Wolters Kluwer, 2012).

Garberí Llobregat, J et al, *Los Procesos Civiles*, vols 1 and 2, 2nd edn (Thomson Reuters Aranzadi, 2011).

García Rubio, MP and Otero Crespo, M, 'Rebuilding the Pillars of Collective Litigation in Light of the Commission Recommendation: The Spanish Approach to Collective Redress' in E Lein et al (eds), *Collective Redress in Europe – Why and How?* (The British Institute of International and Comparative Law, 2015) 133–51.

Garcimartín Alférez, FJ, *Derecho Internacional Privado*, 3rd edn (Civitas, 2016).
—— 'Prorogation of Jurisdiction' in A Dickinson and E Lein (eds), *The Brussels I Regulation Recast* (Oxford University Press, 2015) 277–306.
Garner, BA, *Black's Law Dictionary*, 9th edn (Thomson Reuters, 2009).
Gascón Inchausti, F, 'Specific Problems of Cross-Border Consumer ADR: What Solutions?' in M Stürner et al (eds), *The Role of Consumer ADR in the Administration of Justice* (Sellier European Law Publishers, 2015) 31–65.
—— *Tutela Judicial de los Consumidores y Transacciones Colectivas* (Thomson Reuters-Civitas, 2010).
Gaudemet-Tallon, H, *Compétence et exécution des jugements en Europe – Règlement 44/2001, Convention de Bruxelles (1968) et de Lugano (1988 et 2007)*, 4th edn (Lextenso éditions, 2010).
—— *Recherches sur les origines de l'article 14 du code civil – Contribution à l'histoire de la compétence judiciaire internationale* (Presses universitaires de France, 1964).
Geiger, C, *Kollektiver Rechtsschutz im Zivilprozess – Die Gruppenklage zur Durchsetzung von Massenschäden und ihre Auswirkungen* (Mohr Siebeck, 2015).
Gidi, A, 'Notas Críticas Al Anteproyecto De Código Modelo De Procesos Colectivos Del Instituto Iberoamericano De Derecho Procesal' in A Gidi and E Ferrer (eds), *La Tutela de los Derechos Difusos, Colectivos e Individuales Homogéneos*, 2nd edn (Editorial Porrúa, 2014) 405–20.
Gonçalves Borges, C and Serra Baptista, M, 'Portugal' in PG Karlsgodt (ed), *World Class Actions: A Guide to Group and Representative Actions around the Globe* (Oxford University Press, 2012) 312–22.
González Beilfuss, C and Añoveros Terradas, B, 'Compensatory Consumer Collective Redress and the Brussels I Regulation (Recast)' in A Nuyts and NE Hatzimihail (eds), *Cross-Border Class Actions: The European Way* (Sellier European Law Publishers, 2014) 241–58.
González Campos, J, 'Diversification, spécialisation, flexibilisation et matérialisation des règles de droit international privé' in *Collected Courses of The Hague Academy of International Law*, Tome 287 (Martinus Nijhoff Publishers, 2000).
Gorywoda, L et al, 'Introduction: Market Regulation, Judicial Cooperation and Collective Redress' in A Nuyts and NE Hatzimihail (eds), *Cross-Border Class Actions: The European Way* (Sellier European Law Publishers, 2014) 1–56.
Guinchard, S et al, *Procédure civile – Droit interne et droit de l'Union européenne*, 32nd edn (Dalloz, 2014).
Gutiérrez de Cabiedes Hidalgo, P, 'Artículo 11' in F Cordón Moreno et al (eds), *Comentarios a la Ley de Enjuiciamiento Civil*, vol 1, 2nd edn (Thomson Reuters, 2011) 185–234.
—— and de Caviedes, H, *La Tutela Jurisdiccional de los Intereses Supraindividuales: Colectivos y Difusos* (Aranzadi, 1999).
Halfmeier, A, 'Litigation Without an End? The *Deutsche Telekom* Case and the German Approach to Private Enforcement of Securities Law' in D Hensler et al (eds), *Class Actions in Context – How Culture, Economics and Politics Shape Collective Litigation* (Edward Elgar, 2016) 279–98.
Harbour, L and Evans, J, 'United Kingdom' in PG Karlsgodt (ed), *World Class Actions: A Guide to Group and Representative Actions around the Globe* (Oxford University Press, 2012) 169–85.
Hazard, GC and Taruffo, M, *American Civil Procedure – An introduction* (Yale University Press, 1993).
Heinrich, C, '§ 32b' in HJ Musielak (ed), *Kommentar zur Zivilprozessordnung*, 7th edn (Verlag Franz Vahlen, 2009) 169–72.
Hensler, DR et al, *Class Action Dilemmas – Public Goals for Private Gains* (Rand Institute for Civil Justice, 2000), available at www.rand.org/pubs/monograph_reports/MR969.html.
Heredia Cervantes, I, 'Artículo 8' in JP Pérez-Llorca et al (eds), *Comentario al Reglamento (UE) nº 1215/2012 relativo a la competencia judicial, el reconocimiento y la ejecución de resoluciones judiciales en materia civil y mercantil* (Thomson Reuters Aranzadi, 2016) 289–90.
Herranz Ballesteros, M, *El forum non conveniens y su adaptación al ámbito europeo* (Valencia, Tirant lo blanch, 2011).
Hess, B, 'Collective Redress and the Jurisdictional Model of the Brussels I Regulation' in A Nuyts and NE Hatzimihail (eds), *Cross-Border Class Actions: The European Way* (Sellier European Law Publishers, 2014) 59–68.

—— *Europäisches Zivilprozessrecht: ein Lehrbuch* (CF Müller, 2010).
—— 'Procedural Harmonisation in a European Context' in XE Kramer and CH van Rhee (eds), *Civil Litigation in a Globalising World* (T.M.C. Asser Press, 2012) 159–73.
—— et al, *Kölner Kommentar zum KapMuG*, 2nd edn (Carl Heymanns Verlag, 2014).
Hodges, C, *Multi-Party Actions* (Oxford University Press, 2001).
—— *The Reform of Class and Representative Actions in European Legal Systems*, Studies of the Oxford Institute of European and Comparative Law, vol 8 (Hart Publishing, 2008).
—— 'Collectivism: Evaluating the Effectiveness of Public and Private Models for Regulating Consumer Protection' in WH van Boom and M Loos (eds), *Collective Enforcement of Consumer Law* (Europa Law Publishing, 2007) 207–28.
—— et al, *Consumer ADR in Europe* (CH Beck/Hart, 2012).
—— et al, *The Costs and Funding of Civil Litigation – A Comparative Perspective* (CH Beck/Hart, 2010).
Holher, A, 'Open-End and Closed-End Funds and Real Estate Investment Trusts' in M Mütze et al (eds), *Real Estate Investments in Germany – Transactions and Development* (Springer, 2007) 279–97.
Homburger, A, 'Private Suits in the Public Interest in the United States of America' in A Homburger and H Kötz (eds), *Klagen Privater im öffentlichen Interesse*, Arbeiten zur Rechtsvergleichung, vol 68 (Metzner, 1975) 9–68.
Just, C, 'Legal Framework for Real Estate Asset Classes' in T Just and W Maennig (eds), *Understanding German Real Estate Markets*, 2nd edn (Springer, 2016) 27–41, 129.
Kagan, RA, *Adversarial Legalism – The American Way of Law* (Harvard University Press, 2003).
Karlsgodt, PG, World Class Actions: A Guide to Group and Representative Actions around the Globe (Oxford University Press, 2012).
Keske, SE, *Group Litigation in European Competition Law – A Law and Economic Perspective* (Intersentia, 2010).
——, 'Financing and Group Litigation' in M Tuil and L Visscher (eds), *New Trends in Financing Civil Litigation in Europe – A Legal, Empirical, and Economic Analysis* (Edward Elgar, 2010) 57–91.
Kessedjian, C, 'Le principe de proximité vingt ans après' in *Mélanges en l'honneur de Paul Lagarde – Le droit international privé: esprit et méthode* (Dalloz, 2005) 507–21.
——, 'The ILA Rio Resolution on Transnational Group Actions' in D Fairgrieve and E Lein (eds), *Extraterritoriality and Collective Redress* (Oxford University Press, 2012) 233–43.
Kiurunen, P, 'Finland' in PG Karlsgodt (ed), *World Class Actions: A Guide to Group and Representative Actions around the Globe* (Oxford University Press, 2012) 214–28.
Klausegger, C, 'Austria' in PG Karlsgodt (ed), *World Class Actions: A Guide to Group and Representative Actions around the Globe* (Oxford University Press, 2012) 252–63.
Klonoff, RH, *Class Actions and Other Multi-Party Litigation in a Nutshell*, 3rd edn (Thomson West, 2007).
Kotzur, M, 'Article 81 TFEU' in R Geiger et al (eds), *European Union Treaties – A Commentary* (CH Beck/Hart, 2015) 437–42.
Kramer, XE, 'Harmonisation of Civil Procedure and the Interaction with Private International Law' in XE Kramer and CH van Rhee (eds), *Civil Litigation in a Globalising World* (T.M.C. Asser Press, 2012) 121–39.
Kropholler, J and von Hein, J, *Europäisches Zivilprozessrecht – Kommentar zu EuGVO, Lugano-Übereinkommen 2007, EuVTVO, EuMVVO und EuGFVO*, 9th edn (Verlag Recht und Wirtschaft GmbH, 2011).
Kulski, R, 'Polish Perspectives and Provisions on Group Proceedings' in V Harsági and CH van Rhee (eds), *Multi-Party Redress Mechanisms in Europe: Squeaking Mice?* (Intersentia, 2014) 225–41.
Lagarde, P, 'Le principe de proximité dans le droit international privé contemporain; cours général de droit international privé' in *Collected Courses of The Hague Academy of International Law*, Tome 196 (Martinus Nijhoff Publishers, 1986).
Laperche, B et al (eds), *Innovation, Evolution and Economic Change – New Ideas in the Tradition of Galbraith* (Edward Elgar, 2006).

Leclerc, M, *Les class actions, du droit américain au droit européen – Propos illustrés au regard du droit de la concurrence* (Editions Larcier, 2012).
Lehmann, M, 'Special Jurisdiction (Article 7(1))' in A Dickinson and E Lein (eds), *The Brussels I Regulation Recast* (Oxford University Press, 2015) 142–55.
Leible, S, 'Art. 81 AEUV' in R Streinz (ed), *Vertrag über die Europäische Union und Vertrag über die Arbeitsweise der Europäischen Union*, 3rd edn (CH Beck, 2018), available on beck-online.
Lein, E, 'Cross-Border Collective Redress and Jurisdiction under Brussels I: A Mismatch' in D Fairgrieve and E Lein (eds), *Extraterritoriality and Collective Redress* (Oxford University Press, 2012) 129–42.
——, 'Jurisdiction and Applicable Law in Cross-Border Mass Litigation' in F Pocar et al (eds), *Recasting Brussels I*, Studi e Pubblicazioni della Rivista di Diritto Internazionale Privato e Processuale 76 (CEDAM, 2012) 159–72.
van Lith, H, *The Dutch Collective Settlements Act and Private International Law* (2010), available at ec.europa.eu/competition/consultations/2011_collective_redress/saw_annex_en.pdf.
López Sánchez, J, *El sistema de las* class actions *en los Estados Unidos de América* (Editorial Comares, 2011).
Lurger, B, 'Art. 169 AEUV' in R Streinz (ed), *Vertrag über die Europäische Union une Vertrag über die Arbeitsweise der Europäischen Union*, 3rd edn (CH Beck, 2018), available on beck-online.
Magnus, U and Mankowski, P, *Brussels I Regulation, European Commentaries on Private International Law*, 2nd edn (Sellier European Law Publishers, 2011).
Malaga, F, 'Spain' in PG Karlsgodt (ed), *World Class Actions: A Guide to Group and Representative Actions around the Globe* (Oxford University Press, 2012) 301–11.
Maletić, I, *The Law and Policy of Harmonisation in Europe's Internal Market* (Edward Elgar, 2013).
Marcus, RL, 'The Big Bad Wolf: American Class Actions' in V Harsági and CH van Rhee (eds), *Multi-Party Redress Mechanisms in Europe: Squeaking Mice?* (Intersentia, 2014) 35–51.
Mayer, P and Heuzé, V, *Droit international privé* (Lextenso éditions, 2010).
McLaughlin, JM, *McLaughlin on Class Actions: Law and Practice* (Thomson West, October 2016 update), available on WestlawNext.
Micklitz, HW, 'Collective Private Enforcement of Consumer Law: The Key Questions' in WH van Boom and M Loos (eds), *Collective Enforcement of Consumer Law: Securing Compliance in Europe through Private Group Action and Public Authority Intervention* (Europa Law Publishing, 2007) 13–33.
Morin, A, 'Les actions collectives transfrontières. Rapport français' in B Stauder (ed), *Les actions collectives transfrontières des organisations de consommateurs – Droit international et droit du marché intérieur*, Actes du colloque organisé avec le Centre d'études juridiques européennes (Schultess, 1997) 69–82.
Mulheron, R, *The Class Action in Common Law Legal Systems – A Comparative Perspective* (Hart Publishing, 2004).
Niboyet, ML and de Geouffre de La Pradelle, G, *Droit international privé* (Lextenso éditions, 2011).
Nowak, JT, 'The New Belgian Law on Consumer Collective Redress and Compliance with EU Law Requirements' in E Lein et al (eds), *Collective Redress in Europe – Why and How?* (The British Institute of International and Comparative Law, 2015) 169–201.
Nuyts, A, 'The Consolidation of Collective Claims Under Brussels I' in A Nuyts and NE Hatzimihail (eds), *Cross-Border Class Actions: The European Way* (Sellier European Law Publishers, 2014) 69–83.
Oakley, JB and Amar, VD, *American Civil Procedure: A Guide to Civil Adjudication in US Courts* (Kluwer Law International, 2009).
Peers, S, *EU Justice and Home Affairs Law* (Oxford University Press, 2011).
Picot, Y, *Code de la consommation commenté* (Dalloz, 2012).
Pinna, A, 'The Assignment and Securitization of Liability Claims' in M Tuil and L Visscher (eds), *New Trends in Financing Civil Litigation in Europe – A Legal, Empirical, and Economic Analysis* (Edward Elgar, 2010) 109–30.
Pinto Monteiro, AP and Judice, JM, 'Class Actions & Arbitration in the European Union – Portugal' in *Estudos em Homenagem a Miguel Galvão Teles*, vol 2 (Coimbra, Almedina, 2012) 189–205.

Planchadell Gargallo, A, *Las 'acciones colectivas' en el ordenamiento jurídico español* (Tirant lo Blanch, 2014).

Posnow-Wurm, M, 'Rethinking Collective Redress, Consumer Protection and Brussels I Regulation' in A Nuyts and NE Hatzimihail (eds), *Cross-Border Class Actions: The European Way* (Sellier European Law Publishers, 2014) 259–76.

Radicati di Brozolo, LG, 'Class Arbitration in Europe?' in A Nuyts and NE Hatzimihail (eds), *Cross-Border Class Actions: The European Way* (Sellier European Law Publishers, 2014) 209–22.

Rechberger, WH, 'Verbandsklagen, Musterprozesse und „Sammelklagen" -Möglichkeiten kollektiven Rechtsschutzes im österreichischen Zivilprozess' in C Fischer-Czermak et al (eds), *Festschrift Rudolf Welser zum 65. Geburtstag* (MANZ Verlag, 2004) 871–88.

Reher, T, 'Specific Issues in Cross-Border EU Competition Law Actions Brought by Multiple Claimants in a German Context' in M Danov et al (eds), *Cross-Border EU Competition Law Actions* (Hart Publishing, 2013) 159–65.

Reich, N, 'Economic Law, Consumer Interests and EU Integration' in HW Micklitz et al (eds), *Understanding EU Consumer Law* (Intersentia, 2009) 1–60, 263–315, 317–62.

Requejo Isidro, M and Otero Crespo, M, 'Collective Redress in Spain: Recognition and Enforcement of Class Action Judgments and Class Settlements' in D Fairgrieve and E Lein (eds), *Extraterritoriality and Collective Redress* (Oxford University Press, 2012) 309–31.

van Rhee, CH and Tzankova, I, 'Collective Redress in The Netherlands' in V Harsági and CH van Rhee (eds), *Multi-Party Redress Mechanisms in Europe: Squeaking Mice?* (Intersentia, 2014) 209–24.

Rigaux, F and Fallon, M, *Droit international privé*, 3rd edn (Larcier, 2005).

Röckrath, L, 'Germany' in PG Karlsgodt (ed), *World Class Actions: A Guide to Group and Representative Actions around the Globe* (Oxford University Press, 2012) 241–51.

Rubenstein, WB, *Newberg on Class Actions*, 5th edn (Eagen, West, December 2016 update), available on WestlawNext.

Rühl, G, 'Aussergerichtliche Streitbeilegung ausser Rand und Band? Zur Kompetenz des europäischen Gesetzgebers zum Erlass der Richtlinie über alternative Streitbeilegung und der Verordnung über Online-Streitbeilegung' in T Ackermann and J Köndgen (eds), *Privat- und Wirtschaftsrecht in Europa*, Festschrift für Wulf-Henning Roth zum 70. Geburtstag (CH Beck, 2015) 459–87.

Safjan, M et al, 'Taking the Collective Interese of Consumers Seriously: A View from Poland' in F Cafaggi and HW Micklitz (eds), *New Frontiers of Consumer Protection: The Interplay Between Private and Public Enforcement* (Intersentia, 2009) 171–206.

Sánchez González, MP, 'Los interéses difusos bajo la óptica del derecho civil' in E Carbonell Porras and R Cabrera Mercado (eds), *Intereses Colectivos y Legitimación Activa* (Thomson Reuters, 2014) 137–61.

Schlesinger, P, 'Introduzione' in *XXV Convegni di studio 'Adolfo Beria di Argentine' Problemi attuai di diritto e procedura civile: Class action: il nuovo volto della tutela collettiva in Italia* (Giuffrè Editore, 2011) 9–22.

Scoles, FE et al, *Conflict of Laws*, 3rd edn (West Group, 2000).

Shavell, S, *Foundations of Economic Analysis of Law* (The Belknap Press of Harvard University Press, 2004).

Sherry, S and Tidmarsh, J, *Essentials Civil Procedure* (Aspen Publishers, 2007).

Sibony, AL, 'A Behavioural Perspective on Collective Redress' in E Lein et al (eds), *Collective Redress in Europe – Why and How?* (The British Institute of International and Comparative Law, 2015) 47–57.

Silberman, LJ et al, *Civil Procedure: Theory and Practice*, 4th edn (Wolters Kluwer, 2013).

Silvestri, E, 'Class Actions in Italy: Great Expectations, Big Disappointment' in V Harsági and CH van Rhee (eds), *Multi-Party Redress Mechanisms in Europe: Squeaking Mice?* (Intersentia, 2014) 197–208.

Sparrman, G and Göransson, L, 'Sweden' in PG Karlsgodt (ed), *World Class Actions: A Guide to Group and Representative Actions around the Globe* (Oxford University Press, 2012) 198–213.

Stadler, A, 'Die grenzüberschreitende Durchsetzbarkeit von Sammelklagen' in M Casper et al (eds), *Auf dem Weg zu einer europäischen Sammelklage?* (Sellier European Law Publishers, 2009) 149–70.

Stefanelli, JN, 'Parallel Litigation and Cross-Border Collective Actions' in D Fairgrieve and E Lein (eds), *Extraterritoriality and Collective Redress* (Oxford University Press, 2012) 143–70.

Storskrubb, E, *Civil Procedure and EU Law – A Policy Area Uncovered* (Oxford University Press, 2008).
Stürner, M, 'ADR and Adjudication by State Courts: Competitors or Complements?' in M Stürner et al (eds), *The Role of Consumer ADR in the Administration of Justice* (Sellier European Law Publishers, 2015) 11–29.
Subrin, SN and Woo, MYK, *Litigating in America – Civil Procedure in Context* (Aspen Publishers, 2006).
Taruffo, M, 'La tutela collettiva nell'ordinamento italiano: lineamenti generali' in *XXV Convegni di studio 'Adolfo Beria di Argentine' Problemi attuai di diritto e procedura civile: Class action: il nuovo volto della tutela collettiva in Italia* (Giuffrè Editore, 2011) 25–40.
Tilp, AW and Roth, TA, 'The German Capital Market Model Proceedings Act as Illustrated by the Example of the Frankfurt Deutsche Telekom Claims' in WH van Boom and G Wagner (eds), *Mass Torts in Europe: Cases and Reflections* (Walter de Gruyter GmbH, 2014) 131–42.
Tzankova, I and van Lith, H, 'Class Actions and Class Settlements Going Global: the Netherlands' in D Fairgrieve and E Lein (eds), *Extraterritoriality and Collective Redress* (Oxford University Press, 2012) 67–94.
Vanleenhove, C, *Punitive Damages in Private International Law: Lessons for the European Union* (Intersentia, 2016).
Virgós Soriano, M and Garcimartín Alférez, FJ, *Derecho Procesal Civil Internacional* (Civitas, 2007).
Visscher, L, 'A Law and Economics View on Harmonisation of Procedural Law' in XE Kramer and CH van Rhee (eds), *Civil Litigation in a Globalising World* (T.M.C. Asser Press, 2012) 65–91.
—— and Schepens, T, 'A Law and Economics Approach to Cost Shifting, Fee Arrangements, and Legal Expense Insurance' in M Tuil and L Visscher (eds), *New Trends in Financing Civil Litigation in Europe – A Legal, Empirical, and Economic Analysis* (Edward Elgar, 2010) 7–32.
Voet, S, 'The Crux of the Matter: Funding and Financing Collective Redress Mechanisms' in B Hess et al (eds), *EU Civil Justice: Current Issues and Future Outlook*, Swedish Studies in European Law, vol 7 (Bloomsbury, 2016) 201–22.
von Mehren, A, 'Theory and Practice of Adjudicatory Authority in Private International Law: a Comparative Study of the Doctrine, Policies and Practices of Common- and Civil-Law Systems: General Course on Private International Law (1996)' in *Collected Courses of The Hague Academy of International Law*, Tome 295 (Martinus Nijhoff Publishers, 2002) 68–94.
Weatherill, S, *EU Consumer Law and Policy* (Elgar European Law, 2005).
Wrbka, S, *European Consumer Access to Justice Revisited* (Cambridge University Press, 2015).
Wright, CA and Miller, AR, *Federal Practice & Procedure (Wright & Miller)* (Thomson Reuters West, April 2017 update), available on WestlawNext.
Yeazell, SC, *Civil Procedure*, 8th edn (Aspen Casebook Series, 2012).
——, *From Medieval Group Litigation to the Modern Class Action* (Yale University Press, 1987).
Yuthayotin, S, Access to Justice in Transnational B2C E-Commerce – A Multidimensional Analysis of Consumer Protection Mechanisms (Springer, 2015).
Zuckerman, A, *Zuckerman on Civil Procedure – Principles of Practice*, 2nd edn (Sweet & Maxwell, 2006).

Articles and Working Papers

Alexander, JC, 'Contingent Fees and Class Actions' (1998) 47(2) *DePaul Law Review* 347–62.
Amrani-Mekki, S, 'L'action de groupe du 21 siècle. Un modèle réduit et réducteur ?' (2015) 45 *La Semaine Juridique* 2029–31.
Andreeva, A, 'Class Action Fairness Act of 2005: The Eight-Year Saga is Finally Over' (2005) 59 *University of Miami Law Review* 385–412.
Añoveros Terradas, B, 'Consumer Collective Redress under the Brussels I Regulation Recast in the Light of the Commission's Common Principles' (2015) 11(1) *Journal of Private International* Law 143–162.
Arons, T, 'Recognition of US Class Actions or Settlements in Europe' (2015) 3 *European Company and Financial Law Review* 462–87.
—— and van Boom, WH, 'Beyond Tulips and Cheese: Exporting Mass Securities Claim Settlements from The Netherlands' (2010) 21 (6) *European Business Law Review* 857–83.

de Bandt, A, 'La négociation et la médiation dans le cadre de l'action en réparation collective' (2014) 6 *Revue de Droit Commercial Belge* 591–605.

Bassett, DL, 'Just Go Away: Representation, Due Process, and Preclusion in Class Actions' (2009) 5 *Brigham Young University Law Review* 1079–126.

Bell, A, 'The Negative Declaration in Transnational Litigation' (1995) 111 *Law Quarterly Review* 674–95.

van den Bergh, R and Visscher, L, 'The Preventive Function of Collective Actions for Damages in Consumer Law' (2008) 1(2) *Erasmus Law Review* 5–30.

Berlioz, P, 'La notion de fourniture de services au sens de l'article 5-1 b) du Règlement de « Bruxelles I »' (2008) 135(3) *Journal du Droit International* 675–717.

Bermann, GA, 'Parallel Litigation: Is Convergence Possible?' (2011) 21 *Yearbook of Private International Law* 21–36.

Biard, A and Amaro, R, Resolving Mass Claims in France: Toolbox & Experience, Working Paper Series No 2016/5, available at https://www.researchgate.net/publication/312173326_Resolving_Mass_Claims_in_France_Toolbox_Experience/download.

Boré, L, 'Les prémisses d'une consécration générale du droit d'action des associations au plan civil' (2008) 47 *Revue Lamy de Droit Civil* 17–18.

Brendan Day, J, 'My Lawyer Went to Court and all I Got Was This Lousy Coupon! The Class Action Fairness Act's Inadequate Provision for Judicial Scrutiny over Proposed Coupon Settlements' (2008) 38 *Seton Hall Law Review* 1085–129.

Bronsteen, J, 'Class Action Settlements: An Opt-In Proposal' (2005) 4 *University of Illinois Law Review* 903–28.

Budnitz, ME, 'The High Cost of Mandatory Consumer Arbitration' (2004) 67 *Law and Contemporary Problems* 133–66.

Burns, JW, 'Decorative Figureheads: Eliminating Class Representatives in Class Actions' (1990) 42 *The Hastings Law Journal* 165–202.

Buschkin, I, 'The Viability of Class Action Lawsuits in a Globalized Economy – Permitting Foreign Claimants to Be Members of Class Action Lawsuits in the U.S. Federal Courts' (2005) 90(6) *Cornell Law Review* 1563–600.

Buxbaum, HL, 'Class Actions, Conflict, and the Global Economy' (2014) 21(2) *Indiana Journal of Global Legal Studies* 585–97.

Calcagno, N, '"Italian Class Action": The Beginning' (2011), available at papers.ssrn.com.

Campuzano Díaz, B, 'El TJUE de nuevo con el foro de la pluralidad de demandados. Nota a la sentencia de 1 de diciembre de 2011 en el asunto Painer' (2012) 4(1) *Cuadernos de Derecho Transnacional* 245–55.

Caponi, R, 'Collective Redress in Europe: Current Developments of "Class Action" Suits in Italy' (2011) 16 *Zeitschrift für Zivilprozess International* 1–17.

Cappelletti, M, 'Vindicating the Public Interest through the Courts: A Comparativist's Contribution' (1975–76) 25 *Buffalo Law Review* 643–90.

Carballo, L, 'Protección de inversores, acciones colectivas y Derecho internacional privado' (2011) 37 *Revista de derecho de sociedades* 207–26.

Cataldi, G, 'La nuova azione di classe' (2009) 3 *Consumatori, Diritti e Mercato* 129–42.

—— 'Le problematiche processuali dell'azione collettiva' (2008) 2 *Consumatori, Diritti e Mercato* 21–32.

Coffee, JC, 'Rescuing the Private Attorney General: Why the Model of the Lawyer as Bounty Hunter is Not Working' (1983) 42(2) *Maryland Law Review* 215–88.

Collins, L, 'Negative Declarations and the Brussels Convention' (1992) 108 *Law Quarterly Review* 545–49.

Cortes, P, 'The Impact of EU law in the ADR Landscape in Italy, Spain and the UK: Time for Change or Missed Opportunity' (2015) 16 *ERA Forum* 125–47.

Dam, K, 'Class Actions: Efficiency, Compensation, Deterrence and Conflict of Interest' (1975) 4 *The Journal of Legal Studies* 47–73.

Danov, M, 'The Brussels I Regulation: Cross-Border Collective Redress Proceedings and Judgments' (2010) 6(2) *Journal of Private International Law* 359–93.

Dayagi-Epstein, O, 'Representation of Consumer Interest by Consumer Associations – Salvation for the Masses?' (2007) 3(2) *The Competition Law Review* 209–49.
Downs, HM, 'Federal Class Actions: Diminished Protection for the Class and the Class and the Case for Reform' (1994) 73 *Nebraska Law Review* 646–711.
Drahozal, CR, 'Arbitration Costs and Forum Accessibility: Empirical Evidence' (2008) 41(4) *University of Michigan Journal of Law Reform* 813–41.
Eidenmüller, H and Engel, M, 'Die Schlichtungsfalle: Verbraucherrechtsdurchsetzung nach der ADR-Richtlinie und der ODR-Verordnung der EU' (2013) 34(36) *Zeitschrift für Wirtschaftsrecht* 1704–09.
Eisenberg, T and Hill, E, 'Arbitration and Litigation of Employment Claims: An Empirical Comparison' (2004) *Dispute Resolution Journal* 44–55.
—— and Miller, GP, 'The Role of Opt-Outs and Objectors in Class Action Litigation: Theoretical and Empirical Issues' (2004) 57(5) *Vanderbilt Law Review* 1529–67.
Emons, W, 'Conditional versus Contingent Fees' (2007) 59(1) *Oxford Economics Papers* 1–14, available at www.researchgate.net.
Erichson, HM, 'CAFA's Impact on Class Action Lawyers' (2008) 156 *University of Pennsylvania Law Review* 1593–627.
Farmer, MB, 'Mandatory and Fair? A Better System of Mandatory Arbitration' (2012) 121 *Yale Law Journal* 2346–94.
Feess, E and Halfmeier, A, 'The German Capital Markets Model Case Act (KapMuG) – A European Role Model for Increasing the Efficiency of Capital Market? Analysis and Suggestions for Reform', available at papers.ssrn.com.
Fiorio, P, 'L'azione di classe nel nuovo art. 140bis e gli obiettivi di deterrenza e di accesso alla giustizia dei consumatori' (2009) 172, available at www.ilcaso.it.
Fitzpatrick, BT, 'Do Class Action Lawyers Make Too Little?' (2010) 158 *University of Pennsylvania Law Review* 2043–83.
—— and Gilbert, RC, 'An Empirical Look at Compensation in Consumer Class Actions', Vanderbilt Public Law Research Paper No 15-3 and Vanderbilt Law and Economics Research Paper No 15-6 (2015), available at papers.ssrn.com.
Frankel, ME, 'Amended Rule 23 From a Judge's Point of View' (1966) 32 *Antitrust Law Journal* 295–305.
Frenz, W and Ehlenz, C, 'Rechtsangleichung über Art. 114 AEUV und Grenzen gem. Art. 5 EUV nach Lissabon' (2011) 16 *Europäische Zeitschrift für Wirtschaftsrecht* 623–26.
Garcimartín, FJ and Sánchez, S, 'El nuevo Reglamento Bruselas I: qué ha cambiado en el ámbito de la competencia judicial' (2013) 48 *Revista española de derecho europeo* 9–35.
Garth, BG and Cappelletti, M, 'Access to Justice: The Newest Wave in the Worldwide Movement to Make Rights Effective' (1978) 27 *Buffalo Law Review* 181–292.
Gascón Inchausti, F, 'Acciones colectivas e inhibitorias para la protección de los consumidores en el proceso civil español: el papel de las asociaciones de consumidores' (2005), available at https://eprints.ucm.es.
—— 'La protección de los consumidores en el proceso civil español' (2005), available at eprints.ucm.es.
—— 'Reconocimiento y ejecución de resoluciones judiciales extranjeras en la ley de cooperación jurídica internacional en materia civil' (2015) 7(2) *Cuadernos de Derecho Transnacional* 158–87.
Gaudet, R, 'Turning a Blind Eye: the Commission's Rejection of Opt-out Class Actions Overlooks Swedish, Norwegian, Danish and Dutch Experience' (2009) 30 (3) *European Competition Law Review* 107–17.
Geber, F, 'Rechtsangleichung nach Art. 114 AEUV im Spiegel der EuGH-Rechtsprechung' (2014) 1 *Juristische Schulung* 20–24.
Giussani, A, 'L'azione di classe aspetti processuali' (2013) 67(1) *Rivista trimestrale di diritto e procedura civile* 341–56.
Gómez Ligüerre, C and Ruiz García, CA, 'Honorarios de abogados, competencia y pacto de quota litis' (2009) 1 *InDret*, available at www.indret.com.
Greenberg, J, 'Civil Rights Class Actions: Procedural Means of Obtaining Substance' (1997) 39 *Arizona Law Review* 575–86.

Grušić, U, 'Jurisdiction in Complex Contracts under the Brussels I Regulation' (2011) 7(2) *Journal of Private International Law* 321–40.
Guernelli, M, 'La nuova azione di classe: profili processuali' (2010) 64(3) *Rivista trimestrale di diritto e procedura civile* 917–34.
Haar, B, 'Investors Protection Through Model Case Procedures – Implementing Collective Goals and Individual Rights Under the 2012 Amendment to the German Capital Markets Model Case Act (KapMuG)' (2014) 15 *European Business Organization Law Review* 83–105.
Halfmeier, A, 'Recognition of a WCAM Settlement in Germany' (2012) 1 *Nederlands Internationaal Privaatrecht* 176–84.
Hantler, SB and Norton, RE, 'Coupon Settlements: The Emperor's Clothes of Class Actions' (2005) 18 *Georgetown Journal of Legal Ethics* 1343–58.
Hay, B and Rosenberg, D, 'Sweetheart and Blackmail Settlements in Class Actions: Reality and Remedy' (2000) 75(4) *Notre Dame Law Review* 1377–408.
van der Heijden, MJ, 'Class Actions/les actions collectives' (2010) 14 (3) *Electronic Journal of Comparative Law* 1–17, available at www.ejcl.org.
Heil, B and Lee, B, 'The Role of Private Litigation' *Comparative Corporate Governance and Financial Regulation*, Paper 7, available at scholarship.law.upenn.edu/fisch_2016/7.
Henderson, WD, 'Clear Sailing Agreements: A Special Form of Collusion in Class Action Settlements' (2003) 77(4) *Tulane Law Review* 813–38.
Hensler, DR and Peterson, MA, 'Understanding Mass Personal Injury Litigation: A Socio-Legal Analysis' (1993) 59 *Brooklyn Law Review* 961–1063.
Hermans, R and de B Leuveling Tjeenk, J, 'International Class Action Settlements in the Netherlands since *Converium*' in *The International Comparative Legal Guide to: Class & Group Actions 2016*, available at iclg.com.
Hess, B, 'Cross-Border Collective Litigation and the Regulation Brussels I' (2010) 2 *Praxis des Internationalen Privat- und Verfahrensrechts* 116–21.
—— 'Der Regierungsentwurf für ein Kapitalanlegermusterverfahrensgesetz – eine kritische Bestandsaufnahme' (2004) 48 *Zeitschrift für Wirtschafts- und Bankrecht – Wertpapiermitteilungen Teil IV* 2329–34.
Higgins, A and Zuckerman, A, 'Class Actions come to England – More Access to Justice and More of a Compensation Culture, but they are Superior to Alternatives' (2016) 35(1) *Civil Justice Quarterly* 1–13.
Hodges, C, 'Collective Redress: A Breakthrough or a Damp Squib?' (2014) 37 (1) *Journal of Consumer Policy* 67–89.
—— 'Current Discussions on Consumer Redress: Collective Redress and ADR' (2012) 13 *ERA Forum* 11–33.
Hoffmann, D, 'Directive "Actions en cessation en matière de protection des intérêts des consommateurs (Dir. 98/27/CE du 19/5/98)"' (2000) 1 *European Review of Private Law* 147–54.
Issacharoff, S, 'Class Action Conflicts' (1997) 30 *U.C. Davis Law Review* 805–33.
Jeretina, U and Uzelac, A, 'Alternative Dispute Resolution for Consumer Cases: Are Divergences and Obstacle to Effective Access to Justice?' (2014) XII(4) *International Public Administration Review* 39–72.
Jiménez Blanco, P, 'El tratamiento de las acciones colectivas en materia de consumidores en el Convenio de Bruselas' (2003) 5709 *Diario La Ley* 1573–83.
Johnson, GW, 'Rule 23 and the Exclusion of Foreign Citizens as Class Members in U.S. Class Actions' (2012) 52(4) *Virginia Journal of International Law* 963–93.
Kanner, A and Nagy, T, 'Exploding the Blackmail Myth: A New Perspective on Class Action Settlements' (2005) 57 *Baylor Law Review* 681–704.
Kerameus, KD, 'Procedural Harmonization in Europe' (1995) 43 *The American Journal of Comparative Law* 401–16.
Kessedjian, C, 'L'action en justice des associations de consommateurs et d'autres organisations représentatives d'intérêts collectifs en Europe' (1997) 2 *Rivista di diritto internazionale privato e processuale* 281–300.

Klauser, A, 'Von der "Sammelklage nach österreichischem Recht" zur echten Gruppenklage' (2005) *Ecolex* 744–47.

Kodek, GE, 'Möglichkeiten zur gesetzlichen Regelung von Massenverfahren im Zivilprozess' (2005) *Ecolex* 751–54.

Kolba, P, 'Die Sammelklage nach össterreichischem Recht im Praxistext – Schadenersatz für Brech-Durchfall-Epidemie' (2009) 4 *ReiseRecht aktuell* 167–69.

——, 'Konsumentenschutz vor und mit der Sammelklage' (2010) *Ecolex* 864–67.

Kramer, XE, 'Securities Collective Action and Private International Law Issues in Dutch WCAM Settlements: Global Aspirations and Regional Boundaries' (2014) 27 *Global Business & Development Law Journal* 235–79.

Krans, B, 'The Dutch Act on Collective Settlement on Mass Damages' (2014) 27 *Global Business & Development Law Journal* 281–301.

Kritzer, HM and Anderson, JK, 'The Arbitration Alternative: A Comparative Analysis of Case Processing Time, Disposition Mode, and Cost in the American Arbitration Association and the Courts' (1983) 8(1) *The Justice System Journal* 6–19.

Kuipers, JJ, 'La loi sur le règlement collectif de dommages de masse aux Pays-Bas et ses ambitions dans l'espace judiciaire européen' (2012) 64(1) *Revue internationale de droit comparé* 213–43.

——, 'Schemes of Arrangement and Voluntary Collective Redress: A Gap in the Brussels I Regulation' (2012) 8(2) *Journal of Private International Law* 225–49.

de Laforcade, A, 'L'évolution du droit d'agir des associations de consommateurs: vers un détachement du droit pénal de leur action en justice' (2011) 4 *Revue trimestrielle de droit commercial et de droit économique* 711–20.

Latz, TW, 'Who Can Tell the Futures? Protecting Settlement Class Action Members Without Notice' (1999) 85 *Virginia Law Review* 531–68.

Leclerc, F, 'Note sur l'arrêt Henkel' (2004) 3 *Journal du droit international* 911–17.

Lindblom, H, 'Group Litigation in Scandinavia' (2009) 10(1) *ERA Forum* 7–35.

Loos, MBM, 'Full Harmonisation as a Regulatory Concept and its Consequences for the National Legal Orders: The Example of the Consumer Rights Directive', Centre for the Study of European Contract Law Working Paper Series No 2010/03, available at papers.ssrn.com.

Macey, JR and Miller, GP, 'The Plaintiffs' Attorney's Role in Class Action and Derivative Litigation: Economic Analysis and Recommendations for Reform' (1991) 58(1) *The University of Chicago Law Review* 1–118.

Marcos Francisco, D, 'Nuevas medidas de defensa de los consumidores en materia de acciones colectivas, asistencia jurídica gratuita, costas y tasas judiciales' (2015) 4 *InDret*, available at www.indret.com.

Marín López, JJ, 'Las acciones de clase en el derecho español' (2001) 3 *InDret*, available at www.indret.com.

McGovern, FE, 'Punitive Damages and Class Actions' (2010) 70 *Louisiana Law Review* 435–62.

Michailidou, C, 'Internationale Zuständigkeit bei vorbeugenden Verbandsklagen' (2003) 3 *Praxis des Internationalen Privat- und Verfahrensrechts* 223–29.

Micklitz, HW, 'Cross-Border Consumer Conflicts – A French-German Experience' (1993) 16 *Journal of Consumer Policy* 411–34.

——, 'Efficacité internationale de l'action en suppression des clauses abusives: point de vue allemand' (2000) 52(4) *Revue internationale de droit comparé* 867–89.

—— and Stadler, A, 'The Development of Collective Legal Actions in Europe, Especially in German Civil Procedure' (2006) 17(5) *European Business Law Review* 1473–503.

de Miguel Asensio, P, 'Ley de la Jurisdicción Voluntaria y Derecho Internacional Privado' (2016) XVI *Anuario Español de Derecho Internacional Privado* 147–97.

Miller, AR, 'Of Frankenstein Monsters and Shining Knights: Myth, Reality, and the "Class Action Problem"' (1979) 92 *Harvard Law Review* 664–94.

Miller, GP, 'Overlapping Class Actions' (1996) 71 *New York University Law Review* 514–46.

——, 'Some Agency Problems in Settlement' (1987) 16 *The Journal of Legal Studies* 189–215.

—— and Singer, LS, 'Nonpecuniary Class Action Settlements' (1997) 60(4) *Law & Contemporary Problems* 97–154.

Molfessis, N, 'L'exorbitance de l'action de groupe à la française' (2014) 16 *Recueil Dalloz* 947–53.

Montesinos García, A, 'Últimas tendencias en la Unión Europea sobre las acciones colectivas de consumo. La posible introducción de fórmulas de ADR' (2014) 12 *Revista electrónica del Departamento de Derecho de la Universidad de La Rioja* 87–112.

Mulheron, R, 'Justice Enhanced: Framing an Opt-Out Class Action for England' (2007) 70 *The Modern Law Review* 550–80.

—— 'Some Difficulties with Group Litigation Orders – and why a Class Action is Superior' (2005) 24 *Civil Justice Quarterly* 40–68.

—— 'The Case for an Opt-out Class Action for European Member States: A Legal and Empirical Analysis' (2009) 15(3) *Columbia Journal of European Law* 409–53.

—— 'The Recognition, and Res Judicata Effect, of a United States Class Actions Judgment in England: A Rebuttal of Vivendi' (2012) 75(2) *Modern Law Review* 180–211.

Mullenix, LS, 'Ending Class Actions As We Know Them: Rethinking the American Class Action Rule' (2014) 64 *Emory Law Journal* 399–449.

Murtagh, MP, 'The Rule 23(b)(3) Superiority Requirement and Transnational Class Actions: Excluding Foreign Class Members in Favor of European Remedies' (2011) 1 *Hastings International and Comparative Law Review* 1–47.

Nagy, CI, 'Comparative Collective Redress from a Law and Economics Perspective: Without Risk There is no Reward!' (2013) 19(3) *Columbia Journal of European Law* 469–98.

——, 'The European Collective Redress Debate After the European Commission's Recommendation – One Step Forward, One Step Back?' (2015) 22(4) *Maastricht Journal of European and Comparative Law* 530–52.

Otero, P, 'A acção popular: configuração e valor no actual direito português' (1999) 59 (3) *Revista da Ordem dos Advogados* 871–93.

Perreau Saussine, L, 'Quelle place pour les class actions dans le règlement de Bruxelles I ?' (2011) 20 *La Semaine Juridique – Édition Générale* 992–96.

Pinna, A, 'Recognition and Res Judicata of US Class Action Judgments in European Legal Systems' (2008) 1(2) *Erasmus Law Review* 31–61.

Power, TJ, 'Tearing Down a House of Coupons: CAFA's Effect on Class Action Settlements' (2012) 9 *University of Saint Thomas Law Journal* 906–32.

Rabiej, JK, 'The Making of Class Action Rule 23 – What Were We Thinking?' (2005) 24 *Mississippi College Law Review* 323–92.

Rebeyrol, V, 'La nouvelle action de groupe' (2014) 16 *Recueil Dalloz* 940–46.

Rémy-Corlay, P, 'Note sur l'arrêt Henkel' (2003) 4 *Revue critique de droit international privé* 690–98.

Rott, P, 'The Protection of Consumers' Interests After the Implementation of the EC Injunctions Directive Into German and English Law' (2001) 24 *Journal of Consumer Policy* 399–439.

Rowe, TD, 'State and Foreign Class-Action Rules and Statutes: Differences From – And Lessons For? – Federal Rule 23' (2007) 35(1) *Western State University Law Review* 101–26.

Rubenstein, WB, 'On What a "Private Attorney General" Is – and Why Does it Matter?' (2004) 57(6) *Vanderbilt Law Review* 2129–73.

Rutledge, PB, 'Whither Arbitration?' (2008) 6 *The Georgetown Journal of Law & Public Policy* 549–90.

Sandstrom Simard, L, 'Foreign Citizens in Transnational Class Actions' (2011) 97(1) *Cornell Law Review* 87–129.

Scheuba, E, '"Sammelklage" – Einklang mit der ZPO erbeten' (2005) 10 *Ecolex* 747–50.

Scheuerman, SB, 'Two Worlds Collide: How the Supreme Court's Recent Punitive Damages Decisions Affect Class Actions' (2008) 60(3) *Baylor Law Review* 880–940.

Schwartz, DS, 'Mandatory Arbitration and Fairness' (2009) 84(3) *Notre Dame Law Review* 1247–341.

Sherman, EF, 'Class Actions and Duplicative Litigation' (1987) 62(3) *Indiana Law Journal* 507–59.

Silver, C, 'We're Scared to Death: Does Class Certification Subject Defendants to Blackmail?' (2003) 78(4) *New York Law Review* 1357–430.

Sorabji, J, 'Reflections on the Commission Communication on Collective Redress' (2014) 17(1) *Irish Journal of European Law* 62–76.

Spencer, AB, 'Class Actions, Heightened Commonality and Declining Access to Justice' (2013) 93 *Boston University Law Review* 441–92.

St Antoine, TJ, 'Mandatory Arbitration: Why It's Better Than It Looks' (2008) 41(4) *University of Michigan Journal of Law Reform* 783–812.

Stadler, A, 'A Test Case in Germany: 16 000 Private Investors vs. Deutsche Telekom' (2009) 10(1) *ERA Forum* 37–50.

—— 'Note' (2007) 7 *Zeitschrift für Zivilprozeß International* 284–92.

—— 'The Commission's Recommendation on Common Principles of Collective Redress and Private International Law Issues' (2013) 4 *Nederlands Internationaal Privaatrecht* 483–88.

Sternlight, JR, 'As Mandatory Binding Arbitration Meets the Class Action, Will the Class Action Survive?' (2000) 42 *William and Mary Law Review* 1–126.

—— 'Creeping Mandatory Arbitration: Is It Just?' (2005) 57 *Stanford Law Review* 1631–75.

Strong, SI, 'Does Class Arbitration "Change the Nature" of Arbitration? Stolt-Nielsen, AT&T, and a Return to First Principles' (2012) 17 *Harvard Negotiation Law Review* 201–71.

—— 'Regulatory Litigation in the European Union: Does the U.S. Class Action have a New Analogue' (2012) 88(2) *Notre Dame Law Review* 899–971.

Stuyck, J, 'Class Actions in Europe? To Opt-In or to Opt-Out, That is the Question' (2009) 20 (4) *European Business Law Review* 483–505.

Sustmann, M and Schmidt-Bendun, R, 'Der Referentenentwurf zur Reform des Kapitalanleger-Musterverfahrensgesetzes (KapMuG)' (2011) 31 *Neue Zeitschrift für Gesellschaftsrecht* 1207–13.

Tang, ZS, 'Consumer Collective Redress in European Private International Law' (2011) 7(1) *Journal of Private International Law* 101–47.

Tulibacka, M, 'Europeanization of Civil Procedures: In Search of a Coherent Approach' (2009) 46 *Common Market Law Review* 1527–65.

Tzankova, I, 'Funding of Mass Disputes: Lessons From the Netherlands' (2012) 8 *Journal of Law Economics and Policy* 549–91.

Tzakas, DPL, 'Effective Collective Redress in Antitrust and Consumer Protection Matters: A Panacea or a Chimera?' (2011) 48(4) *Common Market Law Review* 1125–74.

Välimäki, M, 'Introducing Class Actions in Finland – Lawmaking Without Economic Analysis' (2007), available at papers.ssrn.com.

Veljanovski, C, 'Third-party Litigation Funding in Europe' (2012) 8 *Journal of Law, Economics & Policy* 431–33.

Vernadaki, Z, 'Civil Procedure Harmonization in the EU: Unravelling the Policy Considerations' (2013) 9(2) *Journal of Contemporary European Research* 297–312.

Voet, V, 'Consumer Collective Redress in Belgium: Class Actions to the Rescue?' (2015) 16 *European Business Organization Law Review* 121–43.

—— 'Cultural Dimensions of Group Litigation: The Belgian Case' (2013) 41 *Georgia Journal of International and Comparative Law* 433–79.

—— '"Where the Wild Things Are". Reflections on the State and Future of European Collective Redress' forthcoming in M Loos and A Keirse (eds), Ius Commune Europaeum series, available at papers.ssrn.com.

Wagner, G, 'Private Law Enforcement Through ADR: Wonder Drug or Snake Oil?' (2014) 51 *Common Market Law Review* 165–94.

—— 'The Economics of Harmonisation: The Case for Contract Law' (2002) 39 *Common Market Law Review* 995–1023.

Wasserman, R, 'Transnational Class Actions and Interjurisdictional Preclusion' (2011) 86(1) *Notre Dame Law Review* 313–80.

Weber, F, 'Is ADR the Superior Mechanism for Consumer Contractual Disputes? – An Assessment of the Incentivizing Effects of the ADR Directive' (2015) 38 *Journal of Consumer Policy* 265–85.

Wendt, DH, 'Kollektiver Rechtsschutz in Europa – Kompetenzen, Alternativen und Safeguards' (2011) 22(16) *Europaische Zeitschrift für Wirtschatsrecht* 616–22.

Weston, MA, 'The Death of Class Arbitration After *Concepcion*?' (2012) 60 *Kansas Law Review* 767–94.
—— 'Universes Colliding: The Constitutional Implications of Arbitral Class Actions' (2006) 47(5) *William and Mary Law Review* 1711–79.
Willing, TE and Wheatmann, SR, 'Attorney Choice of Forum in Class Action Litigation: What Difference Does it Make?' (2006) 81(2) *Notre Dame Law Review* 591–654.
Winters, BA, 'Jurisdiction over Unnamed Plaintiffs in Multistate Class Actions' (1985) 73(1) *California Law Review* 181–211.
Yung, JC and 'Alison' Park, SB, 'Volkswagen's Diesel Emissions Scandal' (25.10.2016) *Thunderbird International Business Review*, available at onlinelibrary.wiley.com/doi/10.1002/tie.21876/full.

National Reports and Documents

Baegte, D, 'Class Actions, Group Litigation & Other Forms of Collective Litigation – Germany' (2007), available at globalclassactions.stanford.edu.
Bineva, V and Goleminov, T, 'Evaluation of the Effectiveness and Efficiency of Collective Redress Mechanisms in the European Union – Country Report Bulgaria' (2008), available at ec.europa.eu/consumers/solving_consumer_disputes/judicial_redress/index_en.htm.
Brown, A and Dodds-Smith, I, 'England and Wales' in *The International Comparative Legal Guide to Class and Group Actions* (2017), available at iclg.com.
Camera di comercio, industria, artigianato e agricoltura di Torino, 'Li azioni di clase' (2011) 36, available at www.to.camcom.it/sites/default/files/regolazione-mercato/12301_CCIAATO_952011.pdf.
Cavani, R and Fossati, BA, 'Italy' in The International Comparative Legal Guide to Class and Group Actions (2017), available at iclg.com.
Cerutti, C and Guillaume, M, 'Rapport sur l'action de groupe remis le 16 décembre 2005 aux Ministres de l'économie, des finances et de l'industrie et de la justice, garde des sceaux' (2005), available at www.ladocumentationfrancaise.fr/var/storage/rapports-publics/054004458.pdf.
Competition and Markets Authority, Consumer protection enforcement guidance: CMA58 (2016), available at www.gov.uk/government/publications/consumer-protection-enforcement-guidance-cma58.
Dutch Consultation on a draft bill on Redress of Mass Damages in a Collective Action (2014), available at https://www.internetconsultatie.nl/motiedijksma/document/1177.
Ervo, L et al, 'Country Report: Sweden', available at www.collectiveredress.org.
Fairgrieve, D and Biard, A, 'Country Report: France', available at www.collectiveredress.org.
García Rubio, MP and Otero Crespo, M, 'Country Report: Spain', available at www.collectiveredress.org.
Government of The Netherlands, The Dutch 'Class Action Financial Settlement Act' (WCAM), available at www.rijksoverheid.nl/documenten/richtlijnen/2008/06/24/de-nederlandse-wet-collectieve-afwikkeling-massaschade.
Gutiérrez de Cabiedes Hidalgo, P, 'Group Litigation in Spain – National Report', available at globalclassactions.stanford.edu.
Hammarskiöld & Co, Oxford – Leuven Collective Redress Project – Swedish Report (2016), available at www.law.ox.ac.uk/events/empirical-evidence-collective-redress-europe.
Hellbert, K, 'Austria' in The International Comparative Legal Guide to Class and Group Actions (2017), available at iclg.com.
Hodges, C, 'Country Report: England and Wales', available at globalclassactions.stanford.edu.
—— 'Developments in Collective Redress in the European Union and United Kingdom' (2010), available at globalclassactions.stanford.edu.
—— Oxford – Leuven Collective Redress Project – 'British Report' (2016), available at www.law.ox.ac.uk/events/empirical-evidence-collective-redress-europe.
Howells, G, 'Evaluation of the Effectiveness and Efficiency of Collective Redress Mechanisms in the European Union – Country Report United Kingdom' (2008), available at ec.europa.eu/consumers/solving_consumer_disputes/judicial_redress/index_en.htm.
Institut National de la Consommation, 'L'action de groupe: vers une consécration?' (2005) 1348 *INC Hebdo*, available at www.conso.net/sites/default/files/pdf_abonne/1348-action_groupe_255.pdf.

Katzarsky, A and Georgiev, G, 'Bulgaria' in *The International Comparative Legal Guide to Class and Group Actions* (2013), avaiblable at iclg.com.

Kodek, GE, 'Report: Austria', available at www.collectiveredress.org.

Kos, R and Trzaska, A, 'Poland' in The International Comparative Legal Guide to Class and Group Actions (2017), avaiblable at iclg.com.

L'action de groupe à la française : 'parachever la protection des consommateurs', Information Report (2017), available at www.senat.fr/rap/r09-499/r09-49917.html.

Lein, E, 'Country Report: Germany', available at www.collectiveredress.org.

Lindblom, H, 'National Report: Group Litigation in Sweden' (2007), available at globalclassactions.stanford.edu.

——, 'National Report: Group Litigation in Sweden' (2008), available at globalclassactions.stanford.edu.

Loos, MBM, 'Evaluation of the Effectiveness and Efficiency of Collective Redress Mechanisms in the European Union – Country Report The Netherlands' (2008), available at ec.europa.eu/consumers/solving_consumer_disputes/judicial_redress/index_en.htm.

Magnier, V, 'Class Actions, Group Litigation & Other Forms of Collective Litigation Protocol for National Reporters – France', available at globalclassactions.stanford.edu.

—— and Alleweldt, R, 'Evaluation of the Effectiveness and Efficiency of Collective Redress Mechanisms in the European Union – Country Report France' (2008), available at ec.europa.eu/consumers/solving_consumer_disputes/judicial_redress/index_en.htm.

Micklitz, MC and Poncibò, C, 'Evaluation of the Effectiveness and Efficiency of Collective Redress Mechanisms in the European Union – Country Report Italy' (2008), available at ec.europa.eu/consumers/solving_consumer_disputes/judicial_redress/index_en.htm.

—— and Purnhagen, KP, 'Evaluation of the Effectiveness and Efficiency of Collective Redress Mechanisms in the European Union – Country Report Austria' (2008), available at ec.europa.eu/consumers/solving_consumer_disputes/judicial_redress/index_en.htm.

Mulheron, R, 'Reform of Collective Redress in England and Wales: A Perspective of Need', Report submitted to the Civil Justice Council of England and Wales (2008), available at www.judiciary.gov.uk.

Oxford – Leuven Collective Redress Project – 'Bulgarian Report' (2016), available at www.law.ox.ac.uk/events/empirical-evidence-collective-redress-europe.

Pace, NM, 'Class Actions in the United States of America: An Overview of the Process and the Empirical Literature, National Report 9–10' (2007), available at globalclassactions.stanford.edu.

Persson, AH, 'Evaluation of the Effectiveness and Efficiency of Collective Redress Mechanisms in the European Union – Country Report Sweden' (2008), available at ec.europa.eu/consumers/solving_consumer_disputes/judicial_redress/index_en.htm.

Pimentel, J and Judice, JM, 'Portugal' in *The International Comparative Legal Guide to Class and Group Actions 2014*, available at www.csassociados.pt/xms/files/PUBLICACOES/CA14_Chapter-21_Portugal.pdf.

Pirker-Hörmann, B and Kolba, P, 'Österreich: Von der Verbandsklage zur Sammelklage', available at verbraucherrecht.at/cms/uploads/media/Kolba_Pirker_Bamberg.pdf.

Pråhl, J, Oxford – Leuven Collective Redress Project – 'Finnish Report' (2016), available at www.law.ox.ac.uk/events/empirical-evidence-collective-redress-europe.

Principe, G, 'Italian Class Actions – An Update', available at globalclassactions.stanford.edu.

Rajneri, E and Poncibò, C, 'Country Report: Italy', available at www.collectiveredress.org.

Rott, P, 'Evaluation of the Effectiveness and Efficiency of Collective Redress Mechanisms in the European Union – Country Report Germany' (2008), available at ec.europa.eu/consumers/solving_consumer_disputes/judicial_redress/index_en.htm.

Schneider, B and Heppner, H, 'Germany' in *The International Comparative Legal Guide to Class and Group Actions* (2017), available at iclg.com.

Sengayen, M, 'National Report for the Global Class Actions Conference at the Centre for Socio-Legal Studies' (2007), available at globalclassactions.stanford.edu.

Silvestri, E, Oxford – Leuven Collective Redress Project – 'Italian Report' (2016), available at www.law.ox.ac.uk/events/empirical-evidence-collective-redress-europe.

Smith, V and Moeiri-Farsi, M, 'Country Report: England and Wales', available at www.collectiveredress.org.

Sorabji, J et al, 'Improving Access to Justice through Collective Actions – Developing a More Efficient and Effective Procedure for Collective Actions', Civil Justice Council (2008), available at www.ucl.ac.uk/laws/judicial-institute/files/Improving_Access_to_Justice_through_Collective_Actions_-_recommendations.pdf.

Soto Maior, M, 'O Direito de Acção Popular na Constituição da República Portugesa' (1998) 75/76 *Documentação e Direito Comparado*, available at www.gddc.pt/actividade-editorial/pdfs-publicacoes/7576-g.pdf.

Sousa Antunes, H, Class Actions, Group Litigation & Other Forms of Collective Litigation, 'Portugese Report' (2007), available at globalclassactions.stanford.edu.

Specter, Report from the Committee on the Judiciary on the Class Action Fairness Act 2005 (2005) 4–5, available at www.congress.gov/congressional-report/109th-congress/senate-report/14/1.

Sportes, C and Ravit, V, 'France' in The International Comparative Legal Guide to Class and Group Actions (2017), available at iclg.com.

Stadler, A, Oxford – Leuven Collective Redress Project – 'German Report' (2016), available at www.law.ox.ac.uk/events/empirical-evidence-collective-redress-europe.

Storme, ME and Terryn, E, 'Belgian Report on Class Actions', available at globalclassactions.stanford.edu.

Tortell, L, Evaluation of the Effectiveness and Efficiency of Collective Redress Mechanisms in the European Union – Country Report Portugal (2008), available at ec.europa.eu/consumers/solving_consumer_disputes/judicial_redress/index_en.htm.

Tulibacka, M, 'Country Report: Poland', available at www.collectiveredress.org.

—— and Goral, R, 'An Update on Class Actions and Litigation Funding in Poland', available at globalclassactions.stanford.edu.

Tzankova, I, 'Class Actions in The Netherlands, Netherlands National Reports Parts 1 and 2', available at globalclassactions.stanford.edu.

—— et al, 'Country Report: The Netherlands', available at www.collectiveredress.org.

Vale e Reis, R and Mesquita, M, Country Report: Portugal, available at www.collectiveredress.org.

Vanhulst, O, 'Country Report: Belgium, available at www.collectiveredress.org.

Verlinden, J and van Mulders, P, 'Belgium' in *The International Comparative Legal Guide to Class and Group Actions* (2017), available at iclg.com.

Viitanen, K, 'Collective Litigation in Finland', available at globalclassactions.stanford.edu.

Voet, S, 'Class Action Developments in Belgium' (2016), available at globalclassactions.stanford.edu.

——, Oxford – Leuven Collective Redress Project – 'Belgian Report' (2016), available at www.law.ox.ac.uk/events/empirical-evidence-collective-redress-europe.

Posts and Online Newspapers

'Humiliation: A once Proud Firm, Brought Down by its own Flaws, Needs a Thorough Shake-up' (22.04.2014) *The Economist*, available at www.economist.com/node/2611051.

Garcímartin, R, Reconocimiento en España de las class actions extranjeras: el nuevo artículo 47 LCJI, (04.09.2015) *Almacén de Derecho*, available at almacendederecho.org/reconocimiento-en-espana-de-las-class-actions-extranjeras-el-nuevo-articulo-47-lcji.

Gates, G et al, 'How Volkswagen Is Grappling With Its Diesel Scandal' (18.11.2016) *New York Times*, available at www.nytimes.com/interactive/2015/business/international/vw-diesel-emissions-scandal-explained.html.

Moss, G, 'Foundation set up to pursue investor claims against VW in Dutch court' (19.02.2016) *Investment & Pensions in Europe*, available at www.ipe.com/news/esg/foundation-set-up-to-pursue-investor-claims-against-vw-in-dutch-court/10011995.fullarticle.

Murphy, M, 'JJB and Which? settle football shirt case' (10.01.2008) *FT.com*, available at next.ft.com/content/bd0acca2-bf08-11dc-8c61-0000779fd2ac.

Other Online Documents

BEUC, 'Litigation Funding in Relation to the Establishment of a European Mechanism of Collective Redress', available at www.beuc.eu/publications/2012-00074-01-e.pdf.

ECC Denmark, 'Cross-Border Dispute Resolution Mechanisms in Europe – Practical Reflections on the Need and Availability' (2009) 10, available at dokumenter.forbrug.dk/forbrugereuropa/crossborder-dispute-resolution.

European Parliament, 'A European Framework for Private International Law: Current Gaps and Future Perspectives' (2012) 17, available at www.europarl.europa.eu/document/activities/cont/201212/20121219ATT58300/20121219ATT58300EN.pdf.

Manual for Complex Litigation (2004), available at https://public.resource.org/scribd/8763868.pdf

Mulheron, R, 'Costs and Funding of Collective Actions – Realities and Possibilities', Research paper for submission to the European Consumers' Organisation (BEUC) (2011), available at www.law.qmul.ac.uk/media/law/docs/staff/department/71112.pdf.

INDEX

www.ingramcontent.com/pod-product-compliance
Ingram Content Group UK Ltd.
Pitfield, Milton Keynes, MK11 3LW, UK
UKHW020905190926
475560UK00010B/292

9 781509 930296